# Great Ideas in Computer Science

Alan W. Biermann

# Great Ideas in Computer Science

A Gentle Introduction

Second Edition

The MIT Press
Cambridge, Massachusetts
London, England

Second printing, 1998

© 1990, 1997 Massachusetts Institute of Technology

This book was set in Times Roman on the Monotype "Prism Plus" PostScript Imagesetter by Asco Trade Typesetting Ltd., Hong Kong.

Printed and bound in the United States of America.

Library of Congress Cataloging-in-Publication Data

Biermann, Alan W., 1939–
  Great ideas in computer science : a gentle introduction / Alan W. Biermann.—2nd ed.
    p.  cm.
  Includes index.
  ISBN 0-262-52223-3 (pbk. : alk. paper)
  1. Computer science.  I. Title.
QA76.B495   1997
004—dc20                                                      96-41198
                                                                CIP

*To my parents,*
*David and Ruth Biermann*

# Contents

---

\* Each section is labeled A, B, or C, corresponding to introductory, regular, or optional material.

# Preface to the Second Edition

This edition has new chapters on simulation, operating systems, and networks. Two chapters in the original version on transistor theory and Very Large Scale Integration have been deleted, and many of the original chapters have been revised.

This project has been a community effort over the years with a variety of individuals contributing to it. Many clarifications were suggested by friends, instructors, and graduate students who were involved with the course. I would especially like to thank Dietolf Ramm for writing the chapter on networks. Some of the other important contributors were Eric Anderson, Curry Guinn, Mark Holliday, Sally Mason, Peter Wu, Mimi Lee, Benjamin Hardekopf, and anonymous reviewers selected by the publisher. The software for the course was developed by Josh Carter, Chris Connelly, Amr Fahmy, Curry Guinn, D. J. Miller, David Pennock, Steve Wolfman, and Peter Wu. Financial support for the software was provided by Duke University and the National Science Foundation Grants USE 9155897, DUE 9354643, and DUE 9455507.

I am also grateful for the contributions to this book by Anna Drozdowski, our departmental administrator for many years, and I am indebted to my ever-enthusiastic assistant, Denita Thomas, who created many of the figures and typed many of the chapters.

# Preface

This is a book about computers—what they are, how they work, what they can do, and what they cannot do. It is written for people who read about such topics as computer networks or artificial intelligence and want to understand them, for people who need to have data processed on the job and want to know what can and cannot be done, and for people who see the proliferation of computers throughout society and ask about the meaning of it all. It is written for doctors, lawyers, preachers, teachers, managers, students, and all others who have a curiosity to learn about computing. It is also written for computer science students and professionals whose education may not have covered all the important areas, and who want to broaden themselves.

I was asked in 1985 to create a course in computer science for liberal arts students, and I decided that it was my job to present, as well as I could, the great intellectual achievements of the field. These are the "great ideas" that attract the attention of everyone who comes near and that, when collected together, comprise the heart of the field of computer science.

The first and most important of these great ideas is the *algorithm*—a procedure or recipe that can be given to a person or machine for doing a job. The other great ideas revolve around this central one; they give methodologies for coding algorithms into machine-readable form, and they describe what can and what cannot be coded for machine execution. They show how concepts of everyday life can be meaningfully represented by electrical voltages and currents that are manipulated inside a machine, and they show how to build mechanisms to do these computations. They also show how to translate languages that people can use comfortably into languages that machines use so that the machine capabilities are accessible. They show how humanlike reasoning processes can be programmed for machine execution, and they help us to understand what the ultimate capabilities of machines may be.

But it would seem that these great ideas are too complex and too technical to be understood by nonspecialists. Typically, a computer science major studies several years of mathematics and a long list of computer courses to learn these things, and we should not expect ordinary people to pick them up by reading a single book. To condense such extensive studies into a volume that many people can understand, the ideas have been reformulated in substantial ways; nonessential details have been removed, and the vocabulary of the studies has been chosen carefully.

Consider, for example, the traditional coverage of computer programming in a computer science curriculum. Students are taught all the syntactic features of some programming language, numerous implementation details, and a variety of applications. Because there is no time in the course for anything else, those who want a broader view of the field than just programming are frustrated. The treatment in this book, however, uses only a few features of Pascal, and all programs are restricted to these constructions. Since most of the important lessons in programming can be taught within these limitations, the reader's confusion from broad syntactic variety is eliminated.

As another example, the traditional treatment of switching-circuit design involves extensive study of Boolean algebra—equations, minimization, and circuit synthesis. But readers can learn the important ideas without any Boolean algebra at all. They can still address a design problem, write down a functional table for the target behavior, and create a nonminimal switching circuit to do the computation. The whole issue of circuit minimization that electrical engineers spend so much time on need not concern the general readers who simply want to learn something about computers. Similar significant revisions have been made to the traditional treatment of all computer topics. Thus we have Pascal without pointers, compilation without code optimization, computability theory without Turing machines, artificial intelligence without LISP, and so forth.

These revisions have been made to give readers access to the essentials of the great ideas in one book. Readers can learn to write a variety of programs in Pascal, design switching circuits, study a variety of Von Neumann and parallel architectures, hand simulate a compiler to see how it works, examine the mechanisms of an operating system, learn to classify various computations as tractable or intractable, gain an understanding of the concept of noncomputability, and come to grips with many of the important issues in artificial intelligence.

The early chapters introduce topics with motivating material, and each chapter on programming begins with a computational problem and presents lessons in programming as a way of solving the problem. The vocabulary has also been chosen for the general reader. For example, computer scientists tend to use the word "move" in places where ordinary English speakers would say "copy." So the word "move" can cause confusion and has been banned from the book except where it is the only correct word. Dozens of other common vocabulary words have been similarly filtered where they might cause confusion, or they have been carefully defined when they are specifically required. Notations have been included because they are essential to the study of computer science. However, the book introduces relatively few notations, explains them in considerable detail, and uses them repetitively so that even a reader without mathematical experience can become comfortable with them.

Finally, the reader might ask whether the great ideas presented here are the same as those that would be chosen by other authors. In fact, while one would expect some variations in opinions, there is considerable agreement about what constitutes the field of computer science. The central themes presented here would probably be chosen by most experts. As an illustration, one can examine the "intellectual framework for the discipline of computing" as given in "Computing as a Discipline," the report by the Task Force on the Core of Computer Science.\* This report presents a view of the field and makes recommendations about computer science education. Among the contributions of the report is a description of nine subareas that the authors believe cover the field. They are

1. Algorithms and data structures
2. Programming languages
3. Architecture
4. Numerical and symbolic computation
5. Operating systems
6. Software methodology and engineering
7. Database and information retrieval systems
8. Artificial intelligence and robotics
9. Human-computer communication

This book presents an introduction to most of the nine subareas. I would not want to claim that it gives fair and total coverage to all of them, but only that it includes the flavor and some of the important ideas from most of them.

Instructors may find that this volume covers more material than they can fit into a single course. In this case, coverage can be limited, for example, to the first two-thirds of the book with only one or two lectures allocated at the end for overviewing advanced topics. This yields a course on programming and a study of how computers work. Another way to accelerate the study is to cover switching, architecture, and compilers in a single lecture, and then to spend about half the course on chapters 10 through 15. There is a third way to use the book that is applicable when students have already learned programming from another source. In this case, coverage can begin at chapter 7 and proceed to the end. I have used many variations of these strategies in my own course. I usually do not cover recursion or the C-ranked sections of the translation and noncomputability chapters because they are difficult for my students.

It is a pleasure to acknowledge the contributions of many individuals to the preparation of this book. First of all, I am grateful to the Duke University Department of Computer

---

\* Peter J. Denning (Chairman), Douglas E. Comer, David Gries, Michael C. Mulder, Allen Tucker, A. Joe Turner, and Paul R. Young, "Computing as a Discipline," *Communications of the ACM*, Volume 32, Number 1, January, 1989; also in *Computer*, Volume 22, Number 2, February, 1989.

Science, which has given me an exciting environment and plenty of support for scholarly endeavors over the last twenty years. Second, I thank my several hundred students in this course who taught their instructor that he could not include all the things he wanted. They convinced me that I would have to remove much of the material that I dearly loved if any of it were to be understood, and they explained the problems with vocabulary: I might think I was using simple, nontechnical vocabulary, but my words meant something else to them. This book is as much an accomplishment of these patient young people as it is of mine. I am especially appreciative of the efforts of Craig Singer, who did a brilliant job as a teaching assistant over two years, and Michael Hines and Jothy Rosenberg who taught the course other semesters. These people were sensitive to student difficulties and made excellent suggestions for improving the coverage. An early draft of the book was circulated for review among professors at other institutions during the 1987–88 academic year. I am very appreciative of many helpful comments by Shan Chi (Northwestern University), David Frisque (University of Michigan), Rhys Price Jones (Oberlin College), Emily Moore (Grinnel College), Richard E. Pattis (University of Washington), Harvey Lee Shapiro (Lewis and Clark College), Jill Smudski (at that time University of Pennsylvania), and eight anonymous reviewers. On the basis of these reviews and the classroom experiences, the book was reorganized and rewritten.

The new version of the book was brought to the classroom in the fall of 1988, and I am again grateful to my students who filled out questionnaires on four occasions, helping me find weak points in the explanations, and to my teaching assistant, Albert Nigrin, for his help. I would also especially like to thank Elina Kaplan, who spent countless hours on some of the early chapters finding ways to improve the presentation. Where simplicity and clarity occur in these chapters, much is owed to Elina. Many other individuals have contributed by reading chapters and making suggestions. These include Heidi Brubaker, Dania Egedi, Linda Fineman, Chris Gandy, Curry Guinn, Tim Gegg-Harrison, Barry Koster, Anselmo Lastra, Ken Lang, Albert Nigrin, Lorrie Tomek, Tom Truscott, and Doreen Yen. I am especially appreciative of errors found and suggestions made by David M. Gordon, Henry Greenside, Donald Loveland, and Charlie Martin. Many other friends have made suggestions and commented on the chapters.

The book has been given much of its personality by Matt Evans, who created the cartoons at the beginnings of the chapters. I am extremely appreciative of his efforts. I am indebted as well to Ann Davis, who typed the manuscript from my handwritten pages. Her diligence and accuracy greatly eased the burden of creating the book. I would also like to thank Marie Cunningham for typing some of the chapters and Denita Thomas for preparing the index. Barry Koster was kind enough to generate a large number of the figures, and Eric Smith helped me on numerous occasions with library work. My heartfelt thanks go to Robert Prior, Harry Stanton, and the other editors at The MIT Press who understood the dream of my book from the beginning and who have strongly supported my efforts. Finally, I would like to thank my wife, Alice, my daughter, Jennifer, and my son, David, for their enthusiasm and encouragement on this project.

# Studying Academic Computer Science:
# An Introduction

## Rumors

Computers are the subject of many rumors, and we wonder what to believe. People say that computers in the future will do all clerical jobs and even replace some well-trained experts. They say computers are beginning to simulate the human mind, to create art, to prove theorems, to learn, and to make careful judgments. They say that computers will permeate every aspect of our lives by managing communication, manipulating information, and providing entertainment. They say that even our political systems will be altered—that in previously closed societies, computers will bring universal communication that will threaten the existing order, and in free societies, they will bring increased monitoring and control. On the other hand, there are skeptics who point out that computer science has many limitations and that the impact of machines has been overemphasized.

Some of these rumors are correct and give us fair warning of things to come. Others may be somewhat fanciful, leading us to worry about the future more than is necessary. Still others point out questions that we may argue about for years without finding answers. Whatever the case, we can be sure that many issues related to computers are of vital importance, and they are worth trying to understand.

This book is designed to help people understand computers and computer science. It begins with a study of programming in the belief that controlling and manipulating machines is essential to understanding them. Then it takes the reader on a guided tour of the machine internals, exploring its essential functioning, from the movement of electricity through the switches and wires to the architecture and the software that drives it. Finally, the book explores the limitations of computing, the frontiers of the science as they are currently understood.

In short, the book attempts to give a thorough introduction to the field with an emphasis on the fundamental mechanisms that enable computers to work. It presents many of the "great ideas" of computer science, the intellectual paradigms that scientists use to understand the field and that will also enable the reader to comprehend machines.

## Studying Computer Science

Computer science is the study of recipes and ways to carry them out. A recipe is a procedure or method for doing something. The science studies kinds of recipes, the properties of recipes, languages for writing them down, methods for creating them, and the construction of machines that will carry them out. Of course, computer scientists want to distinguish themselves from chefs, so they have their own name for recipes—they call them *algorithms*.

If we wish to understand computer science, then we must study recipes, or algorithms. The first problem is how to conceive of them and how to write them down. For example, we might want a recipe for treating a disease, for classifying birds on the basis of their characteristics, or for organizing a financial savings program. We need to study some sample recipes to see how they are constructed, and then we need practice writing our own. We need experience in abstracting the essence of real-world situations and in organizing this knowledge into a sequence of steps for getting our tasks done.

Once we have devised a method for doing something, we wish to *code* it in a computer language in order to communicate our desires to the machine. Thus, it is necessary to learn a computer language and to learn to translate the steps of a recipe into commands that can be carried out by a machine. This book will introduce the reader to a language called *Pascal*, which is easy to learn and quite satisfactory for our example programs.

The combination of creating the recipe and coding it into a computer language is called *programming*, and this is the subject of the first part of the book, chapters 1 to 6. These chapters give a variety of problem types, their associated solution methods, and the Pascal code, the *program*, required to solve them. The final chapter in the sequence discusses the problems related to scaling up the lessons learned here to industrial-sized programming projects.

While the completion of the programming chapters enables the reader to create useful code, the reader may still view a computer as a magic box that efficiently executes commands. In order to explain why a machine acts as it does, what its limitations are, and what improvements can be expected, the second part of the book addresses the issue of how and why computers are able to compute.

Chapter 7 shows methods for designing electric circuits and describes how to employ these techniques to design computational mechanisms. For example, you will see how to build a circuit for adding numbers. Chapter 8 describes computer architecture and the organization of typical computers. Chapter 9 addresses the translation of a high-level computer language like Pascal into machine language, so that it can be run on the given architecture. An example at the end of chapter 9 traces the significant processing that occurs in the execution of a Pascal language statement from the translation to machine language to the detailed operations of the computational circuits. Chapter 10 introduces concepts related to operating systems; these are the programs that bridge the gap between the user and the many hardware and software facilities on the machine. They make it easy for the user to obtain the computing services that he or she may desire. Chapter 11 introduces computer networks and the many concepts related to having machines talk to each other.

The final chapters of the book examine the limitations of computers and the frontiers of the science. Chapter 12 discusses problems related to program execution time and computations that require long processing times. Chapter 13 describes an attempt to speed up computers to do larger problems, the introduction of parallel architectures. Chapter 14 discusses the existence of so-called *noncomputable* functions, and chapter 15 gives an introduction to the field of *artificial intelligence*.

## Special Software to Help You Learn

Many programs have been developed to illustrate the ideas in this book and you can obtain them via the Internet. There are two storage places for these programs: The MIT Press and the author's World Wide Web page at the Department of Computer Science, Duke University.

Here are some of the programs you can look forward to trying:

- In the simulation chapter, there are two programs in the archives. The first is a car race simulation that enables you to describe a strategy for getting around the track and then to see how well you did. The second is a simulated evolution program that enables you to study generations of simple beings as they evolve in a model environment.
- The chapters on computer hardware and software have an accompanying program called "This-is-how-a-computer-works." It enables you to see the operations of the model computer as it compiles and runs a small program. You will be given enough detail to watch the switches in the central processor jump back and forth and to see the electricity run up and down the wires as the computation proceeds.
- Finally, a Pascal operating system accompanies chapter 10 and you can study, run, and modify it if you wish. Most of the other programs referred to in the book are included in hardcopy where they are discussed.

## An Approach for Nonmathematical Readers

Because people who understand computer science tend to speak their own language and use too much mathematical notation, difficulties in communication lead instructors to the conclusion that ordinary people are not able to understand the field. Books and university courses often skirt the central issues and, instead, teach the operation of software packages and the history and sociology of computing.

This book was written on the assumption that intelligent people can understand every fundamental issue of computer science if the preparation and explanation are adequate. No important topics have been omitted because of their difficulty. However, tremendous efforts were made to prune away unnecessary detail and to remove special vocabulary except where careful and complete definitions could be given.

Because casual readers may not wish to read all the chapters, the book is designed to encourage dabbling. Readers are encouraged to jump to any chapter at any time and read as much as is of interest. Of course, most chapters use some concepts from earlier pages and where this occurs, understanding will be reduced. The programming chapters (1 through 5) are highly dependent on each other, and the architecture chapter (8) should be read before the translation chapter (9). Also, some of the advanced chapters (12 through 15) use concepts of programming from the early chapters (1 to 5). Except for these restrictions, the topics can probably be covered in any order without much sacrifice.

All chapter sections are classified as either A, B, or C to encourage readers to taste much and devour only what they choose. Chapter sections labelled A include only introductory material and make few demands on the reader. One can get an overview of the book in a single evening by reading them. The B sections are the primary material of the book and may require substantial time and effort, but the reader who completes them will have a deep understanding of the major lessons on that topic. The C material answers questions that careful readers may ask and supplements the main portions of the book.

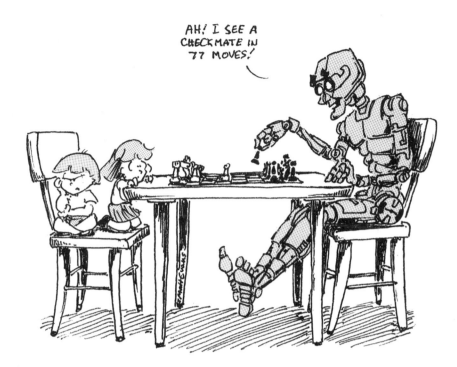

# 1    An Introduction to Programming: Coding Decision Trees

## Good News (A)

In the old days before computers, if we wanted to do a job, we had to do the job. But with computers, we can do many jobs by simply writing down what is to be done. A machine can do the work. If we want to add numbers, search for a fact, format and print a document, distribute messages to colleagues, control an industrial process, or do other tasks, we can write a recipe for what is to be done and walk away while a machine obediently and tirelessly carries out our instructions. Our recipe could also be distributed to many computers, and they could all work together to carry out our instructions. Even after we retire from this life, computers may still be employed to do the same jobs following the commands that we laid down.

The preparation and writing of such recipes is called *programming*, and it implements a kind of "work amplification" that is revolutionizing human society. It enables a single person to do a finite amount of work, the preparation of a computer program, and to achieve, with the help of computers, an unbounded number of results. Thus, our productivity is no longer simply a function of the number of people working; it is a function of the number of people and the number of machines we have.

There is even more good news: computers are relatively inexpensive, and their costs are continuously decreasing. Machines with 64,000 word memories and 1 microsecond instruction times cost $1 million three decades ago. Now we can buy a machine with one hundred times the memory and one hundred times the speed for a few thousand dollars. For the cost of one month of a laborer's time, we can purchase a machine that can do some tasks faster than a thousand people working together.

We wish to study computer programming in this book so that we can experience the work amplification that computers make possible. We will study fundamental information structures and processing techniques that will enable us to develop expertise in abstracting the essence of problem situations into machine code so that our jobs can be done for us automatically.

We will not study programming in the usual fashion, by learning the voluminous details of some particular programming language. We will not, for example, mention all rules for placement of the semicolons and commas, the most general form of every language construct, the number of characters allowed in variable names, or the maximum allowed sizes of numbers or string lengths. We will have all the pleasure of reading and writing simple programs while suffering as little as possible from syntactic precision and encyclopedic completeness.

Our programming examples and exercises use the programming language Pascal. However, we will use only a fraction of the features of Pascal in order to keep the language-learning task under control. If all of Pascal were to be learned, there would be no time for the central theme of this book, the great ideas of computer science. Since only enough details are given here to enable readers to understand the sample programs and to write similar programs as exercises, those who attempt more ambitious programs are advised to have a Pascal manual at hand for reference and study.

If we are to study programming, we must program something. It would be nice to write programs to embody some useful information-processing structure. We also want to write many kinds of programs and be sure that their structure is simple enough to enable easy comprehension and coding by beginners. We want to learn some important ideas that will be fundamental to more advanced studies. The first domain for programming in this book is thus *decision trees*. Decision trees can be used for classifying objects, for interviewing people, and for many other tasks. First we will study decision trees, and then we will learn how to write programs for them.

## Decision Trees (B)

Suppose we wish to decide which book to recommend to a person who intends to get started in computer science. A good way to make the decision is to ask the person a series of questions and to arrive at the appropriate advice. The first question we might ask is whether he or she wants to use a mathematical approach. We formulate a question and then indicate with arrows a direction to follow for the next question:

Book Recommendation
Decision Tree

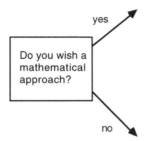

yes

Do you wish a
mathematical
approach?

no

Then we decide what questions should be asked next, depending on the first answer:

Book Recommendation
Decision Tree

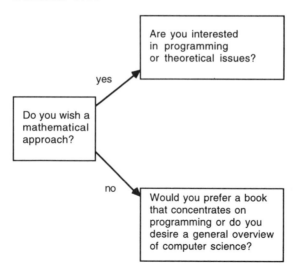

Are you interested
in programming
or theoretical issues?

yes

Do you wish a
mathematical
approach?

no

Would you prefer a book
that concentrates on
programming or do you
desire a general overview
of computer science?

Let us assume that after asking two questions, it is possible to make the appropriate recommendation. Then the decision tree can be completed as follows:

Book Recommendation
Decision Tree

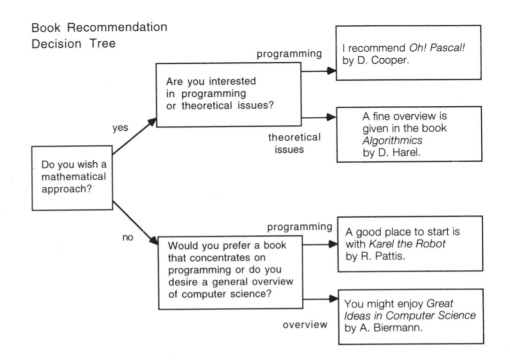

Following through the decision tree, it is possible to trace a sample interaction. Assuming the person is mathematically oriented and interested in theoretical issues, the path through the tree proceeds as follows:

Selecting a book to read in computer science:
Decision tree question: Do you wish a mathematical approach?
Response: yes
Decision tree question: Are you interested in programming or theoretical issues?
Response: theoretical issues
Decision tree advice: A fine overview is given in the book *Algorithmics* by D. Harel.

This tree contains only two sequential questions before arriving at its decision. But it is easy to envision a large tree that asks many questions and recommends a wide variety of books at the end of the path. It is also clear that this type of tree can be used to give advice on almost any subject from medical treatment to fortune-telling. Here are some examples to illustrate the idea:

## Medical Advice Decision Tree

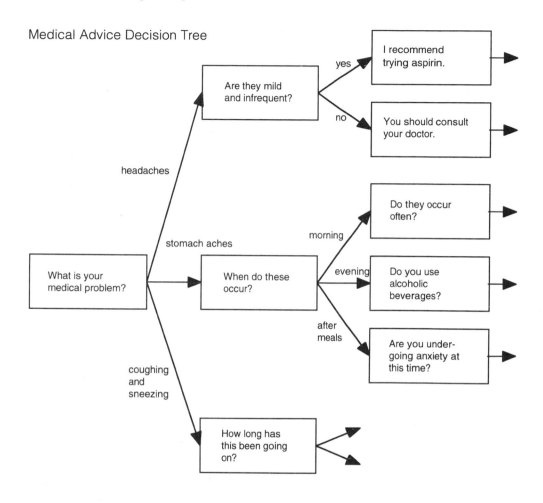

Fortune-Telling Decision Tree

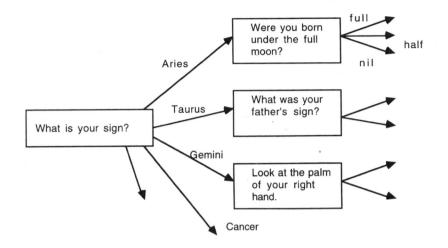

Decision trees can also be used to classify things. Suppose we have information on the characteristics of seagulls, and we wish to determine the exact classification of any specific gull. We could build a tree that might look like this:

Seagull Classification Decision Tree

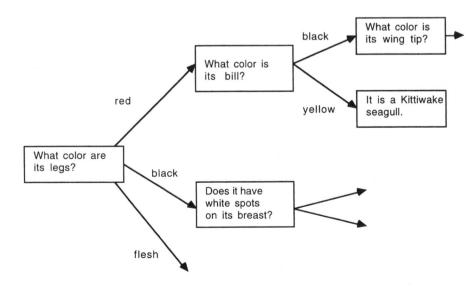

We can even make a decision tree that will help us do our income tax. Here is how a tiny piece of it might look:

Income Tax Helper

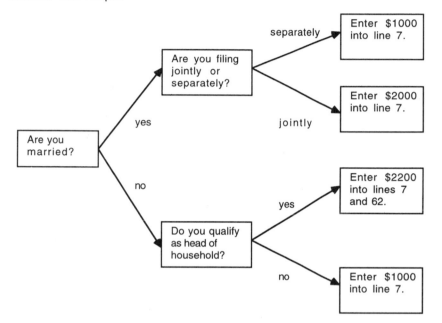

Or what about a game-playing tree? This can be illustrated by the simple game Nim, which has the following rules. The first player can place one, two, or three Xs at the left end of a horizontal ladder; then the opponent can place one, two, or three Os in the next sequential squares. This chain of moves repeats again and again, filling the ladder from left to right, with the winner being the one to place a mark in the last square. As an example, suppose the ladder has seven squares:

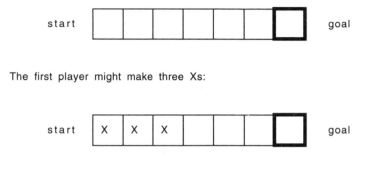

The first player might make three Xs:

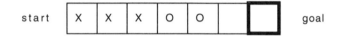

Suppose the second player makes two Os:

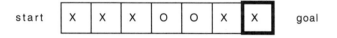

Then the first player could win by placing two more Xs:

start | X | X | X | O | O | X | X |    goal

Here is a decision tree that will play the role of the second player for a Nim ladder of length seven:

Nim Game-Playing Tree

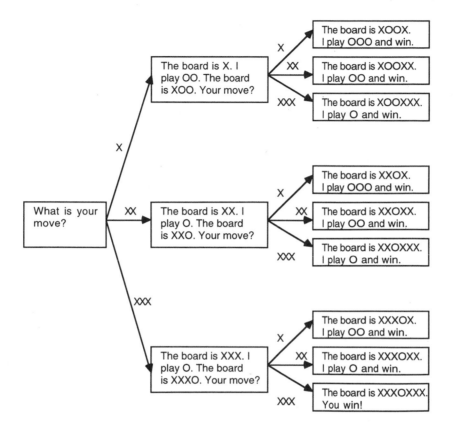

Ordinarily we think of trees as emerging from the ground and spreading their branches toward the sky. The trees in this chapter move from left to right so they will be easier to program. The processing of the tree begins at the left-most box, or *root node*, and proceeds along a path toward the right. At each decision *node*, the user of the tree is asked a question, and the answer given serves to select the next branch to be followed. The path proceeds right until a final *leaf* node is encountered with no outward branches. This leaf node will contain a message giving the result of the sequence of decisions, and it will terminate processing.

Such decision trees are applicable to a multitude of information-processing tasks, including advice giving, classification, instruction, and game-playing activities. Our task in this chapter will be to write programs that will contain these trees, lead a person down the correct paths, and print the results. The ability to design and program these trees is a powerful skill with numerous applications.

### Exercises

1. Complete one of the decision trees that is only partially specified in this section.

2. Design a complete decision tree that will play the part of the second player in Nim with a ladder of nine squares.

3. Specify a problem domain of interest to you and design a decision tree to solve it.

---

## Getting Started in Programming (B)

A *computer program* is a list of commands that can be carried out by a computer. It is a recipe of actions the machine is to perform, and it must be written in a language that the computer can understand. Most programs in this book will be written in Pascal, a popular and convenient language. Sometimes a program or part of a program is called computer *code*. We will use both terms in this book.

Here is a sample program written in Pascal.

```
program FirstCode;
begin
writeln('  Great Ideas  ');
writeln('      in       ');
writeln('Computer Science');
readln;
end.
```

If we want these instructions carried out, we do what is called *running* or *executing* the program on a computer. In order to do this, it is necessary to have the following.

- A computer
- A software system that enables your particular computer to process Pascal
- A manual to help you get the machine turned on and running
- A knowledgeable instructor or friend

Any computer is satisfactory if you can obtain a Pascal system for it, but two popular machines are the Apple Macintosh and the IBM Personal Computer. Every computer has its own machine language so you must always have a software system that can translate the language of choice, Pascal in this case, into that machine's language. The translator is a computer program called a *compiler*, which usually comes on a disk and can be bought at a computer store. The examples in this book have been written in Turbo Pascal, a dialect of the Pascal language developed by Borland International. If you choose to use some other Pascal system, you will probably find that most of the programs run as they are shown. For example, Think Pascal on Apple Macintosh machines runs the same as Turbo except for a few features, most of which will be mentioned as they are encountered in later chapters. For other Pascal versions, you may need help getting a few of the programs to run because there are significant differences.

The manual is necessary because it will tell you which buttons to push on your computer to turn it on and to get your program typed in and running. Finally, you need an instructor or friend to tell you what the manual did not. Computer science, like many disciplines, has an oral tradition, and some of the most important facts are passed only by word of mouth. You may be able to get along without this help, but learning is usually easier if it is there.

To get maximum benefit from this chapter, you should type in and run some of the programs given here and observe their behaviors. For instance, if the above sample is run, the following lines will be printed:

```
   Great Ideas
        in
Computer Science
```

This program is very simple from some points of view, but there are many details related to its form and execution that need to be understood. These include the composition of the program in terms of statements, the order of execution of the statements, and their meaning and structure.

**Program Form**

The primary parts of this program are its *header*, the keyword *begin*, a series of statements followed by semicolons, and the keyword *end* followed by a period. The header must always begin with the word *program*, and it includes a name for the program followed by a semicolon. Thus the first line,

```
program FirstCode;
```

tells the computer that this is a program with the name "FirstCode." The second line

```
begin
```

tells the computer that some programming statements follow. Next are four lines of code, each containing a program statement. The final line of the program is the marker telling the computer where the program ends.

```
end.
```

| The Program | Comments |
| --- | --- |
| `program FirstCode;` | The program header |
| `begin` | Indicator that code will follow |
| `writeln(' Great Ideas ');` | Statement followed by semicolon |
| `writeln(' in ');` | Statement followed by semicolon |
| `writeln('Computer Science');` | Statement followed by semicolon |
| `readln;` | Statement followed by semicolon |
| `end.` | Indicator that code has ended |

**Statements**

A program statement is an individual command to the computer. It corresponds to an imperative sentence in English. It says to the computer, "You do this." The example program has four statements. The first one is this:

```
writeln(' Great Ideas ')
```

It tells the computer to write the words "Great Ideas" on the screen. Some spaces are typed around these words because we would like to see those spaces when they are printed. (Literally, the instruction *writeln* means "write a line.") Each statement in a program is usually followed by a semicolon, so the statement will appear as follows:

```
writeln(' Great Ideas ');
```

The second and third statements are also "write" statements.

The fourth statement instructs the computer to stop and wait for the computer user to type something. It says *readln*, or "read a line." This statement is not necessary for the program, but it serves the purpose of requiring the machine to stop and wait before doing anything else. Without the *readln* statement, typical Turbo Pascal systems would quickly write the three lines and exit to do another job before we have a chance to read what was written. In this book, most programs will include a *readln* statement before the final *end* statement to give you a chance to study the output messages before the program is terminated.

Thus, this program types three lines and halts, waiting for the user to type something. After the user types anything, usually just a single carriage return, the program exits.

**Program Execution**

The computer functions by executing the statements in order. It executes the first statement, the second, and so forth. It always executes statements in order unless special statements require it to do something else.

**Statement Meaning and Structure**

The particular statement

```
writeln(' Great Ideas ');
```

has two parts: the command syntax that specifies exactly what ordering of characters is necessary for the command and some data that the programmer has inserted:

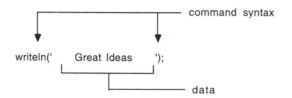

The command tells the machine to write whatever characters are between the quotation marks and then move to the next line. If the program is being run on a video display terminal, the write command will put the characters on the screen in an area designated for writing.

When you type a program into the machine, all command syntax must be perfect. No typographical errors are allowed. None of the following programs will run properly because correct programming syntax has been violated:

```
program FirstCode;
begin
writein(' Great Ideas ');
writeln('    in      ');
writeln('Computer Science');
readln;
end.
```

(The first *writeln* is misspelled.)

```
program FirstCode;
begin
```

```
writeln('  Great Ideas  ');
writeln('     in       ')
writeln('Computer Science');
readln;
end.
```

(There is a missing semicolon.)

```
program FirstCode;
begin
please writeln('  Great Ideas  ');
writeln('     in       ');
writeln('Computer Science');
readln;
end.
```

("Please" is illegally used in this context.)

Most programming languages require perfect syntax, although a few allow some flexibility. Languages of the future will probably be less demanding.

If the command syntax is correct, the program will carry out the commands regardless of what is included as data. Thus the following program will execute normally.

```
program FirstCode;
begin
writeln('   Grit Iders   ');
writeln('      on        ');
writeln('C#7a-%%*         ');
readln;
end.
```

The machine has no basis on which to judge the correctness of the data and will obediently carry out the instructions without regard to what is being manipulated. The computer will do precisely what you say even though it may not be what you want.

One way a correct program can be modified without changing its correctness relates to its spacing. Spaces can be inserted at most places in a program without affecting its behavior. The following program is equivalent to the first one given above. Even though a blank line and many extraneous spaces have been inserted, it will run perfectly.

```
program
    FirstCode;
                    begin
    writeln
        ('  Great Ideas  ');
```

```
     writeln('       in         ');
             writeln('Computer Science');
readln;          end.
```

You would certainly not want to type a program with such random spacing because of its poor readability. But this example does show how complete your freedom is for moving things around on the page and you may want use this freedom to format your code in some special way.

Do not insert spaces in the middle of keywords such as *begin* or *end* or in names or data.

This section has presented a computer program to print three lines and halt. A careful understanding of this simple code is a huge step in the direction of understanding all computer programs. It is important to understand the form of the programs and the concept of the programming statement as the fundamental unit of command. Each statement specifies an action; the sequence of statements specifies a sequence of actions and the order of their execution. The formatting of each statement is precise and unforgiving except for the allowance of spacing between its parts.

Here is a program that performs another printing task:

```
program SecondCode;
begin
writeln('***************************');
writeln('*                         *');
writeln('*      Decision Trees      *');
writeln('*                         *');
writeln('***************************');
readln;
end.
```

You should now be able to write a program that will print almost anything.

### Exercises

1. Write a program that will print your name and address.

2. Write a program that will print the letters PEACE in block format.

```
PPPP  EEEEE     A        CCC  EEEE
P   P E        AAA      C   C E
PPPP  EEE    A   A  C        EEE
P     E     AAAAAAA  C   C E
P     EEEE A       A  CCC  EEEE
```

3. Draw a picture of a cottage in the woods with a path leading to the front door. Convert the picture to an array of characters as is done with the word PEACE above, and write a program to print it.

---

## Reading and Storing Data (B)

The previous section introduced the concept of data—the information being manipulated by the program. In the previous examples, the data items were strings of characters that were being written out. Examples of such strings are "Computer Science", "***************", and "C#7a-%%*". This section will show how to get your program to collect such data from the keyboard; it will read the keystrokes from typed input and store the data in the computer memory.

Before studying the read statement, however, it is necessary to talk about locations in memory. Such locations are like pigeonholes with names where information can be stored and then retrieved when needed. For example, you might like to have a place in memory where a sequence of characters can be stored, and you might choose to name it "position1."

position1 [                        ]

You can then store data in that location and use the data in various ways. You could instruct the machine to write the data in *position1* or move the data in *position1* to some other location.

The correct way to indicate in the Pascal language that such a memory location is to be set up is with the *var* declaration, as follows:

```
var
    position1:string;
```

This declaration tells the machine that a location is to be set up in memory called "position1," which can hold a string of characters. It is included in the program after the header. The name *position1* is called a *variable*.

Once such a memory location is set up, you can refer to it in other statements. The new statement to be studied has the form

```
readln(position1)
```

and it means

1. Receive the characters that are typed (ending with a carriage return).
2. Put this sequence of characters into the place named *position1*. (These characters will also appear on the terminal screen as they are typed.)

Suppose that the machine executes the statement

```
readln(position1)
```

and that the user types the words "A Gentle Introduction" (but without the quotation marks and followed by a carriage return). Then the location named "position1" will receive the information as shown:

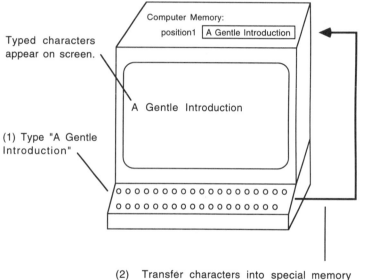

(2)  Transfer characters into special memory location.

Thus, a method for storing some information into the computer memory proceeds as follows. First, put in a declaration to create and name the desired memory location. Then include a *readln* statement to gather the keystrokes and enter them into that location. Finally, if you wish to check whether the data are there, include a write statement. Here is the complete program:

```
program ReadData;
var
   position1 :string;
```

```
begin
readln(position1);
writeln(position1);
readln;
end.
```

Its operation proceeds by first waiting for some typed characters. Suppose you type

```
Very Gentle
```

followed by a carriage return. This will be stored away in the location *position1*.

position1 | Very Gentle |

Then the contents of *position1* will be printed on the screen. Finally, the program will wait for you to type one more thing, say a carriage return, and then exit.

Some Pascal systems require that the word *string* in the previous program be followed by an integer in parentheses telling the maximum length of the strings that may appear in this location. For example, suppose the strings to be entered into the location *position1* are allowed to hold up to 100 characters. Then the declaration would be given as follows:

```
var
   position1:string[100];
```

Turbo Pascal assumes that the longest string will be 255 characters or fewer unless otherwise specified.

The program can be modified so that it will make more sense to the user. *Writeln* statements can be added to tell what is happening:

```
program ReadWriteDemo;
var
   position1:string;
begin
writeln('Please type in some data.');
readln(position1);
writeln('The data have been stored.');
writeln('Next the data will be printed.');
writeln(position1);
writeln('This completes the run.');
readln;
end.
```

Let us run this program to be sure that we understand it:

```
Please type in some data.      (computer message to user)
An Introduction                (the user types the data)
The data have been stored.     (computer message to user)
Next the data will be printed. (computer message to user)
An Introduction                (the computer writes the data)
This completes the run.        (computer message to user)
(carriage return)              (final user input)
```

Notice that two different forms of the *writeln* statement are being employed. If quotation marks are used, the characters between the quotes will be printed. Thus, in

```
writeln('position1')
```

the characters "position1" will be written (without the double quotation marks). But if there are no quotation marks, the processor will go to the memory location with the given name and write the contents of that location. Therefore, the statement

```
writeln(position1)
```

will print "An Introduction" if *position1* contains those characters.

If *writeln* is asked to print something not enclosed in quotation marks and not declared as a memory location, an error results, as in the case

```
writeln(An Introduction)
```

A combination of input and output statements can be used to write a simple interactive program. Here is an illustration. Can you tell what it does?

```
program GetNameTown;
var
    PositionOfName, PositionOfTown:string;
begin
writeln('Hi, tell me your name.');
readln(PositionOfName);
writeln('What town do you live in?');
readln(PositionOfTown);
writeln('Can you tell me something?');
writeln(PositionOfName);
writeln('How do you like living in');
writeln(PositionOfTown);
writeln('???');
readln;
end.
```

The names of the places in memory can be almost anything as long as they begin with an alphabetic letter, include only alphabetic and numeric characters, and are properly declared. For example, the names *A17* and *c8Zi* could be used:

```
program GetNameTown;
var
    A17, c8Zi:string;
begin
writeln('Hi, tell me your name.');
readln(A17);
writeln('What town do you live in?');
readln(c8Zi);
writeln('Can you tell me something?');
writeln(A17);
writeln('How do you like living in');
writeln(c8Zi);
writeln('???');
readln;
end.
```

There are two rules to follow with names: First, they are not allowed to contain spaces. Second, there is a set of *reserved words* for your Pascal system that may not be used as names. Some examples of such words are *program, begin, end, if, else, and,* and *or.* You should consult your Pascal manual for the complete list.

Programmers commonly give a location the name of the object to be stored in that location. In this example, the two locations of interest could be *name* and *town* since they store, respectively, the name and town of a person. This makes the program most easily understood:

```
program GetNameTown;
var
    name, town: string;
begin
writeln('Hi, tell me your name.');
readln(name);
writeln('What town do you live in?');
readln(town);
writeln('Can you tell me something?');
writeln(name);
writeln('How do you like living in');
writeln(town);
writeln('???');
```

```
readln;
end.
```

An important fact is that storage positions should not be used until something is loaded into them, as is done by the input statements. Then they will continue to hold that information until they are reloaded, perhaps by other input statements. If they are reloaded, the earlier information is destroyed and lost forever. This is demonstrated by the following program. What does it do?

```
program LoadDemo;
var
    x, y: string;
begin
writeln('Input x.');
readln(x);
writeln('Input y.');
readln(y);
writeln('Contents of x and y.');
writeln(x);
writeln(y);

writeln('Input x.');
readln(x);                          *
writeln('Contents of x and y.');
writeln(x);
writeln(y);
writeln('Input y.');
readln(y);                          **
writeln('Contents of x and y.');
writeln(x);
writeln(y);
end.
```

Here is an example of its behavior:

```
Input x.                  (printed message)
Jack                      (input to x)
Input y.                  (printed message)
Jill                      (input to y)
Contents of x and y.      (printed message)
Jack                      (contents of x)
Jill                      (contents of y)
```

```
Input x.              (printed message)
Sam                   (input to x)
Contents of x and y.  (printed message)
Sam                   (contents of x)
Jill                  (contents of y)
Input y.              (printed message)
Sally                 (input to y)
Contents of x and y.  (printed message)
Sam                   (contents of x)
Sally                 (contents of y)
```

The first two read statements of the program enter information into $x$ and $y$. Next, $x$ and $y$ are printed. The statement marked by * reads into $x$, destroying its contents. When $x$ and $y$ are printed, the change can be seen. The statement marked by ** replaces the contents of $y$, and the final write statement shows the result.

This section has introduced two ideas that are essential to computer programming—inputting data from the keyboard and storing the data in the computer memory. Because of their subtlety, you should study them carefully. The next section will introduce one more programming concept and show you how to program decision trees.

### Exercises

1. Write a program that reads your first and last names and then prints them out.

2. Write a program that will gather data from a prospective college student regarding academic background, standardized test scores, and so forth. Then the program should print the information in summary form for the college admissions office.

## Programming Decision Trees (B)

Let us begin by programming the simplest possible tree, one with only one branching node:

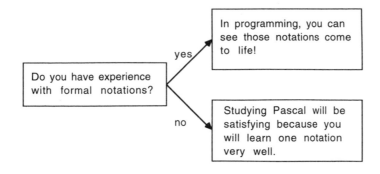

We learned in the previous sections how to make the machine print these kinds of messages and how to make it read the user's answers. But one additional feature is needed, the *if-then-else* statement, which will enable us to build the yes-no branch of the program.

The needed statement for the decision tree is typed on several lines and has the following form:

```
if answer = 'yes' then
    Pascal code A
else
    Pascal code B
```

Here *Pascal code A* and *Pascal code B* are sequences of Pascal statements. These sequences are called *compound statements* and are defined in the next paragraph. Assume that the program has executed

```
readln(answer)
```

where *answer* has been declared as a string location and that the program has stored either "yes" or "no" into *answer*. This code will execute *Pascal code A* if *answer* contains "yes" and *Pascal code B* otherwise.

Now we are able to write a computer program for this simple decision tree.

```
program FirstTree;
var
    answer:     string;
begin
writeln('Do you have experience with formal notations?');
readln(answer);
if answer = 'yes' then
    begin
    writeln('In programming, you can see those notations');
```

```
   writeln('come to life!');
   end
else
   begin
   writeln('Studying Pascal will be satisfying because');
   writeln('you will learn one notation very well.');
   end;
readln;
end.
```

Notice that *Pascal code A* has become a four-line sequence as follows:

```
begin
writeln('In programming, you can see those notations');
writeln('come to life!');
end
```

It contains two *writeln* statements, which are preceded by the keyword *begin* and followed by the keyword *end*. The same is true for *Pascal code B*. In general, any sequence of statements contained between the keywords *begin* and *end* is called a *compound statement*; this is the format allowed in the positions called *Pascal code A* and *Pascal code B*. A variation of this rule will be mentioned in chapter 4. (Actually, this program has three compound statements in all—the two just mentioned and the main part of the program itself, which is also a sequence of statements bounded by *begin* and *end*.)

Although this short program seems easy to understand, you should study it carefully. What would happen if you answered the initial question by typing "Yes, some," instead of "yes" or "no"? What would happen if you typed "Yes" instead of "yes"?

Two extremely important issues are related to this program. The first concerns the indentation policy. Each line of code can be spaced in from the left margin any amount without affecting its execution. However, the readability of the program is enhanced tremendously by indenting the branch portions of each *if* statement. The eye is immediately drawn to the significant sections of code, and the flow of control in the program is easy to follow. You should write computer programs as clearly as you would write a natural language such as English or Russian. If a careful indentation policy is ignored in writing a program, the offense is just as serious as the omission of section headings and paragraphs in a paper or article.

The other important issue relates to the placement of the semicolons. This book will follow the rules of placing semicolons (1) at the end of the header and the declaration, and (2) at the end of every statement within each compound statement.

This rule is easy to apply in the earlier programs because they include only one compound statement—the main sequence of statements that are bracketed by *begin* and *end*.

If we remember that *begin* and *end* are not themselves statements, the placement of semicolons is straightforward:

```
program ReadData;
var
   position1 :string;
begin
readln(position1);
writeln(position1);
readln;
end.
```

But the semicolons in FirstTree need careful attention. First, check that the header and declaration have semicolons. Next, apply rule (2) to each statement in the main program, disregarding the compound statements within the if-then-else construction (which are indented and are surrounded by *begin* and *end*). Finally, examine each indented compound statement and check that its contained statements are followed by semicolons. Consider first the main program, which begins and ends at the positions marked with Ms, and the four associated statements marked with labels M1 through M4:

```
       program FirstTree;
       var
          answer: string;
{M}    begin
{M1}   writeln('Do you have experience with formal notations?');
{M2}   readln(answer);
{M3}   if answer = 'yes' then
          begin
          writeln('In programming, you can see those notations');
          writeln('come to life!');
          end
       else
          begin
          writeln('Studying Pascal will be satisfying because');
          writeln('you will learn one notation very well.');
          end;
{M4}   readln;
{M}    end.
```

All four statements begin at the same indentation level as their *begin-end* brackets. Each statement needs to end with a semicolon. But where are the ends? In three cases, the ends are at the right end of the line, but the *if-then-else* statement stretches over ten lines. Its end is the *end* that precedes the final *readln*. So rule (2) specifies that the positions marked *endM1, endM2, endM3,* and *endM4* require semicolons.

```
      program FirstTree;
      var
          answer:  string;
{M}   begin
{M1}  writeln('Do you have experience with formal notations?');
{endM1}
{M2}  readln(answer); {endM2}
{M3}  if answer = 'yes' then
          begin
          writeln('In programming, you can see those notations');
          writeln('come to life!');
          end
      else
          begin
          writeln('Studying Pascal will be satisfying because');
          writeln('you will learn one notation very well.');
          end; {endM3}
{M4}  readln; {endM4}
{M}   end.
```

Rule (2) also requires that each statement within the indented compound statements be terminated with a semicolon. For example, the compound statement surrounded by the *begin* and *end* keywords labeled with Ns is found to include two statements, N1 and N2. Their ends must have corresponding semicolons:

```
      program FirstTree;
      var
          answer: string;
{M}   begin
{M1}  writeln('Do you have experience with formal notations?');
{endM1}
{M2}  readln(answer); {endM2}
{M3}  if answer = 'yes' then
{N}       begin
{N1}      writeln('In programming, you can see those notations');
{endN1}
{N2}      writeln('come to life!'); {endN2}
```

```
{N}     end
    else
        begin
        writeln('Studying Pascal will be satisfying because');
        writeln('you will learn one notation very well.');
        end; {endM3}
{M4} readln; {endM4}
{M}  end.
```

Finally, examine the last compound statement to see that its two statements have semicolons. If you learn to follow these two rules rigorously, you will have no trouble with semicolons. But if you make mistakes in their application, your program will either not run at all or do unexpected things.

A helpful double check on the correctness of your semicolons is the following: Look at each *else* in your program and check that no semicolon comes immediately before it on the current line or the previous line. If you follow the rules given above, you will never place a semicolon just before an *else*.

(If you read a standard Pascal manual, you will encounter a slightly different view of semicolons than that presented here. There semicolons are viewed as *separators* of statements within a compound statement. A compound statement is considered to be a sequence of statements between *begin* and *end*, and semicolons are placed between each pair of statements, as follows, where *s* stands for "statement":

```
begin s ; s ; s ; s end
```

When this is typed in the usual form for programs, it looks like this:

```
begin
s;
s;
s;
s
end
```

The last statement is not followed by a semicolon. This is sometimes confusing to students so this text uses the more uniform rule that every statement between the *begin* and *end* will be followed by a semicolon:

```
begin
s;
s;
s;
```

```
s;
end
```

The functioning of the programs is the same in both cases.)

Returning to decision trees, we find that all others are programmed similarly, but they may have more branches to keep track of. Let us program the book advice example. It begins very much like the previous one:

```
program BookAdvice;
var
    answer1: string;
begin
writeln('Do you wish a mathematical approach?');
readln(answer1);
if answer1 = 'yes' then
   Put code here to handle "yes" branch.
else
   Put code here to handle "no" branch. ;
readln;
end.
```

Next consider the code to handle the "yes" branch:

```
begin
writeln('Are you interested in programming');
writeln('or theoretical issues?');
readln(answer2);
if answer2 = 'programming' then
   begin
   writeln('I recommend "Oh! Pascal!" by');
   writeln('D. Cooper and M. Clancy.');
   end
else
   begin
   writeln('A fine overview is given in');
   writeln('the book "Algorithmics"');
   writeln('by D. Harel.');
   end;
end
```

Now we can insert the "yes" branch code into the appropriate position in the main program:

```
program BookAdvice;
var
    answer1, answer2: string;
begin
writeln('Do you wish a mathematical approach?');
readln(answer1);
if answer1 = 'yes' then
   begin
   writeln('Are you interested in programming');
   writeln('or theoretical issues?');
   readln(answer2);
   if answer2 = 'programming' then
      begin
      writeln('I recommend "Oh, Pascal!" by');
      writeln('D. Cooper and M. Clancy.');
      end
    else
      begin
      writeln('A fine overview is given in');
      writeln('the book "Algorithmics"');
      writeln('by D. Harel.');
      end;
   end
else
   Put code here to handle "no" branch. ;
readln;
end.
```

Similarly, we can write the code for the "no" branch and insert it into the main program to make the code complete:

```
program BookAdvice;
var
    answer1, answer2, answer3: string;
begin
writeln('Do you wish a mathematical approach?');
readln(answer1);
if answer1 = 'yes' then
    begin
    writeln('Are you interested in programming');
    writeln('or theoretical issues?');
```

```
      readln(answer2);
      if answer2 = 'programming' then
         begin
         writeln('I recommend "Oh, Pascal!" by');
         writeln('D. Cooper and M. Clancy.');
         end
   else
         begin
         writeln('A fine overview is given in');
         writeln('the book "Algorithmics"');
         writeln('by D. Harel.');
         end;
      end
else
         begin
         writeln('Would you prefer a book that');
         writeln('concentrates on programming or do you');
         writeln('desire a general overview of computer');
         writeln('science?');
         readln(answer3);
         if answer3 = 'programming' then
            begin
            writeln('A good place to start is with');
            writeln('"Karel the Robot" by R. Pattis.');
            end
         else
            begin
            writeln('You might enjoy "Great Ideas in');
            writeln('Computer Science" by A. Biermann');
            end;
         end;
readln;
end.
```

Different memory locations—*answer1*, *answer2*, or *answer3*—are used to store the different responses to questions. It is wise to keep these separated to avoid confusion in writing more complicated programs. Remember to declare all these locations.

Another version of the *if* statement is useful in programming decision trees with more than two branches at some nodes:

```
if condition then
    compound statement
```

If the condition is satisfied, the associated compound statement will be executed. If it is not, this statement will cause nothing to happen, and the program will proceed as if the statement did not exist.

The seagull classification decision tree gives a good example of this kind of programming. The initial version of the code can be written as follows:

```
program SeagullClass;
var
    answer1: string;
begin
writeln('What color are its legs?');
readln(answer1);
if answer1 = 'red' then
    Code for the case of red legs. ;
if answer1 = 'black' then
    Code for the case of black legs. ;
if answer1 = 'flesh' then
    Code for the case of flesh legs. ;
if answer1 = 'green' then
    Code for the case of green legs. ;
end.
```

If this program is continued, the code for the individual cases can be filled in as follows:

```
program SeagullClass;
var
    answer1, answer2: string;
begin
writeln('What color are its legs?');
readln(answer1);
if answer1 = 'red' then
    begin
    writeln('What color is its bill?');
    readln(answer2);
    if answer2= 'black' then
       begin
       writeln('What color is its wing tip?');
       readln(answer3);
           More code.
       end;
```

```
      if answer2 = 'yellow' then
         begin
         writeln('It is a Kittiwake seagull.');
         end;
   end;
if answer1 = 'black' then
   Code for the case of black legs. ;
if answer1 = 'flesh' then
   Code for the case of flesh legs. ;
if answer1 = 'green' then
   Code for the case of green legs. ;
end.
```

All decision trees, those discussed here and any others, can be programmed similarly. The only programming constructions needed are *writeln, readln, if-then-else, if-then*, and the program header and declarations. But even these programs are more complicated than is necessary, as we will see in chapter 4 when the subroutine is introduced.

At this point, it would be helpful for you to run some of these programs on a machine and to try some new ones as well. But before running any program, check it extensively to make sure that it expresses your intent properly. There are two kinds of reexamination to carry out: First, verify the syntax of the program to be sure it precisely follows the language rules; second, execute the code by hand to check whether the statements actually do what they are intended to do.

Let us do these two kinds of checks on the BookAdvice program, beginning with the syntax verification. Are all the statements well formed according to the rules of the language? Are the semicolons placed properly? The program will not run unless every detail is correct. We should also check the spacing and line indentations to be sure the program is clear and readable. Do the line indentations display the program's significant parts maximally? Spacing will not affect what the program does, but we must be careful to organize the code so that it is easy to understand.

Second, we execute the code by hand to be sure that it does what we want. The declaration at the beginning tells what memory locations must be maintained, so the hand calculation begins by writing these down.

```
answer1:
answer2:
answer3:
```

Then we start with the begin marker, read every line of code, and decide whether it is correct:

```
writeln('Do you wish a mathematical approach?');
```

After deciding that this is the correct first action, we go on to the second statement:

```
readln(answer1);
```

Is this correct, and is the answer being stored where we want it? Suppose the user types "no." Our hand simulation immediately records the result:

```
answer1:   no
answer2:
answer3:
```

Moving to the next statement, we see that the test *answer1* = "*yes*" is made, and we must methodically look at the location *answer1* and see whether the test succeeds. In this case, it does not, and control will pass to the statement following the *else*. We must now confirm that this action is what we wanted. The hand simulation continues, with every program action being scrutinized carefully.

*Only after thorough and extensive rereading, revising, and repeated verification should a program be committed for translation and execution. Expert programmers know well that errors in programs can cause huge losses of time and other resources, and they wisely spend the great majority of their time in program preparation and hand verification.*

### Exercises

1. Program the income tax helper decision tree shown above.

2. Design a decision tree of interest to you. Write a program for your tree.

3. Write a program for the seven-square Nim player described above.

---

## The Arrow Notation and Its Uses (C)

When we discuss a topic and find ourselves saying the same phrases over and over again, a common practice is to invent a notation that enables us to skip over the repetitive words. As an illustration, we find ourselves saying things like "an example of a legal identifier is *X17*" or "an example of a legal statement is *writeln('Program')*." In order to make these statements simpler and more precise, we will often use the *arrow notation*, which says the same thing, as follows:

```
<identifier> ==> X17
<statement> ==> writeln('Program')
```

This section will introduce the notation and give the rules that specify all the Pascal described in this chapter.

The first new notation uses angle brackets around a name: ⟨identifier⟩. This sequence of symbols "⟨identifier⟩" should be read as "an object called an 'identifier.'" The second notation is an arrow ==>, which in this context means "can be." Using these notations, we can give a general rule for identifiers:

```
<identifier> ==> a sequence of letters and/or digits
                 that begins with a letter
```

Translating this notation into English, we read: An object called an "identifier" can be a sequence of letters and/or digits that begins with a letter. Some examples of identifiers from this chapter are "ReadData" and "position1," and the notation can be used to specify them:

```
<identifier> ==> ReadData
<identifier> ==> position1
```

That is, an identifier can be the sequence of characters "ReadData" or the sequence "position1." Conceptually, identifiers are names given to objects like programs or memory locations.

There are two reasons why this notation is extremely important: (1) It is very useful for talking about and learning the Pascal language. For example, all the Pascal used in this book is summarized in just three pages in the Appendix of this book. Anytime you wish to check on what is legal or how to code a certain construct, a quick reference to the Appendix can often yield the answer. (2) This notation provides the basis for the translation mechanism used in chapter 9 and other mechanisms later in the book. If you use the notation regularly along the way, when you get to those chapters you will be comfortable with it.

Another kind of object in Pascal is called the "string expression." Let us use the arrow notation to define it.

```
<string expression> ==> <identifier>
<string expression> ==> 'any string of printable characters'
```

Paraphrasing these rules, a "string expression" can be an identifier or any string of printable characters surrounded by single quotation marks. Some string expressions from this chapter are:

```
<string expression> ==> position1
<string expression> ==> 'Do you wish a mathematical approach?'
```

String expressions are important because they are the things that can be printed.

We also studied statements in this chapter, and these are represented as ⟨statement⟩. Here are three forms introduced in the early sections:

```
<statement> ==> writeln(<string expression>)
<statement> ==> readln(<identifier>)
<statement> ==> readln
```

The first of these rules states that a statement can be the sequence

```
writeln(<string expression>)
```

where ⟨string expression⟩ is defined as above. Thus, our two examples of string expressions can be substituted here to obtain two legal statements:

```
writeln(position1)
writeln('Do you wish a mathematical approach?')
```

The two *readln* statements work in the same way.

Once statements are defined, we can define a sequence of statements called a "compound statement":

```
<compound statement> ==> begin
                            a sequence of <statement>'s
                            each followed by a semicolon
                         end
```

An illustration of a compound statement from this chapter is:

```
<compound statement> ==> begin
                            readln(position1);
                            writeln(position1);
                            readln;
                         end
```

Some additional kinds of statements are the *if-then-else* and *if-then* forms.

```
<statement> ==> if <boolean expression> then
                    <compound statement>
                else
                    <compound statement>
<statement> ==> if <boolean expression> then
                    <compound statement>
```

The only Boolean expression discussed so far is defined as

```
<boolean expression> ==> <identifier> = <string expression>
```

An example of a Boolean expression is

```
answer1 = 'yes'
```

and it can be used in an *if-then-else* form, as with

```
<statement> ==> if answer1 = 'yes' then
                begin
                writeln('In programming, you can see those');
                writeln('notations come to life!');
                end
           else
                begin
                writeln('Learning Pascal will be satisfying');
                writeln('because you will learn one notation');
                writeln('very well.');
                end
```

We also studied "variable declaration" in this chapter, defined by the rules

```
<variable declaration> ==> nothing
<variable declaration> ==> var
                            list of <identifier>'s :<type>;
              <type> ==> string
```

Thus, a variable declaration may be "nothing"; that is, it may be omitted, or it may be the sequence *var* followed by a list of identifiers, a colon, the type, and a semicolon. Here is a declaration from this chapter:

```
<variable declaration> ==> var
                            answer1, answer2: string;
```

Now we can define "program":

```
<program> ==> program <identifier>;
              <variable declaration>
              <compound statement>.
```

This definition states that an object called a "program" must include the following:

1. The header statement, which gives the program name, and an object called an "identifier" followed by a semicolon

2. The variable declaration
3. The body of statements of the program in the form of a compound statement
4. A period

You can write a program if you know how to fill in the bracketed objects on the right-hand side: ⟨identifier⟩, ⟨declaration⟩, and ⟨compound statement⟩. (The earlier rules have shown you how to do this.)

In order to understand the usefulness of these rules, we will examine how they can *derive* a program in a sequence of steps. For our purpose, the arrow ==> should be read as "can be replaced by," since the derivation of the program will involve a sequence of replacements. The program to be derived will be *ReadData*:

```
program ReadData;
var
   position1: string;
begin
readln(position1);
writeln(position1);
readln;
end.
```

The process begins with ⟨program⟩, and the above rules give the allowed substitutions for the creation of the target program. Beginning with the program rule, we obtain

```
<program> ==> program <identifier>;
             <variable declaration>
             <compound statement>.
```

The identifier rule

```
<identifier> ==> a sequence of letters and/or digits
                 that begins with a letter
```

tells us that ⟨identifier⟩ can be replaced in the program by any sequence of letters and/or digits that begins with a letter. The target program has the sequence *ReadData* in this location, and we know from the identifier rule that

```
<identifier> ==> ReadData
```

This substitution is made into the program:

```
<program> ==> program ReadData;
             <variable declaration>
             <compound statement>.
```

Next we note that the target program declares *position1* as a location for storing a string. Furthermore, the declaration rule make., it possible to generate the proper code:

```
<variable declaration> ==> var
                               position1:string;
```

This substitution is made into the program:

```
<program> ==> program ReadData;
              var
                  position1: string;
              <compound statement>.
```

The rule for compound statement makes it possible to generate a *begin*, any number of statements with semicolons, and an *end*. The target program has three statements, so the following form should be used:

```
<compound statement> ==> begin
                             <statement>;
                             <statement>;
                             <statement>;
                             end
```

This substitution leads to a further development of the program:

```
<program> ==> program ReadData;
              var
                  position1: string;
              begin
              <statement>;
              <statement>;
              <statement>;
              end.
```

Finally, the three rules

```
<statement> ==> readln(position1)
<statement> ==> writeln(position1)
<statement> ==> readln
```

come from the general rules for statements. These can be applied to the program to complete the derivation:

```
<program> ==> program ReadData;
              var
                  position1: string;
              begin
              readln(position1);
              writeln(position1);
              readln;
              end.
```

Notice that the rules have inserted every detail of the program correctly, including the punctuation.

In summary, any program studied in this chapter can be similarly generated. Apply the syntax rules beginning with ⟨program⟩ until the final program is derived. These rules will state precisely the correct format. While programs are not ordinarily generated in this way, if you are ever confused about exactly how to code something, you can use them.

A standard manual on Pascal provides a large number of rules beyond those given here, usually in the form of flowcharts with circles and arrows showing the allowed formats. This book uses only a fraction of the whole Pascal language and therefore includes relatively few syntactic rules.

### Exercises

1. Use the syntax rules to generate two examples of each of the following kinds of objects: ⟨identifier⟩, ⟨string expression⟩, ⟨statement⟩, ⟨compound statement⟩, ⟨boolean expression⟩, ⟨variable declaration⟩, ⟨program⟩.

2. Show how to generate the program *ReadWriteDemo* using the rules.

3. Show how to generate the program *FirstTree* using the rules.

## Summary (B)

This chapter introduced the concept of the decision tree and its many applications to information processing. The concepts necessary for programming decision trees were covered, including the Pascal constructions for writing, reading, *if-then-else, if-then,* declarations, and programs. You should be able to use these ideas to design and program decision trees for numerous applications. A strategy introduced in chapter 4 will make it possible to simplify the coding of these trees so that larger ones can be more easily programmed.

# 2    Text Manipulation and Algorithm Design

## What Is Text Manipulation? (A)

"Something there is that doesn't love a wall."

Who wrote this line, where does it appear, and what was the context? We would like to be able to answer questions like this, but the required effort could be extreme. The only approach may be to collect a pile of books and hope that it will be found in one of them. We must begin with the first book, page through it carefully in our search, and then move through the rest of the books.

Another way to solve this problem is to have our whole library stored on computer files and to let a machine do the work. If this line appears anywhere in any book, it will be straightforward for the machine to do the work, and it can do it thousands of times faster than any human. This is an example of a *text manipulation* problem—the kind of calculation we will examine in this chapter. The computer manipulates the text in some way to get our job done for us. In this case, it grabs each sequential line in every book and compares it with the line we are trying to match.

You may be familiar with the automatic spelling correction feature that is included with many word processors. It enables you to type some text and have the machine highlight any words that it cannot find in its dictionary. This is another example of text manipulation. The machine must be able to find each word in the text and then do the dictionary lookup.

There are numerous examples of other interesting text manipulation problems. One more, an interesting mathematical puzzle that is of particular importance in computer science, will be given here. (Individuals not enthusiastic about such puzzles may skip forward to the next section.) Suppose there are two strings of symbols with the names *string1* and *string2*. Suppose further that there are five operations that modify these strings as follows:

Operation 1: Concatenate b to the right end of *string1* and bbabaa to the right end of *string2*. (Here "concatenate" means "join." Thus concatenating b to the right end of string cdce results in the new string cdceb.)

Operation 2: Concatenate ab to the right end of *string1* and abb to the right end of *string2*.

Operation 3: Concatenate abba to the right end of *string1* and ba to the right end of *string2*.

Operation 4: Concatenate aab to the right end of *string1* and bab to the right end of *string2*.

Operation 5: Concatenate bab to the right end of *string1* and a to the right end of *string2*.

These operations are summarized in the following table:

| Operation | Concatenate to *string1* | Concatenate to *string2* |
|---|---|---|
| 1 | b | bbabaa |
| 2 | ab | abb |
| 3 | abba | ba |
| 4 | aab | bab |
| 5 | bab | a |

The question is, assuming that *string1* and *string2* begin with no symbols, what sequence of one or more operations will result in the two strings being identical?

Let us attempt to find a solution to this problem. We will begin by applying operation 1 to the empty strings:

string1     | b |

string2     | bbabaa |

This is a successful way to begin because the two strings are the same on the first symbol, and we can hope to find a way to apply other operators to make them identical throughout. Next we could apply operator 2:

string1     | bab |

string2     | bbabaaabb |

This was unsuccessful because the second and third symbols are different in the two strings. Operator 2 should not be applied here. But operator 1 could be applied a second time:

string1 | bb |
string2 | bbabaabbabaa |

and then operator 2 could be tried:

string1 | bbab |
string2 | bbabaabbabaaabb |

This is a good start, but *string2* is becoming too long. Are there some operators that would enable *string1* to catch up and achieve equality? Maybe we should have started with a different operator? Or perhaps there is no solution?

This is an example of what is called the *Post Correspondence Problem*, and it has importance in computer science, as will be noted in Chapter 14. For the purposes of the current study, it should be thought of as simply an interesting puzzle that computers can help us solve.

Our main project in this chapter will be to create an editor that will enable you to modify any string in any way you wish. We will also study some important concepts in computer science, including the algorithm, a recipe for doing something, and its design and coding into an executable program.

---

## Algorithms and Program Design for Text Manipulation (B)

An *algorithm* is a method, procedure, or recipe for doing a job. It usually has *inputs*, objects that are to be used by the algorithm, and it always has *outputs*, which are the results of its action. An algorithm also must have a sequence of steps that show what actions must be taken in order to obtain the output. These steps must be well-defined actions like "move an object from one place to another" or "count the (finite) number of objects in a box." They cannot include poorly defined operations such as "compose a beautiful piece of music." The field of computer science may be thought of as the study of algorithms and their automatic execution by machines.

When we study programming, we are studying the process of creating and coding algorithms. Creation involves the discovery of a method for doing a task and coding is concerned with translating that method from a natural language like English into a computer language.

Consider the creation of an algorithm for exchanging the contents of two boxes. If we consider this problem for a moment, we see how to solve it:

1. Move the contents of one box, say box 1, to a temporary storage place.
2. Move the contents of the other box, box 2, to box 1.
3. Move the objects in the temporary storage place into box 2.

(How such programs came into existence in our brains is a mystery.) After we select a method for doing the task, we write down the steps. The inputs to the algorithm are the two boxes with their given contents; the outputs are the same boxes with their contents exchanged.

Next we would like to use a computer language, say Pascal, to code this algorithm. There is no feature in Pascal to move objects as described in these steps, but there is a feature similar enough to be able to code the algorithm directly. This feature is called the *assignment* statement; it is written as

```
x := y
```

where $x$ and $y$ are the names of locations in memory. It means "destroy the contents of $x$ and copy the contents of $y$ into $x$." The main difference between "move" in the algorithm and "copy" is that "move" leaves nothing behind, and "copy" it leaves everything behind. Moving objects from box 1 leaves box 1 empty, and copying from box 1 leaves box 1 unchanged. Another important characteristic of the copy operation is that it destroys or covers up the objects in the destination location. Suppose $x$ and $y$ appear as follows:

x | abc |

y | efgh |

and $x := y$ is carried out. That is, $y$ is copied into $x$. Then the result destroys the contents of $x$ and leaves two copies of the contents of $y$.

x | efgh |

y | efgh |

The three steps of the exchange algorithm can be coded using the assignment statement. Assume the inputs are *box1* and *box2* and that a temporary location for storing information is *temp*. The output is *box1* and *box2* with their contents exchanged:

```
temp:=box1;
box1:=box2;
box2:=temp;
```

To trace the execution of this code on sample data, suppose the locations begin as shown:

box1 | abc |     box2 | efgh |     temp | |

Then the changes are easy to follow for the three statements:

temp := box1;

box1 | abc |     box2 | efgh |     temp | abc |

box1 := box2;

box1 | efgh |     box2 | efgh |     temp | abc |

box2 := temp;

box1 | efgh |     box2 | abc |     temp | abc |

The goal is achieved: the contents of *box1* and *box2* have been exchanged.

Here is the complete program for reading two strings, writing them, exchanging them, and then writing them again:

```
program Exchange;
var
    box1, box2, temp: string;
begin
readln(box1);
readln(box2);
writeln(box1,' ',box2);
temp:=box1;
```

```
box1:=box2;
box2:=temp;
writeln(box1,' ',box2);
readln;
end.
```

In this program the *writeln* statement is used to write three items: the contents of *box1*, the string containing a space, and the contents of *box2*.

In order to be sure that you understand the program *Exchange*, run it on some sample inputs. Here is an example:

| | | |
|---|---|---|
| Typed inputs: | Jack | |
| | Jill | |
| Machine responses: | Jack | Jill |
| | Jill | Jack |

One way to help yourself remember the meaning of the assignment statement is to think of it as a backward arrow. That is, $x := y$ can be thought of as meaning $x <== y$, or $x$ receives the contents of $y$.

Let us consider another problem, the acquisition of a person's name in the following dialogue:

| | |
|---|---|
| Computer: | Tell me your first name. |
| User: | Alan |
| Computer: | Thank you, Alan. Tell me your last name. |
| User: | Turing |
| Computer: | Your full name is Alan Turing. |

The inputs to the algorithm for solving this problem are the user's two names, and the outputs are the three messages shown. Here are the required algorithmic steps:

1. Print "Tell me your first name."
2. Input a string of characters and store them.
3. Create a string beginning with "Thank you," continuing with the characters that were typed in step 2, and ending with ".Tell me your last name."
4. Print the string from step 3.
5. Input another string of characters.
6. Create the string "Your full name is " followed by the string from step 2 followed by a space followed by the string from step 5 followed by the string ".".
7. Print the string from step 6.

Coding this algorithm is as easy as coding the previous one; only one new Turbo Pascal construction is needed, that for concatenation. In order to assemble the strings in steps 3 and 6, we need an operator to glue strings together. The operator is denoted by "+" and it concatenates two strings to produce a third. Thus, the program

```
program t;
var
    x, y, z:string;
begin
x := 'abc';
y := 'defg';
z := x+y;
readln;
end.
```

will put "abc" into *x*, "defg" into *y*, and "abcdefg" into *z*.

If you are using Think Pascal, then an operator called *concat* is used instead of "+". So you would write the above program the same way except that the seventh line would be

```
z := concat(x,y);
```

instead of

```
z := x + y;
```

Using the "+" operator, the seven steps may now be coded:

```
program GetName;
var
    first, last, message1, message2 :string;
begin
writeln('Tell me your first name.');
readln(first);
message1:='Thank you, ' + first + '. Tell me your last name.';
writeln(message1);
readln(last);
message2:='Your full name is ' + first + ' ' + last + '.';
writeln(message2);
readln;
end.
```

In Think Pascal, the seventh line would be

```
message1:=concat('Thank you, ',first,'. Tell me your last name.');
```

This section has explained that programming can be separated into two distinct parts: the creation of the algorithm, which gives the method of solution, and the coding of the steps of the method. Both parts require creativity and hard work. In addition, this section has introduced the assignment statement and the concatenation operator and shown their application in some text manipulation problems.

**Exercises**

1. Write a program that reads a string of symbols and then prints two adjacent copies of that string. For example, if the program reads "think," it will print "thinkthink". Design an algorithm to solve this problem. Remember you must create two copies of the input string and then put them together to obtain the output string. Then code the algorithm in Pascal.

2. Many regular nouns in English can be changed to their plural form by adding an "s" at the end. Write the algorithm that reads such nouns and prints their plural form. Write the code for the program.

3. Write an algorithm that interviews a person to obtain his or her address in the same fashion as the name acquisition program. Write the code.

4. Write an algorithm that does one step of the Post Correspondence Problem. It should input *string1* and *string2* and then ask the user which operation is to be applied. Finally it should apply the selected operation and print the new strings. The algorithm might look something like this:

   1. Write "Input string1 and string2."
   2. Read the strings.
   3. Write "Which operator should be applied?"
   4. Input 1,2,3,4, or 5.
   5. If 1 was input then ...
   6. If 2 was input then ...
          ETC.

   Now write a program to execute your algorithm.

5. Can you find a solution to the Post Correspondence Problem given in the introduction? Create another set of operations similar to those given and find out whether your version of the problem has a solution.

## String and Integer Data Types (B)

A person asked to compute the following quantity may be confused:

```
423 + 51 = ?
```

Is the answer equal to 474, as might have been concluded before reading this chapter? Or is the answer 42351, the result of concatenating the two strings of symbols, 423 and 51? The truth is that we must know whether the data objects 423 and 51 are to be regarded as integers or as strings. In the former case, the operation "+" stands for the addition property that every schoolchild knows. In the latter case, the symbols 51 are placed in sequence with 423.

We can conclude that data can be of various *types* and that the way data are processed depends on what types they are. This book will use three types—*string*, *integer*, and *real*. It is always necessary to tell the Pascal system which type is being used so that it can compute the desired answers. Here is the program to read two strings, concatenate them, and print them:

```
program Concat;
var
    x, y, z: string;
begin
readln(x);
readln(y);
z := x + y;
writeln('z is ',z);
readln;
end.
```

Here is the program to read two integers, add them up, and print the sum:

```
program Add;
var
    x, y, z: integer;
begin
readln(x);
readln(y);
z := x + y;
writeln('z is ',z);
readln;
end.
```

It was very easy to obtain the expected computation in these two cases because we declared the desired data type. However, there is one rule that must always be followed in Pascal: each operator such as "+" functions properly only if it is given the correct types. In the following examples, you will see that if an illegal combination of types is presented to the operator, it will not be able to give a proper answer. Thus, "+" works correctly in these cases

```
(integer) + (integer) = (integer)
```

and

```
(string) + (string) = (string)
```

but there is no definition for the expression

```
(integer) + (string) = ?
```

The following program will not function properly because it attempts to use "+" to operate on an illegal pair of objects:

```
program AddError;
var
    x: integer;
    y, z: string;
begin
readln(x);
readln(y);
z := x + y;
writeln('z is ',z);
readln;
end.
```

There are several other operators applicable to the integer type, including multiplication "*", subtraction "−", and division "div". There are also additional forms that can be used in *if* statements, such as greater than ">" and less than "<", as in the following program, which reads two integers and prints them out with the smallest one first:

```
program SmallestFirst;
var
    x, y: integer;
begin
writeln('Type two integers.');
readln(x);
readln(y);
writeln('In order, they are');
if x > y then
    begin
    writeln(y,' ',x);
    end
```

```
else
    begin
    writeln(x,' ',y);
    end;
readln;
end.
```

It is extremely important that you understand the difference between the various data types and remember that in Pascal each is always restricted to its own well-defined operations. Internally, the various data types are stored in different ways. Integers are stored as binary numbers (or a variant of them), as will be explained in chapter 7, and strings are stored with one character in each of a sequence of memory cells. The following sections will give programs in which both string and integer data types are used.

**Exercises**

1. Design an algorithm that reads an integer and determines whether it is positive. If the integer is positive, it prints "positive," and otherwise it prints "not positive." Code the algorithm.

2. Design an algorithm that reads two integers and prints their sum, difference, product, and quotient. Code the algorithm.

3. Design an algorithm that reads three integers and prints them in order from smallest to largest. Code the algorithm.

## More Text Manipulation (B)

Assignment and concatenation give methods for moving and gluing strings of symbols, but there are other operations that we might like to do. For example, how would we copy several characters out of the middle of a string? If a location contains the string "computer," we would like to have a method to copy the letters "put" from its center. Ideally, the operation should allow us to designate what string to copy characters from, where to begin copying, and how many characters to copy. If "computer" is stored in a location called *A1* and its three-character substring is to be moved into a location *A2*, the image is this:

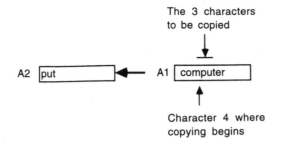

Turbo Pascal includes a convenient feature for doing this job—*copy. Copy* works as we would expect, and, in fact, the previous task is programmed with the following code:

```
A2 := copy(A1,4,3)
```

It means that characters are to be copied from *A1* starting at character number 4 and including a total of three characters. Those characters are to be copied into *A2*. In general, *copy(s,i,j)* means copy from string *s* starting at character number *i* and including a total of *j* characters. If *i* exceeds the length of string *s*, then a string of length zero will be copied.

Here are some more examples of the use of *copy*. If *x* contains "abcdefgh," then *y* will receive the string indicated:

| Statement executed | New contents of y |
|---|---|
| y := copy(x,3,4) | cdef |
| y := copy(x,1,1) | a |
| y := copy(x,6,1) | f |
| y := copy(x,9,2) | (string of length zero) |

Another useful Turbo Pascal feature—called *length*—finds the length of a string. We can find the length of string *x* by typing *length(x)*. Consider the following program:

```
program FindLength;
var
    x: string;
    y: integer;
begin
x := 'abcd';
y := length(x);
```

```
writeln(y);
readln;
end.
```

If this program is run, it will print the number 4. *x* has length 4, *length* will find it, and the second statement will load 4 into *y*. Note that *y* must be an integer.

What does the following program do?

```
program FindIt;
var
    x, y: string;
begin
readln(x);
y := copy(x,length(x),1);
writeln(y);
readln;
end.
```

Suppose *FindIt* reads "abcd." Then *x* will receive this string. Then *length(x)* is 4, and *y* is loaded with *copy(x,4,1)*. So *y* receives "d," and this is printed. In general, this program will read a string and print the last character of the string. Thus, we say *copy(x,length(x),1)* stands for the last character in *x*. Here are some more uses of *copy* and their meanings.

| Expression | Meaning |
| --- | --- |
| copy(x,length(x)-1,1) | The second-to-last character in *x*. |
| copy(x,length(x)-2,1) | The third-from-last character in *x*. |
| copy(x,length(x)-1,2) | The last two characters in *x*. |
| copy(x,1,1) | The first character in *x*. |
| copy(x,1,2) | The first two characters in *x*. |
| copy(x,1,length(x)-1) | All of *x* except the last character. |
| copy(x,2,length(x)-1) | All of *x* except the first character. |
| copy(x,2,length(x)-2) | *x* with its first and last characters removed. |
| copy(x,1,length(x) div 2) | The first half of *x*. |

Suppose we wish to analyze the third expression, *copy(x,length(x)-1,2)*. First, assume that *x* contains the word "network." Since *x* has length 7, we need to compute *copy(x,7-1,2)* which is *copy(x,6,2)*. This means go to the sixth character of *x* and grab two characters. So we take the sixth and seventh characters of "network" and they are "rk." We can repeat this exercise on several examples and finally conclude that *copy(x,length(x)-1,2)* will always grab the last two characters of *x*. This is what the table says it does. Now let us examine *copy(x,2,length(x)-1)*. Assume again that *x* has "network" in it. Then we are computing *copy(x,2,7-1)* or *copy(x,2,6)*, which yields "etwork." So this finds the string in *x* and removes its first character. You can try a few and see that it always does.

These substring features can be used to write many interesting programs. Consider the following sample nouns and their plural forms:

| Nouns | Plural forms |
| --- | --- |
| bird | birds |
| whale | whales |
| cow | cows |
| pony | ponies |
| bunny | bunnies |
| sheep | sheep |
| mouse | mice |

By now you will have discovered certain patterns. Many nouns are made plural by adding an "s," as in the first three cases. However, nouns that end in "y" form their plural by changing "y" to "i" and adding "es." Others follow neither rule and can be classed as special cases.

A way to design the pluralization algorithm is to have it first check whether the incoming noun is a special case. If it is special, find its plural form and stop. If it is not special, then apply the correct rule.

1. Input a noun.
2. Check whether it is a known special case. If so, select its plural form, and mark the task done.
3. If the task is not done, check whether the noun ends in "y".
   (a) If so remove the "y" and add "ies".
   (b) Otherwise, add "s".
4. Print the plural form.

The program can then be coded using the string operations. (We assume for brevity that the only known special cases are those in the table.)

```
program Plurals;
var
    noun, plural, task: string;
```

```
begin
writeln('Input a noun.');
readln(noun);
task := 'not done';
if noun = 'mouse' then
    begin
    plural := 'mice';
    task := 'done';
    end;
if noun = 'sheep' then
    begin
    plural := 'sheep';
    task := 'done';
    end;
if task = 'not done' then
    begin
    if copy(noun,length(noun),1)='y' then
        begin
        plural := copy(noun,1,length(noun)-1) + 'ies';
        end
    else
        begin
        plural := noun + 's';
        end;
    end;
writeln('The plural version is ',plural,'.');
readln;
end.
```

You should study this code carefully to be sure that you understand it. Can you explain why the code *task* := *'done'* is included after a special case (such as *plural* := *'mice'*)? You can see the purpose of *task* := *'done'* more clearly if you remove it and run the program on the input "mouse".

The last feature for string manipulation we will discuss in this chapter is *position*, which finds the position of one string inside another. It is written as *pos*, and *pos(x,y)* means "find the position of the first character in the first occurrence of *x* in string *y*." If *x* is not in *y*, then *pos(x,y)* will give 0. Here are some sample evaluations.

| x | y | pos(x,y) |
|---|---|---|
| cde | abcdef | 3 |
| de | abcdef | 4 |
| def | abcdef | 4 |
| aa | abcdef | 0 |
| bc | abcbcbc | 2 |
| cbc | abcbcbc | 3 |
| a | abcdef | 1 |
| abcd | abc | 0 |

Let us suppose that we are to type a string into the computer but no hyphens are allowed. We could use the *pos* to check for hyphens and give an error message if one occurs. Here is the program:

```
program HyphenCheck;
var
    x:string;
begin
writeln('Type a string.');
readln(x);
if pos('-',x) > 0 then
    begin
    writeln('Sorry but a hyphen is not allowed.');
    end
else
    begin
    writeln('Your string is acceptable.');
    end;
readln;
end.
```

### Exercises

1. Tell exactly what each program will do if the string *s1* is read as "cdef". (Where applicable, if an integer *i* is read, assume it is 3. Where a string *s2* is read, assume it is "abcdefgh".) Then tell in simple English what the program does on inputs in general.

```
program G1;
var
    s1:string;
begin
readln(s1);
s1 := s1 + 'aaaa';
writeln(s1);
readln;
end.

program G2;
var
    s1:string;
begin
readln(s1);
s1 := s1 + copy(s1,1,1);
writeln(s1);
readln;
end.

program G3;
var
    s1:string;
begin
readln(s1);
s1 := copy(s1,length(s1),1) + copy(s1,2,length(s1)-2) +
    copy(s1,1,1);
writeln(s1);
readln;
end.

program G4;
var
    s1:string;
    i:integer;
begin
readln(s1);
readln(i);
s1 := copy(s1,i,length(s1)-i+1);
writeln(s1);
readln;
end.
```

```
program G5;
var
    s1,s2:string;
    i:integer;
begin
readln(s1);
readln(s2);
i := pos(s1,s2);
s2 := copy(s2,i,length(s2)-i+1);
writeln(s2);
readln;
end.

program G6;
var
    s1:string;
    i:integer;
begin
readln(s1);
readln(i);
s1 := copy(s1,1,i-1) + '*' + copy(s1,i,length(s2)-i+1);
writeln(s1);
readln;
end.
```

2. Design an algorithm that reads a string and prints the string with its first and last characters removed. Write the Pascal code.

3. Design an algorithm that reads a string and a number. Then it prints the first part of the string, specifically the number of characters indicated by the number. Write the code.

4. Design an algorithm that reads a string and a number. Then it prints the last part of the string, the number of characters indicated by the number. Write the code.

5. Design an algorithm that reads two strings. If the first string is found to be a substring of the second, it outputs "yes" ; otherwise it outputs "no." Write the code.

---

## Programming Text-Editing Functions (B)

The following examples and exercises will teach you how to construct parts of a text-editing program. We will design code for inserting and deleting text and for other simple operations. The next section will show you how to combine these individual parts to produce a simple text-editing system that enables users to type text into a computer and to modify it or print it conveniently.

Our editor will use the concept of a *pointer* (or *cursor*), which is an indicator of where changes are to be made. Suppose that we have the text "Mary had a little lamb" and wish to make a change just at the position of the word "little." We will set the pointer, represented by a #, to indicate the first letter of that word:

```
Mary had a little lamb.
          #
```

Suppose we decide to insert "very" at the position of "little"; then we will do an insert command and type "very":

```
Mary had a very little lamb.
          #
```

Now suppose that we change our mind and wish to delete "very little" starting at the position of the pointer; we will do a delete instruction and indicate that twelve characters are to be deleted. We are deleting "very" followed by a space and "little" followed by a space.

```
Mary had a lamb.
          #
```

Here is how the actual dialogue with our proposed editor will proceed:

```
Computer:  Command:
User:      i                              (This means "insert." )
Computer:  Insert what?
User:      Mary had a little lamb.
Computer:  Mary had a little lamb.
           #
Computer:  Command:
User:      p                              (This means "point." )
Computer:  Point to what?
User:      little                         (The pointer will move to "little." )
Computer:  Mary had a little lamb.
                      #
Computer:  Command:
User:      i                              (Insert.)
Computer:  Insert what?
User:      very
```

Computer:    `Mary had a very little lamb.`
                            `#`
Computer:    `Command:`
User:        `d`                                    (This means "delete.")
Computer:    `Delete how many characters?`
User:        `12`
Computer:    `Mary had a lamb.`
                            `#`

Individual routines must be written for each operation—to insert, to move the pointer, and to delete. Let us write the insert routine first. In the dialogue given above, the job of the insert routine is to do the sequence of actions that follow the i command. Before the i command is given, we have the text "Mary had a little lamb" with the pointer at the twelfth character. Then we have this interaction:

Computer:    `Insert what?`
User:        `very`

This results in the text "Mary had a very little lamb" and the pointer is still at the twelfth character.

We need to write code that will make these things happen. (All our considerations will assume that the string of characters being manipulated is contained in a location called *text* and that an integer variable called *ptr* tells which character is being pointed to.) Here is the algorithm:

1. Print "Insert what?"
2. Input a string and put it into *new*.
3. Construct the string of characters in *text* up to the position to the left of the pointer, followed by *new*, followed by the rest of the characters in *text*. Copy this modified string into *text*.

Next we write the code for insert. First, translate expressions like "the string of characters in *text* up to the position to the left of the pointer" into Turbo Pascal. The *copy* feature provides the necessary mechanism:

| English | Translation |
| --- | --- |
| the string of characters in *text* up to the position to the left of the pointer | copy(text,1,ptr − 1) |
| the rest of the characters in *text* | copy(text,ptr,length(text) − ptr + 1) |

Here is the code:

```
begin
writeln('Insert what?');
readln(new);
text:=copy(text,1,ptr-1) + new + copy(text,ptr,length(text)-ptr+1);
end
```

We can also program the move pointer routine. The algorithm is straightforward:

1. Print "Point to what?"
2. Input a string and put it into *target.*
3. Put into the integer location called *ptr* the position of the first character of *target* in *text.* (This can be done with *ptr:=pos(target,text).*)

**Exercises**

1. Code the algorithm for setting the pointer, as described above. Test your code by putting it into this main program:

```
program edtest;
var
    text, command:string;
    ptr:integer;
begin
writeln('Input text:');
readln(text);
writeln('Input the pointer value:');
readln(ptr);
writeln('Command:');
readln(command);
if command = 'p' then
    begin
    Put your code for setting the pointer here.
    end
writeln(text);
writeln(ptr);
readln;
end.
```

Here is an example of how this program should run:

```
Input text:
Jack and Jill went up the hill.
Input the pointer value:
3
Command:
p
Point to what?
Jill
Jack and Jill went up the hill.
10
```

(The pointer now gives the first character of the word "Jill.")

2. Design an algorithm for executing the delete operation described above. This algorithm should input the number of characters to be deleted and then remove the required number of characters starting at the pointer. Code the algorithm and put it into a test main program like that in problem 1 except that your code should execute if command = 'd' instead of command = 'p'. The resulting program should, for example, be able to execute this interaction:

```
Input text:
Jack and Jill went up the hill.
Input the pointer value:
6
Command:
d
Delete how many characters?
9
Jack went up the hill.
6
```

The strategy for doing this is as follows: The new string should be made up of a string of the characters to the left of the deleted characters followed by a string of the characters to the right of the deleted characters. You need to use *copy* to compute the first string, *copy* to compute the second string, and then concatenate them together: *text* := *copy*( , , ) + *copy*( , , ).

3. Design an algorithm for an operation called "change" that will be invoked using the code "c." This operation will read a number telling how many characters following the pointer are to be changed. Write the code and place it into a main routine similar to that in problem 1. Here is an example of how your total program should work:

```
Input text:
Jack and Jill went up the hill.
Input the pointer value:
10
Command:
c
Change how many characters?
4
To what?
Sally
Jack and Sally went up the hill.
10
```

4. Sometimes it is useful to have a command "s" that will insert a space at the pointer position if one is needed. Here is how it should work, again using a main program like that in problem 1.

```
Input text:
Jack andJill went up the hill.
Input the pointer value:
9
Command:
s
Jack and Jill went up the hill.
9
```

## First Attempts at a Loop (B)

The editor program depends on repetition:

```
input command
carry out command
input command
carry out command
input command
carry out command
- -
```
(and so forth)

We need a program construction called a *loop* to provide this cyclic action:

> input command
>
> carry out command

The Pascal language offers a very easy way to program this loop. We simply mark the beginning of the code to be repeated with *while true do*:

```
while true do
     input command
     carry out command
```

"While true do" may seem like a strange way to ask for repetitions, but it will not seem so after some additional examples. If the codes for "input command" and "carry out command" are filled in properly, the program will execute these commands endlessly.

There are two ways to stop a loop of this kind. The first is to hit an "interrupt" key on your computer. Consult your computer manual or friend to find out how to stop a looping program. The other way is to change the *while* statement in a way that tells it when to stop (or "exit"). We will see how to do that later in this section.

The loop feature should be tested before it is used in the editor. Here is its simplest possible form:

```
program Repetition;
begin
while true do
     begin
     writeln('Begin the loop.');
     writeln('Here is some more.');
     end;
end.
```

Execution of this program yields the following two messages, which will appear on your screen as fast as it can print them:

```
Begin the loop.
Here is some more.
Begin the loop.
Here is some more.
Begin the loop.
Here is some more.
  - -
  - -
```

Notice we follow an indentation policy with looping code similar to that established for *if-then* code. We also place *begin* and *end* markers around the indented code. Here is another program to try:

```
program RepeatAs;
var
    cursor: string;
begin
cursor := '#';
while true do
    begin
    cursor := 'A' + cursor;
    writeln(cursor);
    end;
end.
```

Can you explain the behavior of this program? Each time the loop code is repeated, a string is created by the computation *'A' + cursor*. Then this new string is placed into *cursor*.

Let us revise this program slightly. We will type an integer and then add *A*s only until the length of the string equals that number.

```
program RepeatAs2;
var
    cursor: string;
    i,ptr:integer;
begin
writeln('How many characters?');
readln(ptr);
cursor := '#';
i := 1;
while i < ptr do
    begin
    cursor := 'A' + cursor;
    writeln(cursor);
    i := i + 1;
    end;
readln;
end.
```

Here the integer *i* is set to 1 before the loop is begun. Then each time around the loop, *i* is increased by 1. The loop will continue "while" *i* has value less than *ptr*.

As you will see below, this particular loop is very important because we will use it in our editor to place the cursor exactly where we want it. We will use the code that appears here except that we will replace the *A* by a blank space.

**Exercises**

1. Run the program Repetition given above.

2. Run the program RepeatAs given above.

3. Run the program RepeatAs2 given above.

4. Revise the program RepeatAs2 so that it adds spaces to the front of *cursor* in place of As and have it print the result only once at the end. Here is an example of how it should look:

```
How many characters?
10
         #
```

## Building the Editor (B)

Returning to the editor, we can now be more precise about the behavior we seek. The dialogue in the previous section shows that in order to receive our command, a write statement *writeln('Command:')* must begin the code and be followed by an input statement. Then if we type "i," the program will carry out the insert code developed in the previous section. However, if we type another command, such as "p," "d," "c," or "s," a different code should be executed. Here is the plan for the program:

```
print the word "Command:"
input the user's command
if the user typed "i", then
    carry out an insert operation
if the user typed "p", then
    do a pointer move operation
if - - -
if - - -
- - -
print the text with the new change
print the cursor in the correct position
```

Here is some of the code:

```
begin
writeln('Command;');
readln(command);
if command = 'i' then
    begin
    writeln('Insert what?');
    readln(new);
    text := copy(text,1,ptr-1) + new +
            copy(text,ptr,length(text)-ptr+1);
    end;
if command = 'p' then
    put pointer code here from problem 1 above ;
if command = 'd' then
    put delete code here from problem 2 above ;

(and so forth)

writeln(text);
cursor := '#';
i := 1;
while i < ptr do
    begin
    cursor := ' ' + cursor;
    i := i + 1;
    end;
writeln(cursor);
end
```

But the program is not complete; it will execute only one command. To tell the machine to repeat command after command after command we must insert the loop instruction. We might also want to write a message at the beginning and end of the program to remind ourselves of the entrance and exit of the program. Now the variables *text* and *ptr* should be given some initial values. (Because of peculiarities of the programming system we are using, they may contain something that we do not want.) All the instructions assume *text* contains something, so let us put a string of length zero into it, which will be represented by two single quotes typed next to each other. The code also assumes *ptr* always has a value, so let us put one into it. We will initialize the command as * which means "no command."

```pascal
program Editor;
var
    text,new,target,command,cursor:string;
    i,ptr:integer;
begin
writeln('Enter Editor.');
text := '';
ptr := 1;
command := '*';
while true do
    begin
    writeln('Command;');
    readln(command);
    if command = 'i' then
        begin
        writeln('Insert what?');
        readln(new);
        text := copy(text,1,ptr-1) + new +
                copy(text,ptr,length(text)-ptr+1);
        end;
    if command = 'p' then
        put pointer code here ;
    if command = 'd' then
        put delete code here ;

    (put other commands here )

    writeln(text);
    cursor := '#';
    i := 1;
    while i < ptr do
        begin
        cursor := ' ' + cursor;
        i := i + 1;
        end;
    writeln(cursor);
    end;
writeln('Exit Editor.');
readln;
end.
```

It is often helpful to write comments about a program in order to keep the various parts of the code in mind; they can also be useful to another person who may use the code or need to revise it. Pascal offers a means for entering these comments. If they are surrounded with curly brackets "{" and "}," they can be placed anywhere in the code without affecting execution because the computer will not process characters nested within these brackets. Some detailed suggestions are given in chapter 4 about where comments should be placed and what information they should contain. Here is another copy of the program with comments added to aid readability:

```
program Editor;              {This is the editor program for chapter 2.}
var
    text,                    {This holds the text to be edited.}
    new,                     {This will hold new text to be inserted.}
    target,                  {This will hold a string to be searched for.}
    command,                 {This will hold the command.}
    cursor:string;           {This will hold the string that has the cursor #.}
    i,ptr:integer;           {These will hold an index and the pointer.}
begin
writeln('Enter Editor.');    {This begins the main routine.}
text := '';                  {We initialize text as a string of length zero.}
ptr := 1;                    {We initialize ptr to point to the first character.}
command := '*';              {We initialize command.}
while true do
    begin
    writeln('Command;');
    readln(command);         {Read the command.}
    if command = 'i' then    {Execute the insert command.}
        begin
        writeln('Insert what?');
        readln(new);
        text := copy(text,1,ptr-1) + new +
                copy(text,ptr,length(text)-ptr+1);
        end;
    if command = 'p' then    {Execute the point command.}
    put pointer code here ;
    if command = 'd' then    {Execute the delete command.}
        put delete code here ;

    (put other commands here )

    writeln(text);           {Write the text showing the recent change.}
    cursor := '#';           {Create a string with the cursor located.}
```

```
    i := 1;
    while i < ptr do
        begin
        cursor := ' ' + cursor;
        i := i + 1;
        end;
    writeln(cursor);               {Write the cursor.}
        end;                       {End loop. Go get another command.}
writeln('Exit Editor.');
readln;
end.                               {Exit the editor program.}
```

The editor now has five commands: i, p, d, c, and s. The last command we will discuss in this chapter is the "q" command, "quit," which causes the machine to exit the loop and end the run. What we are saying to the machine is this: "While the command is not 'q,' continue going around the loop." In Pascal, the test of whether the command is not "q" is written as *command<>'q'*. This test can be entered into the while loop statement to obtain the desired behavior, and we will revise our editor again to include this change:

```
program Editor;                    {This is the editor program for chapter 2.}
var
    text,                          {This holds the text to be edited.}
    new,                           {This will hold new text to be inserted.}
    target,                        {This will hold a string to be searched for.}
    command,                       {This will hold the command.}
    cursor:string;                 {This will hold the string that has the cursor #.}
    i,ptr:integer;                 {These will hold an index and the pointer.}
begin
writeln('Enter Editor.');         {This begins the main routine.}
text := '';                       {We initialize text as a string of length zero.}
ptr := 1;                         {We initialize ptr to point to the first character.}
command := '*';                   {We initialize command.}
while command <> 'q' do
    begin
    writeln('Command;');
    readln(command);              {Read the command.}
    if command = 'i' then         {Execute the insert command.}
        begin
        writeln('Insert what?');
        readln(new);
        text := copy(text,1,ptr-1) + new +
                copy(text,ptr,length(text)-ptr+1);
        end;
```

```
        if command = 'p' then      {Execute the point command.}
            put pointer code here ;
        if command = 'd' then      {Execute the delete command.}
            put delete code here ;

        (put other commands here )

        writeln(text);             {Write the text showing the recent change.}
        cursor := '#';             {Create a string with the cursor located.}
        i := 1;
        while i < ptr do
            begin
            cursor := ' ' + cursor;
            i := i + 1;
            end;
        writeln(cursor);           {Write the cursor.}
        end;                       {End loop. Go get another command.}
writeln('Exit Editor.');
readln;
end.                               {Exit the editor program.}
```

Except for some details, your editor program is now complete. Your job is to fill in those details and then try out your editor.

## Exercises

1. Assemble the complete editor with the commands i, p, d, c, s, and q. Try it on your machine.

2. It is easy to forget the commands available on your editor or on any other computer program. A common practice is to include a command "help," which causes a message to be printed telling the user what the commands are. Program a "help" command, and add it to your editor. It should work as follows:

```
Computer:  Command:
User:      help
Computer:  The available commands are
           c        change
           d        delete
           help     print all commands
           i        insert
           p        move the pointer
           q        quit
           s        add a space
```

3. The editor still has some shortcomings. For example, if the string is "abcdabcd," the p command is unable to set the pointer to the last character. (Try it.) A second command "pl" that means "point to last character in a typed string" can be added to give more flexibility in setting the pointer. For example, the "pl" command would be used as follows to set the pointer:

```
Computer:  Command:
User:      pl
Computer:  Point to last of what?
User:      dabcd
Computer:  abcdabcd
                  #
```

4. Run your editor on some examples to see how well it performs. Think of a command that will help you to manipulate the text, and add it to your editor.

5. Some Pascal systems allow you to use the following code to place your cursor:
   *writeln('#':ptr);*
   Try it on your system. If it works, use this trick to simplify your editor.

6. In a previous section, code was designed to do a single step of the Post Correspondence Problem. Embed this code in a loop and construct a program for doing any number of Post Correspondence Problem steps. Your program should repeatedly ask the user which operator to apply next and then apply it.

---

## Building a Conversation Machine (C)

Some constructions introduced in this chapter can be employed in decision tree programs to achieve more interesting performances. Consider the following decision tree, which carries out a "conversation" with the user:

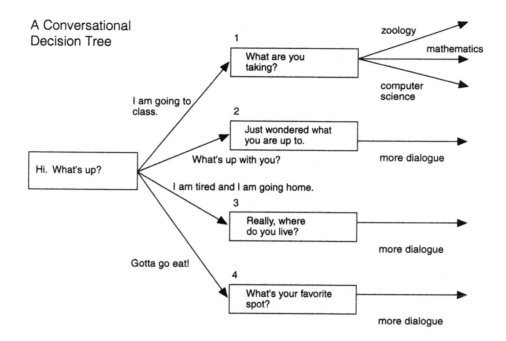

A Conversational Decision Tree

To make this program work, the trick is to look for keywords in each user response. If the user says anything about "class," the program will go to node 1 and respond, "What are you taking?" If the user mentions the word "eat," the program will respond, "What's your favorite spot?" If designed carefully, the program may be able to carry on a plausible conversation for some time.

Keywords are located using the *pos* feature. Thus, if we wish to check whether "class" is in the *answer*, we use

```
if pos('class',answer) > 0 then
```

which says "find the position of 'class' in *answer* and if any position is found (greater than zero) then do the following."

Here is how to get started constructing such a program:

```
program Conversation;
var
    answer1, answer2: string;
begin
writeln('Hi. What is up?');
readln(answer1);
```

```
if pos('class',answer1) > 0 then
    begin
    answer1 := '#';
    writeln('What are you taking?');
    readln(answer2);
        further processing
    end;
if pos('you', answer1) > 0 then
    begin
    answer1 := '#';
    writeln('Just wondered what you are up to.');
    readln(answer2);
        further processing
    end;
if pos('home',answer1) > 0 then
    begin
    answer1 := '#';
    writeln('Really, where do you live?');
    readln(answer2);
        further processing
    end;
if pos('eat',answer1) > 0 then
    begin
    answer1 := '#';
    writeln('What is your favorite spot?');
    readln(answer2);
        further processing
    end;
readln;
end.
```

If one of the keywords—"class," "home," etc.—is found in the program, the user's answer is replaced by "#" to prevent a second reference to this answer. Without this change, the user's sentence could result in going down one path of the decision tree and then later following a second path. This would occur at the first node with the sentence, "I am going to class, and then I will eat."

Here are some of the kinds of "conversations" this program can have:

```
Computer:  Hi. What's up?
User:      I'm taking this wonderful class!
Computer:  What are you taking?
User:      The mathematics of evolutionary systems.
```

Computer:    `Mathematics is the queen of the sciences.`
             etc.

Or

Computer:    `Hi. What's up?`
User:        `I am going to math but I left my problems at home.`
Computer:    `Really, were do you live?`
User:        `In the Old Manor Apartments near Irwin Road.`
             etc.

A program of this type appears to do something—understand English—it cannot really do. It should be thought of as a kind of computer game. However, it cannot ethically be presented to serious users without a proper warning. But in the last chapter on artificial intelligence we will describe computer programs that really do understand simple English.

### Exercise

1. Design a decision tree for some kind of conversational program. Write the program.

---

## Turbo Pascal Summary (C)

Chapter 1 concluded with a discussion of the Pascal constructions used in that chapter and gave a set of rules describing them. More Pascal was introduced here and we will use our arrow notation to summarize all the Pascal covered so far.

### Statement:

```
<statement> ==> writeln(list of <expression>'s separated
                by commas)
<statement> ==> readln(<identifier>)
<statement> ==> readln
<statement> ==> if <boolean expression> then
                      <compound statement>
                else
                      <compound statement>
<statement> ==> if <boolean expression> then
                      <compound statement>
```

```
<statement> ==> <identifier> := <expression>
<statement> ==> while <boolean expression> do
                         <compound statement>
```

**Expression:**

```
<expression> ==> <string expression>
<expression> ==> <integer expression>
```

**Identifier:**

```
<identifier> ==> a sequence of letters and/or digits
                 that begins with a letter
```

**Boolean expression:**

```
<boolean expression> ==> <identifier> <comp> <expression>
<boolean expression> ==> true
<comp> ==> one of >, <, >=, <=, =, or <>
```

**String expression:**

```
<string expression> ==> <identifier>
<string expression> ==> 'any string of printable characters'
<string expression> ==> <string expression> +
                         <string expression>
<string expression> ==> copy(<string expression>,
                 <integer expression>,<integer expression>)
```

**Integer expression:**

```
<integer expression> ==> any integer
<integer expression> ==> <identifier>
<integer expression> ==> <integer expression> <intop>
                 <integer expression>
<integer expression> ==> length(<string expression>)
<integer expression> ==> pos(<string expression>,
                 <string expression>)
<intop> ==> one of +, *, -, or div
```

**Program:**

```
<program> ==> program <identifier>;
              <variable declaration>
              <compound statement>.
```

**Variable declaration:**

```
<variable declaration> ==> nothing
<variable declaration> ==> var a sequence of
               <identifier:type>'s each followed by a
               semicolon
<identifier:type> ==> <identifier list> : <type>
<identifier list> ==> a list of  <identifier>'s separated
               by commas
```

**Type:**

```
<type> ==> string
<type> ==> integer
```

**Compound statement:**

```
<compound statement> ==> begin
                    a sequence of <statement> 's
                      each followed by a semicolon
                    end
```

---

## Summary (B)

This chapter introduced many new Pascal features related to text manipulation and showed how to combine them to build a simple text editor. It described some of the mechanisms built into well-known word processing systems and analyzed their construction.

This chapter also introduced some ideas related to good programming practice. The programmer is wise first to design an algorithm to do the task and then to write down the steps in English or some other language. Finally, the code should be prepared using a computer language.

The concept of "type" was introduced, and two types were discussed. The first type, strings, can be input, printed, concatenated (+), cut into substrings (*copy*), assigned (:=), measured for length (*length*), and searched (*pos*). The second type, integers, can be input, printed, assigned (:=), or operated on by integer operations (+,−,*, *div*).

The quotation at the beginning of the chapter is the first line of the poem "Mending Wall" by Robert Frost.

# 3    Numerical Computation and a Study of Functions

---

## Let Us Calculate Some Numbers (A)

Having finished our study of text processing, let us turn our attention to numerical computation. How much would a young person have to save each month in order to save a million dollars in a lifetime? More specifically, suppose the person is twenty years old and wishes to achieve the goal by the age of sixty. Furthermore, suppose the person has a tax free municipal bond program that pays an annual rate of 6 percent, compounded monthly. We could make a quick guess at the needed monthly payments by ignoring the interest and dividing a million dollars by the number of months (480). The answer is $2083.33 per month. But this guess is high because the regular compounding of interest makes a significant difference.

In order to find an accurate answer, we must do a very long and laborious computation. One way to do it would be to propose a monthly payment, and then for each of the 480 months, compute the interest on the existing account and add in the contribution for that month. After 480 repetitions of this computation, the total amount saved would be known for that level of payment. Then other payment levels could be tried until the right one is found. But another way to solve this problem is to write a program and let a machine find the answer. This is the solution proposed in this chapter.

Another class of interesting tasks is the set of *optimization* problems where we try to find the best value for a parameter in some situation. As an illustration, suppose we wish to construct a cylinder made from 1000 centimeters of tin, and we want to find the correct dimensions so that the cylinder has the largest possible volume. In our attempts to maximize volume, we might propose to build a very tall cylinder. But since the total amount of material is limited, this could lead to a very narrow shape. The cylinder might not hold much:

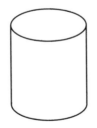

Next, we might propose that the cylinder should be very fat. The material limitation would this time result in a very short container. Again, the total volume might not be large:

Perhaps some intermediate level with moderate height and moderate diameter would be best:

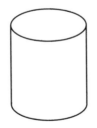

A computer can make it easy to find the dimensions for the cylinder such that volume is maximized and the total material is exactly 1000 square centimeters. Writing a program to solve this problem, we will learn a technique for solving optimization problems. (Readers who know calculus will have an analytical solution to this problem. However, our methodology is general and can be applied to problems that do not have such solutions.)

## Simple Calculations (B)

A new number type is necessary for numerical computing. In our discussions of text processing, we used integers, which are useful for counting, for referencing specific characters in a string, and for other numbering situations. But this number type cannot take on fractional values, as in 2 1/5, and the values cannot be too large in a positive or negative direction. On many machines, an integer may not be larger than 32,767 or smaller than −32,768, and on all machines, there will be limitations on the maximum and minimum values. In general computational applications, we need a number type that can take on fractional as well as very large and very small values.

The answer to this need is the *real* type, which represents numbers in two parts: the *significant digits* and an *exponent*. The number 177 might be represented as $1.77 * 10^2$ where 1.77 gives the significant digits and 2 is the exponent. The actual value of the number can always be retrieved from the representation ($1.77 * 10^2 = 1.77 * 100 = 177$) and the representation can be efficiently stored in the machine. This number type, which solves the two problems posed by integers and requires relatively little computer memory, is used almost universally on modern computers. We will not discuss in detail exactly how the numbers are stored except to say that two storage areas are needed, one to hold the significant digits and one to hold the exponent, and the sizes of these areas are sufficient for most applications. For example, if we use the real type with typical versions of Turbo Pascal, the largest number will be around $10^{38}$, the smallest number will be around $10^{-45}$, and the number of significant digits will be about 11 or 12.

We can start using reals by doing a declaration:

```
var
    x, y, z: real;
```

This results in three locations for real numbers being set up in memory with the appropriate names:

```
x  ┌─────────────────┐
   ├─────────────────┤
y  ├─────────────────┤
z  └─────────────────┘
```

Then we can load a number into a location

```
x := 12.0
```

to obtain

| | |
|---|---|
| x | $1.2 * 10^1$ |
| y | |
| z | |

or add two numbers together, putting the sum into memory,

```
y := 13.3 + x
```

to obtain

| | |
|---|---|
| x | $1.2 * 10^1$ |
| y | $2.53 * 10^1$ |
| z | |

Or we can do a complicated calculation using addition (+), multiplication (*), subtraction (−), and division (/):

```
z := (x + 17.2) * (121 - (y / x))
```

| | |
|---|---|
| x | $1.2 * 10^1$ |
| y | $2.53 * 10^1$ |
| z | $3.471637 * 10^3$ |

As a more practical example, consider the problem of computing the volume of a cylinder using the formula

$$V = \pi r^2 h$$

where $V$ is the volume, $\pi$ is a constant approximately equal to 3.14159, $r$ is the radius of the cylinder base, and $h$ is the height. In Pascal, this would be written as

$$V := 3.14159 * r * r * h$$

A computer program to compute the volume of a cylinder is easy to write. The algorithm is

find the radius $r$
find the height $h$
calculate $V = \pi r^2 h$
print the volume $V$

and the program is

```
program CylinderVolume;
var
   r, h, V: real;
begin
writeln('Give the cylinder radius.');
readln(r);
writeln('Give the cylinder height.');
readln(h);
V := 3.14159 * r * r * h;
writeln('The volume is ', V);
readln;
end.
```

In most cases, I emphasize simplicity and clarity in this book and this sometimes leads to programs unnecessarily pedantic and long. Here is a shorter version of the code:

```
program CylinderVolume;
var
   r, h: real;
begin
writeln('Give the cylinder radius and height.');
readln(r,h);
writeln('The volume is ', 3.14159 * r * r * h);
readln;
end.
```

As another example of a numerical calculation, we can write a formula for how much money a savings account will hold after receiving interest compounded once. Suppose you put $100 into an account that pays 12 percent interest per year. We will write 12 percent as a fraction 0.12. Then at the end of the year, you could expect to have $100 plus the interest, which would be $100 * 0.12 = $12. You would have exactly $112: Thus at the end of the year, the new savings is $100 + (100 * 0.12) = 112$ or in formula form:

newsavings = savings + (savings * interest)

In Pascal, you can perform the calculation on the right and store it back into the same location, *savings*:

```
savings := savings + (savings * interest)
```

This can be embedded in a program to find the amount in an account after one interest period. The algorithm is

find the original amount in the account
find the interest rate as a decimal for the time period
compute the new amount after one time period using the formula
print the result

and the program is

```
program FindSavings;
var
    savings, interestrate: real;
begin
writeln('Give the original amount in the account.');
readln(savings);
writeln('Give the interest rate.');
readln(interestrate);
savings := savings + (savings * interestrate);
writeln('After one time period, the amount is ',
    savings:6:2);
readln;
end.
```

A demonstration of the program shows the form of the input and output numbers:

```
Give the original amount in the account.
100.00
Give the interest rate.
0.09
After one time period, the amount is 109.00.
```

The numbers may be typed as integers even though they are to be stored in the computer as reals with both a significant digits part and an exponent.

In this program a new form for printing reals is introduced. Specifically, two integers are placed just after the variable name in the *writeln* statement. They indicate (1) how many characters wide the field is to be where the real number is to be printed and (2) how many digits are to be to the right of the decimal place. In the program above, the *writeln* statement *writeln(savings:6:2)* requires that the number *savings* be printed in a field six places wide with two digits to the right of the decimal place.

It is easy to write useful programs of this kind, but two hazards need to be mentioned. The first is that the order of the arithmetic operations may be ambiguous. That is, if $x = 2$, $y = 3$, $z = 4$ and we write

```
result := x + y * z
```

what will be loaded into *result*? We ourselves might add $x$ to $y$ (obtaining 5) and multiply by $z$ to get 20. Or we might multiply $y$ times $z$ (obtaining 12) and then add $x$ to get 14. Which will the machine do? In fact, Pascal and most other programming languages employ a precedence mechanism that requires, in ambiguous situations, that multiplication and division be done first, followed by addition and subtraction:

*Precedence order*
multiplication, division
addition, subtraction

Thus, the second of the two results given is correct, 14.

In a series of computations of equal precedence, the program moves from left to right. For example, if $x = 6$, $y = 2$, and $z = 3$, then

```
result := x / y * z
```

will yield the computation $6/2*3 = 3*3 = 9$. The program will not compute the value of $6/2*3 = 6/6 = 1$.

If precedence is a problem, we can always use parentheses to force the order of actions to achieve our goals. Thus

```
result := (x + y) * z
```

will force the addition of $x$ to $y$ before multiplication by $z$, and

```
result := x + (y * z)
```

will force the multiplication before the addition.

The second hazard related to calculation with real numbers is that the machine will make errors. The simple integers 1 and 3 can be stored in a machine precisely, so we can have confidence in their integrity. However, if we divide one by the other, the quotient is

```
0.33333333333333333333333333333333. . . . .
```

Because this is an infinite decimal expansion that will not fit in a computer register, only an approximation to the correct answer is stored—the first dozen or so significant digits:

```
0.333333333333
```

For most purposes, this is not a concern because we need only a few places of accuracy.

However, in some complicated calculations, these errors can build up and greatly distort answers. Consider the following program, which should read a number and print the same number:

```
program ErrorDemo;
var
   data, extra: real;
begin
readln(data);
readln(extra);
data := data + extra;
data := data - extra;
writeln(data:20:2);
readln;
end.
```

The only function of the program is to add a number called *extra* to *data* and then subtract it away again. One would hope that this program would read a value for *data* and then print out the same number. For small values of *extra* and ordinary *data* (like 100), the program will work correctly. However, if *extra* is large, *data* will be destroyed. Here is a table showing the performance of this program on a particular computer that maintains approximately 20 significant digits for real numbers:

| data (input) | extra (input) | data (output) |
|---|---|---|
| 100 | 100 | 100 |
| 100 | 1000 | 100 |
| 100 | 10000 | 100 |
| 100 | 100000 | 100 |
| — | — | — |
| — | — | — |
| 100 | 100000000000000000000 | 100 |
| 100 | 1000000000000000000000 | 96 |
| 100 | 10000000000000000000000 | 128 |
| 100 | 100000000000000000000000 | 0 |
| 100 | 1000000000000000000000000 | 0 |

If the values of *data* and *extra* are moderate, then the program always gives the correct answer. But when *extra* is raised to a value requiring more than 20 digits, the value in *data* is altered in unpredictable ways.

You can see what is happening by working through the details in the last line of the table. The following sum is computed in the seventh line of program *ErrorDemo*:

$$\frac{\begin{array}{r}1000000000000000000000000\\100\end{array}}{1000000000000000000000100}$$

But the number

1000000000000000000000100

is approximated by the number

1000000000000000000000000

because there are not enough significant digits (more than 20) in the real number representation to get the exact value. Then the following computation occurs in the eighth line of the program:

$$\frac{\begin{array}{l}1000000000000000000000000\\1000000000000000000000000\end{array}}{0}$$

which shows how the roundoff error results in the incorrect answer.

Such a computation in the middle of a formula to compute the strength of an aircraft wing or the trajectory of a spaceship could lead to random results, poor decisions, and loss of life. Thus specialists in numerical analysis are often in charge of large, complicated, and critical calculations. However, for our purposes, the computer will be accurate enough. The reader who would like to explore the characteristics of numerical computations in more detail is encouraged to consult a book on numerical analysis.

**Exercises**

1.  The volume of a sphere is $4/3\pi r^3$. Write a program that reads the value of the radius of a sphere and then computes its volume.

2.  The temperature $f$ in degrees Fahrenheit can be computed from the temperature $c$ in degrees Celsius by the formula $f = 9/5\,c + 32$. Write a program that reads the temperature in degrees Celsius and returns the temperature in Fahrenheit.

3.  Assume that $x=6.0$, $y=7.0$, and $z=3.0$ are real numbers. What will be computed in each case?

    (a) `result := x * y - x * z`
    (b) `result := x * 20.0 / z + y`
    (c) `result := (z * x / y) / x + y`

4. Run the program *ErrorDemo* given above for the case of *data* = 0.00001. How large must *extra* be before the value of *data* is altered in the computation?

5. Here is a program that uses the Pythagorean formula for right triangles: $a^2 + b^2 = c^2$ where $a$ and $b$ are sides of a triangle and $c$ is its hypotenuse. The program assumes that you know $b$ and $c$, and it computes the value of $a$.

```
program findside;
var
    a,b,c:real;
begin
writeln('Give the length of the hypotenuse.');
readln(c);
writeln('Give one of the sides.');
readln(b);
a := sqrt(c*c - b*b);
writeln('a = ',a);
readln;
end.
```

We will now investigate the accuracy of the program. If the values for $c$ and $b$ are 1.01 and 1.00, what value should the program compute for $a$? Do the calculation by hand to obtain four significant digits in your answer and run the program to obtain its answer. How accurate is the answer?

Now repeat the above, holding $b$ at 1.00 but allowing $c$ to be 1.0001. How accurate is the machine? Try again, allowing $c$ to be 1.000001, 1.00000001, 1.0000000001, and so forth. As $c$ comes nearer and nearer to $b$, you will see the accuracy degrade until the error becomes 100 percent.

---

## Functions (B)

A *function* receives inputs and yields, for each input, a uniquely defined output. For example, a function might receive the name of a country and yield the name of its capital. Usually functions have names, and let us call this one $F$. If $F$ receives the name Egypt, it will return the name of its capital Cairo. If it receives Japan, it will return Tokyo. Other examples are the function that receives the name of a person and returns the name of that person's mother, or the function that receives the dimensions of a cylinder and returns its volume.

We will present five methodologies for describing functions: English descriptions, mathematical notation, computer programs, tables, and graphs. Any technique that tells how to find the appropriate output for each given input can define a function.

The usual mathematical notation for a function is to write the input in parentheses following the function name and the output after an "=" sign:

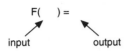

For the country-capital function, which we will call $F$, we would therefore write:

F(Egypt) = Cairo
F(Japan) = Tokyo

In this section, we will concentrate on numerical functions that input and yield numbers. A simple example is a function that doubles an input. If it receives 3, it will output 6. If it receives 17, it will yield 34. Let us call this function $d$ and write down these examples:

$d(3) = 6$
$d(17) = 34$

We can say that $d$ of anything is twice that anything, or

$d(\text{anything}) = 2 * \text{anything}$

Mathematicians prefer to use the variable name $x$ for "anything," so the usual notation for describing the function that doubles is

$d(x) = 2x$

Another numerical function can be used to compute the volume of a cylinder. If the function is named $v$, and it receives $r$ and $h$, we can write

$v(r, h) = \pi r^2 h$

and use the program given on an earlier page to compute this function. Suppose its inputs are $r = 2$ and $h = 3$; then its output will be $3.14159 * 2^2 * 3 = 37.69908$.

Tables provide another way to represent a function. Suppose the double function $d$ is defined to operate only on positive integers. Then it would be written as follows:

| input | output |
| --- | --- |
| x | d(x) |
| 1 | 2 |
| 2 | 4 |
| 3 | 6 |
| 4 | 8 |
| 5 | 10 |
| 6 | 12 |
| — | — |

The cylinder volume function needs a two-dimensional table to represent its value since it has two inputs:

| v(r, h) | h | | | | | |
| --- | --- | --- | --- | --- | --- | --- |
| | 1 | 2 | 3 | 4 | 5 | 6 |
| 1 | 3.14 | 6.28 | 9.42 | 12.57 | 15.71 | 18.85 |
| 2 | 12.57 | 25.13 | 37.70 | 50.27 | 62.83 | 75.40 |
| r  3 | 28.27 | 56.55 | 84.82 | 113.10 | 141.37 | 169.65 |
| 4 | 50.26 | 100.53 | 150.80 | 201.06 | 251.33 | 301.59 |
| 5 | 78.54 | 157.08 | 235.62 | 314.16 | 392.70 | 471.24 |
| 6 | 113.10 | 226.19 | 339.29 | 452.39 | 565.49 | 678.58 |

Finally, we can graph functions. Here is the double function:

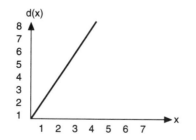

And here is the volume function with one graphical line for each value of *h*:

### Exercise

1. Consider the function that computes the volume of a sphere from its radius. Show how the five given representations can be used to express this function.

## Looping and a Study of Functions (B)

A good way to study functions is to build a program loop that calculates the value of the function repeatedly for many different input values. Suppose we wish to study the *d* function. We could execute the following code:

```
x := 1.0;
d := 2.0 * x;
writeln(x,d);

x := 2.0;
d := 2.0 * x;
writeln(x,d);

x := 3.0;
d := 2.0 * x;
writeln(x,d);
```

and so forth. This is the form of the loop:

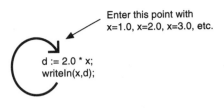

Enter this point with
x=1.0, x=2.0, x=3.0, etc.

d := 2.0 * x;
writeln(x,d);

Pascal offers a format for doing exactly this job:

```
x := 1.0;
while true do
    begin
    d := 2.0 * x;
    writeln(x,d);
    x := x + 1.0;
    end;
```

Conceptually this program sets *x* to 1.0 and then executes

```
d := 2.0 * x;
writeln(x,d);
```

Then it increases *x* by 1.0 and repeats:

```
d := 2.0 * x;
writeln(x,d);
```

This repeats for $x = 3.0$, $x = 4.0$, and so forth. Here is what is printed out:

```
1.0     2.0
2.0     4.0
3.0     6.0
4.0     8.0
5.0     10.0
6.0     12.0
 -       -
 -       -
```

   Since we want to be able to stop the looping, in place of *true* we will introduce a test in the *while* statement. Here is the complete program:

```
program Double;
var
    d, x: real;
```

```
begin
x := 1.0;
while x < = 10.0 do
    begin
    d := 2.0 * x;
    writeln(x:6:1,d:6:1);
    x := x + 1.0;
    end;
readln;
end.
```

The test $x < = 10.0$ means that $x$ must be less than or equal to 10.0 in order for the loop between *begin* and *end* to be executed. The test is made just before the loop body is entered. If the test does not succeed because $x$ is greater than 10.0, the loop body will be skipped and the statement following the *while* loop will be executed, and *readln* will be the next action. Tracing the steps of this program, we can see its detailed operation:

| instruction | | x | d |
|---|---|---|---|
| x := 1.0 | | 1.0 | |
| (test) x <= 10.0 | (yes) | 1.0 | |
| d := 2.0 * x | | 1.0 | 2.0 |
| writeln | | 1.0 | 2.0 |
| x := x + 1.0 | | 2.0 | 2.0 |
| (test) x <= 10.0 | (yes) | 2.0 | 2.0 |
| d := 2.0 * x | | 2.0 | 4.0 |
| writeln | | 2.0 | 4.0 |
| x := x + 1.0 | | 3.0 | 4.0 |
| (test) x <= 10.0 | (yes) | 3.0 | 4.0 |
| — | | — | — |
| — | | — | — |
| writeln | | 9.0 | 18.0 |
| x := x + 1.0 | | 10.0 | 18.0 |
| (test) x <= 10.0 | (yes) | 10.0 | 18.0 |
| d := 2.0 * x | | 10.0 | 20.0 |
| writeln | | 10.0 | 20.0 |
| x := x + 1.0 | | 11.0 | 20.0 |
| (test) x <= 10.0 | (no) | 11.0 | 20.0 |
| readln | | | |

Study the *Double* program with care because it illustrates the looping mechanism that will be used in dozens of programs in the chapters to come. A complete understanding of this code is essential to the comprehension of much of the later material.

It is now easy to approach the problem of finding the perfect dimensions for the cylinder described in the introduction. Its volume is $V = \pi r^2 h$, and its area is $A = 2\pi r^2 + 2\pi rh = 1000$. The second equation can be solved for $h$ and substituted into the first equation to find the volume of the cylinder for each value of $r$;

$$V = 500r - \pi r^3$$

Then a program can be written to compute $V$ for each value of $r$ from 1.0 to 10.0, and we can see how the volume changes:

```
program CylinderVolumes;
var
    r,V: real;
begin
r := 1.0;
while r <= 10.0 do
    begin
    V := 500 * r - 3.14159 * r * r * r;
    writeln(r:8:2,V:8:2);
    r := r + 1.0;
    end;
readln;
end.
```

Running this program obtains the following values for $r$ and $V$, which are graphed to show how $V$ changes for each $r$:

| r | V |
|---|---|
| 1 | 497 |
| 2 | 975 |
| 3 | 1415 |
| 4 | 1799 |
| 5 | 2107 |
| 6 | 2321 |
| 7 | 2422 |
| 8 | 2392 |
| 9 | 2210 |
| 10 | 1858 |

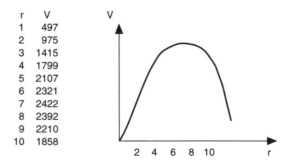

This graph makes it possible to confirm our suspicions at the beginning of this chapter. If the cylinder is extremely tall with a very small radius, the volume will be very small. If the cylinder is very wide with a radius, say, larger than 10, the volume will also not be large. In order to get the largest possible $V$, $r$ should be set to an intermediate level, about 7. We will find a more exact value later. (Experts at differential calculus will have already found a more exact value using analytic methods but that is another story.) The cylinder of maximum volume looks approximately like this:

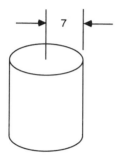

Let us next consider the interest problem from the chapter introduction. At the end of every month, the account will have the funds from the previous month (*savings*) plus the month's interest (*savings* \* *monthint*) plus the new monthly payment (*payment*):

```
savings := savings + (savings * monthint) + payment
```

This calculation needs to be done on the last day of every month for the forty years (40 \* 12 = 480 months). With the *while* loop, it is easy to write a program that will read a proposed monthly payment and compute the total forty-year savings.

Algorithm:
    find out proposed monthly payment
    set savings = 0 and monthint = 0.005 (i.e., 0.06 per year)
    for each of the 480 months compute:
       savings := savings + (savings \* monthint) + payment
    print amount of savings after 40 years

```
Program:
   program Savings40Years;
   var
      payment, savings, monthint, month: real;
   begin
   writeln('What payment do you propose?');
```

```
readln(payment);
savings := 0;
monthint := 0.005;
month := 1;
while month <= 480 do
   begin
   savings := savings + (savings * monthint) + payment;
   month := month + 1;
   end;
writeln(' Total savings after 40 years.', savings:10:2);
readln;
end.
```

**Exercises**

1. Type in the above program *Savings40 Years* and see how much you will save if your monthly payments are $10. Is this enough to collect a million dollars? Try some other values until you find the correct one.

2. Use the methods of this chapter to find the lowest value that the function $f = x^2 - 5x + 4$ can have.

3. Use a program to compute $f = 1/3x^3 - 4x^2 + 15x + 3$ for values of $x$ from 1 to 12. Graph the function.

---

## Searching for The Best Value (B)

With some attention to detail, we can find a more accurate solution to the problem of maximizing the volume of the cylinder. The graph of the previous section would seem to indicate that $r$ should be somewhat greater than 6. If $r$ is exactly 6, the volume is

$$V = 500 * 6 - 3.14159 * 6^3 = 2321.42$$

Let us try $r = 6.01$ and see if the volume is larger:

$$V = 500 * (6.01) - 3.14159 * (6.01)^3 = 2323.02$$

Since the volume did increase when $r$ was increased, our theory was correct. Perhaps $r$ should be increased again to 6.02:

$$V = 500 * (6.02) - 3.14159 * (6.02)^3 = 2324.61$$

Good! A strategy is to increase $r$ repeatedly and see how many times $V$ will continue to increase. If $V$ ever gets smaller, stop. The previous value was the best. In fact, we can write a program to do this task. We are finding the maximum as we did in the previous section, except that we are incrementing by a value other than 1.0 and we are stopping the calculation when the highest value is found.

Here is the method:

set $r$ at some starting value
decide how much $r$ should be increased each cycle
find $V$
increase $r$
find $V$
increase $r$
find $V$
increase $r$
- - - - - -
- - - - - -
if $V$ got smaller, stop
the previous $V$ was the best one found

Clearly the method is very repetitive and needs a loop.

       set $r$ at some starting value
       decide how much $r$ should be increased on each cycle
       find $V$
   ⌐→ increase $r$
   |  find $V$
   └────┘
       if $V$ got smaller, stop
       the previous $V$ was the best one found

Actually, the computer should be told to check, on every cycle through the loop, to see whether $V$ is smaller than the previous $V$.

       set $r$ at some starting value
       decide how much $r$ should be increased on each cycle
       find $V$
   ⌐→ increase $r$
   |  find $V$
   |  if $V$ is less than previous $V$, then stop
   └────┘
       the previous $V$ was the best one found

But before putting this program into Pascal using a while loop, we should try the loop test at the beginning of the loop.

> set $r$ at some starting value
> decide how much $r$ should be increased on each cycle
> find $V$
> ┌→ if $V$ is less than previous $V$, then stop
> │   increase $r$
> │   find $V$
> └─┘
> the previous $V$ was the best one found

This algorithm has a bug in it. Notice its first four actions.

set $r$ at some starting value
decide how much $r$ should be increased on each cycle
find $V$
if $V$ is less than previous $V$, then stop

But there is no previous $V$! Although this test is quite correct each time around the loop, it makes no sense on the first encounter. The solution is to assume an initial value for the previous $V$, which will make the loop work the first time. Assume that $V$ will always be positive since it is a volume. Then let us initialize previous $V$ to be zero so that we can be sure it will be less than $V$.

> set $r$ at some starting value
> decide how much $r$ should be increased on each cycle
> initialize the previous $V$ at zero
> find $V$
> ┌→ if $V$ is less than previous $V$, then stop
> │   increase $r$
> │   find $V$
> └─┘
> the previous $V$ was the best one found

The algorithm is still not complete because the previous $V$ is not systematically maintained. When $V$ is computed each time around the loop, the previous value will be lost unless the program stores it. Thus a statement should be inserted just before the "find $V$" step that saves the current $V$ into a place for the previous $V$.

> set $r$ at some starting value
> decide how much $r$ should be increased on each cycle
> assume the previous $V$ was zero

find *V*
→ if *V* is less than previous *V*, then stop
  increase *r*
  save *V* into a place called "previous *V*"
  find *V*

the previous *V* was the best one found

This completes the design of the algorithm to find the largest value. The care we needed to develop the loop is typical in most programming situations. We can now write the code.

```
program FindBest;
var
    r, V, previousV, increase: real;
begin
writeln('What is the initial value of r?');
readln(r);
writeln('How much should r be increased each time?');
readln(increase);
previousV := 0;
V := 500 * r - 3.14159 * r * r * r;
while V >= previousV do
    begin
    r := r + increase;
    previousV := V;
    V := 500 * r - 3.14159 * r * r * r;
    writeln(r:10:2,V:10:2);
    end;
writeln('The best value is ',previousV:10:2);
readln;
end.
```

You should now type this program and find a better solution to the cylinder maximization problem. Is it possible to find the best possible *r* accurate to three decimal places?

It could happen that this program will not find the best solution if the *V* curve has a strange shape as shown here.

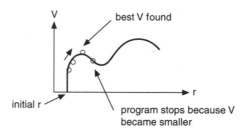

Remember what the program does and notice how it will work on this problem. If it starts at the left side, which is marked "initial $r$," it will keep increasing $r$ and slowly moving right while $V$ increases. But notice that $V$ will start getting smaller where it is marked "best $V$ found." The program will stop and announce it has found the best $V$, but it will be wrong because a larger $V$ exists farther right. In the example of finding the best cylinder this does not occur, but in general we must investigate carefully to be sure the absolute maximum has been found.

This section has demonstrated a method of searching for things with a computer. We were looking for the best possible value of $r$, but we can look for almost anything. The search method builds a loop that repeatedly checks for the desired item. The loop computation is continued until the searched item is found.

(initialize computation)
while item is not found do
    (repetitive portion to get next item)
print item found

**Exercises**

1. Find the dimensions, $r$ and $h$, for a cylinder that has one thousand square centimeters of material and maximum volume. What is the maximum volume that is achieved? Give all answers accurate to three decimal places.

2. Suppose a person deposits $1000.00 into a bank account and then puts in monthly payments of $20.00 regularly for twenty years. Further suppose the bank pays an annual rate of 6 percent, compounded monthly. What will be the total savings at the end of the twenty years?

3. A person has the goal of saving $10,000.00 in ten years. He or she can obtain an annual interest rate of 12 percent, compounded monthly. The plan is to initially deposit $1000.00 and then to make monthly payments for the rest of the ten years. How much should the monthly payments be?

4. Suppose we have two functions $f1 = 2x + 1/(x^3 + x^2)$ and $f2 = x^2 - 6x$. Write a program that will start $x$ at some low value, say $x = 1$, where $f1$ is greater than $f2$, and increment $x$ repeatedly while computing the values of $f1$ and $f2$ each time. The program loop should stop when $f1$ becomes less than $f2$. Find as well as you can what value of $x$ is greater than 1 and makes $f1 = f2$.

5. Write a program that acts as a desk calculator. The program will have a command loop much like the editor program and will have a register that holds the number being manipulated. The commands will operate by manipulating this register, clearing it, entering values into it, adding other numbers to it, and so forth. Each command results in the indicated action, and then it prints the contents of the register to show its current status. Here are the commands:

c     clear the register
e     enter a number into the register
a     add a number to the register
m     multiply a number times the register
d     divide a number into the register
s     subtract a number from the register
h     help

Here is a sample interaction with the desired program:

```
Command: e
17
Register contents: 17
Command: a
14
Register contents: 31
Command: c
Register contents: 0
```

## Storing Information in Arrays (B)

In order to encourage our person in the savings program, we might like to create an electronic savings table that would show the total amount of the savings at the end of each month. The person would be able to check the amount in the account for any month in the future, assuming he or she makes all the payments on time. This record can be constructed by creating an *array* in the computer memory that can hold all the 480 entries in the proposed plan. In this section, we will study the concept of arrays, their utilization, and particularly their usefulness in the savings problem.

Before we can use an array, we must create it in the memory with a declaration. The Pascal method for declaring an array begins with the creation of a new type. Then the array is declared in the usual way with a *var* declaration. For the savings table, an array is needed that holds 480 real numbers, so we will call the new type *realarray480*. The entries of the array will be numbered from 1 to 480, and the complete specification is as follows:

```
type
    realarray480 = array[1..480] of real;
```

If the savings table array is to be given the name *table*, it is declared as

```
var
    table: realarray480;
```

Each individual entry in this array will have its own name. The first is called *table[1]*, the second is *table[2]*, and so forth. Intuitively, the array should be envisioned as follows:

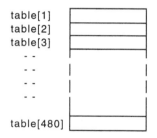

```
table[1]
table[2]
table[3]
  - -
     - -
     - -
  - -
table[480]
```

Before building the electronic savings table, let us study arrays and their manipulation with a few examples. Suppose we have an array called *A* of size 4, and we wish to put the number 10 into each entry. Here is a program to create *A* and make those entries.

```
Program FirstArray;
type
    realarray4 = array[1..4] of real;
var
    A: realarray4;
begin
A[1] := 10;
A[2] := 10;
A[3] := 10;
A[4] := 10;
end.
```

Another way to achieve the same result is to use a *while* loop.

```
Program FirstArray;
type
    realarray4 = array[1..4] of real;
var
    A: realarray4;
    i: integer;
begin
i := 1;
while i <= 4 do
    begin
    A[i] := 10;
    i := i + 1;
    end;
end.
```

Notice that the index *i* for the array must be declared as an integer.

This program creates the array and then executes this sequence.

```
i := 1;
Is i <= 4 ?     Yes.
A[1] := 10;
i := 2;
Is i <= 4 ?     Yes.
A[2] := 10;
i := 3;
Is i <= 4 ?     Yes.
A[3] := 10;
i := 4;
Is i <= 4 ?     Yes.
A[4] := 10;
i := 5;
Is i <= 4 ?     No.
```

If *i* is changed repeatedly through the loop, the item in the array that is being referenced keeps changing as well.

Once some values exist in the array, we can print all those items.

```
i := 1;
while i <= 4 do
    begin
```

```
      writeln(A[i]);
      i := i + 1;
      end;
```

This will print

```
10
10
10
10
```

Here is a program that puts a sequence of integers into an integer array:

```
Program SecondArray;
type
    integerarray4 = array[1..4] of integer;
var
    A: integerarray4;
    i: integer;
begin
i := 1;
while i <= 4 do        {This loop enters values}
    begin              { into the array.         }
    A[i] := i + 10;
    i := i + 1;
    end;
i := 1;
while i <= 4 do        {This loop prints the   }
    begin              {values in the array.   }
    writeln(A[i]);
    i := i + 1;
    end;
readln;
end.
```

This program will set *i* to 1 and then execute

```
A[1]  := 1+10
```

on the first loop repetition. So *A[1]* will receive 11. The other entries will receive 12, 13, and 14, and the program will print

```
11
12
13
14
```

A slightly nicer format will be printed by this version:

```
Program SecondArray;
type
    integerarray4 = array[1..4] of integer;
var
    A: integerarray4;
    i: integer;
begin
i := 1;                    {The first loop fills the array.}
while i <= 4 do
    begin
    A[i] := i + 10;
    i := i + 1;
    end;
writeln('The contents of A.');
writeln('Index      Value');
i := 1;                    {The second loop prints the array.}
while i <= 4 do
    begin
    writeln(i,'      ',A[i]);
    i := i + 1;
    end;
readln;
end.
```

The output in this case will be:

```
The contents of A.
Index      Value
1          11
2          12
3          13
4          14
```

This understanding of arrays makes it possible to build the electronic savings table. A small addition to the first compound interest program, *Savings40 Years*, will create and fill up the needed array.

```
program FillSavingsTable;
type
    realarray480 = array[1..480] of real;
var
    table: realarray480;
    payment,savings, monthint: real;
    month:integer;
begin
writeln('What payment do you propose?');
readln(payment);
savings := 0;
monthint := 0.005;
month := 1;
while month <= 480 do
    begin
    savings := savings + (savings * monthint) + payment;
    table[month] := savings;
    month := month + 1;
    end;
readln;
end.
```

The first time around the loop, *month* will have value 1. So *table[1]* will receive its appropriate entry, the amount of the savings. Each subsequent repetition will increase month by 1 and cause the next table entry to be made.

Code needs to be included to enable the saver to check the savings amount at any month's end. Let us design the program so that it works as follows:

| | |
|---|---|
| Computer: | What payment do you propose? |
| User: | 10.00 |
| Computer: | Good, I have your forty year savings plan prepared. |
| Computer: | What month do you wish to check? |
| User: | 6 |
| Computer: | 61.52 |
| Computer: | What month do you wish to check? |
| User: | 360 |
| Computer: | 34949.60 |
| Computer: | What month do you wish to check? |
| User: | 0 |
| Computer: | This terminates the savings table program. |

The computer allows the person to check the account level at any month and then conclude the session by asking for month 0.

Here is the algorithm for the query routine:

ask "What month do you wish to check?"
input the number of the month
while month is greater than zero do
    print the amount in the account for this month
    ask "What month do you wish to check?"
    input the number of the month

Here is the complete savings table program.

```
program SavingsTable;
type
    realarray480 = array[1..480] of real;
var
    table: realarray480;
    payment,savings, monthint: real;
    month: integer;
begin

                    {First make entries into table.}

writeln('What payment do you propose?');
readln(payment);
savings := 0;
monthint := 0.005;
month := 1;
while month <= 480 do
    begin
    savings := savings + (savings * monthint) + payment;
    table[month] := savings;
    month := month + 1;
    end;

                    {Next enter the query routine.}

writeln('Good. I have your forty year savings plan prepared.');
writeln('What month do you wish to check?');
readln(month);
while month > 0 do
    begin
    writeln(table[month]:10:2);
    writeln('What month do you wish to check?');
    readln(month);
    end;
```

```
writeln('This terminates the savings table program.');
readln;
end.
```

**Exercises**

1. Write a program that has an array capable of holding ten integers. The program should ask the user to type a number and then store it into the array. Then it should ask the user for another number and store it, then another and store it, and so forth, until all ten entries of the array are full. Finally, the program should print the ten entries in the array.

2. Write a program that has an array capable of holding ten integers. The program should ask the user to type in ten integers and then it should store them in the array. Then the program should ask the user to type another integer. If it finds that last integer in the array, it should type FOUND. If it does not find it in the array it should type NOT FOUND.

3. Suppose a bank decides to give each of its customers a key number they must enter before computerized facilities are made available. Then a table must be stored in the computer indicating the key number for each customer so the appropriate check can be made. Write a program that implements this scheme as follows. It will have two tables, one called *name* that holds the names of customers and one called *key* that holds their key numbers. The key numbers will be positive integers. For example, *name[1]* will hold the name of the first customer and *key[1]* will hold that person's key number. The program will first ask how many customers are to be stored with their key numbers. Then it will enable the user to input each name and associated key number. After it has stored these, it will enter a loop designed for customers. It will ask the customer for their name and key number. If it finds the name in the list and sees that the key number is correct, it will print the message "Welcome to the XYZ Bank Automated Teller." If it does not find the name and key number, it will print "Sorry, your name and key numbers are not approved for entry into this system."

4. A shortcoming with the system of problem 3 is that a computer expert might be able to find the table of secret key numbers, print them out, and use them in illegal ways. Let us revise the system so that if an expert found the table, he or she would still have considerable difficulty entering the system. Instead of giving each customer one key number, we will assign each customer two integers which are prime numbers. Our table will not store the numbers themselves but only their *product*. When customers are asked for their name, they will be asked to give their two key numbers. Then the program will check that they are both positive and greater than 1, multiply them together, and note whether this product is in the table.

From the point of view of the customer, the system will work the same way except that two key numbers will be required for entry. However, from the point of view of the bank, the customer's account will be safer. Even if a computer expert has the table of secret *key* numbers, he or she will still need to find two prime numbers that multiply to produce each number in *key*. If the number in *key* is large, this is not an easy problem.

## Finding Sums, Minima, and Maxima (B)

Suppose our hypothetical bank customer makes a deposit on each of four consecutive weeks. Ignoring the issue of interest, we will ask what was the total of the deposits and what were the smallest and largest deposits. In answering these questions, we will examine general methods for accumulating quantities (sums, in this case) and for finding extreme elements (minima and maxima).

Begin by entering the amounts of the deposits:

```
program Deposit;
type
    realarray4 = array[1..4] of real;
var
    deposit: realarray4;
    i: integer;
begin
i := 1;
while i <= 4 do
    begin
    writeln('Enter your deposit.');
    readln(deposit[i]);
    i := i + 1;
    end;
readln;
end.
```

If the entered amounts are 6, 11, 9, 5, then the deposit array will appear as follows:

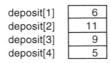

| | |
|---|---|
| deposit[1] | 6 |
| deposit[2] | 11 |
| deposit[3] | 9 |
| deposit[4] | 5 |

Next, develop a method for adding them up:

```
sum := 0
add deposit[1] to sum
add deposit[2] to sum
add deposit[3] to sum
add deposit[4] to sum
```

To add *deposit[1]* to *sum*, add the two quantities together:

deposit[1] + sum

and put the result back into *sum*:

sum := deposit[1] + sum

The methodology becomes:

```
sum := 0
sum := deposit[1] + sum
sum := deposit[2] + sum
sum := deposit[3] + sum
sum := deposit[4] + sum
```

The loop is clear:

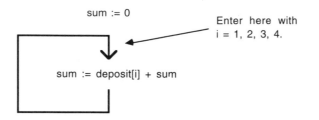

In Pascal, this is written as:

```
sum := 0;
i := 1;
while i <= 4 do
   begin
   sum := deposit[i] + sum;
   i := i + 1;
   end;
```

This program illustrates the format of the basic accumulator program:

initialize accumulator
initialize index
while there are more objects do
     let accumulator = object, operation, accumulator
     increment index

The accumulator can have any name, and the object and operation can have many forms. This basic format can be used to add up deposits, as shown above, or to do other similar tasks. Our first example is a program that adds up the numbers from 1 to *n*:

```
program SumN;
var
    i, n, sum: real;
begin
readln(n);
sum := 0;
i := 1;
while i <= n do
   begin
   sum := i + sum;
   i := i + 1;
   end;
writeln('The sum is ',sum:8:2);
readln;
end.
```

Or we could multiply the numbers from 1 to *n* and obtain *n* factorial. (Remember that *n* factorial means that the numbers 1 * 2 * 3 * . . . * n are to be multiplied together. Thus, 4 factorial is 1 * 2 * 3 * 4 = 24.)

```
program Factorial;
var
   i, n, product: real;
begin
readln(n);
product := 1;
i := 1;
while i <= n do
   begin
   product := i * product;
   i := i + 1;
   end;
```

```
writeln('The factorial is ',product:8:2);
readln;
end.
```

Or we could accumulate a string of *n* As:

```
program Asequence;
var
   i, n: integer;
   asequence: string;
begin
readln(n);
asequence := ''; {Put empty string into asequence.}
i := 1;
while i <= n do
   begin
   asequence := 'A' + asequence;
   i := i + 1;
   end;
writeln('The A sequence is ',asequence);
readln;
end.
```

If we now want to find the largest deposit made by our customer during the month, we will look at the first item and temporarily store it as the largest seen so far. Then we will sequentially examine each later item looking for larger ones. If larger ones are found, we copy them into the "largest-so-far" slot. Here is the code to find the largest deposit:

```
largestsofar := deposit[1];
i := 2;
while i <= 4 do
   begin
   if deposit[i] > largestsofar then
      begin
      largestsofar := deposit[i];
      end;
   i := i +1;
   end;
writeln(largestsofar:8:2);
```

The general pattern for finding such extremes recurs often in programs:

let extremesofar = first item
initialize index
while there are more objects to examine
     if item is more extreme than extremesofar then
        let extremesofar = item
     increment index

This pattern can be used to find the largest number, smallest number, numbers nearest some value, longest and shortest strings, and so forth.

**Exercises**

1. Write a program that reads ten strings and then prints the longest and shortest ones. Then it prints a string that is the concatenation of all of the ten strings.

2. Write a program that reads an integer $n$ and then prints a string of $n$ Os.

3. Write a program that can draw a bar graph for the function $f = 1/4x^2 + x + 2$ for the values of $x$ from 1 to 10. For each value of $x$, it will build a string of Fs with length $f$ using the method of exercise 2. Then it will print the value of $x$ followed by the string. The program will do this for each value of $x$. The output should look something like this:

```
x    bar graph of f value
1    FFF
2    FFFF
3    FFFFF
-    - -
```

4. Use the idea of exercise 3 to build a general program for graphing any function.

## Patterns in Programming (B)

By now you have seen many programs and begun to notice patterns in the code. Programmers often assemble familiar patterns or whole blocks of code adapted in appropriate ways to create new programs. The assembly of programs from larger pieces speeds the process of coding and increases the reliability of the product. These patterns will be called *code patterns* here, and an acquaintance with them will help you in the task of coding. This section will make some of these explicit as a review of previous studies and as an aid to future programming.

The first chapter examined decision trees where a question was asked at each node and, based on the answer, control was passed on to another node. Two formats for coding nodes were presented, one for the case where there were two branches and the other for the case where there were many. Here are the node formats:

Two branches.

```
ask question
input answer
if one answer then
     execute next appropriate node
else
     execute other appropriate node
```

More than two branches.

```
ask question
input answer
if answer=ans1 then
     execute node appropriate to ans1
if answer=ans2 then
     execute node appropriate to ans2
etc.
```

The construction of decision trees involved the repeated nesting of such formats.

Chapter 2 introduced a method for modifying the contents of a location. This was done with a single assignment statement of the form

```
location := location with some change
```

Thus, we added a character A to the right end of string *s1* with

```
s1 := s1 + 'A'
```

and to the left end of *s1* with

```
s1 := 'A' + s1
```

We can remove the last character from *s1* with

```
s1 := copy(s1,1,length(s1)-1)
```

We can increase number $x$ by 1 with

```
x := x + 1
```

and so forth.

Another code pattern that appeared in chapter 2 was the command control loop that enabled the user to request any action:

```
while command is not 'q' do
    ask for command
    input command
    if command = c1 then
        appropriate code
    if command = c2 then
        appropriate code

- - - -
```

Chapter 2 also introduced the simple loop for modifying all the numbers of an array:

```
set index to first item
while index is less than or equal to the number of entries do
    modify entry being indexed
    increment index
```

Earlier sections also gave formats for searching for items and for accumulating and finding extreme values for a set of items.

**Exercises**

1. Find a code pattern that is used commonly in this book but is not shown in this section.

2. Write a program for each code pattern in this section and demonstrate its use.

3. Make up a table of code patterns and show the form, the name, and an example of the use of each pattern. Include all the patterns mentioned in this section as well as some additional ones that you have observed.

---

## Putting Things in a Row and a Special Characteristic of Functions (B)

A number of theoretical issues in computer science will be addressed in later chapters, and it is important to build the foundations along the way. In this section, we discuss an important concept; mathematicians call it *countability*, and this book calls it *putting things in a row*. We will be using this idea in the chapter on noncomputability.

The fundamental idea concerns an unending chain of bins that extends into infinity

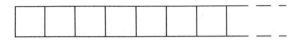

and the question of whether there are enough bins to hold all the elements of a set of objects. We assume every bin is arbitrarily large so it can hold any individual regardless of its size. But the goal for a given set is to put each of its members in some bin in the chain. If we can succeed with a set, we will say we *put this set in a row;* mathematicians would say the set is *countable.*

The first set to consider is the set of positive integers, which can easily be put in a row. Put 1 in the first bin, 2 in the second, and so forth without end:

| 1 | 2 | 3 | 4 | 5 | 6 | 7 | |
|---|---|---|---|---|---|---|---|

There are enough bins to hold every positive integer, and regardless of which integer is chosen, it will be somewhere in the chain. The set of positive and negative integers can also be put in a row, as follows:

| -1 | 1 | -2 | 2 | -3 | 3 | -4 | |
|----|---|----|---|----|---|----|---|

Theoretically, the names of all human beings that have ever been born can be put in a row by placing the name of the lightest person at birth in bin 1, the second lightest in bin 2, and so forth. Where there are ties, they can be ordered on another dimension, such as the number of cells in their body. The set of all molecules in the universe can be arranged in a row by putting one molecule in bin 1, its closest neighbor in bin 2, its second closest neighbor in bin 3, and so forth. Again, a second dimension can be used to settle ties.

In each of these examples we are seeking a rule that will show how to place every member of a set into a different bin in the row. If we can find such a rule, we will say the set can be put in a row.

Consider the set of all finite strings of printable characters such as "computers," "#!−7," and "Let us go." This set can also be put in a row by putting the string of length zero in bin 1, and the strings of length one in bins 2, 3, 4, 5, ...., $n$ since we assume only a finite number of distinct characters. Next the strings of length two can be placed in bins $n+1$, $n+2$, ... etc., and so forth. This set of strings would thus contain all the words in any dictionary, all the sentences that could ever be written, all the books that ever have been or ever will be written, all the books that will *not* be written, and much more. This set can also be put in a row.

At this point, we might think that every set imaginable can be put in a row. However, it turns out that the functions that input a positive integer and yield a positive integer cannot be put in a row. No matter how one tries to squeeze them all into the bins, there will always be more that will not fit. This is an important fact with great implications for computer science. A demonstration of why this is true appears in the next section, and a discussion of its significance is given in the chapter on noncomputability.

**Exercises**

1. Imagine a great two-dimensional checker board that goes on forever in all directions. Is the number of squares on the board countable? That is, can you find a way to put all the squares in a row?

2. Imagine the set of all Pascal programs. Is it possible to put this set in a row?

## Putting the Functions in a Row (C)

Let us try to put functions in a row and see where it leads us. We will consider only functions that accept positive integers as input and yield positive integers as output, and we will represent each function with its input-output table. Here is the beginning of the enumeration:

| x | f(x) | | x | f(x) | | x | f(x) | | x | f(x) |
|---|------|---|---|------|---|---|------|---|---|------|
| 1 | 2    | | 1 | 4    | | 1 | 11   | | 1 | 17  |
| 2 | 4    | | 2 | 7    | | 2 | 11   | | 2 | 109 |
| 3 | 6    | | 3 | 10   | | 3 | 11   | | 3 | 18  |
| 4 | 8    | | 4 | 13   | | 4 | 11   | | 4 | 1   |
| 5 | 10   | | 5 | 16   | | 5 | 11   | | 5 | 512 |
| 6 | 12   | | 6 | 19   | | 6 | 11   | | 6 | 62  |
| 7 | 14   | | 7 | 22   | | 7 | 11   | | 7 | 174 |
| . | .    | | . | .    | | . | .    | | . | .   |
| . | .    | | . | .    | | . | .    | | . | .   |

The first function listed is the double function; the second calculates a simple polynomial; the third always outputs 11 regardless of the input; and the fourth outputs a rather bizarre and unpredictable array of values. All are perfectly legitimate functions and are completely specified by their infinite tables.

Suppose next that an unboundedly patient and speedy creature continues the task begun here and puts all the rest of the functions that exist in a row. Then the task will be complete, and we will have seen how to do yet another large set.

However, consider a new function constructed as shown below. Its table is built as indicated. The first entry of the first function is incremented by one and put into its first output position. The second entry of the second function is incremented and put into its second output position. And, in general, for each $i = 1, 2, 3, \ldots$, the $i$th output position in the $i$th function is incremented and put into the $i$th output position for the new function:

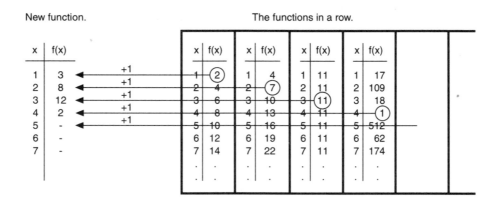

New function.                                    The functions in a row.

This new function is clearly as good as any other function since its table is completely well specified, and therefore our patient and speedy creature must have included it in one of the bins of the row. Let us try to find it. The new function is not in the first bin because it is different on the first entry. It is not in the second bin because it is different on the second entry. Wait a minute! It is different from the $i$th function in the $i$th position for all $i$. The new function is different from every function in the row and is thus not in any bin! So our creature did *not* put every function into the row.

It is easy to find millions of functions that were left out. Consider the functions constructed like the above new function except that 2 or 3 or something else is added to each entry. Consider the function that is built using the second output of the first function, the third output from the second function, and so forth. This function and all of its similar versions will also not be in the row.

The functions that have positive integers for inputs and outputs cannot be put into a row. Mathematicians say this set of functions is *uncountable*. All the other sets discussed in the previous section are *countable*, but this one is not. Most other classes of functions are similarly uncountable, but none needs to be considered here. The fact that these functions cannot be put in a row is an extremely important fact for computer scientists, as we will discover in the chapter on noncomputability.

**Exercises**

1.  Describe various kinds of functions that will not be in the row of functions built in the above construction.

2.  The set of infinite strings of printable characters cannot be put in a row. Show how the above argument can be modified to prove this fact.

3.  Specify which of the following sets can be put in a row and which cannot be. Give a full explanation in each case.
    (a) The set of well-formed English sentences.
    (b) The set of functions that input a positive integer and output a positive integer and that has the following property: For a given function, the output will be the same regardless of what the input is.
    (c) The set of decimal numbers that have an infinite number of digits.
    (d) The set of all creatures that have ever existed or will ever exist.
    (e) The set of all paths down an infinite tree constructed as follows: The root node has two branches below it of length 1 inch. At the end of each branch is a node with two more branches below it of length 1 inch. At the end of those branches are nodes with more branches without end.

---

## Summary (B)

In chapter 3 we learned that integers are not adequate for general numerical computation because they cannot take on fractional or very large or small values. The real number type was introduced along with many examples showing its use. We were warned that numerical computation involves two possible hazards: First, the operators have a precedence that may cause an order of computation that is unexpected by the uninitiated and could therefore yield undesired answers. Second, the computer will make mistakes when computing with real numbers. These mistakes are the round-off errors caused by the limited size of its registers. These errors are typically of little importance in textbook computations, but in some calculations they can combine to undermine the integrity of the answer.

Chapter 3 also introduced functions, a fundamental concept of mathematics and computer science. We learned five different methods for describing functions, and various programs for computing functions were given. The last two sections examined an important class of functions that have the property that they cannot be "put in a row." This unusual property of a set has implications that will be discussed in chapter 14.

Chapter 3 also examined looping programs and showed how to build them. Such programs can be used for studying the properties of a function by repeatedly evaluating the function on different inputs. Looping programs can also be used to calculate complex functions, such as the accumulation from a forty-year savings plan. If a while-loop construction is used for search, the test at the beginning of the while-loop must be designed to stop the repetitions when the searched-for item is found.

Experienced programmers will point out that there are other ways to code loops in Pascal. Thus, the form

```
i := 1;
while i <= n do
    begin
    code
    i := i + 1;
    end;
```

can also be written as

```
for i := 1 to n do
    begin
    code
    end;
```

There is also a *repeat-until* construction similar to the *while* loop except that the test is at the end of the loop instead of the beginning. These and many other features of Pascal are omitted from the current discussions, but anyone who is comfortable with them is encouraged to use them.

This chapter also introduced arrays for storing data and showed their use in various situations. Sample programs illustrated ways to read, print, sum, and find the maximum or minimum values in arrays.

Finally, the concept of the "code pattern" was introduced and the importance of learning common patterns was emphasized. Programming often proceeds by modifying and assembling these patterns of code rather than constructing things from atomic elements.

# 4 Top-Down Programming, Subroutines, and a Database Application

## Let Us Solve a Mystery (A)

As the afternoon sun faded on the village green and Chief Inspector Brown was lighting his evening pipe, an urgent call came in from Dunsmore Manor. It was from a terrified Miss Secrest, who had found Lord Peter Dunsmore collapsed on the drawing room floor. He was dead. Lady Emily had gone to her chambers in shock, and the chief inspector was implored to hurry to the scene. This he did, and upon examining the body, proclaimed the cause of death: a lethal dose of poison administered within the last few hours.

The family and servants seemed too distraught to be questioned, but an elegant computer terminal in the corner of the room gave access to some family data. The inspector sat down and began typing.

```
Who visited the manor today?
```

Machine response:    Mr. Mason visited at 3:00 P.M.
                     The professor visited at 3:00 P.M.
                     Miss Secrest visited at 5:00 P.M.

```
Tell me about Mr. Mason.
```

Machine response:    Mr. Mason has hobby tennis.
                     Mr. Mason visited at 3:00 P.M.
                     Mr. Mason is a chemist.

The inspector typed a long series of questions, slowly puffed his pipe, and finally arrived at a suspect. He was able to identify only one person who had all three prerequisites: a motive, access to the poison, and a way of administering it to the victim.

Although we may want to know who committed the crime, as computer scientists, we are even more interested in knowing how the computer program works. In this chapter, we will study methodologies for creating programs larger than those of previous chapters, like the question-answering program the inspector used. In the process, we will study the method of top-down programming, the use of subroutines, and techniques for keeping the greater complexity of large programs under control. The final sections of this chapter will illustrate the use of these methodologies to solve other sample problems.

## Top-Down Programming and the Database Program (B)

The central issue of computer science is the problem of complexity. There are two important techniques for dealing with it:

1. Represent the problem so it can be dealt with easily.
2. Decompose the problem into simpler subtasks and then repeatedly decompose those subtasks until at the lowest level each remaining subtask is easy to comprehend. Then carefully assemble the subtask solutions to obtain a solution to the whole problem.

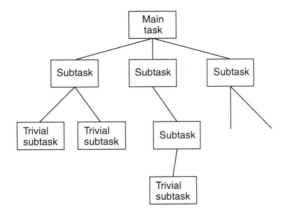

If each decomposition is simple and correct and each lowest level subtask easy to code and also correct, the complete program should be correct.

Let us now apply these ideas to creating the question-answering program the inspector used. A store of information like that on the Dunsmore family computer is called a *database*. A program that stores such information and answers questions about it is called a *database program*. Our current task is to build one. However, the specifications implied by the discussion indicate that this program may become an immense undertaking. If we are to achieve success, we must find ways to reduce the problem's complexity.

Thus, our first task in addressing this problem is to seek a representation that is easy to comprehend and leads to the simplest possible program. As a first simplification, let us assume that the family information is stored as a set of facts represented by declarative sentences such as

Mr. Mason visited at 3:00 P.M.
Mr. Mason is a chemist.

Once this decision is made, we no longer need to grapple with the vague idea of "information," and we can concentrate on finding ways to store and retrieve sentences. We will further simplify by assuming that all questions can be answered by presenting those stored sentences that answer the user's question. Thus, if a user asks a question, the machine need determine only whether facts exist in the database to answer it and to print them out if they do. (We will not consider the case where the program might be asked to make an inference.)

Having settled on a representation that specifies what is meant by "information," we can turn our attention to discovering how to decompose the whole task into a set of easily approached subparts.

The program will need two primary abilities: to read in facts and to answer questions related to them. We will construct it with a command control loop and five commands:

f       find (this command will receive questions and print all relevant facts)
help    help (this command will list the five available commands)
i       input (this command will read facts)
p       print (this command will print all the stored facts)
q       quit (this command will terminate program execution)

The initial version of the program will be

```
program Database;
var
    command: string;
begin
command := 'start';
while command <> 'q' do
    begin
    writeln('Command:');
    readln(command);
```

```
    if command = 'f' then
         find facts to answer a query;
    if command = 'help' then
        print the help message;
    if command = 'i' then
        input a fact;
    if command = 'p' then
        print all of the facts;
    end;
readln;
end.
```

Graphically, the database has been decomposed into a loop with five subtasks, two of them trivial:

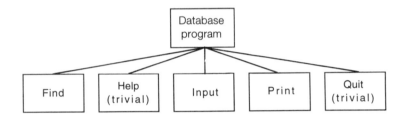

Next we examine the three nontrivial subtasks.

Consider the "input" routine. It will work as follows. First, a new place in memory will be located, and then the fact will be read and placed into that new position:

Input routine:
    find a new place in memory
    read a new fact into that place

The "print" routine will also be easy:

Print routine:
    for each position in memory that has a fact,
    print the contents

The "find" routine will first read the user's question. Then it will check each stored fact and print those facts that help to provide an answer to the question. For example, when the inspector requested general information regarding Mr. Mason, the program printed all the stored facts that used his name.

Find routine:
    read user's question
    for each position in memory that has a fact,
        if that fact helps answer the question, print it

The last part of the "find" routine seems complicated because we do not know when a fact "helps to answer the question." Let us decompose this process again and create a question-fact comparator. This routine will examine the question and the fact and report either "answer" or "no" depending on whether the fact partially answers the question or not. Using this routine, the "find" routine is now quite simple:

Find routine:
    read user's question
    for each position in memory that has a fact,
        call the question-fact comparator
        if the comparator reports "answer" then
            print the fact

Of course, the question-fact comparator may be a complex routine, but that is an issue we will examine later.

   The database program has now evolved to this state:

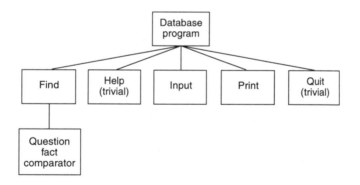

Once we have discovered a way to program the "question-fact comparator," the seemingly complex database program will be reduced to a series of simple subtasks. Before considering these parts further, we will introduce subroutines to help with the decomposition process.

**Exercise**

1. Suppose a program is to read the names and backgrounds of a series of men and women and then pair them up, putting people of similar backgrounds together. The program should print out a list of the couples. How should the data be represented? Show how to decompose this problem into a series of easily programmable subtasks.

## Subroutines (B)

A *subroutine* is a sequence of programming statements. In Pascal, subroutines are called *procedures*, and the two terms will be used interchangeably here. Following is an example of a *subroutine definition* for a routine called *Byline*. (We always associate a name with a subroutine so we can refer to it.) The subroutine prints a message with an author's name and a line of hyphens above and below:

```
procedure Byline;
    begin
    writeln('----------------------------');
    writeln(' This program was written by ');
    writeln(' Lady Emily Dunsmore ');
    writeln('----------------------------');
    end;
```

This subroutine does the job of printing the four lines shown. A programmer who wants those four lines printed need only include the statement

```
Byline
```

This statement *calls* the *Byline* procedure, which in turn, prints the four lines. Suppose that Lady Emily wrote the database program and decided that each time it is used it should begin by printing those four lines and end by printing them again. If her program had this appearance originally:

```
program Database;
declarations
begin                   { Beginning of the main program. }
    -     -     -
    -     -     -
    -     -     -
end.
```

the new version that begins and ends by printing her byline would look like this:

```
program Database;
declarations
begin                    { Beginning of the main program. }
Byline;
      -      -      -
      -      -      -
      -      -      -
Byline;
end.
```

The newly added *Byline* statements are refered to as the *subroutine call* statements.

There is a problem with the new version: it does not include the definition of the procedure. This definition is placed following the other declarations in the program:

```
program Database;
declarations
procedure Byline;
    begin
    writeln('----------------------------');
    writeln(' This program was written by ');
    writeln('     Lady Emily Dunsmore      ');
    writeln('----------------------------');
    end;

begin                    { Beginning of the main program. }
Byline;
      -      -      -
      -      -      -
      -      -      -
Byline;
end.
```

The program executes, as indicated in the figure below, the following sequence: The computation starts at the beginning of the main program after the *begin*. The first statement is *Byline*, which means go to the subroutine *Byline* and carry out the four print statements. After that is done, it will have finished the first call to *Byline*, and it will proceed to do the other parts of the database program. When it is finished, it will execute the second *Byline* statement, which again causes the system to go to the *Byline* subroutine. It will again execute those four print statements before halting.

In the following diagram, these events are graphed, with the thick lines indicating execution and the thin lines indicating jumps. The path shows the two procedure calls and the consequent jumps to the procedure body:

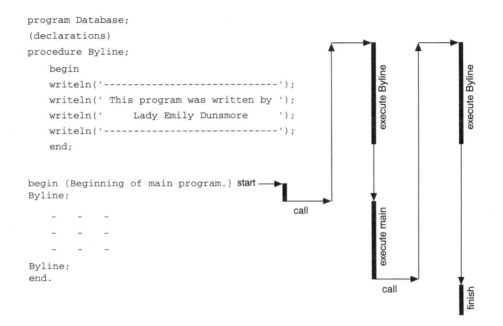

```
program Database;
(declarations)
procedure Byline;
    begin
    writeln('----------------------------');
    writeln(' This program was written by ');
    writeln('      Lady Emily Dunsmore     ');
    writeln('----------------------------');
    end;


begin {Beginning of main program.} start
Byline;

    -    -    -

    -    -    -

    -    -    -
Byline;
end.
```

Subroutines are a tremendous help to programmers for two reasons. *First, they provide a means for avoiding typing the same lines again and again.* The code is typed once in a subroutine definition, and in all other instances it can be used by simply typing the name of the subroutine. Since the total program will be shorter, it will use less memory space inside the computer and will thus be less wasteful of resources. Because subroutines can be dozens of lines long and may be called often, the savings can be substantial.

The second reason that subroutines are useful is even more important than the first: *subroutines enable the programmer to isolate one task from another and thus help simplify problem solving.* For example, the programming problem for "find" in the database program may seem complex. But we simplify the problem greatly by pushing part of the task into the question-fact comparator subroutine. We write code that receives the question and then, for each fact, uses a subroutine, the question-fact comparator, to check whether the fact is a part of the answer. If it is, our code will print it out:

Find routine:
    read user's question
    for each position in memory that has a fact,
        call the question-fact comparator
        if the comparator reports "answer" then
            print the fact

We have cut the problem into parts that are small enough to program easily, and later we can concentrate our energies specifically on the subroutine.

It might be convenient to modify the *Byline* program so it will print anyone's name, not simply Lady Emily's. Here is the appropriate change:

```
procedure Byline2(var name: string);
    begin
    writeln('----------------------------');
    writeln(' This program was written by ');
    writeln(' ', name);
    writeln('----------------------------');
    end;
```

The new variable *name* references the name we wish to print, which could be any sequence of characters. The variable *name* is called a subroutine *parameter*, and it is identified as such when it is placed between parentheses in the subroutine definition after the subroutine name *Byline2*.

The variable *name* is very different from an ordinary variable in a program, such as *y* in

```
program Demo;
var
    y: string;
```

This is because *subroutine parameters declared as shown here are not assigned associated places in memory*. A subroutine parameter such as *name* refers to the place in memory created for some other variable. Consider, for example, the execution of this program:

```
program SecondSubroutine;
var
    n1, n2: string;

procedure Byline2(var name: string);
    begin
    writeln('----------------------------');
    writeln(' This program was written by ');
    writeln(' ', name);
    writeln('----------------------------');
    end;
```

```
begin                    { Beginning of main program. }
n1 := 'Lord Dunsmore';
n2 := 'Miss Secrest';
Byline2(n2);
Byline2(n1);
end.
```

The variables *n1* and *n2* will have their associated locations in memory because they have been declared at the top of the program. But *name*, which is a subroutine parameter, will not. We will graphically represent these declared locations in the usual way but will indicate a parameter as an arrow that will point to some other entity:

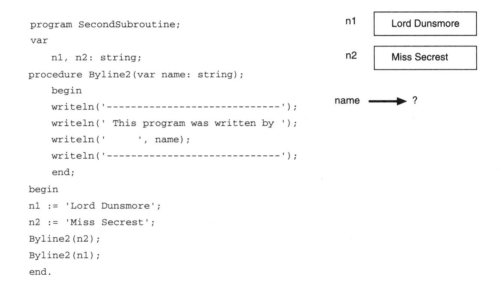

```
program SecondSubroutine;
var
    n1, n2: string;
procedure Byline2(var name: string);
    begin
    writeln('----------------------------');
    writeln(' This program was written by ');
    writeln('       ', name);
    writeln('----------------------------');
    end;
begin
n1 := 'Lord Dunsmore';
n2 := 'Miss Secrest';
Byline2(n2);
Byline2(n1);
end.
```

Now consider the execution of the program. The first and second statements of the main program will cause *n1* and *n2* to be loaded as shown. The third statement will cause control to pass to the subroutine. Notice that *n2* is the memory location referenced in the call statement. Here *n2* is called the subroutine *argument*, and it gives the memory location referred to by *name* in the subroutine:

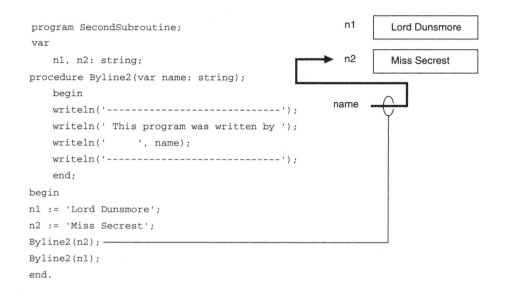

So *name* and *n2* refer to the same memory location at this point in time. That is, the *Byline2* call statement has the function of linking the subroutine parameter *name* to the memory location *n2* at the time the subroutine is run.

After the subroutine has done its work and printed the byline message for Miss Secrest, the main routine will go on to its fourth statement, *Byline(n1)*. This time *name* is linked to *n1*, and Lord Dunsmore's name will be printed:

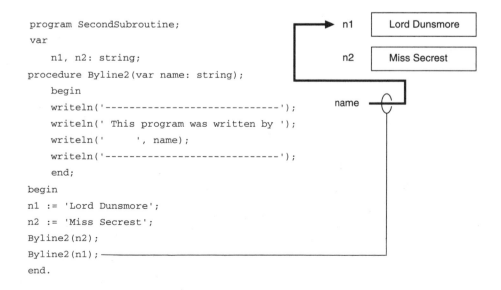

To summarize, the parameters of a subroutine do not create new memory locations when they are declared as shown here. Rather, they refer to existing memory locations. These memory locations are linked to the subroutine parameters at the time of the subroutine call. The execution of the previous program will result in the following printout:

```
--------------------------
This program was written by
        Miss Secrest
--------------------------
--------------------------
This program was written by
        Lord Dunsmore
--------------------------
```

Let us reinforce these ideas by changing the program again. This time a subroutine will be included to read a person's name, and then the *Byline2* routine will print that name in the usual format:

```
program ThirdSubroutine;
var
    n1: string;

procedure Byline2(var name: string);
    begin
    writeln('--------------------------');
    writeln(' This program was written by ');
    writeln(' ', name);
    writeln('--------------------------');
    end;

procedure GetName(var authorname: string);
    begin
    writeln('Type your name.');
    readln(authorname);
    end;

begin
Getname(n1);
Byline2(n1);
end.
```

Remember that *name* and *authorname* do not have associated memory locations. When *Getname* is called, it will link *authorname* to *n1* and the input name will be stored in *n1*. Then when *Byline2* is called, it will link *name* to *n1*, and the contents of *n1* will be printed.

Suppose this program is written erroneously without proper communication between the two procedures. That is, *Getname* and *Byline2* are called with two different arguments:

```
program ThirdSubroutine1;
var
   n1, n2: string;

procedure Byline2(var name: string);
   begin
   writeln('----------------------------');
   writeln(' This program was written by ');
   writeln(' ', name);
   writeln('----------------------------');
   end;

procedure GetName(var authorname: string);
   begin
   writeln('Type your name.');
   readln(authorname);
   end;

begin
Getname(n1);
Byline2(n2);
end.
```

In this case, *Getname* will read the name and put it into *n1* as before. But notice that *Byline2* will print whatever is in *n2*. However, since *n2* has not been loaded, its content is unknown and *Byline2* may print almost anything.

**Exercises**

1. Write a procedure that prints your name. Write a program that calls the subroutine three times and thus prints your name three times.

2. Write a procedure called *Clip* that has two string parameters. It will receive a string in the first parameter, remove the first and last characters from the string, and then return the answer as the second parameter. Here is the main program:

```
Program Test;
var
    n1, n2: string;
```

```
procedure Clip(var s1,s2:string);
   - - -
   - - -
   end;

begin
writeln('Type a string.');
readln(n1);
Clip(n1,n2);
writeln('The clipped string is ',n2);
readln;
end.
```

---

## Subroutines with Internal Variables (B)

Let us study the case where a subroutine may need to have memory locations for its own internal use. Suppose a programmer is sketching a new piece of code and needs to compute factorial on several occasions. (The factorial of positive integer n is the product $1*2*3* \ldots *(n-1)*n$. Thus, the factorial of 4 is $1*2*3*4 = 24$.)

```
(code)
 - -
z3 := the factorial of x
 - - -
y := the factorial of m
 - - -
num1 := the factorial of y
 - - -
```

Then a subroutine can be written that has two arguments: the answer resulting from the calculation and the input. If the name of the routine is *Factorial*, then the code can be written as follows:

```
(code)
 - -
Factorial(z3,x);
 - - -
Factorial(y,m);
 - - -
Factorial(num1,y);
 - - -
```

The subroutine itself is straightforward to define using the accumulation pattern. Notice that the routine needs a memory location *i* as a counter in the loop:

```
procedure Factorial(var out,n:integer);
var
    i: integer;
begin
out := 1;
i := 1;
while i <= n do
    begin
    out := i * out;
    i := i + 1;
    end;
end;
```

In addition to the memory locations referenced by the parameters, this procedure also needs location *i* during the calculation. The declaration of *i* follows the procedure statement and has the same form as a declaration after a program statement. This declaration tells the machine to set up a properly named memory location to be used by this subroutine only during its execution. We will follow the policy here that *all variables in a subroutine will either be parameters of that subroutine or declared as variables in that subroutine*. Pascal allows variations from this rule, but they introduce numerous dangers.

The cause for confusion if this rule is not followed is easy to illustrate. Suppose one executes

```
i := 6;
writeln(i);
```

It seems reasonable to believe that a "6" will be printed. However, if

```
i := 6;
Factorial(r,s);
writeln(i);
```

is executed, one would again expect a "6" to be printed because there is no immediately visible reason why it should not. Unfortunately, if *Factorial* does use *i* in some way without having its own declaration of *i*, the following sequence could occur: $i := 6$; would load "6" into *i*; the routine *Factorial* could change *i* to some new value, say "10," and the *writeln* statement would print "10." Error! This is a very hard-to-find bug because *i* was changed in a separate, possibly distant place without any obvious indications. To avoid spending hours looking for the cause of an unexpected change in some location, you should always write obviously correct code with no subtle behaviors.

Thus, the rule to follow is that every variable in a subroutine should be specified either by subroutine parameters or by declarations in that routine. When it is, you can be sure that the subroutine can be inserted into a main program without affecting anything in the main program except items specifically listed in the parameter list.

**Exercises**

1. Write a procedure called *Checker* that reads an integer and prints "Okay" if the integer is greater than 0 and less than 100. It should print "Not okay" otherwise. It should be called by the following program:

```
program Test1;
procedure Checker;
    - - -
    - - -
    end;
begin
Checker;
readln;
end.
```

When the program is run, it should work as follows:

Machine:   Please type a number.
User:      17
Machine:   Okay

2. Modify the program in exercise 1 so that the main program reads the integer and prints the result. The integer read should be passed to the procedure through the parameter list, and the string to be printed should be passed back to the main program through the parameter list. Here is the main routine:

```
program Test2;
var
    int:integer;
    str:string;

procedure Checker(var i:integer;var s:string);
    - - -
    - - -
    end;
begin
```

```
writeln('Please type a number.');
readln(int);
Checker(int,str);
writeln(str);
readln;
end.
```

3. Write a procedure that has two arguments, an integer and a string. The procedure will check whether the integer is a prime number. If it is, it will return the string "Yes" in its second parameter. Otherwise it will return "No." Write a main routine to call your subroutine. It should read the number, call the subroutine, and then print the answer returned by the subroutine.

   **Note:** A prime number is an integer greater than 1 that is not evenly divisible by any positive integers except 1 and itself. Thus 2, 3, 5, and 7 are prime numbers, but 4 is not because it is divisible by 2. In Pascal, we can check whether $i$ divides $j$ by checking whether *( j div i)* \* $i$ equals $j$. If they are equal, then $i$ divides $j$; otherwise it does not. The subroutine can do its job by having a while loop that checks whether $i$ divides $j$ for every $i$ from 2 to $j - 1$. If none is found, then $j$ is prime.

4. Subroutines can greatly simplify the decision trees of chapter 1. The strategy begins by coding the root of the decision tree into the main program. Then every other node is given a name, and a procedure by that name does the processing of that node. Here is the main program for the book advice decision tree. Can you finish the program?

```
program BookAdvice;
var
    answer1: string;

procedure Math;
    Put code here to process the case of individuals who
    wish a mathematical approach.

procedure Nonmath;
    Put code here to process the case of individuals who
    wish a nonmathematical approach.
begin
writeln('Do you wish a mathematical approach?');
readln(answer1);
if answer1 = 'yes' then
    begin
    Math;
    end
```

```
else
    begin
    Nonmath;
    end;
readln;
end.
```

5. Pick out a decision tree from chapter 1 with at least one long path of decisions. Show how subroutines simplify the code even when the tree is deeply nested.

## Subroutines with Array Parameters (B)

Subroutines can have arrays as parameters using roughly the methodology described above for individual locations. The syntax will be explained in the context of a program to add up a series of integers. We will create two procedures: *ReadArray* to read the integers and *AddArray* to add them. These routines will assume that the main program has declared *integerarray100* to be an array type as follows:

```
type
    integerarray100 = array[1..100] of integer;
```

Here is the *ReadArray* procedure:

```
procedure ReadArray(var n:integer;var B:integerarray100);
    var
        i: integer;
    begin
    writeln('How many entries?');
    readln(n);
    i := 1;
    while i <= n do
        begin
        writeln('Input entry.',i);
        readln(B[i]);
        i := i + 1;
        end;
    end;
```

The specification of the array *B* in the parameter list follows the same format as for other parameters, except that a declared rather than a basic type is used.

Suppose that this routine is called as

```
ReadArray(m,A)
```

where *A* has been declared as an array of type *integerarray100*, and *m* is an integer. Then *ReadArray* will go through its steps entering into *m* the number of entries to be read and entering into *A[1], A[2], A[3], ..., A[m]* the integers to be read.

This same routine can be used again and again to read entries into other arrays, as with

```
ReadArray(Num,grades)
```

to read *Num* values into array *grades*, or with

```
ReadArray(NN,DayTemperatures)
```

to read *NN* values into array *DayTemperatures*.

Next, the subroutine for summing the values in an array can be written:

```
procedure AddArray(var n: integer;var C:integerarray100;
                   var answer: integer);
    var
        i: integer;
    begin
    answer := 0;
    i := 1;
    while i <= n do
        begin
        answer := C[i] + answer;
        i := i + 1;
        end;
    end;
```

Similarly, this routine can be used to add up the elements of all the arrays mentioned previously:

```
AddSub(m,A,ans1);
AddSub(Num,grades,ans2);
AddSub(NN,DayTemperatures,ans3);
```

where the answers are placed into *ans1*, *ans2*, and *ans3*, respectively.

The following program uses these two procedures to read values into an array and then add them up:

```
program ReadAddArray;
type
    integerarray100 = array[1..100] of integer;
var
    n, answer: integer;
    A: integerarray100;
procedure ReadArray( . . . .);
    copy from above ;

procedure AddArray(. . . . );
    copy from above ;

begin
writeln('Read:');
ReadArray(n,A);
writeln('Add up.');
AddArray(n,A,answer);
writeln('The answer: ',answer);
readln;
end.
```

**Exercises**

1. Write a procedure *PrintArray(n,A)* similar to the *ReadArray* routine above. It should print the entries in array *A*.

2. Write a procedure *DoubleArray(n,A)* that doubles all the entries in array *A*.

3. Write a procedure *CopyArray(n,A,B)* that copies all the *n* entries in array *A* into array *B*.

4. Write a main routine that uses the above routines, *ReadArray*, *DoubleArray*, *Copy-Array*, and *PrintArray*, to do the following:

   - It reads *n* values into array *XX*.
   - It prints the array *XX*.
   - Then it doubles the values in *XX* and prints them again.
   - Then it moves the values in *XX* to array *YY* and prints *YY*.
   - Finally, it doubles the values in *YY* and prints them again.

   Your program should be very easy to write because it will contain no executable statements other than procedure calls. The procedures will do all the work.

## Subroutine Communication Examples (B)

Because communications with subroutines can be confusing, several examples of different types of communication will be included here. In each case, the subroutine will be named *double*, and it will double some real number. The interesting points will be how it gets its input and what it does once the number is doubled.

The first example is a case where there is no communication at all. The subroutine doubles an entry with nothing in it and does nothing with the result:

```
program communication1;
procedure double;
   var
      r1, r2: real;
   begin
   r2 := 2 * r1;
   end;
begin
double;
end.
```

Here is a graphical representation:

communication1

This unsuccessful program can be fixed by putting read and write statements into the subroutine:

```
program communication2;
procedure double;
    var
        r1, r2: real;
```

```
    begin
    readln(r1);
    r2 := 2 * r1;
    writeln(r2);
    end;
begin
double;
end.
```

The picture now shows the information passing from the keyboard into the subroutine, where it is doubled and then printed:

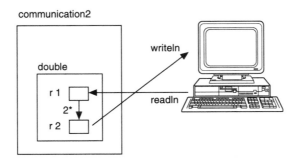

Next we could pass the information to the subroutine through the parameter list and then have the routine print its answer as before:

```
program communication3;
var
    num: real;
procedure double(var x: real);
    var
        r1, r2: real;
    begin
    r1 := x;
    r2 := 2 * r1;
    writeln(r2);
    end;
begin
readln(num);
double(num);
end.
```

communication3

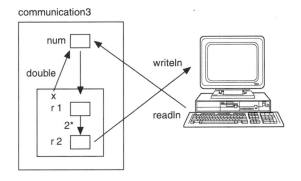

Also, we could modify the program to send its output back via the parameter list:

```
program communication4;
var
     num, ans: real;
procedure double(var x,y: real);
     var
         r2: real;
     begin
     r2 := 2 * x;
     y := r2;
     end;
begin
readln(num);
double(num,ans);
writeln(ans);
end.
```

communication4

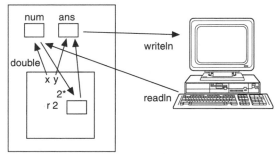

A shorter version omits the variable declared inside the subroutine:

```
program communication5;
var
    num, ans: real;
procedure double(var x,y: real);
    begin
    y := 2 * x;
    end;
begin
readln(num);
double(num,ans);
writeln(ans);
end.
```

communication5

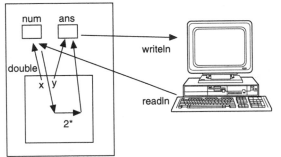

Finally, the subroutine can be revised to receive a number from the main routine and then return its answer to the same location:

```
program communication6;
var
    num: real;
procedure double(var x: real);
    begin
    x := 2 * x;
    end;
begin
readln(num);
double(num);
```

```
writeln(num);
end.
```

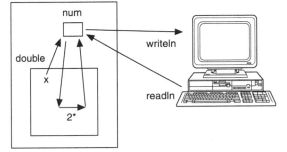

communication6

**Exercise**

1. Repeat the examples of this section except that the subroutine should add up a real array instead of doubling a location.

## Storing and Printing Facts for the Database (B)

We must now develop a systematic plan for storing database facts of the kind given at the beginning of this chapter:

Mr. Mason is a chemist.
The professor visited at 3:00 P.M.

It is important to notice that most of these facts are of the form

(noun phrase) (relationship) (noun phrase)

We will discover later that the question-answering task is made easier if we separate each fact into these three parts:

(Mr. Mason)(is)(a chemist.)
(The professor)(visited at)(3:00 P.M.)

We will call the first part *noun1* (for noun phrase 1), the second part *relation* (for relationship), the last part *noun2* (for noun phrase 2), and declare these as string variables. This strategy would store the first fact in Pascal with these statements:

```
noun1 := ' Mr. Mason';
relation := 'is';
noun2 := 'a chemist.';
```

In order to read a fact into these locations, you can use the statements:

```
readln (noun1);
readln (relation);
readln (noun2);
```

Thus, the fact should be typed in this form:

Mr. Mason
is
a chemist.

The separation of the statement onto three lines enables the program to divide the string of characters into three strings for the three sequential locations.

But the database program needs to store many facts, so the three locations should be expanded into arrays. This can be done with the following declaration, which specifies that each array should hold 100 strings and each string may contain up to 30 characters:

```
type
    stringDB = string[30]; {All strings limited to length 30.}
    stringarray100 = array[1..100] of stringDB; {Only 100 facts allowed.}
var
    noun1A, relationA, noun2A: stringarray100;
```

| noun1A[1] | Mr. Mason | noun1A[1] | is | noun2A[1] | a chemist. |
|-----------|-----------|-----------|-----|-----------|-----------|
| noun1A[2] | The professor | noun1A[2] | visited at | noun2A[2] | 3:00 PM. |
| - - | | | - - | | - - |
| - - | | | - - | | - - |

Let us create a location called *last* that gives the position of the last fact in the tables. If only two facts are stored, then this location would be

last | 2 |

and if a place is needed for a new fact, we would increase *last* to 3 and put the new fact in position 3.

Now it is possible to write rough draft code for the database input routine described above in English:

Input routine:
>   find a new place in memory
>   read a new fact into that place

The code is

```
procedure InputFact;
    begin
    writeln('Input a fact. Type three fields on sequential lines.');
    last := last + 1;
    readln(noun1A[last]);
    readln(relationA[last]);
    readln(noun2A[last]);
    end;
```

This routine is correct except that its communication to the main program needs to be ensured. This is done with parameters. Here is the revised code:

```
procedure InputFact(var noun1A,relationA,noun2A:stringarray100;
                    var last:integer);
    begin
    writeln('Input a fact. Type three fields on sequential lines.');
    last := last + 1;
    readln(noun1A[last]);
    readln(relationA[last]);
    readln(noun2A[last]);
    end;
```

That is, *InputFact* places information into three arrays that are specified in its parameter list and updates *last*, the location of the last fact. (This routine assumes the arrays are large enough to store as many facts as the user will ever type. We might wish to revise the subroutine to print the message "Too many facts" if the user types more facts than can fit into the arrays.)

The print routine for the database program can be written similarly.

We have now made progress in building the database program. A way of storing facts has been devised and we found that it is straightforward to write subroutines to store facts and to print them. The only remaining task is to write the "find" routine which will enable the user to obtain the answers to questions.

**Exercises**

1. Write the print routine for the database program.

2. Revise *InputFact* so that if the user attempts to type more facts than there is room, the system will refuse to make the error and print the message, "Too many facts."

## Representing Questions and Finding Their Answers (B)

Suppose a large number of facts are stored in the machine using the method of the previous section. The next problem to consider is how someone who does not know those facts can access information. The problem will be approached very conservatively, and then a seemingly narrow technique will be expanded to become a powerful query-handling mechanism.

Suppose someone wishes to ask the question,

Is it true that Mr. Mason is a chemist?

What this question means is that the user wishes to know whether the fact

(Mr. Mason)(is)(a chemist.)

is in the database. We will write code so the system will ask the user for a query, and the user will type the fact he or she wishes to check for. Then the system will respond by typing that fact again if it is found.

Let us use the model begun in a previous section to write code to solve this simple problem. The version given above is

Find routine:
     read user's question
     for each position in memory that has a fact,
          call the question-fact comparitor
          if the comparitor reports "answer" then
               print the fact

We can now write the code for the find routine. Remember that the parameters can have any names and that they are not initially associated with any specific memory location. Only when the program is called are the parameters associated with memory locations.

Here the arrays holding the facts are called *n1*, *r*, and *n2* in the parameter list, and they will eventually be referencing *noun1A*, *relationA*, and *noun2A*:

```
procedure Find(var n1,r,n2:stringarray100;var last:integer);
    var
        noun1, relation, noun2, result: stringDB;
        i: integer;
    begin
    writeln('Give the query. Type three fields on sequential lines.');
    readln(noun1);
    readln(relation);
    readln(noun2);
    writeln('THE RELATED FACTS:');
    i := 1;
    while i <= last do
        begin
        QFCompare(noun1,relation,noun2,n1[i],r[i],n2[i],result);
        if result = 'answer' then
            begin
            writeln(n1[i],' ',r[i],' ',n2[i]);
            end;
        i := i + 1;
        end;
    end;
```

The job of *QFCompare* is to return *result* = "answer" if the query fact is identical to the given database fact. That is, we must check whether *noun1 = n1[i]* and *relation = r[i]* and *noun2 = n2[i]*. The routine is written with parameter names that make as much sense locally as possible, regardless of how they may be used later. Here "Q" and "F" have the meaning "query" and "fact" to help make the procedure understandable:

```
procedure QFCompare(var Qnoun1,Qrel,Qnoun2,Fnoun1,Frel,Fnoun2,
                    an:stringDB);
    begin
    if (Qnoun1 = Fnoun1)
        and (Qrel = Frel)
            and (Qnoun2 = Fnoun2) then
        begin
        an := 'answer';
        end
```

```
    else
       begin
       an := 'no';
       end;
    end;
end;
```

This code will function as expected. If the user wishes to search for a given fact, that fact is typed as the query. If the fact is found, the system will print it:

```
Give the query. Type three fields on sequential lines.
Mr. Mason
is
a chemist.
THE RELATED FACTS:
Mr. Mason is a chemist.
```

We have developed the code to determine whether a given fact is in the database. If the fact is found, it is printed. If it is not found, the program will print nothing after the message "THE RELATED FACTS." However, this is not an exciting capability and certainly would not be very helpful to the inspector. How can we write code to answer more interesting types of questions?

Suppose it is known that someone visited today at 3:00 P.M. but it is not known who. That is, we question whether any fact appears of the form

(        ) (visited at)( 3:00 P.M.)

Because the answer to the question will be found in the first of the three fields, the way to find the answer is to search the database and print any fact that matches on the second and third fields. A good way to type this question into the machine is

?
visited at
3:00 P.M.

where the question mark means "the user does not know this information." Here is a modification to the *QFCompare* routine to handle this query:

```
procedure QFCompare(var Qnoun1,Qrel,Qnoun2,Fnoun1,Frel,Fnoun2,
                    an:stringDB);
   begin
   if ((Qnoun1 = Fnoun1) or (Qnoun1 = '?'))
       and (Qrel = Frel)
           and (Qnoun2 = Fnoun2) then
```

```
            begin
            an := 'answer';
            end
        else
            begin
            an := 'no';
            end;
        end;
```

If the first field *Qnoun1* of the question is not "?," then the code will function as before. If *Qnoun1* is a "?," then the routine will return result *an* = "answer" whenever *Qrel* = *Frel* and *Qnoun2* = *Fnoun2*. Thus it will ignore the first field and print any fact that agrees on the second and third fields. Here is how it will look to the user:

```
Give the query. Type three fields on sequential lines.
?
visited at
3:00 P.M.
THE RELATED FACTS:
The professor visited at 3:00 P.M.
```

Success! This program is clearly going to be of use to the inspector! Let us try another one:

```
Give the query. Type three fields on sequential lines.
?
has hobby
tennis.
THE RELATED FACTS:
Lord Dunsmore has hobby tennis.
Mr. Mason has hobby tennis.
```

This greatly improved system was achieved by allowing a question mark in the first field of any query. The question mark means that the user does not know what belongs in that field and the system should print all facts that match on the other two fields. The next obvious extension is to allow a question mark in any field. With this change, one may ask a huge variety of questions:

| Question | Form for typed query |
|---|---|
| Mr. Mason visited at what time? | Mr. Mason<br>visited at<br>? |
| What was Mr. Mason doing at 3:00 P.M.? | Mr. Mason<br>?<br>3:00 P.M. |
| Give me every fact about Mr. Mason. | Mr. Mason<br>?<br>?<br>and<br>?<br>?<br>Mr. Mason. |
| Who visited today and at what time? | ?<br>visited at<br>? |
| What happened at 3:00 P.M.? | ?<br>?<br>3:00 P.M. |
| Tell me everything you know. | ?<br>?<br>? |

Although this chapter began with the seemingly insoluble problem of writing a program that would help the chief inspector find his prime suspect, our query system is now quite satisfactory for his use. We solved our problem by formulating the task as storing and retrieving facts and by discovering a powerful method for doing the retrieval. The coding effort was cut down to manageable proportions through a decomposition into subtasks, which were then implemented using subroutines.

**Exercises**

1. Show how to modify the *QFCompare* procedure to handle a question mark in every field.

2. Design a procedure called *FindAll* that receives one string from the user such as "Mr. Mason" and then prints all facts that contain that string in any field. Thus, in this case it would print facts such as

Mr. Mason visited at 3:00 P.M.
The Inspector is a customer of Mr. Mason.

## Assembling the Database Program and Adding Comments (B)

The work of coding the database program is now almost complete, but to finish the program in a professional manner, we need to document the code properly for anyone who may later wish to read it or change it. We should include sufficient information regarding its input-output characteristics and method of operation to enable a new reader of the code to use it, understand its functioning, and modify it if necessary. The program comments should also identify the author and give other nominal information such as the date and application.

Most of the programs in this book do not have many comments because the surrounding text includes the necessary information and comments might distract attention from the code. In other situations, however, programs must stand alone so the programmer should carefully add enough information to preserve their usefulness. Most industrial organizations have standards for their programmers specifying how code should be written and documented.

A reasonable policy for code documentation includes three kinds of comments:

1. The program header. This appears at the beginning of the program and includes (a) the programmer's name and other nominal information, (b) the input-output specification for the program, and (c) a brief description of how the code works.
2. Code block headers. Well-written code is always organized into "blocks" of self-consistent code that do well-defined tasks such as reading, sorting, or calculating. Each block should begin with enough comments to identify its purpose and its essential operation. Blocks are usually 5 to 20 lines in length and in many cases are organized as subroutines. In some cases, the author of a block may not be the same as the main author, and proper credit should be included in the header.
3. Line comments. Although you should write code that is so straightforward that its operation is obvious to any reader, occasionally you might want to add a short comment just to the right of a line of code to clarify its meaning. Comments are especially helpful at array declarations or at assignment statements where key computations occur.

Adherence to these standards should result in a program that can be read, used, or modified by any competent programmer. Here is the database program fully commented:

```
{                      Database Program                     }
{                     by Alan W. Biermann                   }
{                        January 1997                       }
{                                                           }
{ Inputs: In input mode (command i), "facts" are read in three fields }
{   noun phrase, relationship, noun phrase. For example, "John is a    }
{   boy." is separated into three parts, "John," "is," and "a boy."    }
{   These parts are typed into the machine on three sequential lines:  }
{                                                           }
{       Input a fact. Type three fields on sequential lines. }
{       John                                                }
{       is                                                  }
{       a boy.                                              }
{                                                           }
{                                                           }
{   In query mode (command f), queries are read in the same format as }
{   facts except that some fields may have a question mark instead of  }
{   data.                                                   }
{                                                           }
{ Outputs: In query mode (command f), the program prints all facts     }
{   that match the query on fields that do not have question marks.     }
{                                                           }
{ Method of operation: The facts are stored in three arrays called      }
{   noun1A, relationA, and noun2A. The ith fact has its first, second, }
{   and third fields in the ith entries of, respectively, noun1A,       }
{   relationA, and noun2A. The program answers a query by sequentially }
{   examining every stored fact and printing it if it matches the       }
{   query on the fields that do not contain a question mark.            }
{                                                           }
{                                                           }
program Database;
type
    stringDB = string[30]; {All strings limited to length 30.}
    stringarray100 = array[1..100] of stringDB;
                                {Only 100 facts allowed.}
var
    noun1A, relationA, noun2A: stringarray100;
                                {Facts are stored in these. }
    command:stringDB;
    last: integer;
                                {"last" tells how many facts are stored.}
```

```
procedure InputFact(var n1,r,n2:stringarray100;var last:integer);
    { This procedure inputs a fact and inserts it into the database,   }
    { which is stored in n1, r, and n2 as described. "last" tells      }
    { where in these arrays the last stored fact is placed. The method }
    { of operation is to increase "last" by one and insert the new     }
    { fact into that position.                                         }
    begin
    writeln('Input a fact. Type three fields on sequential lines.');
    last := last + 1;
    readln(n1[last]);
    readln(r[last]);
    readln(n2[last]);
    writeln('Total number of facts (not to exceed 100):',last);
    end;

procedure PrintFacts(var n1,r,n2:stringarray100;var last:integer);
    { This procedure prints all of the database facts stored in n1, r, }
    {  n2.                                                             }

        This code is left as an exercise. ;

procedure QFCompare(var Qnoun1,Qrel,Qnoun2,Fnoun1,Frel,Fnoun2,
                        an:stringDB);
    { This procedure is called "query-fact compare" or QFCompare and   }
    { it determines whether the query represented by the three strings }
    { Qnoun1, Qrel, Qnoun2, matches the fact represented by strings    }
    { Fnoun1, Frel, Fnoun2 on all fields that do not have a question   }
    { mark in the query. If there is a match, then "an" is loaded      }
    { with "answer" ; otherwise it is loaded with "no."                }

        Put code here as described above. ;

procedure Find(var n1,r,n2:stringarray100;var last:integer);
    { This procedure reads a query in the same format as a fact.       }
    { However, some fields of the query may contain question marks.    }
    { It examines each fact in the database stored in n1, r, n2, and   }
    { if QFCompare reports result = "answer" for that fact, it         }
    { prints that fact.                                               }

        Put code here as described above. ;

{ The main program begins here. It reads a command in the location  }
{ "command" and then calls the corresponding procedure.             }
```

```
begin
writeln('Entering Database.');
last := 0;                          { The database begins with no facts.}
command := 'start';
while command <> 'q' do
    begin
    riteln('Command:');
    readln(command);
    if command = 'help' then
        begin
        writeln('The commands are');
        writeln('    f          find facts which match query');
        writeln('    help       help');
        writeln('    i          input fact');
        writeln('    p          print facts');
        writeln('    q          quit');
        end;
    if command = 'i' then
        begin
        InputFact(noun1A,relationA,noun2A,last);
        end;
    if command = 'p' then
        begin
        PrintFacts(noun1A,relationA,noun2A,last);
        end;
    if command = 'f' then
        begin
        Find(noun1A,relationA,noun2A,last);
        end;
    end;
writeln('Exiting database.');
readln;
end.
```

In this program, the *QFCompare* routine is declared before the *Find* routine because it is used in the *Find* routine. As the translator moves down the code, it encounters the definition of *QFCompare* and then the call to *QFCompare* inside *Find*.

The above code can be shortened by following a rule allowed by Pascal. Whenever the form

```
begin
a single statement;
end
```

falls within an *if-then-else, if-then,* or *while* statement, it can be replaced by

*a single statement*

Thus the *begin* and *end* are not needed if only one statement is being used. As an example, we can apply this rule to

```
if command = 'i' then
   begin
   InputFact(noun1A,relationA,noun2A,last);
   end;
```

to obtain this equivalent and shorter code:

```
if command = 'i' then
    InputFact(noun1A,relationA,noun2A,last);
```

However, we will not use this rule here to shorten code because it might cause confusion.

The time has finally come for us to discover the prime suspect for the murder mystery. Here is the database the inspector used to draw his conclusion. Use the program to store the information and then type the queries you need to find the prime suspect.

Lord Dunsmore is married to Lady Emily.
The gardener is married to the maid.
Poison can be gotten by a person for a blood relative.
Mr. Mason visited at 3:00 P.M.
A shared hobby causes friendship.
The gardener was recently dismissed by Lord Dunsmore.
Lord Dunsmore has hobby tennis.
The maid set tea on the table at 2:45 P.M.
Lord Secrest has hobby philosophy.
The gardener has hobby music.
Lord Dunsmore has rival Lord Secrest.
Mr. Mason is a chemist.
The Inspector is a customer of Mr. Mason.
Lord Secrest has daughter Miss Secrest.
The butler owes 10,000 pounds to Lord Dunsmore.
The butler helped serve lunch at 12:00.
The professor has hobby philosophy.

The professor visited at 3:00 P.M.
Lord Secrest is a customer of Mr. Mason.
The professor often brings gifts to Lady Emily.
Tea is always taken at 3:00 P.M.
Miss Secrest visited at 5:00 P.M.
Poison is sold by a chemist.
Lady Emily has hobby music.
Poison can be gotten by a person for a friend.
Mr. Mason has hobby philosophy.
Poison takes one hour to take effect.
The professor was once a suitor of Lady Emily.

The set of three-field facts in this problem is known as a *relation*, and the database system is referred to as a *relational database* system. (This technical definition of "relation" should not be confused with more ordinary uses of the word that may appear elsewhere in this book.) Complex relational database systems, in which there are dozens of relations and dozens of fields in each relation, are commonly used in commercial applications.

One shortcoming of the database system described here is that no inference system was programmed. Suppose that "Jill is a sister of Nancy" and "Nancy is a sister of Barbara" are facts in a database. If a query requests the sisters of Jill, although both Nancy and Barbara are listed, the database of this chapter will not discover that Jill is a sister of Barbara. An inference is required of the form

"If X is a sister of Y and Y is a sister of Z, then X is a sister of Z."

Commercial database systems usually do include inferential capabilities, and another programming system with such abilities is described at the end of chapter 9.

### Exercises

1. Complete the assembly of the database program, and try it on a simple problem.

2. Which character in the story is most likely to have had a motive, access to the poison, and an opportunity to lace the lord's food? Can you reconstruct the events that probably led to the crime?

3. A problem with the database program is that it provides no method for deleting facts. A simple way to delete a fact is to replace all its fields with an asterisk. Add a command to the system that requests the number of the fact to be deleted and then replaces its three fields with asterisks. Then change the print routine so that it skips over asterisks when they are encountered.

4. Write a delete program similar to the one described in exercise 3, but use a deletion procedure that is not so wasteful of space.

5. Prepare a database for the courses taught in a university department. The database should include what times the courses are taught, the names of instructors, and the prerequisites. A user should be able to obtain answers to such questions as

   Which professors are teaching this semester?
   Who is teaching Psychology 11?
   What are the prerequisites to Psychology 207?
   Are there any courses being taught at 4 P.M.?

6. Some relationships are called "symmetrical" because the order of the noun groups does not affect meaning. An example of such a relationship is sisterhood. If one can say

   Julie is the sister of Ann

   then one can also say

   Ann is the sister of Julie.

   The database program does not account for this possibility and will thus answer some questions incorrectly. If the single fact

   (Julie) (is the sister of) (Ann.)

   is stored, it will not correctly answer the question, "Who is the sister of Julie?"

   ?
   is the sister of
   Julie.

   Design a feature for the database program that can ask which relationships are symmetrical and then use this information to process queries that refer to them.

7. Solve some retrieval problems with the database program. Discover some of its shortcomings, and write code to correct them.

## Another Application: Drawing a Picture with Pascal (C)

Once you have learned the form of Pascal, you can use it to do a variety of tasks. This section will show you how to draw a picture by calling the correct graphics functions.

Our goal will be to draw a picture of the following building:

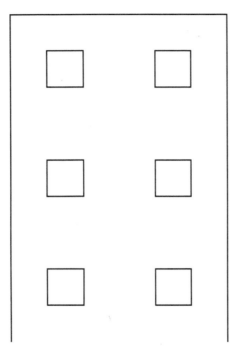

Because this program requires drawing dozens of lines on the screen at precisely the correct locations, it will involve a lot of complexity. We will begin by remembering the two
steps from the beginning of this chapter for dealing with complexity:

1. Represent the problem so that it can be dealt with easily.
2. Decompose the problem into simpler subtasks and then decompose these into even
   simpler ones until at the lowest level each subtask is easy to comprehend.

Here representation will be simple since we will be using only straight lines and Pascal is
quite capable of drawing these, as will be seen below.

The issue of decomposition is much more interesting. Let us think of the building as a
top with a set of floors:

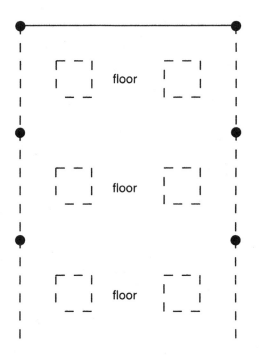

The task decomposition looks like this:

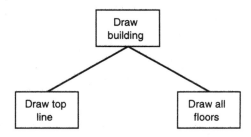

Next we need to figure out how to draw a floor. One floor should look like this:

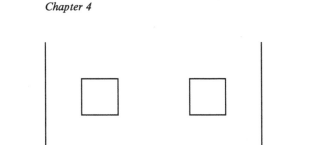

At the lowest level, the floor routine will repeatedly call a single routine that is capable of

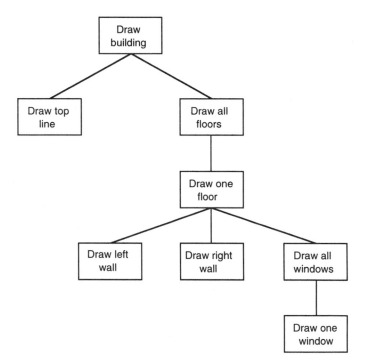

drawing a window. So now the task decomposition looks like this:

An examination of this tree shows us how to write the code. If our decomposition was successful, each part of the coding job will be easy and the combination of them will solve the problem. The next few paragraphs will show the details.

In order to get started with using the Turbo Pascal graphics facility, you must first learn some things. The screen in graphics mode is mapped out as a 640 by 480 grid as shown and you can draw items where you want them on the screen by referencing these coordinates. For example, if you want to draw a straight line from the point with coordinates x = 100, y = 100 to the point with coordinates x = 200, y = 100, then this code will do the job:

```
moveto(100,100);
lineto(200,100);
```

The first line says essentially "put your pen down at x = 100, y = 100," and the second line says "draw a straight line to x = 200, y = 100." All distances on the screen are measured in the same units, usually pixels.

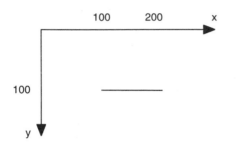

The next thing you must learn is how to put your machine into graphics mode so that such commands will actually work. Here is the calling protocol as explained in the Turbo Pascal manual:

```
program graphics;
uses
    Graph; {This links in the graphics facilities.}
var
    GraphDriver, GraphMode, ErrorCode:integer;
            {These variables are needed by the graphics
            system.}
begin
GraphDriver := Detect;
InitGraph(GraphDriver,GraphMode,'C:\tp\bgi');
            {This initializes the graphics mode on the
            machine.}
ErrorCode := GraphResult;
if ErrorCode <> grOK then
            {This code checks that graphics is operative.}
```

```
      begin
      writeln('Graph error:', GraphErrorMsg(ErrorCode));
      writeln('Program aborted . . ');
      readln;
      Halt(1);
      end;
moveto(100,100);
            {Here is our first try at drawing something.}
lineto(200,100);
readln;
end.
```

Try this program to see if it will run properly on your machine. If you have problems with it, the cause could be that the filename C:\tp\bgi is wrong. It is supposed to tell where the graphics routines reside on your machine. Consult your manual or friend to find out how to load and link your graphics routines.

If you use Think Pascal, you do not need to include special code to go into graphics mode. In fact, the following program will do the job:

```
program graphics;
begin
moveto(100,100);
            {Here is our first try at drawing something.}
lineto(200,100);
readln;
end.
```

Now we are ready to create the program that will draw the building described above. We want to specify the dimensions, the number of floors, and the number of windows on each floor. Here is the main routine. Before going into graphics mode, it asks a series of questions to find out the parameters for the building. Then it enters the graphics mode and calls one routine that will draw the building.

```
program build;
uses
    Graph; {This links in the graphics facilities.}
var
    GraphDriver, GraphMode, ErrorCode:integer;
            {These variables are needed by the graphics
            system.}
    x,y,height,width,numfloors,nwinfloor:integer;
            {These variables are needed by our building
            routine.}
```

```
{The subroutines need to be typed here.}

begin         {This codes sets all variables.}
writeln('Input x.');
              {This gives the x coordinate of the}
readln(x);   {upper left corner of the building.}
writeln('Input y.);
              {This gives the y coordinate of the}
readln(y);   {upper left corner of the building.}
writeln('Input height.');
              {This gives the height of the building.}
readln(height);
writeln('Input width.')
              {This gives the width of the building.}
readln(width);
writeln('Input number of floors.');
readln(numfloors);
              {This gives the number of floors.}
writeln('Input number of windows per floor.');
readln(nwinfloor);
              {This gives the number of windows on each
              floor.}

GraphDriver := Detect;
              {This is the graphics initialization code.}
InitGraph(GraphDriver,GraphMode,'C:\tp\bgi');
              {This initializes the graphics mode on the
              machine.}
ErrorCode := GraphResult;
if ErrorCode <> grOK then
              {This code checks that graphics is operative.}
    begin
    writeln('Graph error:', GraphErrorMsg(ErrorCode));
    writeln('Program aborted . . ');
    readln;
    Halt(1);
    end;
              {The next routine draws the building.}
building(x,y,height,width,numfloors,nwinfloor);
readln;
end.
```

The next step is to write the subroutine that draws the building. We will begin by drawing a line across the top of the building, starting at the coordinates x, y given by system parameters passed down from the main program. Then the routine will enter a loop to draw a floor just below the top line, then another floor below that, and so forth.

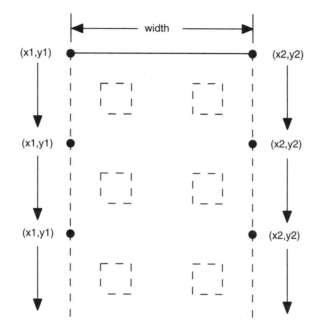

The algorithm for the program must carry out these steps:

Find the values for x1 and y1. They give the upper left corner of the building and they are equal x and y from the main routine.
Find the values for x2 and y2. x2 is x1 plus the amount of the width of the building and y2 is just the same as y1.
Find the heighth for each floor. This is the height of the building divided by the number of floors.
Draw the line across the top of the building.
i := 1;
while there are more floors to draw
    Draw a floor starting at the coordinates x1,y1.
    Find a new values for x1 and y1.
    i := i + 1;

Here is the code:

```
procedure building(var x,y,height,width,nfloors,
                       nwinfloor:integer);
{ This procedure draws a building starting with its upper left corner  }
{ at x,y with dimensions height and width and number of floors nfloors }
{ and number of windows per floor nwinfloor.}
var
   x1,x2,y1,y2,hfloor,i:integer;
begin
x1 := x;
y1 := y;                              {x1, y1 specify the upper left corner.}
x2 := x1 + width;
y2 := y1;                             {x2, y2 specify the upper right corner.}
hfloor := height div nfloors;
                                         {Find the height of each floor.}
moveto(x1,y1);
lineto(x2,y2);                            {Draw the top of the building.}
i := 1;
while i <= nfloors do                        {Draw all the floors.}
    begin
    floor(x1,y1,hfloor,width,nwinfloor);        {Draw this floor.}
    y1 := y1 + hfloor;              {Find coordinates for next floor.}
    i := i + 1;
    readln;
    end;
end;
```

We now know how to build the building but not how to draw a floor. Here is what we want on each floor:

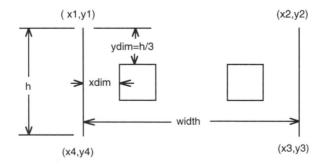

Here is the strategy:

Find the coordinates of the four corners: x1,y1 and x2,y2 and x3,y3 and x4,y4.
Find the dimensions xdim and ydim which will give the sizes of the windows and also the coordinates for their placement. We will use just 1/3 of the linear distance available for each window.
Draw the left vertical line delineating the left wall.
Draw the right vertical line delineating the right wall.
Find the coordinates xwin,ywin of the first window location.
i := 1;
while i <= the number of windows
    Draw a window with its upper left corner at xwin,ywin.
    Update the values of xwin,ywin for the next window.
    i := i + 1;

Here is the code:

```
procedure floor(var x,y,h,width,num:integer);
{ This routine draws a floor of the building starting at the upper      }
{ left corner coordinates x,y and drawing it with dimensions h and      }
{ width and with the number of windows given by num.                    }
var
    x1,y1,x2,y2,x3,y3,x4,y4,xwin,ywin,xdim,ydim,i:integer;
begin
x1 := x;            y1 := y;                {Compute the coordinates for}
x2 := x1 + width;   y2 := y1;                      {the four corners.}
x3 := x2;           y3 := y2 + h;
x4 := x3 - b;       y4 := y3;
xdim := width div (3*num);          {These are the window dimensions}
ydim := h div 3;                    {and the window spacing distances.}
moveto(x1,y1);
lineto(x4,y4);                                      {Draw the left wall.}
moveto(x2,y2);
lineto(x3,y3);                                     {Draw the right wall.}
xwin := x1 + xdim;                 {Find where to draw first window.}
ywin := y1 + ydim;
i := 1;
while i := num do                              {Draw all of the windows.}
    begin
    window(xwin,ywin,xdim,ydim);                    {Draw this window.}
    xwin := xwin + (width div num);
                                   {Find coordinates for next window.}
```

```
        i := i + 1;
        end;
end;
```

We need to write a final subroutine to draw just one window. The figure and the algorithm will be left for you to figure out. Here is the code to do the job:

```
procedure window(var x,y,xd,yd:integer);
        { This routine draws a window starting with its upper left corner  }
        { at x,y and with dimensions xd and yd.                            }
var
        x1,y1,x2,y2,x3,y3,x4,y4:integer;
begin
x1 := x;                    y1 := y;
x2 := x1 + xd;              y2 := y1;
x3 := x2;                   y3 := y2 + yd;
x4 := x3 - xd;             y4 := y3;
moveto(x1,y1);
lineto(x2,y2);
lineto(x3,y3);
lineto(x4,y4);
lineto(x1,y1);
end;
```

This completes the code to draw the building shown at the beginning of this section. In the final assembly of the code the important point to remember is that the Pascal system will expect the subroutines to be ordered so that when any routine calls another routine, the called routine will already have been defined. Thus, when the *building* routine calls *floor*, *floor* should already be defined, and when *floor* calls *window*, *window* should already be defined. Thus, the ordering in our program should be *window* first, *floor* next, and *building* last.

### Exercises

1. Draw the figure and write down the algorithm for the *window* procedure given above. Check the correctness of the code.

2. Modify the code in the above program so that it draws one window on the top floor, two windows on the next floor, and so forth.

3. Write a program that uses the code in this section to draw something like the New York skyline.

4. Show how to revise the code in this section to draw a more realistic version of a building.

5. Read about the graphics features of your programming system and use some of them to draw a picture of interest to you. This might include elements like circles, arcs, colors, sound, and motion.

## Recursion (C)

As we have seen, a major strategy for solving a problem is to divide it into parts, solve the parts, and then combine the solutions of the parts to obtain a solution to the whole. If we wish to compute the factorial of 5 ($5*4*3*2*1 = 120$), we can split it into two parts, 5 and $4*3*2*1$, and calculate each part separately: $5 = 5$ and $4*3*2*1 = 24$. Then we can combine the parts to obtain the answer: $5*24 = 120$. This strategy can be represented with the following notation:

factorial(5) = 5 * factorial(4)

More generally, if $n$ is greater than zero, we can write

factorial(n) = n * factorial(n − 1).

This is a very special calculation because it is circular in nature. The strategy for computing *factorial(n)* requires finding *factorial(n − 1)* first. But how do we compute *factorial(n − 1)*? The answer is that we must compute *factorial(n − 2)* and so forth.
But the formula

factorial(n) = n * factorial(n − 1)

fails if $n = 0$. In the case $n = 0$, we write

factorial(n) = 1.

In fact, the general definition of factorial is

factorial(n) =
    if n = 0 then
       1
    else
       n * factorial(n − 1)

This is called a *recursive* calculation because the function being defined is used in the definition. Here is a general format for such calculations:

A method for doing computation $C$ on data $D$ to obtain result $R$.

if the calculation is trivial then
    do it and return the result R
else
      begin
      divide D into two parts D1 and D2
      do part of the calculation on D1 to obtain R1 (possibly using C)
      do part of the calculation on D2 to obtain R2 (possibly using C)
      combine R1 and R2 to obtain the result R
      end

This can be illustrated by showing how it works on factorial:

    A method for computing the factorial of $n$ to obtain result $f$.

if $n = 0$ then
    $f := 1$
else
      begin
      separate n into parts $D1 = n$ and $D2 = n - 1$
      do part of the calculation on D1 to obtain $R1 := D1$
      compute the factorial of D2 to obtain R2
      combine R1 and R2 to obtain $f := R1 * R2$
      end

Here is the factorial program:

```
procedure factorial(var n,f:integer);
    var
        D1,D2,R1,R2:integer;
    begin
    if n = 0 then
        f := 1
    else
        begin
        D1 := n;
        D2 := n-1;
        R1 := D1;
        factorial(D2,R2);
        f := R1 * R2;
        end;
    end;
```

This, of course, uses more data locations than are necessary. The program can be shortened to this:

```
procedure factorial(var n,f:integer);
    var
        i:integer;
    begin
    if n = 0 then
        f := 1
    else
        begin
        i := n - 1;
        factorial(i,f);
        f := n * f;
        end;
    end;
```

(Note: If this program is run, it will overflow the integer variables for values of *n* that are not small.)

You can better understand this program for factorial if you carry through a computation by hand. Here is a trace of its major actions when it computes the factorial value for 3. All computations from a single call are indented equally.

Call factorial(3,f)
    i := 2;
    Call factorial(2,f)
        i := 1;
        Call factorial(1,f)
            i := 0;
            Call factorial(0,f)
                f := 1;
                Exit.
            f := 1 * (f from previous call) = 1 * 1 = 1
            Exit.
        f := 2 * (f from previous call) = 2 * 1 = 2
        Exit.
    f := 3 * (f from previous call) = 3 * 2 = 6
    Exit.

Recursion is a difficult concept to learn, but when you master it, you will find it easy to code many difficult programs. Let us use recursion to sort a list:

A method for sorting a list *L*.

if L has length 1 or less then
    do nothing

else
      begin
      choose a member x of L
      let D1 be the members of L less than x
      let D2 be the members of L greater than or equal to x
            (but D2 does not contain x)
      rearrange L so that D1 is to the left of x and D2 is to the right of x
      sort D1 to obtain R1
      sort D2 to obtain R2
      the final sorted list is R1 followed by x followed by R2
      end

   Suppose, as an illustration, the list 2,5,7,6,3,1,4 is to be sorted. The method of calculation chooses one member of the list—let us say the last one, 4—and moves the numbers less than 4 to the left end of the array and the numbers greater than 4 to the right: 2,3,1,4,5,7,6. Here we have $x = 4$, $D1 = 2,3,1$, and $D2 = 5,7,6$. Next, $D1$ is sorted to obtain 1,2,3, and $D2$ is sorted to obtain 5,6,7. The final sorted list is $D1$ followed by $x$ followed by $D2$: 1,2,3,4,5,6,7.

   Here is the subroutine for this sorting algorithm. It is a famous sorting method known as *quicksort*. The routine *quicksort(ar,i,j)* sorts the integer array *ar* beginning at entry *i* and ending at entry *j*:

```
procedure quicksort(var ar:intarray;var i,j:integer);
    var
        b1,e1,b2,e2:integer;
                    {b1 and e1 begin and end sublist D1.}
                    {b2 and e2 begin and end sublist D2.}
    begin
    if i < j then
        begin
        b1 := i;
        e2 := j;
        rearrange(ar,b1,e1,b2,e2);
        quicksort(ar,b1,e1);
        quicksort(ar,b2,e2);
        end;
    end;
```

   There are many strategies for coding *rearrange*. Here is one Pascal version of this routine you may wish to study:

```
procedure rearrange(var ar: intarray;
                    var b1,e1,b2,e2:integer);
```

```
    var
        mover:string;
        i1,i2:integer;
    procedure exchange(var i,j:integer);
        var
            temp:integer;
        begin
        temp := i;
        i := j;
        j := temp;
        end;
    begin

    i1 := b1;
    i2 := e2;
    mover := 'i1';
    while i1 < i2 do
        if mover = 'i1' then
            if ar[i1] > ar[i2] then
                begin
                exchange(ar[i1],ar[i2]);
                mover := 'i2';
                end
            else
                i1 := i1 + 1
        else
            if ar[i1] > ar[i2] then
                begin
                exchange(ar[i1],ar[i2]);
                mover := 'i1';
                end
            else
                i2 := i2 - 1;
    e1 := i1 - 1;
    b2 := i1 + 1;
    end;
```

This procedure declaration should precede the declaration for *quicksort* so that references to *rearrange* in *quicksort* will be well defined when they are encountered. (*Rearrange* differs slightly from our original definition, but its effect is the same.)

The method of dividing a problem into simpler parts and solving each separately was explored earlier in this chapter. In this section, the strategy for computing function *C* divides the data into parts, calculates partial results using *C*, and combines these results to obtain the final answer. This subtle and powerful strategy is called recursion. Some writers also refer to the methodology of splitting the data into parts and solving the *divide and conquer* methodology.

Recursion can often be used as an alternative to writing ordinary looping programs. Although you can easily write a program to compute factorial without recursion, other problems may be extremely difficult to write unless you use recursion. An example of such a problem is given in exercise 4 below, where you are asked to compute all the orderings of a set of symbols. The tree-searching problems described in the chapter on artificial intelligence also need recursion for a straightforward solution.

**Exercises**

1. Study the routine *rearrange* and explain how it works. Write a program that reads a series of integers and then uses the quicksort program to sort them.

2. The *n*th Fibonacci number is computed by adding the $(n-1)$th and the $(n-2)$th Fibonacci numbers. The first two are 0 and 1, and the Fibonacci numbers can be enumerated as $0,1,1,2,3,5,8,13,21, \ldots$ Write a recursive program that reads a number *N* and then prints the *N*th Fibonacci number. (Note that when this program is run, its execution time can be long if *N* is not small. Why is this? Program execution time will be studied more in chapter 12.)

3. The sum of *n* numbers in an array can be computed as follows: Add the first $n-1$ numbers, and then add that sum to the last number. Use this method to design and program a recursive procedure for adding an array.

4. Write a program that receives an array of symbols and then prints every arrangement (permutation) of those symbols. For example, if the program receives the array a,b,c, it will print out

   a,b,c
   a,c,b
   b,a,c
   b,c,a
   c,a,b
   c,b,a

   Use a recursive strategy to solve this problem.

## Object-Oriented Programming (C)

A popular style of programming that differs from the methodologies described here is called *object-oriented programming*. This methodology organizes a program as a set of *objects*, each of which contains the key data related to some significant computational entity. The computation is done by routines called *methods* that are contained within the objects. The objects communicate during the computation by passing *messages* back and forth.

A central idea in object-oriented programming is the concept of *class*, a template from which objects can be created. For example, the class *person* would specify the form that objects in this class must have. If we wish to organize a group of people to do a task and must keep track of their schedules, we could define the class *person* to specify two data items: the individual's name and the individual's schedule.

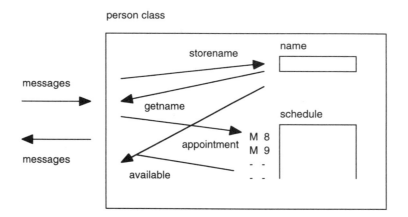

Subroutines that manage the data items are called *methods* (or *member functions*). In our example, let us assume that we need the following four methods:

| | |
|---|---|
| storename(W) | Stores *W* into the *name* location. |
| getname | Retrieves from *name* location. |
| appointment(U,V) | Schedules appointment *U* at time *V*. |
| available(T1,T2) | Returns *name* if this individual is available during the time interval *T1* to *T2* (and null otherwise). |

A user of any object from this class would not be able to examine this data directly, but only call the methods to use the data. It is the task of the methods to maintain the data and to hand it to the outside world when appropriate. The exact form of the internal data may never be known by the user. When a computation makes a call to a method in an object, it is said to send a *message* to the object. Sometimes this is referred to as *calling a member function*. In our example, we could create an object *P1* of type *person*, which would make it possible to enter the name "Smith" into *P1* with the code

```
X := 'Smith';
P1.storename(X);
```

This sends a message to object *P1* that it should store "Smith" in its *name* field.

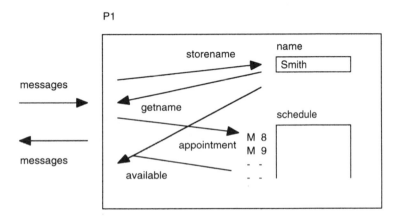

The class *person* is not used directly for computation but to create objects that will do the computation. As an example, we can instantiate the above class repeatedly to create objects in its image. Each newly created object has the exact form of the class template given above, and it has the additional property that it can take part in a computation. Thus, we might decide to do a computation requiring three people and generate the following objects: (Notice that we have also used methods *storename* and *appointment* to make entries into the object data locations.)

P1

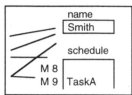

P2

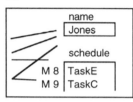

P3

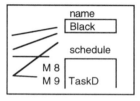

    Each object represents a different person, and computations related to the objects can be performed by sending messages to them. Suppose we wish to schedule a job that needs to be done between 8:00 and 9:00 on Monday and we need someone to help out. We could create an object to send messages to all the available objects of type *person* giving the requested time. Those objects that show free schedules during the given time would then return the appropriate names. The scheduling object would then collect the list of available people.

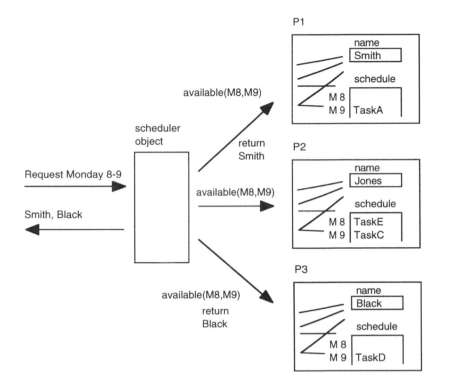

The advantages of doing programming in this way are many. First, if people have done similar computations in the past and have created a class like *person* in the class library, it may be much better than any code we would have written. Perhaps it was refined over the years during extensive use by professionals and has features we would not have thought of and reliability we could not have hoped for. Second, because the data is *encapsulated* in the object, it is protected by the object from erroneous modification. If we access the data in an object by prescribed methods, the data will be properly managed and will be unaltered by erroneous external coding. Third, object-oriented programming enables the user of a class to interact with the class without knowing the details of the internal processing. The same message sent to different objects could require entirely different internal processing while the result for the user is the same. This is known in the literature as *polymorphism*.

We will finish our discussion of object-oriented programming techniques with the concept of *inheritance*. Suppose we would like to augment the *person* class given above to include each employee's starting date and job classification. Then we can declare an *employee* class as a *subclass* of the *person* class. This new class will use the *person* class and will have its own additional fields.

employee class

inherit from person class

start date

m1 [            ]

job classification

m2 [            ]

We can then use the *employee* class to define many employee objects. Each would have *name* and *schedule* data structures inherited from the *person* class, and *start date* and *job classification* data structures from its own declaration. Here is an example of type employee with all its structures and methods:

P4

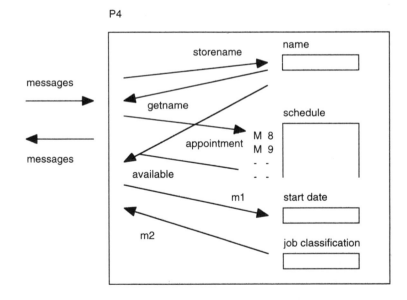

We could continue the inheritance to a third level and define a class called *manager* that inherits from *employee* and contains fields indicating what department the individual manages, who his or her secretary is, and related information. Possibly we would also want other classes inheriting from the *employee* class, such as *salesperson* and *engineer*. This results in the following inheritance tree:

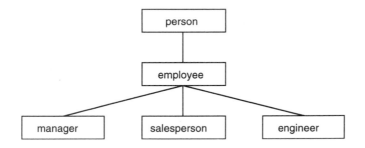

Many programmers are now using the object-oriented techniques described here. Because such coding methods enable them to mimic the structure of the problem being solved, they can create objects and communication paths that resemble those in the domain. The correspondence between the code and the real world makes the code easier to understand, to create, and to debug.

**Exercises**

1. Create a class called *animal* for a set of objects that will enable you to represent animals. Use as a model the *person* class shown above. Give both data structures and methods that you consider appropriate. Next, create subclasses of *animal* called *bird* and *mammal* that will have the same data structures and methods as *animal* but will also have additional structures associated with the classes of birds and mammals. Create other classes called *robin* and *chicken* that will inherit from the *bird* class.

2. Show with a diagram objects M1 and M2 of type *manager* with all their data structures and methods. Show what happens if one executes

```
Y := 'Bill';
M1.storename(Y);
M2.storename(Y);
```

Trace the call to the method *storename* through the inheritance hierarchy, from the definition of *manager* to the point where the definition of *storename* occurs.

---

## Summary (B)

The central problem of computer science is to discover methods for managing complexity. The two techniques that have proven most effective are finding the best representation for the problem and decomposing it into simpler parts. These strategies seem applicable to all problem-solving situations, and their mastery is fundamental to all education.

This chapter has illustrated both strategies. The first illustration was the database problem, where the original statement of the task seemed to involve programming far beyond the grasp of novice programmers. Yet with careful structuring of the solution, a way was found to achieve the target behaviors with a single loop program and relatively little additional complexity. The building-drawing problem and sorting problems gave additional examples of the development of a representation and a solution through problem decomposition.

Pascal and most other programming languages provide syntactic support for the decomposition process through the subroutine feature. A subroutine is a module of programming that solves a part of the total problem. Whenever the solution to any task seems complex, we section off parts of it into subroutines that will be written later. Each part of the solution should be sectioned off until the subroutine seems straightforward and obviously correct.

The use of the subroutine feature requires care in designing communication between the subroutine and its calling program, and this communication is carried out through the parameter list. The higher-level program needs to have a job done on its data structures, and it calls the subroutine to do it. Through the parameter list, the subroutine references only the structures needed in the calling program. If the subroutine needs additional memory locations to do its work, it should have them declared internally.

The database program developed here introduces the concept of the relational database and shows how it organizes data. An excellent way to retrieve information from such a database is to search for data patterns where some but not all of the fields are specified. One of the shortcomings of the program studied here is its inability to do inferences when the needed facts are not explicitly in the memory. A later chapter will reexamine this shortcoming and describe a method for overcoming it.

Another method of program modularization, which is not discussed at length in this book, is object-oriented programming. In this case, the modules are the objects and their associated methods. If you wish to study more about this approach, you can examine the object-oriented features of your Turbo Pascal system or consult the references given below.

This chapter completes our study of the Pascal language. The features described in chapters 1 to 4 do not include the whole language but they are sufficient to do essentially any program. A description of the syntax used in these chapters appears in the Appendix. The full Pascal language includes many other features, but they are primarily embellishments of the constructions covered here: additional looping, branching, and subroutine constructions and additional data structure types and declaration facilities.

In the early days of computing, an interesting competition arose over the power of computer languages. One researcher would show that his or her language could be used to compute every function that some other language could compute. Then someone else would show that the second language could compute everything that the first could. The implication was that neither language could compute anything more than the other; both were capable of computing the same class of functions. Such comparisons occurred many times with the same surprising result: *any nontrivial computer language that one can invent is apparently capable of computing no more and no fewer functions than all the other non-trivial programming languages.* This is known as the Church-Markov-Turing thesis, and it applies to the part of Pascal described in this book. You have learned all the computational features needed to compute any function that can be programmed by any language yet invented. Additional features provide convenience but not increased computational capability.

The Church-Markov-Turing thesis has even more profound implications. Consider the portion of the English language appropriate for discussing computation in very concrete terms. This widely used sublanguage includes such sentences as, "Find the largest number in this finite set that is prime" and "Sort the set of records on the fifth field." Let us call this portion of English *C-English* and think of it as just another programming language. As far as anyone can tell, the power of C-English is similar to any other programming language; it is capable of describing any calculation that any standard programming language can do and no more. The Church-Markov-Turing thesis in its extended form asserts that *any algorithm that can be described in a natural language can be translated into any modern programming language.* This thesis is embraced by most computer scientists, and it implies a kind of completeness to modern programming languages. It says that if you can specify an algorithm concretely in English, you can program it. Modern computer languages are powerful enough; no new languages will enable us to compute more functions than are now possible unless some currently unimaginable new paradigm for computing is created.

This has been only a brief introduction to programming. If you wish to become an accomplished programmer, learn the rest of the Pascal features, as well as one or two other languages. Then undertake an extensive study of data structures and learn the multitude of ways that data can be represented in computers. You must learn to analyze the execution times of programs so you can create efficient, as well as correct, programs, and you must also learn methodologies for proving the correctness of programs so they can be guaranteed to meet the specifications claimed for them. Finally, you should practice applying all these skills to the analysis and coding of a variety of problems.

# 5  Simulation

---

## Predicting the Future (A)

Scientists predict that the sun will continue to burn in roughly its current state for perhaps 5 billion more years. When it begins to exhaust its resources, it will enter a "red giant" phase and expand its diameter from less than a million miles to possibly over 50 million miles. Instead of being a small disk in our sky, it will be large fraction of our sky. It will burn itself out in this phase and eventually collapse to a "white dwarf," which will be tiny in comparison to its current size.

This chapter will introduce a powerful tool for studying complex systems like the sun and for understanding their mechanisms. Knowing the current basic facts about the sun, or any other system, we would like to make predictions about it. What will happen next? How long will each phase last, and what will its characteristics be? The answers to these kinds of questions can often be found by *simulation*.

The methodology follows three steps:

1. We will devise a model that captures the essence of the characteristics of the system we wish to study. It usually consists of some equations or other relationships that indicate how the significant measures of the system relate to each other.
2. We will develop a next-step function. The input for this function will be a listing of the significant information about the system at a given time. The output will be the state the model will change to after a given interval of time.
3. We will set the model in an initial state and apply the next-step function repeatedly to discover future states.

Simulation enables us to observe a system as it goes through a sequence of steps. A simulation can help scientists understand a system; it can help a designer of a system to predict behavior so that design decisions can be optimized; it can provide us with a subjective view of a proposed system so that we can enjoy, appreciate, and understand it even though it does not exist in reality.

## Winning an Auto Race (B)

Suppose we wish to run a race over the track given below. Our car can start anywhere along the start line, as shown, and must drive towards the right, around the barrier in a right-hand turn. In order to win, we need to know how to reach the finish line in the shortest amount of time. Let us suppose that our car is capable of accelerating and decelerating at 3 meters per second per second and that it has no maximum speed. We will assume that the lateral acceleration on the curve may also not exceed 9 meters per second per second without losing traction and sliding off the track. A simulation will allow us to propose any strategy we wish in order to find the fastest route to the finish line.

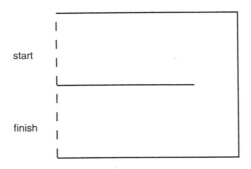

To devise a simulation, we must follow the three steps listed above. First, we need a model that represents the position of the car, its velocity, its direction, and its status (running normally, skidding, crashed into the wall, etc.).

State description     $x$ coordinate
                      $y$ coordinate
                      $x$ velocity
                      $y$ velocity
                      $x$ component of the direction vector
                      $y$ component of the direction vector
                      running state (1 for under control;
                           0 for skidding)
                      completion code (0 for not terminating;
                           1 for crashed;
                           2 for successful completion)
                      $t$ time in seconds since the beginning of the race

The model must also include a description of the race track that indicates where the walls and finish lines are. Let us decide that the start and finish lines are at $x = 500$. The top and bottom lines will be at $y = 1800$ and 200, respectively. The far wall in the $x$ direction will be at $x = 2500$. The dividing line in the middle will be at $y = 1000$ and extend from $x = 500$ to $x = 2000$.

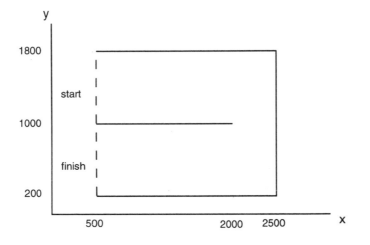

Second, we need a next-step function. This function will receive as input a state description of the auto as given in the paragraph above, and it will compute the next state after one second of driving. The name of this function will be *drive* and it will have three arguments as follows:

*state*     This will be an array that will contain the list of parameters given above characterizing the current state of the auto.

*a*     This will give the acceleration that we have decided to apply. It may not exceed 3 in a positive or negative direction. (A negative acceleration corresponds to applying the brake.)

*turnr*     This will give the turn radius. For example, *turnr* = 100 means turn right in an arc with a center that has a distance of 100 meters from the vehicle. A negative turn radius means the same thing except turn left. If *turnr* is zero, the system will go on a straight course.

What will *drive(state,a,turnr)* do? It will receive the values of the position, velocity, and so forth, which specify the state as well as the desired acceleration $a$ and turn radius *turnr*. It will then compute the new values of position, velocity, etc. after one second of driving and enter them as the new state.

For example, suppose *state* holds the position ($x = 1000$, $y = 1400$) and velocity 30 meters per second in the $x$ direction. Suppose also that $a = 0$ and *turnr* $= 0$. Then *drive(state,a,turnr)* will compute a new state with position ($x = 1030$, $y = 1400$) and velocity in the $x$ direction of 30 meters per second.

Now we can program the simulation to do any driving sequence. As a first test of the system, let us place the auto at the location $x = 500.1$, $y = 1400$, with velocity zero aimed in the $x$ direction. (We place the car just inside the edge wall at $x = 500$.) Then let us accelerate for 10 seconds at a rate of 3 meters per second per second in a straight line.

```
a := 3;
turnr := 0;
time := 1;
while (time <= 10) & (not complete) do
    begin
    drive(state,a,turnr);
    time := time + 1;
    end;
```

This should get the car moving at a rate of 30 meters per second in the $x$ direction down the track. (If you accelerate at 3 meters per second per second for 10 seconds, you will be travelling at 30 meters per second.) In the location "not complete" of the program, we place a test to check that the race has not just ended with a success or a crash.

Next, let us drive at a steady rate until we are even with the corner. (Here *corner* has the value 2000.)

```
a := 0;
turnr := 0;
while (x < corner) & (not complete) do
    begin
    drive(state,a,turnr);
    end;
```

Next let us turn with a radius of 400 meters until we are going in the opposite direction. Since we are 400 meters from the end of the middle barrier, we will be rotating around that corner.

```
a :=0;
turnr := 400;
while (((y > middle) | (x > corner)) & (not complete)) do
    begin
    drive(state,a,turnr);
    end;
```

(The symbols "&" and "|" stand for "and" and "or.") Finally, we should accelerate maximally in a straight line until we cross the finish line.

```
a := 3;
turnr := 0;
while (not complete) do
   begin
   drive(state,a,turnr);
   end;
```

That is the program. We simply join together the above four pieces of code and insert them into the simulation program. Let us run the simulation and observe the path and the total time required to finish the course.

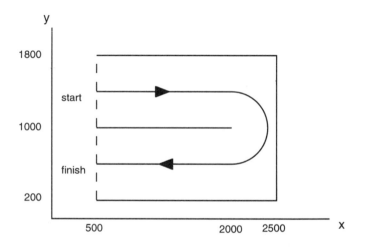

The total time was 121 seconds. (If you actually run this simulation, you will find the car stays on the curve around the track a bit too long and does not make a perfectly straight path toward the finish. The reason for this and how to fix it is left to you to figure out.)

To summarize, we proposed a strategy for completing the course and coded the simulation. Then we ran the simulation and determined that the car finished the course successfully in a time of 121 seconds. Presumably, if this course and automobile actually exist somewhere, someone could drive the sequence we have programmed and, assuming the model is accurate, they could complete the path shown above in 121 seconds.

Of course, in order to win the race we need a strategy that will do better than our first attempt. Let us accelerate the car continuously from the start line to the curve. Then we will hold that speed around the curve before accelerating maximally again to the finish. The code in this case begins with

```
a := 3;
turnr := 0;
while (x < corner) & (not complete) do
    begin
    drive(state,a,turnr);
    end;
```

and finishes with the last two segments in the previous strategy.

Unfortunately, when we run the new version, the car goes into a skid at the turn and crashes into the far wall at $x = 2500$. It was travelling too fast at the curve to make the turn. There must be a better strategy, and we will leave it for you to find.

You can obtain the Turbo Pascal program for this simulation on the Internet, as described in the introductory chapter, "Studying Academic Computer Science."

**Exercises**

1. Write a program to simulate the following racing strategy. Begin at the same position as above. Accelerate maximally in the $x$ direction until reaching the point $x = 1000$. Then decelerate maximally to a velocity in the $x$ direction of 30 meters per second. Then make the curve as before but with a radius of 300 meters and accelerate maximally across the finish.

2. Find the best strategy you can for completing the race course in minimum time.

## Avoiding the Plague (C)

A problem of great interest to public health officials is the life cycle of a contagious disease: how many people will be infected, how long the disease will be a problem, and how our preventative and curative efforts may change the situation. A way to study these questions is to develop a model of the disease characteristics and run a simulation to try to predict their behavior.

Our first step is to devise a model of a population and of the way the disease spreads. We will use a simple model that is easy to program and shows a variety of interesting behaviors. We will think of our population as a linear set of individuals and model it as a linear array. We will place a 0 in each individual's entry if that person is well and a positive integer if the person becomes infected. The positive integer will indicate the number of days since the individual was infected.

The model will work as follows: all individuals will start in the well condition with 0s in their associated locations. One individual in the population will be infected by placing a 1 in that individual's location. It will look like this:

00000000000000000000000000000001000000000000000000000000000000000

You can think of it as a row of houses with one containing a sick person. Or it could be a row of tomato plants.

Then a contagion rule will model the process of infecting other individuals. It will randomly select individuals near the currently ill individual and place 1s in their locations. They will become ill on the next day and the individual who is already ill will have the number of days incremented:

0000000000000000000001000000002010000000000000000100000000000000

On the third day, the newly infected individuals will infect additional individuals, and the number of ill individuals will multiply.

00000000000000010100201100000030201001001010100200000000000000

We will then model the process of getting over the disease and include an immune period afterward. We will have a parameter called *infectious* that will give the number of days that the illness will last. We will have a parameter called *immune* that will tell the number of days past the first day of infection when the individual cannot be reinfected. Thus, if an individual is ill for 3 days after infection and remains immune to the disease until 7 days after the infection began, we will set *infectious:= 3* and *immune:= 7*.

Having completed the model, we can consider the next-step function. The core of this is the computation that finds which individuals will be infected by an existing ill individual. This will be done by a routine called *infect* that will receive as input the number of the individual who is infecting and that will make entries into the array showing which new individuals are becoming infected on the current day. Here is a first attempt at writing the *infect* routine. Variable *k* tells which individual is doing the infecting.

```
procedure infect(var B:arraytype;var k, rate:integer);
    var
        i,j:integer;
    begin
    i := 1;
    while i <= rate do
        begin
        {select individual j to be infected}
        B[j] := 1;
        i := i + 1;
        end;
    end;
```

This routine will infect several individuals, namely the number given by *rate*. It will infect individuals by placing 1s into their associated array entries.

We need to decide how to compute *j* each time a new individual is to be infected. We will do this by calculating a *pseudo random number*, a number that is computed by a carefully designed function and that will deliver a variety of numbers if it is used repeatedly. (The design of this computation is complex and will not be discussed here.) Here is the revised subroutine with the pseudo random-number generator:

```
procedure infect(var B:arraytype;var k, iInc, rate:integer);
    var
        i,j:integer;
    begin
    i := 1;
    while i <= rate do
        begin
        {select individual j to be infected and infect it}
        iInc := ((iInc * 23) mod 31);
        j := k + iInc -13;
        if (j > 0) and (j <= 60) then
            begin
            B[j] := 1;
            end;
        i := i + 1;
        end;
    end;
```

Our next step, which begins with a matrix of individuals, some well, some ill, and some immune, calls *infect* repeatedly on all the ill individuals to infect new ones. In our current study, let us choose the infection rate to be 3. (The complete code for the simulation is given in Appendix B.)

Let us execute our simulation and see what we can expect from a disease with the given characteristics: *infectious := 3; immune := 7; rate := 3*. The printout will show each sick individual with an asterisk *, each immune individual with a 1, and all others with a 0.

day 1  OOOOOOOOOOOOOOOOOOOOOOOOOOOOOO*OOOOOOOOOOOOOOOOOOOOOOOOOOOOOO

day 2  OOOOOOOOOOOOOOOOOOOOO*OOOOOOOO*O*OOOOOOOOOOOOO*OOOOOOOOOOOOO

day 3  OOOOOOOOOOOOOOO*O*OO*O**OOOOO*O*O*OO*OO*O*O*OO*OOOOOOOOOOOOO

day 4  OOO*OO*OOOO**OO*O*******O***O1O***O****O*O*****OOOOO*O**OOO

day 5  OO**OO****O***O*****1***O****1*1**************1***O*O*O****O

day 6  *O***O********O1*1**1*11*****1*1*1**1**1*1*1**1***********

day 7  ***1*O1****11**1*1111111*111*1*1111*1111*1*11111*****1*11***

day 8  **11**1111*111*111111111*11101111111111111111111*1*1*1111*

day 9  1*111*11111111*11111*111111101*1111111111111101111111111111

Here is a statistical summary of what happened over the nine days:

Wellness summary

| day | well | ill | immune |
|-----|------|-----|--------|
| 1 | 59 | 1 | 0 |
| 2 | 56 | 4 | 0 |
| 3 | 47 | 13 | 0 |
| 4 | 27 | 32 | 1 |
| 5 | 11 | 45 | 4 |
| 6 | 3 | 44 | 13 |
| 7 | 1 | 26 | 33 |
| 8 | 1 | 11 | 48 |
| 9 | 2 | 5 | 53 |

The simulation shows that the whole population eventually becomes infected by the disease. However, the immune period after the sickness enables every individual to become immune, and the disease appears to die out. (Actually, it might not die out. This is left as an exercise.)

In summary, we wanted to investigate the progress of a contagious disease as it makes its way through a population. We built a model for the population and devised a rule for the spread of the disease. Then we ran the simulation and saw what would happen and when. The exercises involve further investigations with this model.

**Exercises**

1. Does the disease modelled above die out as expected? Investigate this and explain. Use the program given in Appendix B.

2. What happens in the above model if the immunity period is longer, say until 8 or 9 or 10 days after the first infection? What happens if the immunity period is shorter?

3. It is quite possible that the contagion rate selected above is not correct in a given situation. If the disease is modelled by infectious = 3 and immune = 7, show what happens if the infection rate changes.

4. Can you discover a systematic relationship between any two variables, such as contagion rate and the probability that the disease will die out?

5. Suppose that a very infectious disease has arrived in town. It has the property that if a given house on a street becomes infected, then both neighbors (one on each side) become infected on the next day. Write a new *infect* routine that has this property and replace the existing one with yours. Using the same model described above (infectious = 3, immune = 7) and your new infection routine, discover what the life cycle of the disease is.

6. A better simulation might result if the state is stored in a two-dimensional array measuring, perhaps, 20 by 20 in size. Revise the simulation program to handle this model. Repeat a set of experiments of the kinds suggested above.

---

## Observing Evolution (C)

In order to study evolution, let us create a model world and populate it with creatures called *neds*. Then let's watch the beings survive in the world and evolve to become a better species. We will design an 8 by 8 grid and propose that neds can wander around the grid looking for food and, from time to time, mating. (This simulation was developed by Joshua D. Carter.) Each ned must eat some food each day, and we will say that the amount of food is an integer computed by (age div 20) + 1, where age gives the number of days the ned has lived. Thus, a ned of age 25 days would eat 2 units of food per day. There will be three more rules related to food. First, each of the grid squares will start with some food units and have more food units added to it each day. The amounts will be controlled by a random-number generator. Second, a ned can pick up as many as three units of food each day and store what it doesn't need. (Its food requirements will not allow it to reach an age a lot older than 40 days. The reason for this is left as an exercise.) Third, the ned uses up two extra units of food if it mates.

The activities of a ned on a given day are, first, to eat the required amount and, second, to make a move given by one of the following codes:

00    move forward one step (if a wall is hit, stand still)
01    rotate right by 1/8 of a full turn
10    mate (if a member of the opposite sex is present in the same square)
11    mate (if a member of the opposite sex is present in the same square)

How the ned gets these codes is the next question to address.

Each ned is created with a gene code, its DNA, so to speak. This is a 40-bit binary string of digits created as follows. When the mating of its parents, a male and a female, occurs, a random number $i$ is selected between 1 and 40. Then the first $i$ bits from one parent are combined with the bits starting from $i + 1$ on to the end for the other parent. This becomes the gene code for the new ned. As an example, suppose the parents have these gene codes.

0000010000110000011110101111111111100111
1111111101110101010101010101010101010101

And suppose that the random number selected is 17. Then the new gene code would be

0000010000110000010101010101010101010101

Each ned's behavior is governed by its gene code. Specifically, it executes the first two bits in its code on one day using the activity code given above, the next two bits on the next day, and so forth. Thus, the new child ned would follow these actions on its first few days:

day 1    00    move forward one step
day 2    00    move forward one step
day 3    01    rotate
day 4    00    move forward one step
day 5    00    move forward one step
day 6    11    mate

Here is a diagram of its path:

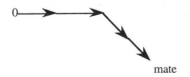

mate

Now let us run the simulation and see what kinds of neds evolve. We will use a random-number generator to create four neds with random genetic codes. Then we will place them in random cells on the grid and watch the action. Here are the neds, two males and two females. Watch what happens in the first three days.

Day 1

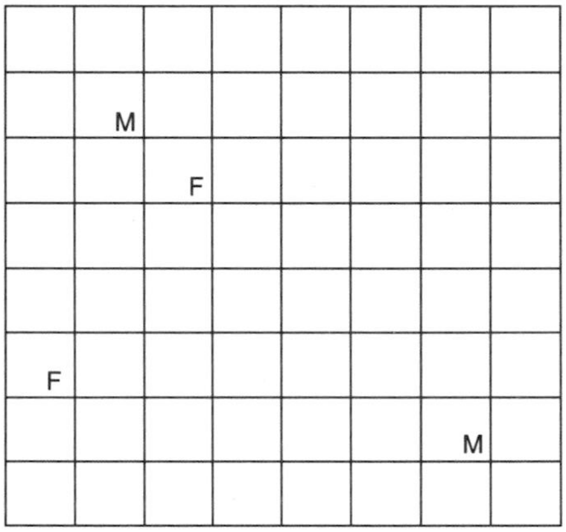

An asterisk means an attempted mate. A dollar sign means death from lack of food.

Day 2

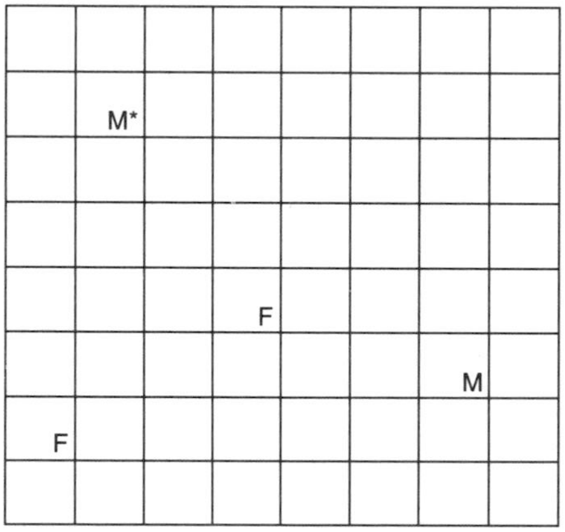

Day 3

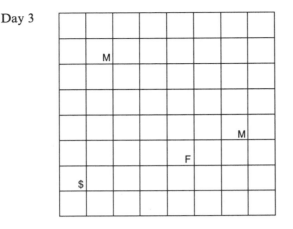

These neds are not doing very well. There are not enough of them to find each other and mate. The simulation goes only a few steps until the last lonely ned dies from lack of food.

Let us start again with 20 neds. This time the simulation lasts for about 100 days before they die out. After trying a number of similar simulations, we find one that lasts for 491 days. This is an unusually long period, which suggests that the neds in the last generation had developed a fairly good genetic code. Here is the code for the last surviving ned. You should, as an exercise, analyze this ned and describe why its genetic code enabled it to survive.

100000101101110110100100100101101111010

In summary, we wanted to observe evolution in action. We watched creatures in a very severe environment attempt to survive. Those that survived passed on their genes to later generations. Those with poor genetic codes disappeared. The methodology was the same as for the car race and the plague. First a model was designed, then the next-step function was created, and finally the system was set in an initial state and run. We started with random codes and allowed the evolution to proceed. After a number of attempts, one population survived an unusually long time and we had the opportunity to see what its code had become. We can now use this model to study evolution as an abstract phenomenon. We can vary the many parameters and mechanisms in the system and observe the results.

You can obtain a program in C to do this computation. Use the Internet as described in the introductory chapter, "Studying Academic Computer Science."

**Exercises**

1. Analyze the code of the final ned and tell why its design succeeded as well as it did.

2. Repeat the simulation described above with parameters that you set. Try to evolve a creature whose genetic code is more succesful than the one studied in problem 1.

---

## What Will It Look Like? (C)

There are many scientific, engineering, and even recreational reasons to want to view something that does not, in reality, exist. With computers, we can create an object in *information space* and then use the graphical capabilites of the system to view that object. An the architect can create a building graphically that people with head-mounted displays can actually "walk through." They can try out the design, critique its functionality and aesthetics, and make suggestions for improvement.

In this section, we will create a program that allows us to enter new world of both recreational and scientific interest. It is the world of fractals, and it is a study that could not progress practically until computer graphics came into existence.

We will begin our study with the concept of a point transformation on a geometric plane. We will represent such a transformation with the functional notation $f$. Suppose we have the point $z0$ on the x,y plane; then $f(z0)$ will find a new point on the the plane. Our example for the moment will be as follows; if $(x,y)$ gives the coordinates of a point on the plane, we will define $f((x,y))$ to be $(x1,y1)$ where

```
x1 = x*x - y*y + c1
y1 = 2*x*y + c2
```

and $c1$ and $c2$ are constants. Thus, if we choose $c1 = 0.36$ and $c2 = 0.10$, then the point $(0,0)$ is transformed into the point $(0.36, 0.10)$ by the function $f$. This is shown on the following diagram by the arrow from $(0,0)$ to $(0.36,0.10)$:

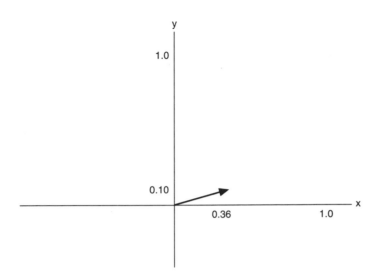

We can then apply the function *f* to the point (0.36, 0.10) and obtain yet another point.

```
x1 = (0.36)² - (0.10)² + 0.36 = 0.48
y1 = 2*(0.36)*(0.10) + 0.10 = 0.17
```

We can apply *f* again and again to the new points as they are generated and obtain a sequence:

```
f( 0.36, 0.10) = ( 0.48, 0.17)
f( 0.48, 0.17) = ( 0.56, 0.27)
f( 0.56, 0.27) = ( 0.60, 0.40)
f( 0.60, 0.40) = ( 0.57, 0.58)
f( 0.57, 0.58) = ( 0.34, 0.76)
f( 0.34, 0.76) = ( -0.10, 0.62)
f( -0.10, 0.62) = ( -0.01, -0.02)
f( -0.01, -0.02) = ( 0.36, 0.10)
f( 0.36, 0.10) = ( 0.48, 0.17)
    etc.
```

Here is a graph of the sequence of points:

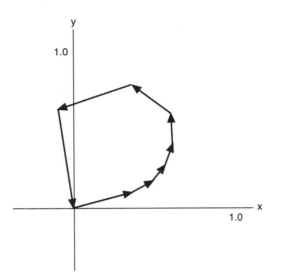

Notice that this sequence has the property that it bends back on itself. The last two points given above are, in fact, the same as the first two points (to the level of accuracy that is shown).

In the theory of fractals, we are interested in points that have converging sequences like (0,0) where the resulting sequence of points stays close to the origin of the plane. We are also interested in diverging sequences where the later generated points go off into infinity. An example of one of these points is (0.70,0.70), which results in the following:

```
f( 0.70, 0.70) = ( 0.36, 1.08)
f( 0.36, 1.08) = ( -0.68, 0.88)
f( -0.68, 0.88) = ( 0.05, -1.09)
f( 0.05, -1.09) = (-0.83, 0.00)
f(-0.83, 0.00) = ( 1.04, 0.10)
f( 1.04, 0.10) = ( 1.43, 0.31)
f( 1.43, 0.31) = ( 2.32, 1.00)
f( 2.32, 1.00) = ( 4.75, 4.72)
f( 4.75, 4.72) = ( 0.69, 44.97)
f( 0.69, 44.97) = (-2021.58, 62.48)
f(-2021.58, 62.48) = (4,082,867.15,-252,602.95)
    etc.
```

Here is a graph of the sequence of points:

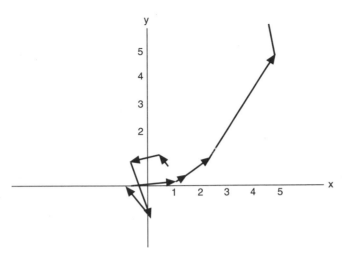

Using the tranformation *f* given above, let us color black all points that result in converging sequences and white all points that result in diverging sequences. We know that (0,0) should then be colored black and (0.70, 0.70) should be colored white. Here is the beginning of our diagram:

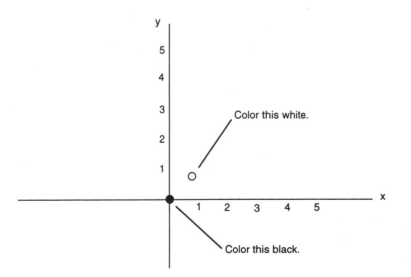

If we apply this rule to the coloring of all the points on the plane using $c_1 = 0.360284$ and $c_2 = 0.100376$, here is what we get: (This is from *Chaos, Fractals, and Dynamics* by Robert L. Devaney.)

This figure is known as a fractal. By varying the constants $c_1$ and $c_2$, we can obtain an astounding variety of complex figures. (The program is given in Appendix B so you can try it out yourself.) By varying the way the figures are drawn, we can get full color and an even wider variety. An interesting characteristic of fractals is that they have endlessly interesting detail. If a part of the figure is generated in a magnified form, it is as complex as the overall figure, no matter how great the level of magnification.

Fractals have proved very interesting to mathematicians in recent years. They give us a bridge from the very simple, as exemplified by the equations given above, to the very complex, as shown in the figure. Although we might suspect that only complex generators can produce complex phenomena, fractals are an amazing example to the contrary.

A possible application for fractals is in coding theory. If we wish to transmit information over a channel, how many bits do we need to convey a picture like the one given above? (A bit is defined as a single binary digit, 0 or 1.) The answer is that millions of bits of information might be needed. But how much information is needed to transmit the equations for the generation given above? Possibly only a few hundred. So a strategy for transmitting pictures might be to code a picture into fractal images in some way, transmit the equations of the fractals, and then reconstruct the picture at the other end using those equations. This could lead to dramatic reductions in the number of bits required to transmit pictures.

**Exercises**

1. Repeat the experiment described above using the constants $c_1 = -1.0$ and $c_2 = 0$. Try $c_1 = 0.3$ and $c_2 = -0.4$. Try $c_1 = -0.1$ and $c_2 = 0.8$. (These examples are from Robert L. Devaney, *Chaos, Fractals, and Dynamics.*)

2. Look for other examples of $c_1$ and $c_2$ values that produce interesting figures.

# Summary (A)

With computer simulation, we can try out our ideas. Whether we are building a structure, composing a symphony, creating a new government, or studying the sun, we can often, at not too high a cost, get a close enough approximation to the future to help us with the present.

The process of doing a simulation usually follows the three steps illustrated in this chapter. First, we build a mathematical model of the phenomenon to be simulated and then we devise a next-step function. Finally, we place the system in an initial state and apply the next-step function repeatedly to discover what will occur over a period of time. This chapter presented simulations of a car race, a disease epidemic, and a species evolution. It also demonstrated simulation techniques in the creation of the complex graphical constructions known as a fractals.

2 MONTHS INTO 6 MONTH PROGRAMMING EFFORT

4 MONTHS INTO 6 MONTH PROGRAMMING EFFORT

6 MONTHS INTO THE PROGRAMMING EFFORT

# 6  Software Engineering

---

## The Real World (A)

A recent honors graduate in computer science from a prestigious university, whom we shall call Brian, accepted an industrial programming job. Brian, an able programmer, had worked in that capacity in university laboratories during his student days and had earned a string of As in computer courses. He was accustomed to looking at a problem, sketching out a solution method, and accurately estimating both the size of the desired program and the amount of time needed to write and debug the code. For planning purposes, he was wise enough to multiply estimates by a factor of two to make sure he had "breathing room," and even then he sometimes found himself up late the night before the deadline getting things into perfect order. But he had a reputation for doing a good job, and he was usually on time.

After he began working at his new position, Brian was given a specification for a program and asked to develop a plan for getting it done. He followed his usual procedures and then went to his boss with a set of algorithms for the various subroutines, data structure descriptions, and a time schedule. He told his boss that he could finish the job in three months and described at length how he would do it. His boss, whom he respected immensely, listened carefully to the plan and studied the problem. Then he made an announcement that astounded Brian: he assigned five programmers to the job and set the deadline for a year.

Brian went home that night confused and amazed. How, he wondered, can a company afford to spend such tremendous resources on this program? He believed that they should fire the five programmers and let him do it.

But Brian's boss had had plenty of experience in the industrial world, and he knew the difference between personal computing and industrial computing. He knew about standards that had to be met, interfaces that had to be negotiated, documentation that had to be written, and revised specifications that might be introduced from time to time. He had seen deadlines like Brian's set and then slipped. He had seen the number of programmers on a project doubled and later doubled again, and he had seen deadlines pushed back ever further. He had seen a system running except for a few bugs, but when those bugs were fixed, the changes introduced new bugs in an unending chain. He knew that entering into an industrial-scale programming project was a fiscally dangerous undertaking and that it had to be done with care.

Such is the case for large-scale programming projects. Experiences that are gained with one or two people writing programs a few pages long do not extrapolate well into massive efforts. The needs for extensive communication among programmers, requirements for documentation, the intrinsic complexities of large programs, and many other factors greatly reduce efficiency. Too many times large programming efforts have marched forward to produce a product that still has bugs, is many months late, and overruns the budget. Frederick Brooks in *The Mythical Man-Month* likens the world of industrial programming to the tar pits of old where "many great and powerful beasts have thrashed violently" only to become more and more entangled.

It is important to know that large-project programming is shockingly different from personal programming. It is important to understand the characteristics of such projects, the problems that can occur, and the remedies that can be tried. The following sections describe lessons that have been learned from large-scale projects, improved technologies that lead to better team effectiveness, and the life cycle of an industrial program.

## Lessons Learned from Large-Scale Programming Projects (B)

The first lesson is that a *program* is much easier to produce than a *programming system*, which in turn is easier to produce than a *programming system product*. Brooks (in *The Mythical Man-Month*) has defined these three entities and estimated that each higher stage is at least three times more expensive to produce than the previous one. A *program* is the entity that students write in universities. Its specifications are given in a small document, and it computes the target behavior on a single machine and under the control of its author. A *programming system* involves a group of interacting components coordinated to do a central task. Each component must have carefully designed interfaces that match specifications with other components and may need to conform to other specifications. For example, components may have to meet restrictions related to size and speed. A *programming system product* is a programming system that is documented thoroughly, usable in many environments, and robust in its operation. It must be sufficiently well described that its maintenance, revision, and operation can be carried on in the absence of the author. It is the most typical goal of an industrial project, and, by Brooks's estimate, is at least nine times as costly to produce as a simple program. In fact, this factor alone is nearly sufficient to account for the heavy investments that Brian's boss was prepared to make.

The second lesson is that programming is not an easily divisible task. If Brian's boss is not to wait several years for Brian to produce a programming system product, more programmers will be needed. But these additional people will be communicating with each other and perhaps arguing about how the design should proceed. They will have to develop precise specifications of the interfaces between their different parts of the code and may have to do additional work to meet these demands. Testing and debugging of the interacting modules may be more complex than it would be for the more unified architecture that a single person would build. Thus, the per person productivity for a multi-person effort will usually be lower than it would be for a single programmer. Halving the time required to finish a project might require more than doubling the number of programmers.

Researchers have found that the more programmers interact with each other in order to do a job, the lower their productivity will be. Brooks presents the following rough guidelines (by Joel Aron) for programmer productivity, in terms of numbers of instructions written per programmer-year for design and coding (Brooks, chapter 8):

| Numbers of interactions | Instructions per year |
| --- | --- |
| Very few interactions | 10000 |
| Some interactions | 5000 |
| Many interactions | 1500 |

These figures roughly summarize the kinds of results that have been observed in various studies of programmer productivity. They can be off by a factor of two or more in some situations, but they give the order of magnitude for typical performance.

Programmers do not spend all of their time planning and writing code, so these figures may be high as an overall performance measure. Brooks (chapter 2) estimates that in the course of a project programmers spend roughly half their time in testing and debugging activities.

Since the addition of programmers to speed up a project increases the complexity of the programming task, it does not result in time improvements proportional to the number of people added. In fact, too many additional programmers can saturate the team and yield no improvement whatsoever, and most programming tasks require a certain minimum amount of time to reach maturity regardless of the number of programmers assigned.

Large programs may also be disproportionly more complex. That is, a large program, say 500,000 lines of code, may require more than twice as much effort as a project of half that length. This effect may occur regardless of the number of programmers.

The combination of these effects sends average programmer productivity plummeting in a way that Brian could not be expected to appreciate. While he was able to write and debug comfortably 100 lines of code per day, the figures indicate (assuming 200 working days per year) that industrial programmers may code as few as 7 lines of code per day.

If Brian's original estimate had been used, he would probably have worked very hard for a month or two only to realize that he was not generating a product to meet the required standards. He might then have asked for additional programmers and an extra two months. Because he would try to convince the new people that he had much of the task completed, he would spend time teaching them his theory of operation and his code. By the time they got into the swing of the project, the second deadline would be hard upon them. They would then ask for another slippage of the deadline. They also might ask for more programmers, who would also have to be trained and integrated into the effort.

**Exercises**

1. Assume that you are a manager and need to have a simple stand-alone program coded that will be approximately 500 instructions in length. How many programmers will you assign to the job, and when, based on figures given above, can you expect to have the program completed?

2. Suppose you are a manager and wish to have a programming-system product coded that will be approximately 40,000 instructions in length—for example, the size of a compiler for a programming language. Assuming the above guidelines are applicable to your situation, how many programmers might you need in order to complete the job in three years? How would you revise your estimate if the time allotted were only two years? If your boss demanded that the program be completed within three months, how would you respond?

3. Repeat exercise 2 for the case where the target program will be approximately 200,000 instructions. This might be the length of an operating system for a moderate-sized machine.

4. What can you say about the amount of programming effort required for a large program such as a modern telephone switching system that could involve 10 million instructions? Assume that the time allowed for coding is four years.

---

## Software Engineering Methodologies (B)

The tremendous cost of software has become a major concern of the computing industry. In the mid-1950s, software costs were less than 20 percent of total computing costs, but now they exceed 80 percent. This has led to a major emphasis on discovering ways to improve programming methodologies and to the birth of a new field, *software engineering*. The goal has been to change programming from a hit-or-miss, one-person-at-a-time operation to a sophisticated science where groups of people work together to produce, reliably and efficiently, a worthy product. Three areas of software engineering will be discussed here: the development of strategies to improve the correctness of programs, the invention of new organizational schemes for programmers, and the creation of better programming tools.

**Correctness**

The specification of a system will often state the allowed error rates. For example, the specification might require that the software system process input successfully at some high rate, say, 99.95 percent of the time. Software engineers enter into a project with the sobering knowledge that the ultimate product will be rejected if it does not achieve such a high level of reliability.

Therefore, successful designers and coders have to adopt a philosophy that brings correctness to the forefront, from the early stages of design to the day of product delivery. The philosophy asserts that correctness cannot be added as an afterthought but must be meticulously designed in at every stage. It disallows common attitudes that errors are natural and inevitable and insists that errors exist in programs because people put them there. It asserts that correctness is a consequence of responsible programming practice and that no alternative should be contemplated. The generation of correct programs is important because the ultimate product must be correct and the cost of removing errors from running code can be tremendous.

Correctness considerations begin with the design of the program specifications, which must be a careful, detailed, and exact description of every aspect of the product behavior. These specifications prescribe every detail that the external world will see but say nothing about how the program will actually work. It is the job of the implementors to produce code that performs precisely as guaranteed in the program specifications. At these early stages, correctness must be carefully attended to, since errors here will radiate into the product in unpredictable ways. Barry Boehm has estimated (in *Software Engineering Economics*, chapter 4) that specification errors repaired in the later stages of software development can cost as much as 100 times more to fix than if they were caught at specification time.

Next, the system designers build an image of how the internals of the system will work and write specifications for the various modules proposed to do the job. Then smaller groups of programmers will be assigned these modules. Their task is to produce code with behaviors that are guaranteed to match the interface specifications. This means that programmers must have verification techniques for checking that the code advances through the proper steps and delivers precisely what is specified. These techniques usually involve studying each sequential statement, considering every possible situation, and showing that, in every case, the statement does the right thing. During the 1970s, methodologies evolved that made it possible to prove mathematically that a program achieves its specifications, but such rigorous procedures are too expensive for most applications and are used only in rare situations where extreme measures are justified.

Top-down structured programming, which encourages clear and systematic thinking about large programs, plays an essential role in writing correct code. Before the days of structured programming, programming methodologies allowed the use of a "go to" statement that enabled programmers to write code that would make many jumps from place to place, which sometime resulted in programs that were a nightmare to understand and debug. The elimination of the "go to" statement forces a programmer to use constructs with a more straightforward flow of control so they can be read in a linear fashion from beginning to end.

Another technology that has improved correctness is the development of adequate test procedures for programs. Once a program has gone through the laborious design, coding, and verification procedures, it can be run on a carefully constructed set of inputs that will exercise every branch, activate every combination of submodules, and explore endpoints and extreme values. Where failures occur, the responsible programmers will be called upon to do the repair.

**Organizational Schemes**

The second area for improved programming methodology concerns the way programmers are organized. Various innovations have evolved that encourage people to help each other and that attempt to utilize the special talents of each. A way to encourage good group dynamics in a programming environment is to break up the sense of ownership that programmers have in the code they have written. Consider, as an example, the case of a student who has spent countless hours designing a program, writing the code, and adding some much-loved special features. If later this program is said to be of poor quality or is discovered to have errors, the student justifiably will feel threatened or uncomfortable. In the environment of a programming team, the student could become protective, secretive, and defensive about the code when the goals of the group require openness and cooperation.

This can be prevented by encouraging *egoless programming*, where the code is considered to be a product of the group activity and where criticism and improvements from any member are always welcome. It may be that person A wrote the first draft, person B rewrote the code and got it running, and person C found some errors and made some improvements. All three individuals accept each other as both contributors and mistake-makers, and the code is viewed as a separate entity that can be praised or criticized without threatening any one of them. All team members want to get it right, and the best talents of each are aimed at the common goal. (Some software engineers object to the idea of egoless programming because they have found that if no single person is answerable for a code, its correctness and performance does not get proper attention.)

Often an organization has programmers who are star performers, and it makes a special arrangement to utilize their talents. Since in programming the highest achiever may be ten times more productive than lesser contributors, good management requires that they be free to practice their trade and that others do everything possible to help. This gives rise to a *chief programmer team*, which centers all activities around a single person.

Such a team begins with the *chief programmer* whose job is to conceive of the code, write it, debug it, and perhaps write the major documentation. The second most important member of the team is the *backup programmer*, who observes every action of the chief and knows the code and documentation. This person performs support activities such as verification of correctness, development of required subroutines, background research, and documentation. If the chief programmer becomes unavailable at any point, the backup must step in and keep things going forward without delays. The third most important member is the *programming librarian*, who types, formats, stores, and retrieves code and documentation for the group. The team may also contain various other members who may program, test, write documentation, or do other tasks. The chief programmer team idea has been used on numerous occasions, often breaking records for programmer productivity and for quality of the final product.

## Programming Tools

The creation of better software tools has also aided productivity and reduced costs. The new image of a programmer is no longer of a person with a pencil, paper, and terminal. Instead, it centers on a large-screen workstation that displays windows into a variety of facilities—libraries of code, a language editor, a run-time monitor, a debugging package, programming manuals, a theorem prover for verification activities, graphics subsystems, communications facilities to other programmers, and much more.

In this modern environment, a programmer may write relatively little code. Instead, he or she will have an extensive knowledge of existing software and will attempt to find ways to assemble the target program from these pieces. A complete programming task might begin with a coder writing a top-level program to organize the computation. Then the programmer peruses the code library for the correct subroutines to finish the programming job. In the future, a programmer may be able to check some menu items and have the routines automatically specialized to the application.

With the code assembled, the programmer might generate test data automatically, and then immediately run the code on the examples. If an error is observed, the programmer would study the code in one window, the data structures in another, the computation history in another, and so forth, to try to determine the cause of failure. Later, with the code fixed and running, the programmer might signal another team member of the accomplishment through computer mail, and send the revised code to that member's machine for verification, modification, or use. Later he or she might receive the code back with comments and updates, and it might then be archived and indexed for later use.

Not all the facilities mentioned here are in routine use in all programming organizations, but more organizations are adopting them each year.

**Exercises**

1. Select a program from an earlier chapter or from your own experience, and carry out a detailed study of its correctness:
   (a) Write exact specifications for the class of legal inputs to the program. State explicitly every characteristic a legal input must have, including the lengths of allowed input strings, the number of significant digits, the sizes of allowable numbers, and so forth. Give examples of legal and illegal inputs.
   (b) Write complete and exacting specifications for the outputs of the program. Tell clearly what is to result in every possible computation that could result from the inputs specified in part a.
   (c) Study every line of code and write down careful arguments to show that it will do the proper action, assuming the input meets the specifications given. Show with your arguments that the collection of the statements, in fact, computes the outputs exactly as they have been given in part b. Be sure to check behaviors at endpoints where inputs may have length zero or otherwise stretch the performance of the program.

2. Study the topics covered in this section and suggest a field of software engineering that you believe should be studied but is not described here. What kinds of results do you think could be obtained if this field were studied?

## The Program Life Cycle (B)

Software engineering is not restricted to the program synthesis task. Economic investments with regard to a program begin early and may continue for many years after the program is written. This is because a program may have a long life cycle that substantially engages the organization at every stage. Decision making should account for this larger picture and attempt to optimize benefits for the long term. A system architecture optimized at the design stage but not amenable to later upgrade or maintenance will not be successful. A set of terminal specifications written to make programming easy but without regard to later training and usage requirements can lead to catastrophe. Thus, the software engineer must keep the larger picture in mind at each stage to achieve a long-term success. We will briefly examine the life cycle of a typical software product and note some of the concerns that appear at each stage.

### Defining the Product

The first question to ask is what need is to be addressed. The answer may be in terms of new information the client needs to compile, labor-intensive jobs that need to be automated, or the improvement of some already automated function. Extensive interviews with the client and market surveys might need to be carried out to determine the nature of the need.

Automated solutions to the problem can then be proposed and measured against the need. Rough estimates can be made about cost and effectiveness, and judgments can be made about desirability. Sometimes an inexpensive prototype for a proposed system can be assembled and tested in the user environment to determine its value. The most desirable alternative can be selected, and the organization can begin its implementation.

### Selecting the Programming Team

If the decision is to code a programming product to solve the problem, the organizers can begin choosing the members of the programming groups and making estimates about the kind and numbers of people needed. As system specification and architecture develop, better estimates will become possible and more team members can be chosen.

### Developing the Program Specification

Here the rough estimates of the earlier stages are made precise. An exact specification of the system's external characteristics is written down in a possibly voluminous document. In some cases, certain features of the ultimate product have not been decided. When this occurs, the required "hooks" are defined where later features can be inserted.

### Designing the System Structure

The form of the system organization needs to be designed and the major data structures must be specified. At first the design will be sketched in rough form, but these ideas must then be solidified in another set of specifications. These working documents, which could be longer than the external specifications, will set forth the list of the subcomponents and their complete interface characteristics. Individual programming teams will be given these subcomponents as tasks and will have little guidance except what is stated in these documents.

**Coding the System**

Next the staff will write the program. Typically the implementation effort results in the discovery of errors or poor decisions at earlier stages, which must be corrected. The original specifications and other working documents will probably be revised as the group changes its view of the whole project. If the original conception was good, changes will have only second-order effects, and the basic form of the architecture will remain.

**Testing the Code**

As individual parts of the system become operative, they can be tested to confirm that they meet the requirements given in the working documents. Many times special software is written to test system modules. Testing often results in revisions to the code, but truly professional programmers can usually achieve early, if not immediate, convergence on acceptable performance. As larger subsystems come into existence, parts that were finished and tested earlier can be integrated into the whole.

**Revision**

As members of the group mature in their conceptualization of a system, improvements may be made in the system design. Even updates to the original system behavioral specifications may be made from time to time. This involves modifying documentation and rewriting parts of the code.

**Documentation**

All stages of the project require documentation, especially when many programmers are involved. In addition to the documentation of code, user manuals must be created for training and explanation of the principles of operation, installation, and maintenance. These documents will accompany the product into the user environment.

**Delivery and Training**

The product needs to reach the user and come into useful operation. This may involve sending project participants to the user organization to help with installation, early operation, and the training of users.

**Maintenance and Upgrade**

Once a product is in field operation, the organization can expect to receive notification of errors in its behavior and requests for additional features. It is quite common for the vendor to keep a group of programmers working on the project for many years after its original development to carry on these maintenance and upgrade activities. Users can be sold contracts for such services so these efforts can be profitable ventures on their own.

**Positioning for the Next Product**

Success on one project engenders opportunities for others. A reputation gained by delivering one successful system can open the door to projects that complement the original one or lead to later follow-on projects.

To summarize, the life cycle of a programming project includes many, varied stages that can span a period of years. In order for a system to be successful, decision making must account for the whole life cycle and consider the best long-term interests of the project.

**Exercise**

1. Draw a set of boxes on a page and label each by one of the headings in this section. Then show the time flow of the stages in a product life by drawing arrows from box to box. Notice that in realistic situations the flow may not be linear, as indicated above.

---

# Summary (B)

Software engineering is the collection of disciplines that enable a group of people to build and maintain computer software systems. These include mathematical subfields that deal with program correctness and performance, numerous technologies related to programming languages and systems, some economics, and the psychology and sociology of team efforts.

The industrial programming of a software product is a substantially more ambitious undertaking than the kind of individual program students or laboratory workers may assemble. While isolated programmers may be able to assemble hundreds of lines of code per day to satisfy their own needs, programmers in an industrial project may average fewer than ten lines of code in a programming systems product per day.

Numerous technologies have developed to aid the task of industrial programmers, including strategies for designing correctness into programs, methods for organizing programming groups, object-oriented programming methodologies, and automated systems for assembling code.

# 7     Electric Circuits

## How Do Computers Work? (A)

In the previous chapters, we studied how to write Pascal programs. We learned to write code to input characters and numbers, to concatenate, to add and subtract, to modify iteratively, to print results, and so forth. But how does the machine actually do these operations? How does a computer receiving the statement

```
Z := (X + Y);
```

actually find $X$ and $Y$, add them, and put the result into the correct place? How does one organize electricity to make it calculate?

The purpose of this chapter and the next two is to answer these questions. In this chapter, we learn that program actions, such as the execution of the above statement, can be broken down into elementary *machine operations*. In typical processing, the Pascal statement is translated into *assembly language* and then converted to basic machine operations. Then electric circuitry executes these elementary operations:

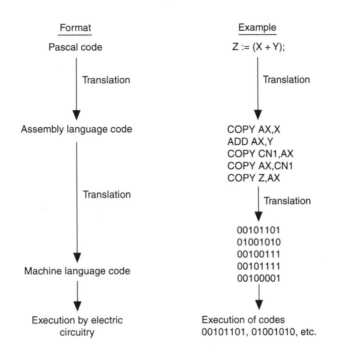

For example, the statement

```
Z := (X + Y);
```

may translate into something like this (as will be shown in chapter 9):

| | |
|---|---|
| Put the quantity called X into register AX. | COPY AX,X |
| Get Y and add it to the quantity in AX. | ADD AX,Y |
| Store the result in a location called CN1. | COPY CN1,AX |
| Take the result. | COPY AX,CN1 |
| Put it into Z. | COPY Z,AX |

The translator has the job of changing the input $Z := (X + Y)$; into an equivalent set of assembly language operations, here listed as *COPY AX,X*, etc. Then these operations are converted to binary codes such as 00101101, 01001010, .... Finally, basic electrical circuits execute these binary codes in sequence to get the job done. (Note: The experienced reader will wonder why the statement compiles into five instructions instead of the expected three. The answer is that we are being consistent here with the compiler presented in chapter 9.)

This chapter will show how those basic electrical circuits can be built to do the machine operations. Chapters 8 and 9 will show how computers are organized and how the translation is done from a source language like Pascal into machine language. These three chapters will show all the essential mechanisms involved in the execution of a program written in a language such as Pascal. They are graphically illustrated by the program called "This-is-how-a-computer-works," which you can obtain on the internet as described in the introductory chapter, "Studying Academic Computer Science."

## Computer Organization (B)

This chapter will show how to build electric circuits that do primitive machine operations such as adding two numbers. Computers are organized, as illustrated below, with circuits, called registers, that store information, and circuits that calculate things to put into those registers. One special register, the instruction register, holds the code (like 00101101) that tells what is to be done. For example, it might be a code telling the computer to add certain numbers and put the answer into computation register AX. The set of code deciphering circuits will receive this code. One of them will turn on its associated circuit; in our example the add circuit near the bottom would be turned on since 00101101 is a command to add. The other code deciphering circuits will receive this code and turn off their associated circuits. Since the add circuit has been turned on, it will do the calculation called for by 00101101 and send the result to AX.

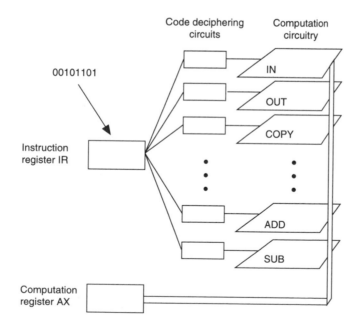

The computation in this example would proceed as follows: (1) Put the first instruction code (00101101) into the instruction register, (2) decipher it, and (3) call on the correct machine operation to do the job. Then load the next instruction code (01001010) into the instruction register and repeat the same actions. Continue loading and executing all sequential instructions until the task is complete.

This section previews the story of this chapter. It will all be much clearer soon.

## Circuits for Computing Primitive Functions (B)

Our study of electric circuits begins with the simplest possible circuit—a battery connected to a light bulb:

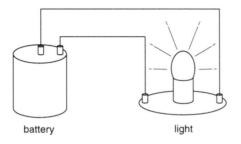

battery                              light

If a battery is connected to a properly rated electric bulb, the bulb will light up. It is beyond the scope of this chapter to discuss the chemical and physical processes that create the electrical pressure within the battery and guide the electricity through the wires to light the bulb. We note only that batteries do exist, that they can force electric current through a wire, and that the current can light a bulb.

We can view a battery as a pump for electrons, the tiny negatively charged particles that make up an electric current. The pump attempts to push the electrons out of the terminal marked minus (−) and to collect them from the terminal marked plus (+). Think of a battery as acting like a water pump, with little whirling paddles grabbing electrons from the input path and pushing them out the output:

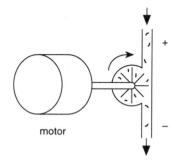

motor

Think of the electric wires as pipes and the light bulb as a very thin pipe that turns a glowing white hot if the electrons are forced through at a fast enough pace. The total circuit may then be visualized as a simple loop, with electrons flying around the circle at high speed under the pressure of relentless paddle blades, causing the thin part to glow brightly:

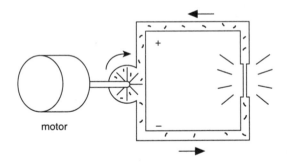

motor

It is helpful to have a symbolic form for such a circuit, so we will use parallel lines for the battery and a circle with filament for the bulb:

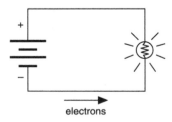

electrons

The electrons move from the shortest line on the battery symbol and proceed around the circuit back to the longer line on the battery symbol.

We can now modify this circuit to compute something. Specifically, we can insert a switch that acts like a water valve to turn the current off and on:

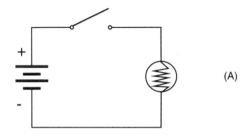

(A)

This modified circuit, if left alone in the state shown, will not carry an electric current and will not light the bulb. The electrons cannot travel around the loop because the conducting path at the top is broken. However, if we push the switch conductor down, we restore the original circuit, and the light will come on.

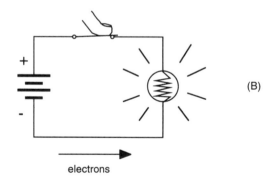

(B)

electrons

We will assume that the switch is made of spring material and that it will bounce back to position A if we remove our finger.

We can think of this circuit as a very simple computer. Suppose people are entering a room, and that someone pushes the switch conductor down only if the current person entering the room is tall; if a nontall person enters, the switch is not pushed down. We can say this circuit computes "tallness" because the bulb will shine if the person entering is tall and will remain off otherwise. (In the upcoming section on relays, we will address the issue of whose finger pushes the button.)

We need a notation for representing such computations and will use the variable $x_t$ to represent the property of tallness. If a person is tall, we will write $x_t = 1$; otherwise, we will say $x_t = 0$. We will then label the switch with the symbol $x_t$ and note that the released position A corresponds to the assignment $x_t = 0$, and the depressed position B corresponds to $x_t = 1$. Variables that can take on only two values, such as $x_t$, are called *Boolean variables*.

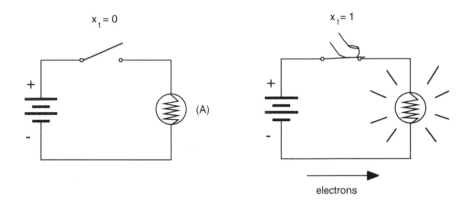

The circuit with a single switch is not a very exciting computer. We do such "computations" quite often when entering dark rooms and do not ordinarily think of them as such. A much more interesting computation is possible if we have two variables and thus two switches. Assume that people entering the room may be handsome as well as tall, and consider the following circuit, where $x_t$ represents "tallness" and $x_h$ represents "handsomeness":

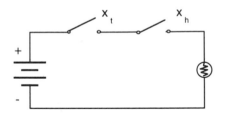

Clearly, the light will not shine when $x_t = 0$ and $x_h = 0$ because the electric current will not have a path to flow around the loop. Furthermore, if either switch is depressed individually ($x_t = 1$, $x_h = 0$ or $x_t = 0$, $x_h = 1$), the light will continue to remain off. Only if both $x_t$ and $x_h$ are depressed simultaneously will a current flow to light the bulb. The important word to note is "and"; if two switches are wired in series as shown, they compute the function $f_{and}(x_t, x_h)$, which has value 1 if both $x_t$ and $x_h$ are 1 and value 0 otherwise.

| $x_t$ | $x_h$ | $f_{and}$ |
|---|---|---|
| 0 | 0 | 0 |
| 0 | 1 | 0 |
| 1 | 0 | 0 |
| 1 | 1 | 1 |

We can also have an "and" function of three variables. It will be called $f(x_1, x_2, x_3)$ and it will have value 1 only when all three ($x_1$ and $x_2$ and $x_3$) have value 1. Otherwise, $f(x_1, x_2, x_3) = 0$:

| $x_1$ | $x_2$ | $x_3$ | $f(x_1, x_2, x_3)$ |
|---|---|---|---|
| 0 | 0 | 0 | 0 |
| 0 | 0 | 1 | 0 |
| 0 | 1 | 0 | 0 |
| 0 | 1 | 1 | 0 |
| 1 | 0 | 0 | 0 |
| 1 | 0 | 1 | 0 |
| 1 | 1 | 0 | 0 |
| 1 | 1 | 1 | 1 |

If the above circuit had been wired differently, another interesting function would have been computed:

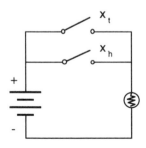

In this configuration, there is still no path for the electrons around the loop. However, if either $x_t$ or $x_h$ is depressed ($x_t = 1$, $x_h = 0$ or $x_t = 0$, $x_h = 1$), a path is provided. If both switches are depressed ($x_t = 1$, $x_h = 1$), the electrons can flow through the bulb and through both switches back to the battery. This circuit thus computes the function $f_{or}(x_t, x_h)$, which has value 1 if either $x_t$ or $x_h$ is 1 or if both are 1:

| $x_t$ | $x_h$ | $f_{or}(x_t, x_h)$ |
|---|---|---|
| 0 | 0 | 0 |
| 0 | 1 | 1 |
| 1 | 0 | 1 |
| 1 | 1 | 1 |

We could also have an "or" function of three arguments $f(x_1, x_2, x_3)$, which has value 1 if at least one of $x_1$, $x_2$, or $x_3$, is 1:

| $x_1$ | $x_2$ | $x_3$ | $f(x_1, x_2, x_3)$ |
|---|---|---|---|
| 0 | 0 | 0 | 0 |
| 0 | 0 | 1 | 1 |
| 0 | 1 | 0 | 1 |
| 0 | 1 | 1 | 1 |
| 1 | 0 | 0 | 1 |
| 1 | 0 | 1 | 1 |
| 1 | 1 | 0 | 1 |
| 1 | 1 | 1 | 1 |

We have finished our examination of circuits for computing the "and" and "or" functions. Learning one more type of circuit, the following "not" circuit, will make it possible for us to compute any function of binary variables:

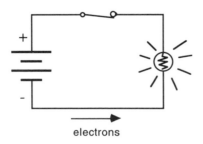

electrons

Here a new kind of switch is needed that will conduct electricity whenever the circuit is left alone. If a finger depresses the switch, the circuit is broken and the flow stops:

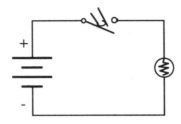

Assume a finger depresses the switch whenever a tall person enters the room. Then the bulb will light whenever it is *not* true that a tall person is entering the room. If $x_t$ stands for tallness, we will continue the convention that $x_t = 1$ corresponds to pushing down on the switch. However, this time $x_t = 1$ will result in the bulb going off. Here is the functional table for $f_{not}(x_t)$, which outputs 1 if $x_t = 0$ and 0 if $x_t = 1$:

| $x_t$ | $f_{not}(x_t)$ |
| --- | --- |
| 0 | 1 |
| 1 | 0 |

   The following section will show you how to combine the three functions, "and," "or," and "not," to compute *any* function of binary variables.

**Exercises**

1. Suppose a circuit has two switches; one is pushed if the person entering the room is tall and the other if the person is handsome. Find a circuit that will light a bulb only if the entering person is tall but not handsome and will have the bulb off otherwise.

2. Suppose two switches are available; one is depressed if a person is older than 18, and the other is depressed if the person is accompanied by a parent. Draw a circuit that will light a bulb if the person can be admitted to a film rated R.

3. Suppose three switches are available. The first is depressed if your friend Bob has received a million dollars, the second if he was robbed of everything, and the third if he has a huge debt. Construct a circuit that will light a bulb if Bob is rich.

4. Given the following circuit, fill in the table showing the function that it computes.

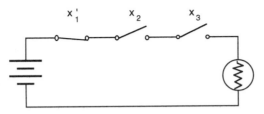

| $x_1$ | $x_2$ | $x_3$ | $f(x_1,x_2,x_3)$ |
|-------|-------|-------|------------------|
| 0 | 0 | 0 | ? |
| 0 | 0 | 1 | ? |
| 0 | 1 | 0 | ? |
| 0 | 1 | 1 | ? |
| 1 | 0 | 0 | ? |
| 1 | 0 | 1 | ? |
| 1 | 1 | 0 | ? |
| 1 | 1 | 1 | ? |

## Circuits for Computing Complex Functions (B)

Suppose we have the following circuit and we want to determine what function $f_1$ it computes.

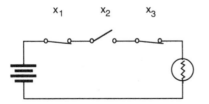

If $x_1 = 0$, $x_2 = 0$, and $x_3 = 0$, we see that none of the switches will be pushed down. Current will not flow because $x_2$ will not conduct, and the bulb will remain off. We conclude that $f_1(x_1,x_2,x_3) = 0$. If we try another example, $x_1 = 0$, $x_2 = 0$, $x_3 = 1$, we get the same result because both $x_2$ and $x_3$ will be nonconducting. Switch $x_2$ is normally nonconducting, and $x_3$ will not conduct because it is pushed down ($x_3 = 1$). If we continue the analysis, the following functional table emerges:

| $x_1$ | $x_2$ | $x_3$ | $f_1(x_1,x_2,x_3)$ |
|-------|-------|-------|--------------------|
| 0     | 0     | 0     | 0                  |
| 0     | 0     | 1     | 0                  |
| 0     | 1     | 0     | 1                  |
| 0     | 1     | 1     | 0                  |
| 1     | 0     | 0     | 0                  |
| 1     | 0     | 1     | 0                  |
| 1     | 1     | 0     | 0                  |
| 1     | 1     | 1     | 0                  |

The only situation that yields $f(x_1,x_2,x_3) = 1$ is $x_1 = 0$, $x_2 = 1$, $x_3 = 0$. Switches $x_1$ and $x_3$ are not pushed down, but $x_2$ is.

The way to see the relationship between the circuit and the table is to look at the table row where the output is 1. The inputs at this row are 0, 1, 0, and they are related to the switches in the circuit. An input of 0 corresponds to a normally closed switch (a *not* switch). An input of 1 corresponds to a normally open switch. Since the inputs are $x_1 = 0$, $x_2 = 1$, $x_3 = 0$ in that row with output 1, the circuit is built with switches normally closed, open, and closed, respectively, as shown.

Similarly, another circuit can be analyzed that computes $f_2$:

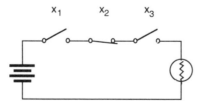

If we study its tabular function, we can see a simple relationship between the circuit and the table:

| $x_1$ | $x_2$ | $x_3$ | $f_3(x_1,x_2,x_3)$ |
|-------|-------|-------|--------------------|
| 0 | 0 | 0 | 0 |
| 0 | 0 | 1 | 0 |
| 0 | 1 | 0 | 0 |
| 0 | 1 | 1 | 0 |
| 1 | 0 | 0 | 0 |
| 1 | 0 | 1 | 1 |
| 1 | 1 | 0 | 0 |
| 1 | 1 | 1 | 0 |

Again only one 1 appears in the table output. Since the row in the table with a 1 output has the input 1, 0, 1, the circuit must have three sequential switches, which are normally open, closed, and open, respectively. Every similar circuit of three sequential switches will yield such a functional behavior with only a single 1 in the table output.

Now we can consider the "or" combination of these two circuits. It will yield a table with two outputs equal to 1 and a circuit with two series circuits:

| $x_1$ | $x_2$ | $x_3$ | $f_3(x_1,x_2,x_3)$ |
|-------|-------|-------|--------------------|
| 0 | 0 | 0 | 0 |
| 0 | 0 | 1 | 0 |
| 0 | 1 | 0 | 1 |
| 0 | 1 | 1 | 0 |
| 1 | 0 | 0 | 0 |
| 1 | 0 | 1 | 1 |
| 1 | 1 | 0 | 0 |
| 1 | 1 | 1 | 0 |

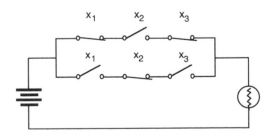

This circuit will light the bulb and thus yield $f_3(x_1,x_2,x_3)=1$ in just the cases $x_1 = 0$, $x_2 = 1$, and $x_3 = 0$ or $x_1 = 1$, $x_2 = 0$, and $x_3 = 1$.

For each line with a 1 output in the above table for $f_3$, there is a series of three switches in the resulting circuit. This makes it easy to create a circuit for a function with any number of 1s in its output. For example, consider $f_4$, which is similar to $f_3$ except that it has three 1s in its output:

| $x_1$ | $x_2$ | $x_3$ | $f_4(x_1,x_2,x_3)$ |
|---|---|---|---|
| 0 | 0 | 0 | 0 |
| 0 | 0 | 1 | 0 |
| 0 | 1 | 0 | 1 |
| 0 | 1 | 1 | 0 |
| 1 | 0 | 0 | 0 |
| 1 | 0 | 1 | 1 |
| 1 | 1 | 0 | 0 |
| 1 | 1 | 1 | 1 |

The associated circuit will have three sequences of three switches each. Can you write this circuit down?

You should now be able to write down a circuit for any binary function of any number of Boolean variables regardless of the number of 1s in the output. The circuit will light a bulb for any value of the input variables that yields a 1 output. As a final example, suppose the following function $f$ is to be computed. Here is the appropriate switching circuit:

| $x_1$ | $x_2$ | $x_3$ | $x_4$ | $f(x_1,x_2,x_3,x_4)$ |
|---|---|---|---|---|
| 0 | 0 | 0 | 0 | 0 |
| 0 | 0 | 0 | 1 | 0 |
| 0 | 0 | 1 | 0 | 0 |
| 0 | 0 | 1 | 1 | 0 |
| 0 | 1 | 0 | 0 | 0 |
| 0 | 1 | 0 | 1 | 1 |
| 0 | 1 | 1 | 0 | 0 |
| 0 | 1 | 1 | 1 | 0 |
| 1 | 0 | 0 | 0 | 1 |
| 1 | 0 | 0 | 1 | 0 |
| 1 | 0 | 1 | 0 | 0 |
| 1 | 0 | 1 | 1 | 0 |
| 1 | 1 | 0 | 0 | 0 |
| 1 | 1 | 0 | 1 | 1 |
| 1 | 1 | 1 | 0 | 0 |
| 1 | 1 | 1 | 1 | 0 |

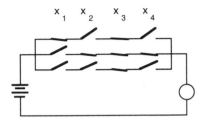

**Exercises**

1. Find the circuit to compute $f_4$, given above.

2. Suppose that $a$, $b$, and $c$ are integers such that the sum of $a$ and $b$ is $c$: $a + b = c$. Suppose $x_a$ is a Boolean variable that has value 1 if $a$ is an even integer and value 0 if $a$ is odd. Suppose $x_b$ is similarly defined for $b$. Design a circuit that will light a bulb if and only if $c$ is even. Hint: Fill out the following table to determine the desired function:

| $x_a$ | $x_b$ | $f(x_a,x_b)$ |
|-------|-------|--------------|
| 0 | 0 | ? |
| 0 | 1 | ? |
| 1 | 0 | ? |
| 1 | 1 | ? |

Then construct the desired circuit.

3. Repeat problem 1 using the assumption that $a$ times $b$ is $c$.

4. A corporation has developed the following personnel classification scheme:

$x_m = 1$     if a person has management training
$x_m = 0$     otherwise

$x_s = 1$     if a person has sales skills
$x_s = 0$     otherwise

$x_t = 1$     if a person has a strong technical competence
$x_t = 0$     otherwise

The following table indicates the required qualifications for three job types: salesperson, manager, and technical adviser.

| $x_m$ | $x_s$ | $x_t$ | Salesperson | Manager | Technical Adviser |
|-------|-------|-------|-------------|---------|-------------------|
| 0 | 0 | 0 | 0 | 0 | 0 |
| 0 | 0 | 1 | 0 | 0 | 1 |
| 0 | 1 | 0 | 1 | 0 | 0 |
| 0 | 1 | 1 | 1 | 0 | 0 |
| 1 | 0 | 0 | 0 | 0 | 0 |
| 1 | 0 | 1 | 1 | 0 | 1 |
| 1 | 1 | 0 | 1 | 0 | 0 |
| 1 | 1 | 1 | 1 | 1 | 0 |

We can see from line 2 of this table that if a person has no management training or sales skills but is technically competent, he or she may be used as a technical adviser. However, from line 4 we see that if the person also has sales abilities, he or she should not be used as a technical adviser but should be moved to the sales department.

(a) Draw a circuit that will light a bulb if the person is qualified as a salesperson.

(b) Design a circuit to indicate management qualifications.

(c) Repeat for technical adviser qualifications.

5. A computer is to be designed to operate an elevator in a two-story building where the stories are labeled 0 and 1. The system has four inputs, as follows:

$x_0 = 1$      if the floor 0 elevator button is pushed
$x_0 = 0$      otherwise

$x_1 = 1$      if the floor 1 elevator button is pushed
$x_1 = 0$      otherwise

$x_e = 1$      if the elevator internal button is pushed
$x_e = 0$      otherwise

$x_f = 1$      if the elevator is at floor 1
$x_f = 0$      if the elevator is at floor 0

The elevator has three possible actions:

Action 1: Go to floor 1, open door, pause, close door.
Action 2: Go to floor 0, open door, pause, close door.
Action 3: Open door, pause, close door.

As elevator designers, we need to decide under what conditions each action is to be taken. For example, if the elevator is at floor 0 ($x_f = 0$) and the button at floor 1 is pushed ($x_1 = 1$), we would like the elevator to rise to floor 1, open the door, pause, and close the door (action 1). (This assumes no one is pushing the floor 0 button or the internal button: $x_0 = 0$, $x_e = 0$.) The following table gives a reasonable specification of every other possible situation and the appropriate action.

| $x_0$ | $x_1$ | $x_e$ | $x_f$ | Action 1 | Action 2 | Action 3 |
|---|---|---|---|---|---|---|
| 0 | 0 | 0 | 0 | 0 | 0 | 0 |
| 0 | 0 | 0 | 1 | 0 | 0 | 0 |
| 0 | 0 | 1 | 0 | 1 | 0 | 0 |
| 0 | 0 | 1 | 1 | 0 | 1 | 0 |
| 0 | 1 | 0 | 0 | 1 | 0 | 0 |
| 0 | 1 | 0 | 1 | 0 | 0 | 1 |
| 0 | 1 | 1 | 0 | 1 | 0 | 0 |
| 0 | 1 | 1 | 1 | 0 | 0 | 1 |
| 1 | 0 | 0 | 0 | 0 | 0 | 1 |
| 1 | 0 | 0 | 1 | 0 | 1 | 0 |
| 1 | 0 | 1 | 0 | 0 | 0 | 1 |
| 1 | 0 | 1 | 1 | 0 | 1 | 0 |
| 1 | 1 | 0 | 0 | 0 | 0 | 1 |
| 1 | 1 | 0 | 1 | 0 | 0 | 1 |
| 1 | 1 | 1 | 0 | 0 | 0 | 1 |
| 1 | 1 | 1 | 1 | 0 | 0 | 1 |

Design a circuit that will light a bulb whenever action 1 is required. Repeat for actions 2 and 3.

## Relays (B)

But whose fingers are going to push all the switches described in the previous section? In an ordinary calculation with a computer, thousands of switches get turned, and we know our own fingers do not do it. The answer is that electrical circuits turn the switches. In this chapter we will examine two kinds of electrically operated switches: *relays*, which were the basis for computers and telephone systems in the first half of the twentieth century, and *transistors*, which were introduced in the 1950s and have been used ever since. (A third kind of switch, *vacuum tubes*, was important in the 1940s and 1950s but will not be discussed here.)

Relays are switches moved by electromagnets. As we learned as children, if we wind a piece of insulated wire around a nail many times and connect it to a battery, the nail becomes magnetic. If the wire is disconnected, most of the magnetism disappears:

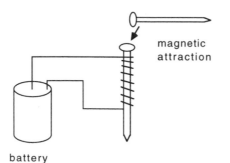

If the magnetic attraction from the electromagnet causes a switch to move, the electric current to the magnet will control the movement of the switch:

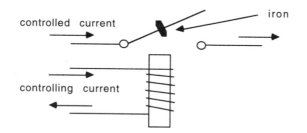

A piece of magnetic material, usually iron, must be attached to the electrical conductor of the switch. If the controlling current flows, it will magnetize the iron core in its coil and pull the movable switch iron downward, closing the switch. If the controlling current is turned off, the magnetism disappears, and the switch spring action will return it to the "up" position.

   All the switches in the previous sections could be moved by incoming electrical currents instead of by human hands. For example, we can repeat the circuit for $f_3$ given above on the assumption that electrical circuits control the switches. Suppose circuit 1 passes current whenever $x_1 = 1$ and ceases when $x_1 = 0$. Similarly, circuits 2 and 3 are controlled by $x_2$ and $x_3$. Then $f_3$ is computed by this circuit:

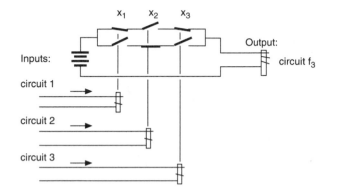

This circuit is shown symbolically. The vertical lines drawn downward from the switches show which switches will be pushed down by which magnets. (In practical relays, the magnets are always extremely close to the switches.) Also notice that the light bulb has been replaced by the circuit output labelled "circuit $f_3$." Thus, if this output is connected to another electromagnet, that magnet will come on when $f_3(x_1, x_2, x_3) = 1$ and will turn off otherwise.

Using these techniques, we can compute arbitrarily complicated functions. We can write down the functional table for any target behavior with any number of binary input variables. The associated circuit can then be constructed with its electrical inputs and outputs. The inputs may be the results of other calculations, and the outputs may feed into many other circuits. Any individual circuit will act like a subroutine to the whole calculation, and a large network of such circuits can perform huge tasks.

### Exercises

1. Repeat the action 1 portion of the elevator problem. Assume the inputs are provided by electrical currents and the output is a current to activate action 1. Fill in the following diagram to show all wires, relays, and batteries to drive the action 1 circuit.

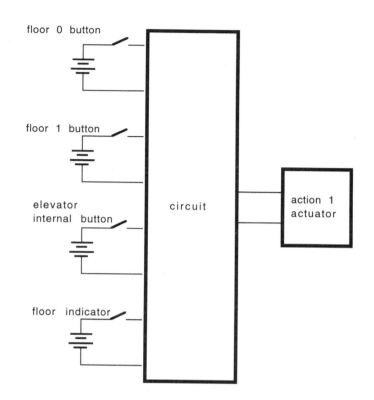

2. Suppose a three-floor elevator system is to be built similar to the one in exercise 5 of the previous section. Develop a complete design using the methodologies of this and previous sections.

## The Binary Number System (B)

The internal mechanisms of most digital computers involve devices that flip back and forth between two states. The relays of the previous section are either off or on, the electrical wires either carry current or do not, and so forth. Since the components of the computer are only two-valued, a reasonable way to represent states is with two-valued notation, which is why information is coded into binary form. This section shows how nonnegative integers can be coded into binary numbers and manipulated.

We first examine the familiar decimal number system and notice its construction. In a three-digit number, the left-most digit tells how many 100s are in the number, the second digit tells how many 10s are in the number, and the last digit tells how many 1s. Thus 327 decimal has 3 100s plus 2 10s plus 7 1s. The binary number system functions similarly, except that the sequential digits may be only 0s and 1s and they have this meaning in an eight-digit number.

| | |
|---|---|
| Left-most digit | Number of 128s |
| Second from left-most digit | Number of 64s |
| Third from left-most digit | Number of 32s |
| Fourth from right-most digit | Number of 16s |
| Fifth from right-most digit | Number of 8s |
| And so forth. | |

This provides an easy way to convert any binary number to its decimal form. Simply write the binary digits in a column with the left-most digit at the top. Then add up the contributions of all digits, as is shown below for the binary number 00010010:

$$
\begin{array}{rcl}
0 * 128 &=& 0 \\
0 * 64 &=& 0 \\
0 * 32 &=& 0 \\
1 * 16 &=& 16 \\
0 * 8 &=& 0 \\
0 * 4 &=& 0 \\
1 * 2 &=& 2 \\
0 * 1 &=& 0 \\
\hline
& & 18
\end{array}
$$

The decimal form of 00010010 is 18.

A Pascal program to do this calculation is given here:

```
program BinaryToDecimal;
var
     length,base,decimal,bit,i:integer;
begin
writeln('Read the number of binary digits.');
readln(length);
base := 1;
i := 1;                        {First compute 2^(length-1)
                                putting result into base.}
while i < length do
    begin
    base := base * 2;
    i := i + 1;
    end;
```

```
decimal := 0;
while base >=1 do              {For each binary bit, add its
                                contribution.}
    begin
    writeln('Input next binary digit.');
    readln(bit);
    decimal := decimal + base * bit;
    base := base div 2;    {Set base to half of its previous
                                value.}
    end;
writeln('The decimal value is ',decimal);
readln;
end.
```

The conversion from decimal to binary is equally easy. To convert 18 into 8-bit binary, begin with the left-most binary digit. How many 128s are in 18? None, so the left-most digit is 0. How many 64s are in 18? None. The second digit is 0. Similarly, there are no 32s in 18 so the third digit is 0. How many 16s are in 18? One, so the next digit is 1, and we subtract away the 16 just found: $18 - 16 = 2$. How many 8s are in 2? None, so 0 is next. How many 4s are in 2? None, so 0 is next. How many 2s are in 2? One, so choose the next digit to be 1 and subtract out 2: $2 - 2 = 0$. How many 1s are in 0? None, so the last digit is 0.

This calculation is better understood if it is kept in a tabular form, as follows:

| Number being considered | How many of these? | Resulting digit |
|---|---|---|
| 18 | 128 | 0 |
| 18 | 64 | 0 |
| 18 | 32 | 0 |
| 18 | 16 | 1 (subtract from number) |
| 2 | 8 | 0 |
| 2 | 4 | 0 |
| 2 | 2 | 1 (subtract from number) |
| 0 | 1 | 0 |

Now that we understand the binary number system, we can study the manipulation of binary numbers. For example, how do we add the binary form of 5 to the binary form of 7? The process is identical to adding decimal numbers. The right-most digits are added and possibly a carry is added to the second from right-most column. Then that column is added, possibly leading to another carry, and so forth.

5 decimal is 0101 binary
7 decimal is 0111 binary

Adding the right-most column: $1 + 1 = 10$. (That is, adding 1 in binary to 1 in binary yields 2 in binary.) The result is 0 with a carry of 1:

```
carry        1
5        0 1 0 1
7        0 1 1 1
         ─────────
             0
```

Adding the second from right-most column, $1 + 0 + 1 = 10$. The result is 0 with a carry of 1:

```
carry      1 1
5        0 1 0 1
7        0 1 1 1
         ─────────
           0 0
```

Adding the third from right-most column yields $1 + 1 + 1 = 11$. The result is 1 with a carry of 1:

```
carry    1 1 1
5        0 1 0 1
7        0 1 1 1
         ─────────
         1 0 0
```

Adding the final column yields 1:

```
carry    1 1 1
5        0 1 0 1
7        0 1 1 1
         ─────────
         1 1 0 0
```

The answer is 1100 binary, which can be converted back to decimal to obtain 12.

Other operations on binary numbers can also be carried out similarly to those on decimal numbers, but they need not be discussed further here.

**Exercises**

1. Convert decimal 77 to 8-bit binary form.

2. Convert decimal 101 to 8-bit binary form.

3. Find the decimal forms of the binary numbers 1010111 and 11110010.

4. Find the sum of the numbers in exercise 3 using binary addition.

5. Write a program that reads a decimal number and prints its binary equivalent.

6. A circuit is to be designed to input the binary form of one of the digits 0 to 9 and to present a digital display of the digits. The digital display is represented below as a seven line segment object where each line segment may be individually illuminated. Thus, if the circuit inputs a binary 5, which is 0101, it will display the array shown below. (The darkened lights are the ones that are illuminated.)

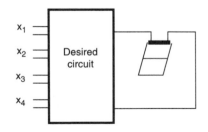

The digital display has seven linear light sources, and any of the ten digits can be presented by illuminating the correct ones. The table on the following page shows the digits and their associated displays.

Each of the seven lights of the digital display must have a switching circuit to turn it on for the appropriate inputs. For example, the middle light is always on except for the inputs 0000, 0001, and 0111.

Design a circuit that illuminates the top light of the display for all appropriate inputs.

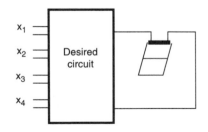

The driver for the complete digital display clearly needs seven such circuits.

| | Input in Binary Form | | | | |
|---|---|---|---|---|---|
| Digit | $x_1$ | $x_2$ | $x_3$ | $x_4$ | Display |

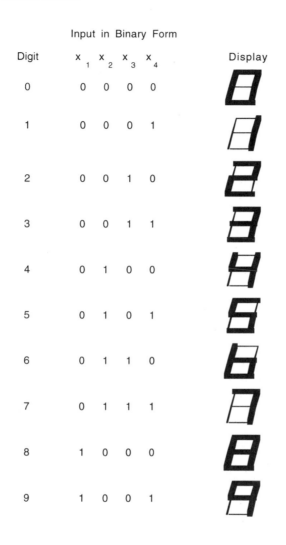

| Digit | $x_1$ | $x_2$ | $x_3$ | $x_4$ |
|---|---|---|---|---|
| 0 | 0 | 0 | 0 | 0 |
| 1 | 0 | 0 | 0 | 1 |
| 2 | 0 | 0 | 1 | 0 |
| 3 | 0 | 0 | 1 | 1 |
| 4 | 0 | 1 | 0 | 0 |
| 5 | 0 | 1 | 0 | 1 |
| 6 | 0 | 1 | 1 | 0 |
| 7 | 0 | 1 | 1 | 1 |
| 8 | 1 | 0 | 0 | 0 |
| 9 | 1 | 0 | 0 | 1 |

## The Circuits for Adding Two Digits (B)

We would like to build an electric circuit that will add up binary numbers. In order to get started, let us examine our earlier sample computation and rethink the exact steps of the addition. We will call the numbers to be added *X1* and *X2*.

```
carry     1110
X1        0101
X2        0111
          ————
sum       1100
```

The method is to examine the right-most column and produce two results, the sum digit and the carry digit. Then examine the next column and produce two results, the sum digit and the carry digit. And so forth.

Since two results, the sum digit and the carry digit, are computed at each step, we will need two switching circuits, one for each result. Let us first concentrate on the switching circuit that computes the sum digit. From studying the example, we learn that if the carry digit is 0 and the $X1$ digit is 1 and the $X2$ digit is 1, then the sum digit is 0. This comes from the right-most column. Let us write this in a clear notation:

if *carry* $= 0$, $X1 = 1$, $X2 = 1$     then *sum* $= 0$

From the other three columns we get these:

if *carry* $= 1$, $X1 = 0$, $X2 = 1$     then *sum* $= 0$
if *carry* $= 1$, $X1 = 1$, $X2 = 1$     then *sum* $= 1$
if *carry* $= 1$, $X1 = 0$, $X2 = 0$     then *sum* $= 1$

Let us fill these values into a table in preparation for building a switching circuit.

| carry | X1 | X2 | sum |
|-------|----|----|-----|
| –     | –  | –  | –   |
| –     | –  | –  | –   |
| –     | –  | –  | –   |
| 0     | 1  | 1  | 0   |
| 1     | 0  | 0  | 1   |
| 1     | 0  | 1  | 0   |
| –     | –  | –  | –   |
| 1     | 1  | 1  | 1   |

This looks like the tables we used earlier for designing switching circuits, except that there are some missing entries. For example, in the first row, we have if *carry* $= 0$, $X1 = 0$, $X2 = 0$, then *sum* is 0. You should be able to fill in the rest of the rows.

| carry | X1 | X2 | sum |
|-------|-----|-----|-----|
| 0 | 0 | 0 | 0 |
| 0 | 0 | 1 | 1 |
| 0 | 1 | 0 | 1 |
| 0 | 1 | 1 | 0 |
| 1 | 0 | 0 | 1 |
| 1 | 0 | 1 | 0 |
| 1 | 1 | 0 | 0 |
| 1 | 1 | 1 | 1 |

We will need one additional feature for our adder. It will be an on-off switch that will turn the adder on when we want to add and off when we do not. So we will add another input to the table that guarantees a 0 output if the on-off switch is 0 but allows normal addition when the on-off switch is 1.

| on-off | carry | X1 | X2 | sum |
|--------|-------|-----|-----|-----|
| 0 | 0 | 0 | 0 | 0 |
| 0 | 0 | 0 | 1 | 0 |
| 0 | 0 | 1 | 0 | 0 |
| 0 | 0 | 1 | 1 | 0 |
| 0 | 1 | 0 | 0 | 0 |
| 0 | 1 | 0 | 1 | 0 |
| 0 | 1 | 1 | 0 | 0 |
| 0 | 1 | 1 | 1 | 0 |
| 1 | 0 | 0 | 0 | 0 |
| 1 | 0 | 0 | 1 | 1 |
| 1 | 0 | 1 | 0 | 1 |
| 1 | 0 | 1 | 1 | 0 |
| 1 | 1 | 0 | 0 | 1 |
| 1 | 1 | 0 | 1 | 0 |
| 1 | 1 | 1 | 0 | 0 |
| 1 | 1 | 1 | 1 | 1 |

This table gives 0 whenever the on-off switch is 0 and it is identical to the previous table when the on-off switch is 1.

Now we can apply our technology from the early part of this chapter to produce the switching circuit for the sum digit.

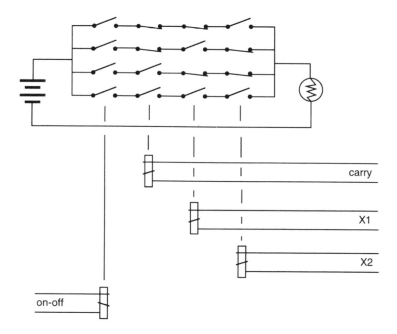

We can check whether this circuit turns the sum light bulb on when it is supposed to. If the on-off switch is on, that is *on-off* = 1, and the right-most column from the above example *carry* = 0, *X1* = 1, *X2* = 1 is computed, the result is that the light bulb does not go on, the sum digit is 0. This is a correct computation. You should check the other possible inputs to see whether they also compute the correct answers.

But two circuits are needed to compute the sum of a column of three binary digits. We have just created one of the circuits but the other, the carry circuit, is needed to calculate the carry digit to be placed at the top of the next column. We will call this *ncarry*. The reasoning sequence that produced the sum circuit will work for the carry circuit. The completion of this circuit is the goal of the exercises that follow.

**Exercises**

1. Let us build the circuit for *ncarry*. The first step is to create a table of inputs and outputs that tells what the carry circuit should compute. Let us go back to the sample computation at the beginning of the section and look at the carry digits that were computed. In the right-most column, the inputs were *carry* = 0, *X1* = 1, *X2* = 1, and the carry digit, which we will call *ncarry*, that was put at the top of the second from right column was 1. We will tabulate this information:

if *carry* = 0, *X1* = 1, *X2* = 1     then *ncarry* = 1

Now you should tabulate the other carry computations observed in that calculation. Next you should fill out the complete table for the carry computation.

| carry | X1 | X2 | ncarry |
|-------|-----|-----|--------|
| 0 | 0 | 0 | ? |
| 0 | 0 | 1 | ? |
| 0 | 1 | 0 | ? |
| 0 | 1 | 1 | ? |
| 1 | 0 | 0 | ? |
| 1 | 0 | 1 | ? |
| 1 | 1 | 0 | ? |
| 1 | 1 | 1 | ? |

Finally, you should introduce the idea of the on-off switch and create a table that has four inputs (*on-off*, *carry*, *X1*, *X2*) and one output (*ncarry*). This table should always indicate *ncarry* = 0 if the on-off switch is 0 (off) and it should be the same as the above table if the on-off switch is 1 (on).

2. Create the switching circuit that computes *ncarry* as described in problem 1. Assume four inputs: *on-off*, *carry*, *X1*, and *X2*.

3. This section has created two switching circuits, one for the adder and one for the carry digit. Let's check to see if they work. We will carry out the computation 5 + 7 in binary.

0101
0111
‾‾‾‾

(a) Use the sum circuit shown above to find the right-most sum digit. Assume the carry from the previous column (there is none) is 0. Enter your answer on the page.
(b) Use your carry circuit from problem 2 on the right-most column to compute the carry digit called *ncarry*. Put it at the top of the second column from the right.
(c) Use the sum circuit to find the sum digit for the second from right-most column. Enter your answer on the page.
(d) Use your carry circuit on the second from right-most column to compute the carry digit. Put it at the top of the third column from the right.
(e) Finish the computation as indicated by the method so far.
(f) Check that the answer computed is correct.

## The Adder Circuit (B)

Our goal is to add up two many-digit binary numbers. The circuits of the previous section do the necessary work to add numbers but they are not yet organized to do the job. We must lay down an array of these circuits and connect them together. Space limitations restrict us to handling two three-digit numbers in our figures.

Before looking at the adder, it is necessary to understand the idea of a binary register. A three-digit binary register will be displayed here as follows:

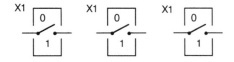

This register has the name X1. Each switch can be either in the position shown to indicate a zero or it can be pushed down to indicate a one. The register X1 above is shown in the configuration of containing three zeros, 000, and in the following case, it contains 011.

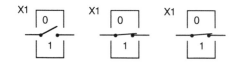

The collection of circuits capable of adding two numbers is shown below. It is called the *adder circuit* and its parts are as follows:

(a) This is the X1 register. It can hold three binary digits and its contents are to be added to the X2 register.
(b) This is the X2 register. It can also hold three binary digits and it holds the second number that is to be added.
(c) This is the register AX. It is to receive the sum of X1 and X2 when the circuit is activated.
(d) These are the carry digits. When *ncarry* is computed by any carry circuit, the answer goes into one of these digit locations.
(e) These are the circuits from the previous section that compute *sum*. You should check back to be sure they are the same circuit. (The switches are drawn upside down for reasons that will be given below.)
(f) These are the circuits that compute the carry as worked out in the exercises of the last section. Each computed result is passed on to the carry digit in the next column.
(g) This is the instruction register that receives the next command to be executed.

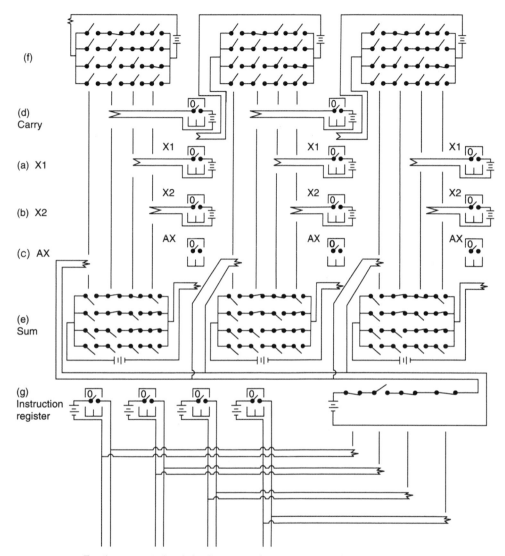

(f)

(d)
Carry

(a) X1

(b) X2

(c) AX

X1

X2

AX

(e)
Sum

(g)
Instruction
register

To other computational circuits: copy, sub, etc.

The functioning of the adder is described below. We will use the following codes to show switch movements:

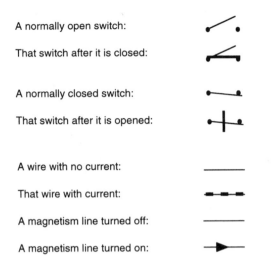

A normally open switch:

That switch after it is closed:

A normally closed switch:

That switch after it is opened:

A wire with no current:

That wire with current:

A magnetism line turned off:

A magnetism line turned on:

These codes have two purposes. First, they enable us to see the before and after configurations for each switch. Second, these codes are easy to use because we can make several copies of this adder and practice working through the computations by hand.

The calculation proceeds as described below. (Remember to obtain a copy of "This-is-how-a-computer-works" as described in the introductory chapter so you can see it all happen in full color animation.)

1. First we will enter numbers into the two registers X1 and X2. Let us add 3 to 1 in this example. We must convert them to binary numbers and then load them into the registers as indicated above. They are 011 and 001 in binary, and the following diagram shows them entered. Notice that when these numbers are entered, switches that allow current to flow in the circuits are closed. The current will activate magnets that pull on switches straight above and below the magnet, as shown by the lines. This turns several switches in the add and carry circuits. (All these actions are shown in the diagram below.)

2. Second, we enter an operation code into the instruction register. This is a four-digit binary number that tells the computer what to do. If someone wants the computer to do a subtraction, they can enter 0110 into the instruction register. This code will cause the subtraction circuits to subtract X2 from X1 and put the result into AX. (None of that circuitry is shown on our diagram.) However, if 0100, the code for addition, is entered, we can see in the diagram below that current flows down serial wires and all the on-off switches in the add and carry circuits are turned on.

3. If we look at the summing circuit for the right-most column, we see that it computes a 0. Notice that the right-most digit in register AX also contains a 0. If we look at the carry circuit for the right-most column, we see that it computes a 1, which is entered in the carry digit at the top of the second column from the right. Then we can examine the sum and carry digits in the second from right-most column and so on, until all the columns are processed.

4. After the processing is done, we can look at the digits in the AX register and find 100, which is the correct answer. We added 3 to 1 and obtained 4.

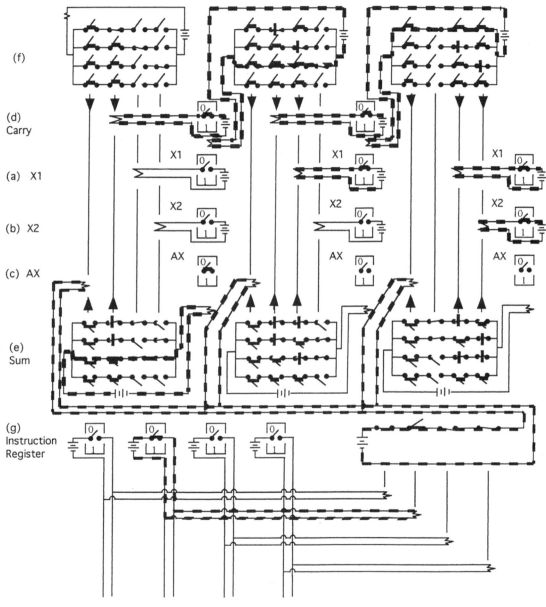

(f)

(d)
Carry

(a)  X1

(b)  X2

(c)  AX

(e)
Sum

(g)
Instruction
Register

X1

X2

AX

To other computational circuits: copy, sub, etc.

Before completing this section, we will examine the instruction register and the adder circuit in relation to the rest of a computer. We can think of the instruction register as a choir director and the adder circuit and other circuits for doing computations as the choir members. The instruction register gets a sequence of binary codes such as 1100, 0110, 0100, and these codes turn on the individual computation circuits as they arrive. If the code 0100 arrives, as in the above diagram, it turns on the adder and an addition is done. When other codes arrive, they turn on other circuits to do subtraction, multiplication, and other types of computation. Together, the instructions comprise a total computation that gets useful work done for the computer user.

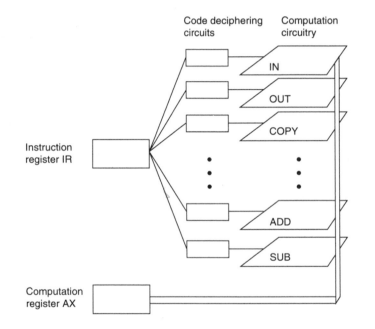

### Exercises

1. On a copy of the above adder circuit, enter the operation code 0011 and tell what happens.

2. On a copy of the adder circuit, enter the numbers 3 and 3 into registers X1 and X2. Enter the code 0100 into the instruction register. Show all current movement by darkening the appropriate wires and switch movements using the method described above. What answer does the circuit compute? Is this correct?

3. Show how the adder adds the numbers 1 and 1.

4. A user was doing an addition with a damaged version of this circuit and noticed that when it added 000 to 001, the result was 011. It was incorrect. Study the circuit and find the wires and switches that, on the basis of this observation, could be causing the problem.

---

## Storing Characters in Memory (C)

This chapter has shown how a computer represents binary numbers and computes with them. An issue that has been ignored for the sake of simplicity is that machines can also store and manipulate characters. While we will not discuss characters at length, we will at least mention that they do have their own coding in the machine, and they are stored in registers in the same manner as binary numbers.

The most common coding for characters uses eight binary digits, as specified by the American Standard Code for Information Interchange (ASCII). Here is a part of the ASCII code, the representations for the capital letters and the space (which is also a legitimate character):

| | |
|---|---|
| A | 01000001 |
| B | 01000010 |
| C | 01000011 |
| D | 01000100 |
| E | 01000101 |
| F | 01000110 |
| G | 01000111 |
| H | 01001000 |
| I | 01001001 |
| — | — |
| — | — |
| — | — |
| Z | 01011010 |
| (space) | 00100000 |

The complete code specifies representations for the lower case alphabet, the digits, and a variety of punctuation and other symbols. Using this code, you can see, for example, how to store the word "BE" in a sixteen bit register:

0100001001000101

**Exercise**

1. Fill in the rest of the table for the capital letters. Show how these codes would be used to spell out your name.

---

## Transistors and Very Large Scale Integration (B)

The circuits in this chapter have been built out of relays. Relays are switches that can be turned off and on by an electrical current that magnetizes an iron core and moves the switch conductor. The problem with relays is that they are very large, typically measuring almost an inch on each side; they are also slow, being able to switch on and off a few dozen times per second; and they require a lot of electrical power. In building computers, we want switches that are much smaller than a period on this page, that turn off and on millions of times per second, and that use practically no power at all. The fulfillment of these specifications comes from the *transistor*, one of the most astounding inventions in history.

Transistors and their fabrication into Very Large Scale Integrated Circuits are *the* invention that has made modern computing possible. Without the ability to assemble machines with millions of fast switches in physically very small volumes, it would not be possible to build any modern computer. Many important recent accomplishments—the space program, the computerization of industry, and the simulation of economic and physical systems—were made possible by computers built from transistor technologies.

A transistor is a three-layer semiconductor device that can achieve the switching function using forces at the level of electrons rather than at the level of moving mechanical parts. The three parts, called the *emitter*, the *base*, and the *collector*, carry on the functions, respectively, of emitting electrons, controlling them, and collecting them.

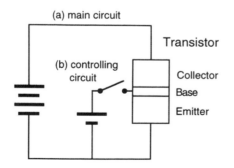

The switching function works roughly as follows. A battery tries to push electrons around the main circuit (a), which is made up of electrical conducting material and, in the transistor itself, a semiconductor material. But the electrons cannot cross the middle base region of the transistor because it is constructed to have a lack of free electrons to carry electricity. Only if the controlling circuit for the base of the transistor supplies the free electrons can current flow. But if the switch at (b) is turned on, current will flow in the controlling circuit. It will travel through the small battery through the emitter and base materials and back to the small battery. This will supply electron carriers to the base region, which then allows current to flow in the main circuit. Thus, the controlling circuit can turn the main circuit off and on by supplying, or failing to supply, carrier electrons in the base region of the transistor.

Once this wonderful idea was discovered, engineers found ways to embed thousands of these tiny switches into semiconductor material. This is the technology that has become known as *very large scale integration ( VLSI )*. The most common semiconductor is silicon, and conductors and transistors can be etched by the hundreds of thousands onto a silicon surface that measures a fraction of an inch square. The primary tool for doing the etching is light, and the methodology resembles the photography business more than the electronics industry.

## Summary (B)

This chapter gives the fundamental principles of designing a computer with relays, and the methodology is adequate to build machines of great complexity and functionality. In our study of how electric circuitry computes, we covered many important topics, including circuit synthesis from specifications, coding information into binary form and the binary number system, and the design of circuitry and codes to drive machine operations.

Computer design is a refined and well-developed discipline, and much is necessarily omitted from this chapter. For example, switching-circuit theorists emphasize representing functions with Boolean algebra and minimizing the number of switches required. Also many VLSI technologies have special characteristics that require innovative design methodologies. Many designs presented in this chapter help to clarify fundamental ideas but are not necessarily typical of actual modern machines.

THE INSTRUCTIONS COME IN FROM
MEMORY OVER THERE. THEN
THEY ARE DECODED DOWN THERE.

THE DECODING CIRCUITRY TELLS
THE COMPUTATION REGISTER WHAT
DATA TO USE AND WHICH
OPERATION TO CARRY OUT.

INSTRUCTION
REGISTER
DEPT.

DECODING
DEPT.

• ADD
• SUB.
• MULT.
• DIV.
• COPY

IN

COMPUTATION
DEPT.

# 8    Machine Architecture

## Let Us Build a Computer (A)

We have learned how to build simple circuits that compute functions, and our next task is to study the assembly of such circuits into a computer. Most computer architectures have two major subparts, the machine *central processing unit (CPU)* and the *memory*. The CPU executes the calculations, and thus has *computational registers* wired to do the arithmetic operations and other manipulations on data. It contains the instruction register introduced in chapter 7 and its associated decoding circuitry. It contains all the mechanisms for retrieving instructions to be executed, sequencing them through the instruction register, and getting the individual instructions executed.

The memory has no ability to compute anything. It is simply a huge array of low-cost registers where information can be stored. The registers are numbered, usually from 0 to $n$; each location holds 8, 16, or some other number of bits, and the values of $n$ may be large, say, from 32,767 to hundreds of millions.

The central processor needs two kinds of information that are stored in the memory: its own instructions and the data that it works on. Its instructions are stored in the memory as a sequence of binary-coded machine instructions, and they are sequentially brought into the central processor for execution. The resulting computations utilize the other kind of information stored in the memory, the data. These data contain the character sequences and the numbers the user wants to manipulate.

Some digital machines have only one computational register in the CPU and a few instructions, and others have dozens of such registers and hundreds of instructions. A sample architecture is the CPU for the IBM personal computer, which uses the Intel class VLSI chip as its central processor. Recent versions of this are the Intel 286, 386, 486, and Pentium. This architecture has about a dozen registers and about a hundred instructions that do a variety of arithmetic, logical, and character operations. The speeds of these machines vary from a few million to a few hundred million instructions per second.

Another way of varying the architecture is to have several copies of the CPU-memory configuration in one machine. This is called a *parallel architecture*, and it enables the programmer to divide a computation into several different parts that can all be worked on simultaneously. (Parallel architectures and their uses are described in chapter 13.)

In this chapter we will study a model machine called the P88 that resembles most contemporary computers. Although it has only one register for manipulating data and twelve instructions, its instructions are nearly identical to those of the Intel class of machines. It contains the configuration constructed in the last chapter, the instruction register (IR), decoding circuits, computation circuits, and the computation register (AX).

The instruction register will contain the whole binary-coded instruction, both the code to tell which operation to perform, such as 0010, and any extra bits to tell what registers and memory locations are to be referenced. There will also be another register, the condition flag (CF), which will be explained below, and an instruction pointer (IP), which will tell from where in the memory the machine should fetch the next instruction to be executed. Finally, there will be the memory itself.

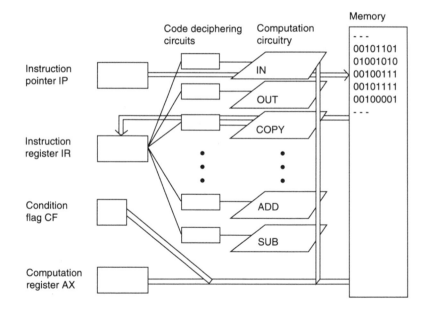

For our purposes in this chapter, we can remove most of the details. We will not, for example, use binary codes in our discussion. When a typical instruction like *COPY AX,X* is stored in the memory, it is usually coded as a binary number, such as 00101101. However, we will write simply *\*COPY AX,X\** where the surrounding asterisks indicate that the instruction has been translated into binary code. That is, *COPY AX,X* is an instruction to the machine, and *\*COPY AX,X\** represents its binary code.

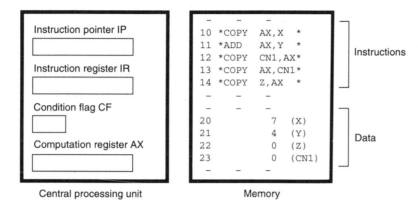

Central processing unit                    Memory

You can run a simulator for the P88 if you obtain a copy of the program called "This-is-how-a-computer-works," as described in the introductory chapter.

## A Sample Architecture: the P88 Machine (B)

The P88 computer contains the components shown above: an instruction pointer register (IP), an instruction register (IR), a condition flag (CF), the computational register (AX), and the memory.

The computer proceeds by repeatedly executing the following two steps:

Repeat without end:

1. (Fetch) Find the instruction in memory at the address given by IP and put that instruction into IR. Increment IP to give the address of the next instruction.
2. (Execute) Execute the instruction in IR.

These two steps comprise what is called the *fetch-execute cycle*, and they can best be understood by going over an example. Suppose that the machine instruction codes

```
*COPY AX,X  *
*ADD AX,Y   *
*COPY CN1,AX*
*COPY AX,CN1*
*COPY Z,AX  *
```

reside in the memory at locations 10 through 14 and that the machine is about to execute these codes. Then the address (10) of the first such code *COPY AX,X* will be in IP:

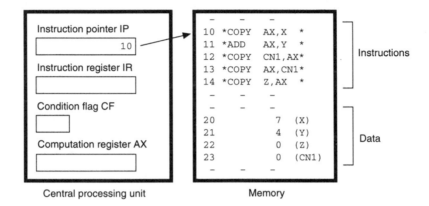

The first step of the fetch-execute cycle loads IR from the location given by IP. Then IP is incremented to give the address of the next instruction:

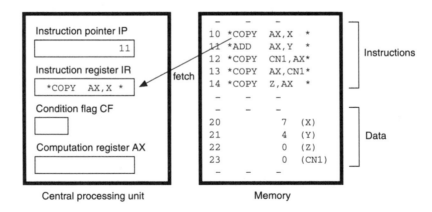

The second step is the execute cycle, which carries out the instruction in the instruction register (IR). In this case, *COPY AX,X* is executed. As is explained below, the contents of memory location X will be copied into the register AX. The circuitry doing this task is the instruction decoding and execution (D&E) circuits, as explained in chapter 7:

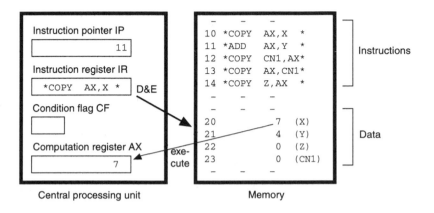

The fetch-execute cycle continues without stopping. On the next cycle, the instruction is fetched from location 11 in the memory. This is an add instruction, *ADD AX,Y*. It adds the contents of memory location *Y* to the contents of register *AX* and leaves the result in register *AX* . Here is the result of this fetch and execute:

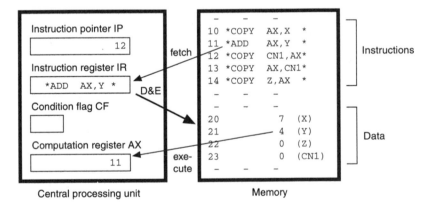

Another pass through the fetch-execute cycle results in the third instruction's being executed. This instruction causes the contents of the *AX* register to be copied into the memory location *CN1*:

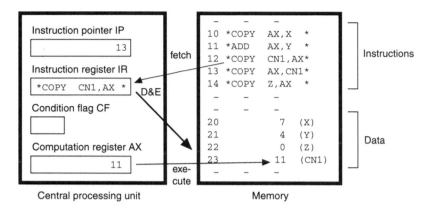

Thus the machine sequentially loads the string of commands in memory and carries them out. Occasionally a "jump" instruction will load a new value into IP, which begins a new sequence of commands. For example, in the above case, it is possible that some instruction would cause 10 to be loaded into IP again and result in another execution of this sequence.

The fundamental operation of every digital computer is built around the fetch-execute cycle as described here. This is, in fact, the only thing that modern digital computers are designed to do—to fetch instructions and execute them. There is no need to be impressed with the intelligence of any modern computer, no matter how large, with its blinking lights, complex displays, and many terminals over which workers huddle. *The giant machine is doing nothing more than fetching instructions and executing them. It never has in the past, cannot now, and never in the future will be able to do more or less than this.*

(Chapter 13 will suggest other architectures, such as neural network computers, that do not use the fetch-execute approach to computing. But that is another story.)

**Exercises**

1. Trace the execution of the final two instructions in the above example—those instructions in memory locations 13 and 14. Show every detail of the fetch-execute cycle.

2. In the example above, the instruction pointer (IP) increases one on each cycle and will apparently soon reach 20. An error will occur if it does. Explain the nature of the error. What instruction must be included after location 14 but before location 20 to avoid this error?

## Programming the P88 Machine (B)

The P88 has 12 instructions, as shown below. Each individual instruction is simple in its operation, as described by its *action* entry. The first instruction is called a "copy" and is written *COPY AX,mem* where *mem* refers to a location in memory. If this instruction is executed, the contents of the memory at location *mem* is copied into register *AX*. Another copy instruction *COPY mem,AX* copies the contents of *AX* to memory location *mem*. As an illustration, we can use these two instructions to move data from memory location *A* to memory location *B*.

```
COPY AX,A
COPY B,AX
```

Here are the instructions:

| Instruction | Format | Action |
|---|---|---|
| copy from mem | COPY AX,mem | AX := mem |
| copy to mem | COPY mem,AX | mem := AX |
| add | ADD AX,mem | AX := AX+mem |
| subtract | SUB AX,mem | AX := AX-mem |
| multiply | MUL AX,mem | AX := AX*mem |
| divide | DIV AX,mem | AX := AX div mem |
| compare | CMP AX,mem | if AX < mem then<br>    CF := B<br>else<br>    CF := NB |
| jump | JMP lab1 | Go to the instruction<br>    with label lab1. |
| jump if not below | JNB lab1 | Go to the instruction<br>    with label lab1 if<br>    CF=NB. Otherwise<br>    go to next instruction. |
| jump if below | JB lab1 | Go to the instruction<br>    with label lab1 if<br>    CF=B. Otherwise go to<br>    the next instruction. |
| input | IN AX | Input an integer into<br>    register AX. |
| output | OUT AX | Output an integer from<br>    register AX. |

The P88 has four arithmetic instructions—*ADD, SUB, MUL,* and *DIV*—which perform their respective operations on *AX* and a memory location and leave the result in *AX*. Thus *ADD AX,B* adds the contents of memory location *B* to *AX* and leaves the result in *AX*.

Notice that the following instruction is illegal: *ADD mem,AX.* The only instructions that allow a reference to memory to follow the instruction name immediately are *COPY, JMP, JNB,* and *JB.*

It also has instructions for reading and printing integers, *IN* and *OUT.* These instructions can be used for writing some P88 programs. Here is a P88 program for reading an integer into register *AX* and then printing it:

```
IN  AX
OUT AX
```

Or we could read an integer, square it, and print the result:

```
IN   AX
COPY M1,AX
MUL  AX,M1
OUT  AX
```

As another example, we could read two numbers, divide the first by the second, and print the result:

```
IN   AX
COPY A,AX
IN   AX
COPY B,AX
COPY AX,A
DIV  AX,B
OUT  AX
```

Another type of instruction is the "jump," which loads a new address into IP and causes the machine to jump to an instruction that is not next in sequence. As an example, consider the following program, which adds the number in memory location *A* to *AX* repeatedly:

```
L1 ADD AX,A
   JMP L1
```

This program adds *A* to *AX,* and then the next instruction causes a jump to the instruction labeled *L1.* Here *A* is again added to *AX.* Then the jump instruction sends the machine back to *L1* again, and so forth. This program loops forever, adding *A* to *AX* an unlimited number of times.

Of course, programmers usually write a loop that will halt after an appropriate number of repetitions. This is done with the combination of the "compare" and conditional jump instructions, *JB* and *JNB*. An example of this type of program is the following code, which prints the numbers from 1 to 10 before exiting. This program assumes the numbers 0,1, and 10 appear in memory locations *M0*, *M1*, and *M10*.

```
   COPY AX,M0
L1 ADD  AX,M1
   OUT  AX
   CMP  AX,M10
   JB   L1
```

The compare instruction *CMP* loads *B* into register *CF* if *AX* is less than (below) *M10*. The "jump if below" instruction *JB* jumps to *L1* if *CF* is *B*, that is, if *AX* is below *M10*. A paraphrase of this program shows its method of operation.

```
   Put 0 into AX.
L1 Add 1 to AX.
   Print the contents of AX.
   Check whether AX is less than 10.
   If it is, go to L1.
```

Another example of a program that uses the compare and jump commands is the following, which reads a number and changes its sign if it is negative. This program computes what is called the "absolute value" in mathematics:

```
     IN   AX
     COPY M1,AX
     SUB  AX,M1
     CMP  AX,M1
     JB   NEXT
     SUB  AX,M1
     COPY M1,AX
NEXT COPY AX,M1
     OUT  AX
```

The final example will be a program to add a series of nonnegative numbers. If a negative number is read at any time, the program prints the sum of all nonnegative numbers read and exits:

```
   IN   AX
   COPY M1,AX
   SUB  AX,M1
   COPY ZERO,AX
   COPY SUM,AX
   COPY AX,M1
```

```
LOOP CMP  AX,ZERO
     JB   FIN
     ADD  AX,SUM
     COPY SUM,AX
     IN   AX
     JMP  LOOP
FIN  COPY AX,SUM
     OUT  AX
```

The language of machine instructions written in symbolic form as described here—*COPY*, *ADD*, *CMP*, and so on—is called *assembly language*. This type of language was heavily used during the 1940s and 1950s before higher-level programming languages like FORTRAN, PL/I, and Pascal were available. Each instruction in assembly language can be directly translated into a binary code, the *machine language*, denoted in this chapter by instructions surrounded by asterisks. The machine language instructions can be loaded into the IR register and executed, as explained here and in chapter 7.

**Exercises**

1. Explain what function the following program computes:

```
     IN   AX
     COPY M1,AX
     SUB  AX,M1
     CMP  AX,M1
     JB   LAB1
     OUT  AX
     JMP  LAB2
LAB1 COPY AX,M1
     DIV  AX,M1
     OUT  AX
LAB2 END
```

2. Write an assembly language program that reads two integers and prints the larger one.

3. Write an assembly language program that reads two integers—a small integer followed by a larger one. Then it prints all the integers between but not including them.

4. A programmer noticed that a machine was running more slowly each day and wondered why. Furthermore, it acted erratically from time to time. She studied the code running in the machine, and after considerable effort, found the following code that she could identify as being of unknown origin:

```
V1       JMP   BEGIN
ZERO     0
ONE      1
TEN      10
FIFTY    50
LENGTH   33
COUNT    0
N1       0
BEGIN    COPY  AX,RANDOM
         COPY  N1,AX
         DIV   AX,TEN
         MUL   AX,TEN
         SUB   AX,N1
         CMP   AX,ZERO
         JB    EXIT
         COPY  AX,ZERO
         COPY  COUNT,AX
LOOP1    COPY  CX,RANDOM
         COPY  AX,COUNT
         CMP   AX,FIFTY
         JNB   EXIT
         COPY  BX,ZERO
LOOP2    CMP   BX,LENGTH
         JNB   NEXT
         COPY  AX,V1+c(BX)
         COPY  c(CX),AX
         ADD   BX,ONE
         ADD   CX,ONE
         JMP   LOOP2
NEXT     COPY  AX,COUNT
         ADD   AX,ONE
         COPY  COUNT,AX
         JMP   LOOP1
EXIT
```

In fact, the programmer had found a computer virus, and your job is to analyze it to discover how it works. This is a program that might be inserted into a computer system by an unfriendly person. It sits quietly in the middle of any program that it is inserted into until the right moment. Then it springs into action and duplicates itself many times around the machine memory.

Can you answer the following questions about the virus: How does it make the decision to go into action? How does it hide when it is not doing anything? What mechanism does it use to duplicate itself? How many times does it duplicate itself? Why does the virus make the machine seem to slow down? Why does it cause the system to act erratically sometimes? What should the programmer do to get rid of this virus? What problem does this virus have in carrying out its destructive job, and how can it be changed so that it can more discreetly sneak around in the machine undetected?

The virus uses some features of the P88 machine not discussed before. It references a location called *RANDOM*, which contains a random number. Every time that location is referenced, it gives a different random number. Two additional registers are assumed: they are called *BX* and *CX*. The notation *c(CX)* refers to the memory location with the address equal to the number in *CX*. Thus, if register *CX* contains 100, then *COPY c(CX),AX* will put the contents of *AX* into location 100 in memory. The expression *V1 + c(BX)* refers to the memory location found by starting at location *V1* at the beginning of the program and counting *BX* locations beyond it.

Note: This virus would not be dangerous in a typical modern computer because such machines usually have memory protection mechanisms that would quickly stop it. A successful virus that runs on contemporary machines will also need a scheme to trick the protection system, an issue not discussed here.

---

## Summary (B)

This chapter describes the classic architecture of most digital computers. They have a CPU that runs the fetch-execute cycle on sequences of instructions, and these instructions are stored in memory with the data of the computation. This is called the *von Neumann* architecture, and the only common deviations from it are the parallel machines that will be described in chapter 13.

This chapter completes another link in the chain of concepts required to understand how computers work. At the lowest level are the transistors, the valves that control electric current flow. Above them are the electric circuits, which we can design to compute functions and store information. Such circuits can be organized to do useful tasks, such as add numbers or manipulate characters. Binary-coded machine language instructions are used to activate the appropriate computational circuits, and such instructions are sequenced through the instruction register (IR) in order to do a nontrivial calculation. The binary-coded machine instructions are actually translations of symbolic assembly-language instructions, which are much more convenient for humans to read. This assembly language, its binary-coded form, and its execution on a machine have been the topic of this chapter.

The final and highest level set of concepts in the chain relates to the translation of a high-level language such as Pascal into assembly language and will be the topic of the next chapter.

Looking at this chain from the top, we can trace the processing of a Pascal statement from its entry into the computer to the detailed switching of electrical currents. Consider, for example, the statement

```
Z := (X + Y)
```

It is translated into assembly language and then into machine language. These instructions are sequenced through the instruction register. *X* is brought in from memory, *Y* is added to it, and the result is placed in *Z*. (All this is illustrated in "This-is-how-a-computer-works.")

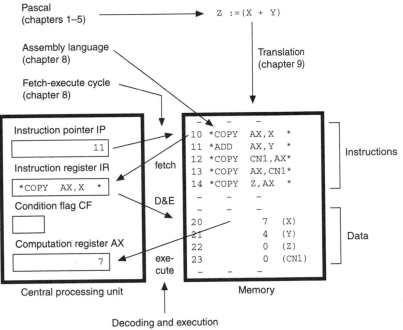

# 9    Language Translation

## Enabling the Computer to Understand Pascal (A)

The primary vehicle for communication is language, which is the chief characteristic that differentiates humans from other animals. A multiplicity of languages has developed over the millennia; the advent of computers has brought many more. But most languages have no meaning to us unless we can translate them into familiar terms. So translation is a process of great importance to people and machines. We wish to understand and use many languages, and the process of translation can give us access to them.

Computer scientists have developed a powerful techology for language translation. This chapter will introduce a general technique applicable to many translation problems, and will thus familiarize you with another "great idea" of the field. The methodology has been quite successful on computer languages and can also handle subsets of natural languages, as you will see in chapter 15.

Our concern here is the translation of a higher level programming language, like Pascal, into a lower level language, assembly language or machine language. Machines cannot process higher level languages but they do process machine language or, with the help of a simple translator, assembly language. For example, we ask how the Pascal statement

```
Z := (X + Y)
```

can be translated into an equivalent assembly language program such as

```
COPY AX,X
ADD  AX,Y
COPY CN1,AX
COPY AX,CN1
COPY Z,AX
```

If we can understand the mechanisms that do this translation, we will understand the fundamental processes of translation in almost any domain. (Note: The assembly language translation shown here is not of minimal length, and you can probably find a shorter program to do the same job. Automatic translators can produce correct translations, but they do not always produce optimum ones, as will be the case for the translator of this chapter.)

This chapter will introduce fundamental ideas in the theory of languages and translation. It will show how to assemble these ideas to build a translator for a small part of Pascal and will give many examples of translation. (Again, you can see an animated view of all the steps described here if you use the "This-is-how-a-computer works" program.)

## Syntactic Production Rules (B)

Language is embodied in sequences of symbols. In order to understand language, we must have a mathematics for sequences of symbols. This mathematics will show how to generate and analyze such sequences and will supply the necessary mechanisms for doing translation.

The first idea is that of the *production rule*. Such rules were introduced in the last section of chapter 1, and additional rules were added in later chapters to describe Pascal syntax. These rules will be discussed in more detail here and will provide the basis for our translation mechanisms. Conceptually, a production rule changes a given object or set of objects into something else—a different object or set of objects. An example of a production rule from chapter 1 is

```
<identifier> ==> a sequence of letters and/or digits that begins with a
                 letter
```

which will be written in a modified form here as

```
R1: <i>ⱼ ==> a sequence of letters and/or digits that begins with a
              letter
```

We will call this rule R1, and it means "change $\langle i \rangle_j$ into a sequence of letters and/or digits that begins with a letter." The term $\langle identifier \rangle$ from previous chapters has been shortened to $\langle i \rangle$ and given a subscript $j$. Each time R1 is used, $j$ will have a specific value, and a specific alphabetic string will be used on the right-hand side of the rule. An example *instantiation* of R1 is

```
<i>₇ ==> HEIGHT
```

which means "change $\langle i \rangle_7$ into HEIGHT."

We can now *apply* this version of R1 to change this string:

```
(<i>₇ + <i>₁₉)
```

The rule $\langle i \rangle_7 ==>$ HEIGHT says that $\langle i \rangle_7$ can be changed to HEIGHT so the result will be

```
(HEIGHT + <i>₁₉)
```

Since the form $(\langle i \rangle_7 + \langle i \rangle_{19})$ has been changed to (HEIGHT + $\langle i \rangle_{19}$), we can write

```
(<i>₇ + <i>₁₉) ==> (HEIGHT + <i>₁₉)
```

The $\langle i \rangle_7$ in the first form has been replaced by HEIGHT, as shown in the second form. If we wish to apply R1 again, we can use the following instantiation

```
<i>₁₉ ==> INC
```

to obtain

```
(HEIGHT + <i>₁₉) ==> (HEIGHT + INC)
```

In these rules, $\langle i \rangle_j$ stands for "identifier name," and the string of symbols generated by $\langle i \rangle_j$ will be an identifier name.

Since it may also be desirable to apply rules to other things besides $\langle i \rangle_j$'s, R2 is another useful rule; it enables us to convert $\langle e \rangle_i$ into $\langle i \rangle_j$:

```
R2: <e>ᵢ ==><i>ⱼ
```

For example, using the version $\langle e \rangle_3 ==> \langle i \rangle_7$ plus the R1 rule given above, we have

```
<e>₃ ==> <i>₇ ==> HEIGHT
```

The asterisk * is used to indicate that any number of rule applications has occurred. Thus, the above two-step derivation could be written

```
<e>₃ =*=> HEIGHT
```

In these rules, $\langle e \rangle_i$ stands for "expression" or "arithmetic expression," as defined in previous chapters. (For example, $(X + Y)$ is an arithmetic expression.)

None of this looks like it has much to do with Pascal. But rule R3 introduces a familiar construction, the assignment statement:

```
R3: <s>ₖ ==> <i>ⱼ := <e>ᵢ
```

This rule says that $\langle s \rangle_k$ can be replaced by "$\langle i \rangle_j := \langle e \rangle_i$." But the real meaning of the rule is that a legal statement $\langle s \rangle_k$ in Pascal is the sequence of symbols "$\langle i \rangle_j := \langle e \rangle_i$" where $\langle i \rangle_j$ is an identifier name and $\langle e \rangle_i$ is an arithmetic expression. Using the combination of rules R1 to R3, we can generate legal assignment statements. As an illustration, consider the generation of the Pascal statement

```
X := Y
```

| Derivation | Rules |
|---|---|
| $\langle s \rangle_1$ | R3: $\langle s \rangle_1 \Longrightarrow \langle i \rangle_2 := \langle e \rangle_3$ |
| $\langle i \rangle_2 := \langle e \rangle_3$ | R1: $\langle i \rangle_2 \Longrightarrow X$ |
| X := $\langle e \rangle_3$ | R2: $\langle e \rangle_3 \Longrightarrow \langle i \rangle_4$ |
| X := $\langle i \rangle_4$ | R1: $\langle i \rangle_4 \Longrightarrow Y$ |
| X := Y | |

In this derivation, we begin with $\langle s \rangle_1$, which means we wish to generate a statement in Pascal. Then we use a case of rule R3 to convert $\langle s \rangle_1$ to something else, namely "$\langle i \rangle_2 := \langle e \rangle_3$." The conversion is done with the rule $\langle s \rangle_1 \Longrightarrow \langle i \rangle_2 := \langle e \rangle_3$. Next, we wish to change the $\langle i \rangle_2$ to $X$, and this is done with R1 of the form $\langle i \rangle_2 \Longrightarrow X$. The result of this change appears on the third line of the derivation: $X := \langle e \rangle_3$. Finally, rule R2 is used to convert $\langle e \rangle_3$ to $\langle i \rangle_4$, and rule R1 is used to convert $\langle i \rangle_4$ to $Y$.

Two more rules, R4 and R5, will make it possible to handle more complex arithmetic expressions:

```
R4: <e>ᵢ ==> ( <e>ⱼ + <e>ₖ)
R5: <e>ᵢ ==> ( <e>ⱼ * <e>ₖ)
```

This set of five rules, which makes up a *grammar* for some assignment statements in Pascal, will provide many interesting examples for this chapter. Here are a few sample derivations:

| Derivation | Rules |
|---|---|
| $\langle s \rangle_1$ | R3: $\langle s \rangle_1 \Longrightarrow \langle i \rangle_2 := \langle e \rangle_3$ |
| $\langle i \rangle_2 := \langle e \rangle_3$ | R1: $\langle i \rangle_2 \Longrightarrow Y$ |
| Y := $\langle e \rangle_3$ | R4: $\langle e \rangle_3 \Longrightarrow ( \langle e \rangle_4 + \langle e \rangle_5)$ |
| Y := ( $\langle e \rangle_4$ + $\langle e \rangle_5$) | R2: $\langle e \rangle_4 \Longrightarrow \langle i \rangle_6$ |
| Y := ( $\langle i \rangle_6$ + $\langle e \rangle_5$) | R1: $\langle i \rangle_6 \Longrightarrow XX$ |
| Y := (XX + $\langle e \rangle_5$) | R2: $\langle e \rangle_5 \Longrightarrow \langle i \rangle_7$ |
| Y := (XX + $\langle i \rangle_7$) | R1: $\langle i \rangle_7 \Longrightarrow YY$ |
| Y := (XX + YY) | |

The following shows the generation of a more deeply nested arithmetic expression:

| Derivation | Rules |
|---|---|
| $\langle s \rangle_1$ | R3: $\langle s \rangle_1 ==> \langle i \rangle_2 := \langle e \rangle_3$ |
| $\langle i \rangle_2 := \langle e \rangle_3$ | R1: $\langle i \rangle_2 ==> $ SUM |
| SUM $:= \langle e \rangle_3$ | R4: $\langle e \rangle_3 ==> (\langle e \rangle_4 + \langle e \rangle_5)$ |
| SUM $:= (\langle e \rangle_4 + \langle e \rangle_5)$ | R5: $\langle e \rangle_4 ==> (\langle e \rangle_7 * \langle e \rangle_8)$ |
| SUM $:= ((\langle e \rangle_7 * \langle e \rangle_8) + \langle e \rangle_5)$ | R2: $\langle e \rangle_7 ==> \langle i \rangle_9$ |
| SUM $:= ((\langle i \rangle_9 * \langle e \rangle_8) + \langle e \rangle_5)$ | R1: $\langle i \rangle_9 ==> $ X |
| SUM $:= ((X * \langle e \rangle_8) + \langle e \rangle_5)$ | R2: $\langle e \rangle_8 ==> \langle i \rangle_{10}$ |
| SUM $:= ((X * \langle i \rangle_{10}) + \langle e \rangle_5)$ | R1: $\langle i \rangle_{10} ==> $ C |
| SUM $:= ((X * C) + \langle e \rangle_5)$ | R2: $\langle e \rangle_5 ==> \langle i \rangle_{11}$ |
| SUM $:= ((X * C) + \langle i \rangle_{11})$ | R1: $\langle i \rangle_{11} ==> $ SUM |
| SUM $:= ((X * C) + $ SUM$)$ | |

Of course, any nesting of multiplication and addition can be generated in the arithmetic expressions:

$\langle s \rangle_1 =*=> $ Y $:= ((XX * YY) + (XY * (YX + XXX)))$

The question of how the indexes are determined arises in all these derivations. For example, if we have the string

X $:= (Y + \langle e \rangle_6)$

and wish to apply the rule $\langle e \rangle_i ==> (\langle e \rangle_j + \langle e \rangle_k)$, what method should we use to determine $i$, $j$, and $k$? The answer is that the index on the left-hand side is determined by the symbol to be replaced. For example, the symbol $\langle e \rangle_6$ is to be replaced in the statement, so the left side of the rule must be $\langle e \rangle_6$: $\langle e \rangle_6 ==> (\langle e \rangle_j + \langle e \rangle_k)$. The indexes on the right-hand side can be anything, as long as they are different from any indexes used previously in this derivation. Suppose that 8 and 9 have not been used. Then we can set $j = 8$ and $k = 9$ to obtain the form $\langle e \rangle_6 ==> (\langle e \rangle_8 + \langle e \rangle_9)$. When we apply this rule, the result is

X $:= (Y + (\langle e \rangle_8 + \langle e \rangle_9))$

To summarize the process for setting the indexes, we will repeat the above example. Suppose we wish to modify this:

X $:= (Y + \langle e \rangle_6)$

And we wish to use this rule:

$$\langle e \rangle_i \implies (\langle e \rangle_j + \langle e \rangle_k)$$

Then we set the index on the left-hand side of the rule to make it match the item to be replaced:

$$\langle e \rangle_6 \implies (\langle e \rangle_j + \langle e \rangle_k)$$

But the rule is not ready until all its indexes are set. Let us put any numbers we want into the other slots, $j$ and $k$, say 8 and 9. (We must be sure that 8 and 9 have not been previously used as indexes.)

$$\langle e \rangle_6 \implies (\langle e \rangle_8 + \langle e \rangle_9)$$

Now let us apply the rule to the original form $X := (Y + \langle e \rangle_6)$.

$$X := (Y + (\langle e \rangle_8 + \langle e \rangle_9))$$

Once a grammar has been established for a language (or, as in our case, part of a language), the grammar can be used for either *generation* of the language or *analysis* (or understanding) of it. The above examples illustrate generation; a person wanting to "say something" in Pascal begins with the decision to "say" a statement and then generates the thing to be said.

$$\langle s \rangle_1 \implies \langle i \rangle_2 := \langle e \rangle_3 \implies X := \langle e \rangle_3 \implies \ \ldots \ \implies X := (Y * X)$$

Each application of a rule further specifies what is to be said until the statement is completely defined. But the rules can also be applied in reverse to analyze (or understand) a statement. Thus, given

$$X := (Y * X),$$

we can use R1 to discover where the identifiers are:

$$\langle i \rangle_1 := (\langle i \rangle_2 * \langle i \rangle_3)$$

Then rules R2 and R4 uncover the structure of the right-hand side:

$$\langle i \rangle_1 := \langle e \rangle_4$$

Finally, R3 tells us that a complete statement has been made:

$$\langle s \rangle_0$$

So the same rules that were used in generation can be used backward to disassemble, analyze, and understand a Pascal statement.

Analogous processes probably account for the human's processing of English. Presumably humans have something like a grammar in their brains and generation proceeds by applying the rules to create well-formed utterances. A person might decide to assert a declarative sentence

(declarative sentence)

and a grammar could indicate that such sentences have subjects and predicates:

(subject) (predicate)

Further rules could enable these symbols to be replaced by actual words:

The boy went to town.

Understanding would involve the reverse process, finding the parts of speech of the spoken words, finding how they assemble to become sentence constituents such as subjects and predicates, and ultimately, finding the structure of the complete sentence. This is discussed further in chapter 15.

This section has addressed the issue of the *syntax* of language. We have examined mechanisms for generating and analyzing the strings of symbols that make up language. The next section concerns itself with the *semantics* of language. There we will study the concept of "meaning" and show how meaning is associated with the syntactic strings of symbols.

**Exercises**

1. Apply the following rules to $\langle s \rangle_1$ to generate strings of symbols:
    (a) Rules R3, R1, R2, R1.
    (b) Rules R3, R1, R5, R2, R1, R2, R1.
    (c) Rules R3, R1, R4, R2, R1, R5, R2, R1, R2, R1.

2. Use rules R1 through R5 to generate each of the following strings of symbols, starting from $\langle i \rangle_1$ or $\langle s \rangle_1$:
    (a) YXY
    (b) JACK
    (c) X := Y
    (d) X := (X * X)
    (e) YYY := (Y * (X + X))
    (f) XX := ((X + XX) * Y)
    (g) X := ((Y * Y) + (X * X))

3. What new rules are needed to generate the following statement?

```
SUM := FACT - X
```

Use your new rules to show the complete generation of this statement.

4. Build a grammar that can generate the following sentences:

The boy knows the girl.
This girl knows that boy.
That boy knows this boy.
Jack knows that boy.
Jill knows Jack.
Jack knows Jill.
etc.

---

## Attaching Semantics to the Rules (B)

The *meaning* of a language entity is a knowledge structure that the users of the language associate with that entity. An example language is English and an example language entity is "John ran to the red house." Its meaning might be a picture that forms in your mind showing John running toward a house that is colored red. Another example of a language is the set of binary numbers and an example member of the language is 101. We could decide that we will take the meaning of each binary number to be its decimal equivalent. Thus the meaning of the string 101 would be 5. The *semantics* of a language refers to the mechanisms that attach meaning to the language entities and to the meanings of those entities.

The language being translated will be called the *source language*, and the language it will be translated into will be called the *object language*. The source language is presumably not usable by the recipient while the object language is. In this section we consider the binary numbers a source language and show how to translate them into decimal numbers, the object language.

We will begin our study of language meaning by studying the semantics of binary numbers. First, let us create a set of rules for generating binary numbers. Here they are:

```
P1: <s>_i ==> <s>_j 0
P2: <s>_i ==> <s>_j 1
P3: <s>_i ==> 0
P4: <s>_i ==> 1
```

We can use these rules to generate any binary number. Here is how you generate 101:

| Derivation | Rules |
|---|---|
| $\langle s \rangle_1$ | P2: $\langle s \rangle_1 \implies \langle s \rangle_2 1$ |
| $\langle s \rangle_2 1$ | P1: $\langle s \rangle_2 \implies \langle s \rangle_3 0$ |
| $\langle s \rangle_3$ 01 | P4: $\langle s \rangle_3 \implies 1$ |
| 101 | |

Begin with $\langle s \rangle_1$ and apply rule P2 to create a 1 on the right end of the string. Then rule P1 creates the 0, and P4 completes the derivation of 101. (All this is a review of the familiar rule mechanism.)

We will now add a semantic part to rules P1 through P4:

| Syntax | Semantics |
|---|---|
| P1: $\langle s \rangle_i \implies \langle s \rangle_j 0$ | $M(\langle s \rangle_i) = M(\langle s \rangle_j) * 2$ |
| P2: $\langle s \rangle_i \implies \langle s \rangle_j 1$ | $M(\langle s \rangle_i) = M(\langle s \rangle_j) * 2 + 1$ |
| P3: $\langle s \rangle_i \implies 0$ | $M(\langle s \rangle_i) = 0$ |
| P4: $\langle s \rangle_i \implies 1$ | $M(\langle s \rangle_i) = 1$ |

Each production rule now has two parts, the syntactic part and the semantic part. The notation $M$ stands for the concept of "meaning," so the semantic part of rule P1 should be read as "the meaning of $\langle s \rangle_i$ is equal to the meaning of $\langle s \rangle_j$ times 2." The other semantic parts can be read the same way. Our next task is to find out how to use this semantic part.

The function of the semantics mechanism can be seen by examining the derivation of the string 101 and its meaning, 5. Here is the derivation from above with the addition of the semantic parts of the rules:

| Derivation | Rules | |
|---|---|---|
| | **Syntax** | **Semantics** |
| $\langle s \rangle_1$ | P2: $\langle s \rangle_1 \implies \langle s \rangle_2 1$ | $M(\langle s \rangle_1) = M(\langle s \rangle_2) * 2 + 1$ |
| $\langle s \rangle_2$ 1 | P1: $\langle s \rangle_2 \implies \langle s \rangle_3 0$ | $M(\langle s \rangle_2) = M(\langle s \rangle_3) * 2$ |
| $\langle s \rangle_3$ 01 | P4: $\langle s \rangle_3 \implies 1$ | $M(\langle s \rangle_3) = 1$ |
| 101 | | |

This is simply a copy of an earlier table with the semantics parts of the rules added according to the definitions given above. Now we will recopy this table, but after every line we will write the current version of the meaning using all the semantics information up to that point.

| Derivation | Rules | |
|---|---|---|
| | **Syntax** | **Semantics** |
| $\langle s \rangle_1$ | P2: $\langle s \rangle_1$ ==> $\langle s \rangle_2 1$ | $M(\langle s \rangle_1) = M(\langle s \rangle_2) * 2 + 1$ |

Using the entry from the line above, we write that the first approximation to the meaning is $M(\langle s \rangle_1) = M(\langle s \rangle_2) * 2 + 1$.

MEANING FOUND: $M(\langle s \rangle_1) = M(\langle s \rangle_2) * 2 + 1$

But this expression for meaning has the unknown quantity $M(\langle s \rangle_2)$. The next entry in the table will help us.

$\langle s \rangle_2 1$        P1: $\langle s \rangle_2$ ==> $\langle s \rangle_3 0$      $M(\langle s \rangle_2) = M(\langle s \rangle_3) * 2$

We used the semantics from rule P1 to tell us the value of $M(\langle s \rangle_2)$ and we can now substitute that value into MEANING FOUND: $M(\langle s \rangle_3) * 2$.

MEANING FOUND: $M(\langle s \rangle_1) = (M(\langle s \rangle_3) * 2) * 2 + 1$

But this expression for meaning has the unknown $M(\langle s \rangle_3)$ in it. The next line of the table will help with that.

$\langle s \rangle_3 01$        P4: $\langle s \rangle_3$ ==> $1$          $M(\langle s \rangle_3) = 1$

Let us substitute the value of $M(\langle s \rangle_3)$ into the MEANING FOUND expression: $M(\langle s \rangle_3) = 1$.

MEANING FOUND: $M(\langle s \rangle_1) = (1 * 2) * 2 + 1 = 5$

This completes the computation of the meaning of 101. The meaning is $M(\langle s \rangle_1) = 5$.

The following table with the MEANING FOUND entries shows every step of the computation that produced the meaning value. You should study this table until you are sure you understand every step.

| Derivation | Rules | |
|---|---|---|
| | **Syntax** | **Semantics** |
| $\langle s \rangle_1$ | P2: $\langle s \rangle_1$ ==> $\langle s \rangle_2 1$ | $M(\langle s \rangle_1) = M(\langle s \rangle_2) * 2 + 1$ |
| | MEANING FOUND: $M(\langle s \rangle_1) = M(\langle s \rangle_2) * 2 + 1$ | |
| $\langle s \rangle_2 1$ | P1: $\langle s \rangle_2$ ==> $\langle s \rangle_3 0$ | $M(\langle s \rangle_2) = M(\langle s \rangle_3) * 2$ |
| | MEANING FOUND: $M(\langle s \rangle_1) = (M(\langle s \rangle_3) * 2) * 2 + 1$ | |
| $\langle s \rangle_3 01$ | P4: $\langle s \rangle_3$ ==> $1$ | $M(\langle s \rangle_3) = 1$ |
| | MEANING FOUND: $M(\langle s \rangle_1) = (1 * 2) * 2 + 1 = 5$ | |
| 101 | | |

In conclusion, we have gone through all the details of finding the meaning for a language entity like 101. First, we found a sequence of syntactic rules that start with $\langle s \rangle_1$ and generate 101. Then we used the semantic parts of those rules to create the meaning $M(\langle s \rangle_1)$.

**Exercises**

1. Use the syntactic parts of the rules P1 through P4 to find a generation of the string 1011. Now add the semantic parts of the rules and use them to compute the meaning (the decimal equivalent) of the original string.

2. Repeat problem 1 for the binary strings 10111 and 00111.

3. Explain the construction of the semantic parts of rules P1 and P2, and tell exactly why they compute the correct value for $M(\langle s \rangle_i)$.

---

## The Semantics of Pascal (B)

The previous section showed how to attach semantics to rules and how to use those semantic parts to compute a meaning for a language utterance. Now it is time to use these ideas on the problem of central importance here, the translation of Pascal into a language that the machine can understand, P88 assembly language or, ultimately, the binary-coded machine language.

The symbols $\langle i \rangle_j$, $\langle e \rangle_j$, and $\langle s \rangle_j$ on the left sides of the grammar rules R1 to R5 discussed earlier in this chapter are called *grammar variables*, and the grammar semantics will assign meaning to them. We will now add semantic parts to each of these rules in the same manner as in the previous section. The result will be a translator for the class of Pascal statements that they represent.

What should be the meaning associated with the simplest rule, R1?

```
R1: <i>j ==> a sequence of letters and/or digits that begins with a
            letter
```

That is, if a variable is called $X$ in the source language, what name should it have in the object language? Let us make things as easy as possible and let the variable have the same name in both languages:

```
R1: <i>j ==> w     M(<i>j) = w
```

where $w$ is some identifier string. Thus, we might have the following instantiation of R1:

```
<i>9 ==> HEIGHT     M(<i>9)= HEIGHT
```

Next we consider the semantics associated with R2. The left-hand variable, $\langle e \rangle_i$, has two parts to its meaning representation, $M(\langle e \rangle_i)$ and $code(\langle e \rangle_i)$. Intuitively, the arithmetic expression $\langle e \rangle_i$ will have a name $M(\langle e \rangle_i)$ and some lines of assembly language code, $code(\langle e \rangle_i)$:

```
R2: <e>_i ==> <i>_j     M(<e>_i) = M(<i>_j)
                        code (<e>_i) = nothing
```

For example, if $\langle e \rangle_1 = * \Rightarrow \text{HEIGHT}$, then $M(\langle e \rangle_1) = \text{HEIGHT}$ and $code(\langle e \rangle_1)$ is a list of instructions (code) of length zero.

Rule R3 provides the first interesting semantics. If $\langle s \rangle_k$ generates a Pascal statement, then $code(\langle s \rangle_k)$ will give its translation in terms of P88 assembly language.

```
R3: <s>_k ==> <i>_j := <e>_i     code (<s>_k) = code (<e>_i)
                                              COPY AX,M(<e>_i)
                                              COPY M(<i>_j),AX
```

Thus, $code(\langle s \rangle_k)$ is the list of all instructions in $code(\langle e \rangle_i)$ followed by the two COPY instructions shown. This says that the code for $\langle s \rangle_k$ should first compute the value of $\langle e \rangle_i$, then copy the result of that calculation into AX and then into the location for $\langle i \rangle_j$.

Notice that this chapter follows a particular notational convention. Fragments of code are typed as similarly indented sequential lines of programming. Such fragments should be regarded as units even though they are spread across several lines. In the above definition, $code(\langle s \rangle_k)$ is defined as

```
code (<s>_k) = code (<e>_i)
                 COPY AX,M(<e>_i)
                 COPY M(<i>_j),AX
```

The convention requires that the three lines of code

```
code (<e>_i)
COPY AX,M(<e>_i)
COPY M(<i>_j),AX
```

be considered as a single unit. Thus, the definition states that $code(\langle s \rangle_k)$ is the three lines of code given, not just the single line $code(\langle e \rangle_i)$. This convention is followed throughout this chapter.

To illustrate the use of the rules R1 to R3 with their semantic components, let us do a complete translation of the statement

```
X := Y
```

into assembly language. From the previous section, it is clear that the sequence of rules R3, R1, R2, R1 is sufficient to derive the source statement. So we write down the derivation that will determine the semantic rules required to find the translation. This derivation is identical to the one carried out in that earlier section except that the semantic portion of each rule is written down beside the syntactic portion.

| Derivation | | Rules |
|---|---|---|
| $\langle s \rangle_1$ | R3: $\langle s \rangle_1 ==> \langle i \rangle_2 := \langle e \rangle_3$ | code($\langle s \rangle_1$) = code($\langle e \rangle_3$) |
| | | COPY AX,M($\langle e \rangle_3$) |
| | | COPY M($\langle i \rangle_2$),AX |
| $\langle i \rangle_2 := \langle e \rangle_3$ | R1: $\langle i \rangle_2 ==> X$ | M($\langle i \rangle_2$) = X |
| X := $\langle e \rangle_3$ | R2: $\langle e \rangle_3 ==> \langle i \rangle_4$ | M($\langle e \rangle_3$) = M($\langle i \rangle_4$) |
| | | code($\langle e \rangle_3$) = *nothing* |
| X := $\langle i \rangle_4$ | R1: $\langle i \rangle_4 ==> Y$ | M($\langle i \rangle_4$) = Y |
| X := Y | | |

The first two columns in this table are taken from the previous section on syntax. The third column is new; it gives the semantic portion of each of the rules used. Now we want to rewrite this table and add the MEANING FOUND entries as before.

| Derivation | | Rules |
|---|---|---|
| $\langle s \rangle_1$ | R3: $\langle s \rangle_1 ==> \langle i \rangle_2 := \langle e \rangle_3$ | code($\langle s \rangle_1$) = code($\langle e \rangle_3$) |
| | | COPY AX,M($\langle e \rangle_3$) |
| | | COPY M($\langle i \rangle_2$),AX |

The beginning of our discovery of meaning involves simply copying the value for code($\langle s \rangle_1$):

MEANING FOUND:   code($\langle s \rangle_1$) = code($\langle e \rangle_3$)
                           COPY AX,M($\langle e \rangle_3$)
                           COPY M($\langle i \rangle_2$),AX

This is a good start, but we wonder what the value of M($\langle i \rangle_2$) will be. The answer is given by the next row of the table, M($\langle i \rangle_2$) = X:

$\langle i \rangle_2 := \langle e \rangle_3$     R1: $\langle i \rangle_2 ==> X$                M($\langle i \rangle_2$) = X

Now we can make that substitution into the MEANING FOUND entry:

MEANING FOUND:   code($\langle s \rangle_1$) = code($\langle e \rangle_3$)
                           COPY AX,M($\langle e \rangle_3$)
                           COPY X,AX

The next row will enable us to fill in values for two more entities in the MEANING FOUND, $M(\langle e \rangle_3)$ and code($\langle e \rangle_3$):

```
X := <e>3        R2: <e>3 ==> <i>4        M(<e>3) = M(<i>4)
                                          code(<e>3) = nothing
```

With those two substitutions, MEANING FOUND becomes

**MEANING FOUND:**  `code(<s>1) = COPY AX,M(<i>4)`
                     `          COPY X,AX`

We still have to complete the evaluation of $M(\langle i \rangle_4)$, which the next row in the table makes possible.

```
X := <i>4        R1: <i>4 ==> Y           M(<i>4) = Y
```

**MEANING FOUND:**  `code(<s>1) = COPY AX,Y`
                     `          COPY X,AX`

The translation rules thus assert that the meaning of $X := Y$ in Pascal is

```
COPY AX,Y
COPY X,AX
```

in P88 assembly language. The Pascal statement says: "Find the value in $Y$ and put it into $X$." The translation says the same thing in P88 assembly language: "Copy $Y$ into $AX$ and then copy $AX$ into $X$." This example is worth careful study because it demonstrates the essential mechanisms of the translator without undue complexity.

In summary, the input to the translation process was the following:

Translation input:

```
X := Y
```

Rules R1, R2, and R3 were applied and resulted in the following semantic relationships (column 3 in the syntax-semantics table):

Semantic Rules:

```
code(<s>1) = code(<e>3)
             COPY AX,M(<e>3)
             COPY M(<i>2),AX
M(<i>2) = X
M(<e>3) = M(<i>4)
code(<e>3) = nothing
M(<i>4) = Y
```

Finally, $code(\langle s \rangle_1)$ was evaluated using these rules:

Translation output:

```
COPY AX,Y
COPY X,AX
```

More interesting translations will be possible only if a semantics is available for our last two rules, R4 and R5.

```
R4: <e>ᵢ ==> (<e>ⱼ + <e>ₖ)    M(<e>ᵢ) = createname
                               code(<e>ᵢ) = code (<e>ⱼ)
                                            code (<e>ₖ)
                                            COPY AX,M(<e>ⱼ)
                                            ADD AX,M(<e>ₖ)
                                            COPY M(<e>ᵢ),AX
R5: <e>ᵢ ==> (<e>ⱼ * <e>ₖ)    M(<e>ᵢ) = createname
                               code(<e>ᵢ) = code (<e>ⱼ)
                                            code (<e>ₖ)
                                            COPY AX,M(<e>ⱼ)
                                            MUL AX,M(<e>ₖ)
                                            COPY M(<e>ᵢ),AX
```

These semantic rules use the function *createname* to create a name that has not been used elsewhere. Thus, if one encounters $M(\langle e \rangle_7) = createname$, the system might create the name *CN1* and assign it $M(\langle e \rangle_7) = CN1$. If later one encounters, say, $M(\langle e \rangle_9) = createname$, the result might be $M(\langle e \rangle_9) = CN2$.

Examining the code semantics for the addition rule R4, we can see that the code segments for $\langle e \rangle_j$ and $\langle e \rangle_k$ are expanded to determine the value of these arithmetic expressions. Then the results are added into the register *AX* by two P88 instructions and stored away to be used by a later calculation. An analogous thing happens with the rule R5.

The use of these rules is demonstrated in the following two derivations. The first is the translation of

```
Z := (X + Y)
```

| Derivation | Rules |
|---|---|

$\langle s\rangle_1$      R3: $\langle s\rangle_1$ ==> $\langle i\rangle_2$ := $\langle e\rangle_3$     code $(\langle s\rangle_1)$=code$(\langle e\rangle_3)$

```
                                            COPY AX,M(<e>₃)
                                            COPY M(<i>₂),AX
```

**MEANING FOUND:**   code $(\langle s\rangle_1)$=code$(\langle e\rangle_3)$

```
                           COPY AX,M(<e>₃)
                           COPY M(<i>₂),AX
```

$\langle i\rangle_2$ := $\langle e\rangle_3$      R1: $\langle i\rangle_2$ ==> Z        $M(\langle i\rangle_2)$ = Z

**MEANING FOUND:**   code $(\langle s\rangle_1)$=code$(\langle e\rangle_3)$

```
                           COPY AX,M(<e>₃)
                           COPY Z,AX
```

Z := $\langle e\rangle_3$      R4: $\langle e\rangle_3$ ==> $(\langle e\rangle_4 + \langle e\rangle_5)$   $M(\langle e\rangle_3)$ = CN1

```
                                        code(<e>₃) = code (<e>₄)
                                                     code (<e>₅)
                                                     COPY AX,M(<e>₄)
                                                     ADD AX,M(<e>₅)
                                                     COPY M(<e>₃),AX
```

**MEANING FOUND:**   code $(\langle s\rangle_1)$=code $(\langle e\rangle_4)$

```
                           code (<e>₅)
                           COPY AX,M(<e>₄)
                           ADD AX,M(<e>₅)
                           COPY CN1,AX
                           COPY AX,CN1
                           COPY Z,AX
```

Z := $(\langle e\rangle_4 + \langle e\rangle_5)$    R2: $\langle e\rangle_4$ ==> $\langle i\rangle_6$       $M(\langle e\rangle_4)$ = $M(\langle i\rangle_6)$

```
                                        code(<e>₄) = nothing
```

**MEANING FOUND:**   code $(\langle s\rangle_1)$=code $(\langle e\rangle_5)$

```
                           COPY AX,M(<i>₆)
                           ADD AX,M(<e>₅)
                           COPY CN1,AX
                           COPY AX,CN1
                           COPY Z,AX
```

Z := $(\langle i\rangle_6 + \langle e\rangle_5)$    R1: $\langle i\rangle_6$ ==> X       $M(\langle i\rangle_6)$ = X

**MEANING FOUND:**   code $(\langle s\rangle_1)$=code $(\langle e\rangle_5)$

```
                           COPY AX,X
                           ADD AX,M(<e>₅)
                           COPY CN1,AX
                           COPY AX,CN1
                           COPY Z,AX
```

| Derivation | Rules | |
|---|---|---|
| Z := (X + $\langle e\rangle_5$) | R2: $\langle e\rangle_5$ ==> $\langle i\rangle_7$ | $M(\langle e\rangle_5) = M(\langle i\rangle_7)$ |
| | | code($\langle e\rangle_5$) = *nothing* |
| | **MEANING FOUND:** | code ($\langle s\rangle_1$)=COPY AX,X |
| | | ADD AX,M($\langle i\rangle_7$) |
| | | COPY CN1,AX |
| | | COPY AX,CN1 |
| | | COPY Z,AX |
| Z := (X + $\langle i\rangle_7$) | R1: $\langle i\rangle_7$ ==> Y | $M(\langle i\rangle_7) = Y$ |
| | **MEANING FOUND:** | code ($\langle s\rangle_1$)=COPY AX,X |
| | | ADD AX,Y |
| | | COPY CN1,AX |
| | | COPY AX,CN1 |
| | | COPY Z,AX |
| Z := (X + Y) | | |

This completes the translation of the original statement. The whole computation can be summarized as follows:

Translation Input:

```
Z := (X + Y)
```

Semantics rules:

(see syntax-semantics table)

Translation output:

```
COPY AX,X
ADD AX,Y
COPY CN1,AX
COPY AX,CN1
COPY Z,AX
```

The nonminimal code in this example, which is often produced by translators, can be optimized by numerous well-known techniques, but such studies are beyond the scope of this book.

Our last example demonstrates the translation of a more complicated arithmetic expression:

```
U1 := (X + (Y * Z))
```

| Derivation | Rules |
|---|---|
| $\langle s \rangle_1$ | R3: $\langle s \rangle_1 \implies \langle i \rangle_2 := \langle e \rangle_3$    code $(\langle s \rangle_1)$=code$(\langle e \rangle_3)$ |

code $(\langle s \rangle_1)$=code$(\langle e \rangle_3)$
    COPY AX,M$(\langle e \rangle_3)$
    COPY M$(\langle i \rangle_2)$,AX

**MEANING FOUND:** code $(\langle s \rangle_1)$ = code $(\langle e \rangle_3)$
    COPY AX,M$(\langle e \rangle_3)$
    COPY M$(\langle i \rangle_2)$,AX

$\langle i \rangle_2 := \langle e \rangle_3$    R1: $\langle i \rangle_2 \implies$ U1    M$(\langle i \rangle_2)$ = U1

**MEANING FOUND:** code $(\langle s \rangle_1)$ = code $(\langle e \rangle_3)$
    COPY AX,M$(\langle e \rangle_3)$
    COPY U1,AX

U1 := $\langle e \rangle_3$    R4: $\langle e \rangle_3 \implies (\langle e \rangle_4 + \langle e \rangle_5)$    M$(\langle e \rangle_3)$ = CN1
    code$(\langle e \rangle_3)$ = code $(\langle e \rangle_4)$
    code $(\langle e \rangle_5)$
    COPY AX,M$(\langle e \rangle_4)$
    ADD AX,M$(\langle e \rangle_5)$
    COPY M$(\langle e \rangle_3)$,AX

**MEANING FOUND:** code $(\langle s \rangle_1)$ = code $(\langle e \rangle_4)$
    code $(\langle e \rangle_5)$
    COPY AX,M$(\langle e \rangle_4)$
    ADD AX,M$(\langle e \rangle_5)$
    COPY CN1,AX
    COPY AX,CN1
    COPY U1,AX

U1 := $(\langle e \rangle_4 + \langle e \rangle_5)$    R2: $\langle e \rangle_4 \implies \langle i \rangle_6$    M$(\langle e \rangle_4)$ = M$(\langle i \rangle_6)$
    code$(\langle e \rangle_4)$ = *nothing*

**MEANING FOUND:** code $(\langle s \rangle_1)$ = code $(\langle e \rangle_5)$
    COPY AX,M$(\langle i \rangle_6)$
    ADD AX,M$(\langle e \rangle_5)$
    COPY CN1,AX
    COPY AX,CN1
    COPY U1,AX

U1 := $(\langle i \rangle_6 + \langle e \rangle_5)$    R1: $\langle i \rangle_6 \implies$ X    M$(\langle i \rangle_6)$ = X

**MEANING FOUND:** code $(\langle s \rangle_1)$ = code $(\langle e \rangle_5)$
    COPY AX,X
    ADD AX,M$(\langle e \rangle_5)$
    COPY CN1,AX
    COPY AX,CN1
    COPY U1,AX

| Derivation | Rules |
|---|---|
| U1 := (X + $\langle e\rangle_5$) | R5: $\langle e\rangle_5$ ==> ($\langle e\rangle_7$ * $\langle e\rangle_8$)    $M(\langle e\rangle_5)$ = CN2 |

$$code(\langle e\rangle_5) = code(\langle e\rangle_7)$$
$$code(\langle e\rangle_8)$$
$$\text{COPY AX,}M(\langle e\rangle_7)$$
$$\text{MUL AX,}M(\langle e\rangle_8)$$
$$\text{COPY CN2,AX}$$

**MEANING FOUND:**  code $(\langle s\rangle_1)$ = code($\langle e\rangle_7$)
code $(\langle e\rangle_8)$
COPY AX,$M(\langle e\rangle_7)$
MUL AX,$M(\langle e\rangle_8)$
COPY CN2,AX
COPY AX,X
ADD AX,CN2
COPY CN1,AX
COPY AX,CN1
COPY U1,AX

| Derivation | Rules |
|---|---|
| U1 := (X + ($\langle e\rangle_7$ * $\langle e\rangle_8$)) | R2: $\langle e\rangle_7$ ==> $\langle i\rangle_9$    $M(\langle e\rangle_7)$ = $M(\langle i\rangle_9)$ |

$$code(\langle e\rangle_7) = nothing$$

**MEANING FOUND:**  code $(\langle s\rangle_1)$ = code($\langle e\rangle_8$)
COPY AX,$M(\langle i\rangle_9)$
MUL AX,$M(\langle e\rangle_8)$
COPY CN2,AX
COPY AX,X
ADD AX,CN2
COPY CN1,AX
COPY AX,CN1
COPY U1,AX

| Derivation | Rules |
|---|---|
| U1 := (X + ($\langle i\rangle_9$ * $\langle e\rangle_8$)) | R1: $\langle i\rangle_9$ ==> Y    $M(\langle i\rangle_9)$ = Y |

**MEANING FOUND:**  code $(\langle s\rangle_1)$ = code($\langle e\rangle_8$)
COPY AX,Y
MUL AX,$M(\langle e\rangle_8)$
COPY CN2,AX
COPY AX,X
ADD AX,CN2
COPY CN1,AX
COPY AX,CN1
COPY U1,AX

| Derivation | Rules |
|---|---|
| U1 := (X + (Y * $\langle e\rangle_8$)) | R2: $\langle e\rangle_8$ ==> $\langle i\rangle_{10}$    $M(\langle e\rangle_8)$ = $M(\langle i\rangle_{10})$ |

$$code(\langle e\rangle_8) = nothing$$

| Derivation | Rules | |
|---|---|---|
| | **MEANING FOUND:** | code $(<s>_1)$ = COPY AX,Y |
| | | MUL AX,M$(<i>_{10})$ |
| | | COPY CN2,AX |
| | | COPY AX,X |
| | | ADD AX,CN2 |
| | | COPY CN1,AX |
| | | COPY AX,CN1 |
| | | COPY U1,AX |
| U1 := (X + (Y * $<i>_{10}$)) | R1: $<i>_{10}$ ==> Z | M$(<i>_{10})$ = Z |
| | **MEANING FOUND:** | code $(<s>_1)$ = COPY AX,Y |
| | | MUL AX,Z |
| | | COPY CN2,AX |
| | | COPY AX,X |
| | | ADD AX,CN2 |
| | | COPY CN1,AX |
| | | COPY AX,CN1 |
| | | COPY U1,AX |
| U1 := (X + (Y * Z)) | | |

This completes the description of the translator for a small class of Pascal assignment statements. The system uses the syntactic portions of the rules to find the structure of the unknown statement. The semantic portions of the rules are functions that compute portions of the meaning. The expansion of these functions and their combination provide the final translation. This general methodology is quite satisfactory for handling many translation problems and is the basis for numerous existing translators.

Programs have been written to do all the translation steps shown above for complete programming languages like Pascal. Such programs are called *compilers*. The following section gives translation rules for the compilation of simple looping programs, which show how the methodology of this chapter can be extended to handle larger programming constructions.

## Exercises

1. Use rules R1 through R5 to translate the following statement into assembly language:

```
HEIGHT := (C * B)
```

2. Use rules R1 through R5 to translate the following statement into assembly language:

```
I := (I + ONE)
```

3. Use rules R1 through R5 to translate the following statement into assembly language:

```
X := ((T * U) * V)
```

4. Use rules R1 through R5 to translate the following statement into assembly language:

```
TOTAL := ((C1 * MAX) + (C2 * MIN))
```

5. Examine the translations given in this section for the statements $Z := (X + Y)$ and $UI := (X + (Y^*Z))$. Can you write assembly-language code that will do the same task with fewer instructions? Can you make a rough estimate of how much shorter minimal assembly-language programs are, on the average, than programs output by the translator? Can you guess how much faster optimal assembly-language programs will be than computer-generated ones?

6. Study the construction of the syntactic and semantic parts of rule R5 and explain the function of every part of the rule.

## The Translation of Looping Programs (C)

The previous sections gave a general approach to the design of translators. This section adds no new ideas to the theory but provides additional examples of rules and shows how larger code segments can be translated.

We need two more rules to translate a sequence of statements rather than a single statement:

```
R6: <q>i ==> <s>j;    code(<q>i) = code(<s>j)
            <q>k                  code(<q>k)
R7: <q>i ==> <s>j;    code(<q>i) = code(<s>j)
```

Here $\langle q \rangle_i$ stands for a "sequence" of statements. To see how these rules work, we will apply R6 several times in a row to $\langle q \rangle_1$:

| Derivation | Rules | |
| --- | --- | --- |
| $\langle q \rangle_1$ | R6: $\langle q \rangle_1 ==> \langle s \rangle_2;$ | $code(\langle q \rangle_1) = code(\langle s \rangle_2)$ |
| | $\langle q \rangle_3$ | $code(\langle q \rangle_3)$ |
| $\langle s \rangle_2;$ | R6: $\langle q \rangle_3 ==> \langle s \rangle_4;$ | $code(\langle q \rangle_3) = code(\langle s \rangle_4)$ |
| $\langle q \rangle_3$ | $\langle q \rangle_5$ | $code(\langle q \rangle_5)$ |
| $\langle s \rangle_2;$ | R6: $\langle q \rangle_5 ==> \langle s \rangle_6;$ | $code(\langle q \rangle_5) = code(\langle s \rangle_6)$ |
| $\langle s \rangle_4;$ | $\langle q \rangle_7$ | $code(\langle q \rangle_7)$ |
| $\langle q \rangle_5$ | | |
| $\langle s \rangle_2;$ | | |
| $\langle s \rangle_4;$ | | |
| $\langle s \rangle_6;$ | | |
| $\langle q \rangle_7$ | | |

The three applications of R6 produce a sequence of three statements, $\langle s \rangle_2$, $\langle s \rangle_4$, $\langle s \rangle_6$, each followed by a semicolon. Now we can apply R7 once to add a final statement to the sequence:

| Derivation | Rules | |
| --- | --- | --- |
| $\langle s \rangle_2 \;;$ | R7: $\langle q \rangle_7 ==> \langle s \rangle_8$ | $code(\langle q \rangle_7) = code(\langle s \rangle_8)$ |
| $\langle s \rangle_4 \;;$ | | |
| $\langle s \rangle_6 \;;$ | | |
| $\langle q \rangle_7$ | | |
| $\langle s \rangle_2 \;;$ | | |
| $\langle s \rangle_4 \;;$ | | |
| $\langle s \rangle_6 \;;$ | | |
| $\langle s \rangle_8 \;;$ | | |

We can apply the semantics rules to determine codes for the four statements $\langle s \rangle_2$, $\langle s \rangle_4$, $\langle s \rangle_6$, and $\langle s \rangle_8$. These are the MEANING FOUND entries for the creation of the final meaning of the set of four statements.

```
code (<q>₁) = code (<s>₂)     by first R6
              code (<q>₃)
            = code (<s>₂)     by second R6
              code (<s>₄)
              code (<q>₅)
```

```
    = code (<s>₂)      by third R6
        code (<s>₄)
        code (<s>₆)
        code (<q>₇)
    = code (<s>₂)      by R7
        code (<s>₄)
        code (<s>₆)
        code (<s>₈)
```

The result is as we expected. The translation of $\langle s \rangle_2$, $\langle s \rangle_4$, $\langle s \rangle_6$, $\langle s \rangle_8$ is

```
code (<q>₁) = code (<s>₂)
                code (<s>₄)
                code (<s>₆)
                code (<s>₈)
```

But Pascal always embeds statement sequences between the keywords *begin* and *end* to form a *compound statement*. A rule is needed for this:

```
R8: <c>ᵢ ==> begin      code(<c>ᵢ) = code(<q>ⱼ)
              <q>ⱼ
              end
```

Using this rule with the others, we can show that

```
<c>₀ =*=> begin
            <s>₂;
            <s>₄ ;
            <s>₆ ;
            <s>₈ ;
            end
```

The semantics rules are the same as in the previous example.

To summarize, if a compound statement of $n$ sequential statements is to be translated, rule R8 should be used once, followed by rule R6 $n - 1$ times and R7 once. This will give $n$ statements whose translation will be $n$ code segments. To illustrate this idea, suppose the following short program is to be compiled.

```
begin
X := Y;
Z := (X + Y);
U1 := (X + (Y * Z));
end
```

These individual statements were translated in the previous section, so those details can be omitted.

| Derivation | Rules | | |
|---|---|---|---|
| $\langle c \rangle_0$ | R8: $\langle c \rangle_0$ ==> begin<br>$\langle q \rangle 1$<br>end | code($\langle c \rangle_0$) = code($\langle q \rangle_1$) | |
| begin<br>$\langle q \rangle_1$<br>end | R6: $\langle q \rangle_1$ ==> $\langle s \rangle_2$ ;<br>$\langle q \rangle_3$ | code($\langle q \rangle_1$) = code($\langle s \rangle_2$)<br>code($\langle q \rangle_3$) | |
| begin<br>$\langle s \rangle_2$ ;<br>$\langle q \rangle_3$<br>end | R6: $\langle q \rangle_3$ ==> $\langle s \rangle_4$ ;<br>$\langle q \rangle_5$ | code($\langle q \rangle_3$) = code($\langle s \rangle_4$)<br>code($\langle q \rangle_5$) | |
| begin<br>$\langle s \rangle_2$;<br>$\langle s \rangle_4$ ;<br>$\langle q \rangle_5$<br>end<br>begin<br>$\langle s \rangle_2$;<br>$\langle s \rangle_4$ ;<br>$\langle s \rangle_6$ ;<br>end | R7: $\langle q \rangle_5$ ==> $\langle s \rangle_6$ ; | code($\langle q \rangle_5$) = code($\langle s \rangle_6$) | |

We can show that

```
code (<c>0) = code (<s>2)
              code (<s>4)
              code (<s>6)
```

where

```
<s>2 =*=> X := Y
<s>4 =*=> Z := (X + Y)
<s>6 =*=> U1 := (X + (Y * Z))
```

(Code($\langle s \rangle_2$), code($\langle s \rangle_4$), and code($\langle s \rangle_6$) were computed in the previous section.) Substituting the results of previous sections, we obtain

```
code (<c>₀) = COPY AX,Y
              COPY X,AX
              COPY AX,X
              ADD AX,Y
              COPY CN1,AX
              COPY AX,CN1
              COPY Z,AX
              COPY AX,Y
              MUL AX,Z
              COPY CN2,AX
              COPY AX,X
              ADD AX,CN2
              COPY CN1,AX
              COPY AX,CN1
              COPY U1,AX
```

(This code is not precisely what is generated by the rules because we did not use new names *CNi* for each new assignment statement as it was generated. This detail does not affect the computation so it will not be discussed here.)

The final rule to be examined in this chapter will make it possible to do looping programs:

```
R9: <s>ᵢ ==> while <i>ⱼ < <e>ₖ do    M(<s>ᵢ) = createname
                  <c>ₕ                M'(<s>ᵢ) = createname
                      code(<s>ᵢ) = M(<s>ᵢ)    code(<e>ₖ)
                                              COPY AX,M(<i>ⱼ)
                                              CMP AX,M(<e>ₖ)
                                              JNB M'(<s>ᵢ)
                                              code(<c>ₕ)
                                              JMP M(<s>ᵢ)
                              M'(<s>ᵢ) NO-OP
```

This rule translates loops that have a single test in them, $\langle i \rangle_j < \langle e \rangle_k$. One new assembly-language instruction, *NO-OP*, appears in the code. It means "no operation" and is included only because a place is needed to put the label $M'(\langle s \rangle_i)$.

Let us collect all the rules for the translator in one place:

| Name | Syntax | Semantics |
|------|--------|-----------|
| R1: | $\langle i \rangle_j$ ==> w | $M(\langle i \rangle_j)$ = w |
|  | where w = *a sequence of letters and/or digits that begins with a letter* | |
| R2: | $\langle e \rangle_i$ ==> $\langle i \rangle_j$ | $M(\langle e \rangle_i) = M(\langle i \rangle_j)$ |
|  |  | code $(\langle e \rangle_i)$ = *nothing* |
| R3: | $\langle s \rangle_k$ ==> $\langle i \rangle_j = \langle e \rangle_i$ | code $(\langle s \rangle_k)$ = code $(\langle e \rangle_i)$ |
|  |  | COPY AX,$M(\langle e \rangle_i)$ |
|  |  | COPY $M(\langle i \rangle_j)$,AX |
| R4: | $\langle e \rangle_i$ ==> $(\langle e \rangle_j + \langle e \rangle_k)$ | $M(\langle e \rangle_i)$ = createname |
|  |  | code$(\langle e \rangle_i)$ = code $(\langle e \rangle_j)$ |
|  |  | code $(\langle e \rangle_k)$ |
|  |  | COPY AX,$M(\langle e \rangle_j)$ |
|  |  | ADD AX,$M(\langle e \rangle_k)$ |
|  |  | COPY $M(\langle e \rangle_i)$,AX |
| R5: | $\langle e \rangle_i$ ==> $(\langle e \rangle_j * \langle e \rangle_k)$ | $M(\langle e \rangle_i)$ = createname |
|  |  | code$(\langle e \rangle_i)$ = code $(\langle e \rangle_j)$ |
|  |  | code $(\langle e \rangle_k)$ |
|  |  | COPY AX,$M(\langle e \rangle_j)$ |
|  |  | MUL AX,$M(\langle e \rangle_k)$ |
|  |  | COPY $M(\langle e \rangle_i)$,AX |
| R6: | $\langle q \rangle_i$ ==> $\langle s \rangle_j$ ; <br> $\langle q \rangle_k$ | code$(\langle q \rangle_i)$ = code$(\langle s \rangle_j)$ <br> code$(\langle q \rangle_k)$ |
| R7: | $\langle q \rangle_i$ ==> $\langle s \rangle_j$ ; | code$(\langle q \rangle_i)$ = code$(\langle s \rangle_j)$ |
| R8: | $\langle c \rangle_i$ ==> begin <br> $\langle q \rangle_j$ <br> end | code$(\langle c \rangle_i)$ = code$(\langle q \rangle_j)$ |
| R9: | $\langle s \rangle_i$ ==> while $\langle i \rangle_j$ < $\langle e \rangle_k$ do <br> $\langle c \rangle_h$ | $M(\langle s \rangle_i)$ = createname |
|  |  | $M'(\langle s \rangle_i)$ = createname |
|  |  | code$(\langle s \rangle_i)$ = $M(\langle s \rangle_i)$  code$(\langle e \rangle_k)$ |
|  |  | COPY AX,$M(\langle i \rangle_j)$ |
|  |  | CMP AX,$M(\langle e \rangle_k)$ |
|  |  | JNB $M'(\langle s \rangle_i)$ |
|  |  | code$(\langle c \rangle_h)$ |
|  |  | JMP $M(\langle s \rangle_i)$ |
|  |  | $M'(\langle s \rangle_i)$ NO-OP |

To illustrate these rules, we will translate a program to compute factorial. This program computes $1^*2^*3^*\ldots^*N$ and leaves the result in *FACT*. Thus, if $N=5$, it will compute $FACT = 1^*2^*3^*4^*5 = 120$. The process of translating variable declarations will not be considered here, but we will assume that *I*, *FACT*, *N* and *ONE* have been declared as integers, that *ONE* contains a 1, and that *N* contains the argument for the calculation:

```
begin
I := ONE;
FACT := ONE;
while I < (N + ONE) do
    begin
    FACT := (FACT * I);
    I := (I + ONE);
    end;
end
```

The compilation of this program using rules R1 to R9 follows. (Some steps are omitted.)

| **Derivation** | **Rules** | | |
|---|---|---|---|
| $\langle c\rangle_0$ | $\langle c\rangle_0 \Longrightarrow$ begin $\langle q\rangle_1$ end | $code(\langle c\rangle_0) =$ | $code(\langle q\rangle_1)$ |
| begin $\langle q\rangle_1$ end | $\langle q\rangle_1 \overset{*}{=}\Rightarrow \langle s\rangle_2$ ; $\langle s\rangle_4$ ; $\langle s\rangle_6$ ; | $code(\langle q\rangle_1) =$ | $code\ (\langle s\rangle_2)$ $code(\langle s\rangle_4)$ $code(\langle s\rangle_6)$ |
| begin $\langle s\rangle_2$ ; $\langle s\rangle_4$ ; $\langle s\rangle_6$ ; end | $\langle s\rangle_2 \overset{*}{=}\Rightarrow$ I := ONE | $code(\langle s\rangle_2) =$ | COPY AX,ONE COPY I,AX |
| begin I := ONE; $\langle s\rangle_4$ ; $\langle s\rangle_6$ ; end | $\langle s\rangle_4 \overset{*}{=}\Rightarrow$ FACT := ONE | $code(\langle s\rangle_4) =$ | COPY AX,ONE COPY FACT,AX |

| Derivation | Rules | |
|---|---|---|
| ```
begin
  I := ONE;
  FACT := ONE;
  <s>6 ;
end
``` | $<s>_6$ =\*=> while $<i>_7$ < $<e>_8$ do<br>          $<c>_9$ | $M(s_6) = CN6$<br>$M'(s_6) = CN7$<br>$code(s_6) = CN6$   $code(e_8)$<br>        COPY AX,M($<i>_7$)<br>        CMP AX,M($<e>_8$)<br>        JNB CN7<br>        code($<c>_9$)<br>        JMP CN6<br>     CN7   NO-OP |
| ```
begin
  I := ONE;
  FACT := ONE;
  while <i>7 < <e>8 do
       <c>9;
  end
``` | $<i>_7$ =\*=> I | $M(<i>_7) = I$<br>$code(<i>_7) = $ *nothing* |
| | $<e>_8$ =\*=> (N + ONE) | $M(<e>_8) = CN8$<br>$code(<e>_8) = $   COPY AX,N<br>                ADD AX,ONE<br>                COPY CN8,AX |
| ```
begin
  I := ONE;
  FACT := ONE;
  while I < (N + ONE) do
       <c>9;
  end
``` | $<c>_9$ =\*=> begin<br>           $<s>_{10}$ ;<br>           $<s>_{11}$ ;<br>        end | $code(<c>_9) = $   $code(<s>_{10})$<br>                   $code(<s>_{11})$ |
| ```
begin
  I := ONE;
  FACT := ONE;
  while I < (N + ONE) do
     begin
        <s>10;
        <s>11;
     end;
  end
``` | $<s>_{10}$ =\*=> FACT := (FACT \* I) | $code(s_{10}) = $   COPY AX,FACT<br>                MUL AX,I<br>                COPY CN9,AX<br>                COPY AX,CN9<br>                COPY FACT,AX |

| Derivation | Rules | |
|---|---|---|
| ```
begin
I := ONE;
FACT := ONE;
while I < (N + ONE) do
    begin
    FACT := (FACT * I);
    <s>₁₁;
    end;
end

begin
I := ONE;
FACT := ONE;
while I < (N + ONE) do
    begin
    FACT := (FACT * I);
    I := (I + ONE);
    end;
end
``` | $<s>_{11}$ =\*=> I := (I + ONE)<br><br>$code(<s>_{11})$ = | COPY AX,I<br>ADD AX,ONE<br>COPY CN10,AX<br>COPY AX,CN10<br>COPY I,AX |

If we applying the semantics rules, we obtain the final translation:

```
code (<c>₀) =    COPY AX,ONE
                 COPY I,AX
                 COPY AX,ONE
                 COPY FACT,AX
          CN6    COPY AX,N
                 ADD AX,ONE
                 COPY CN8,AX
                 COPY AX,I
                 CMP AX,CN8
                 JNB CN7
                 COPY AX,FACT
                 MUL AX,I
                 COPY CN9,AX
                 COPY AX,CN9
                 COPY FACT,AX
                 COPY AX,I
                 ADD AX,ONE
```
```

```
          COPY CN10,AX
          COPY AX,CN10
          COPY I,AX
          JMP CN6
     CN7  NO-OP
```

Comparing the source-language program with its translation, we can see the tremendous gains in clarity and simplicity from using the higher-level language.

**Exercises**

1. Show how rules R1 to R9 can be used to find the translation for the following program:

```
begin
INC := TW;
J := (J + INC);
end
```

2. Fill in the details for the translation of the factorial program.

3. Show how rules R1 to R9 can be used to compute the translation of the following program. Assume that *ZERO* and *ONE* are integers that are initialized at 0 and 1, respectively. Assume that $N$ is a nonnegative integer and $X$ is an integer; both have been initialized as data items, perhaps from read statements:

```
begin
J := ZERO;
POWER := ONE;
while J < N do
    begin
    POWER := (POWER * X);
    J := (J + ONE);
    end;
end
```

What does this program compute?

4. Write a Pascal program that is within the generative scope of rules R1 to R9. Use the rules to find its translation.

5. Design an if-then construction and create a rule R10 to translate it. Write a program using your if-then construction, and show how it can be translated using rules R1 to R9 with your new rule R10.

## Programming Languages (B)

The understanding of compiler design made it relatively easy to invent new higher-level languages and write compilers for them. In the past fifty years, hundreds of computer languages have been developed. A few of the best known will be briefly mentioned here to give a glimpse of the rest of the programming world. To compare them, we will examine the code required to add a column of numbers in each language. The initializations and declarations in the programs are omitted in order to emphasize the lines of code that execute the addition.

We will begin with the language of this book, Pascal. Assume that an array *A* has been declared to hold the numbers to be added. The location *SUM* stores the sum of the numbers, and *I* indexes through the array:

```
SUM := 0;
I := 1;
while I <= N do
    begin
    SUM := A[I] + SUM;
    I := I + 1;
    end;
```

The for-loop feature of Pascal, not described in this book, makes it possible to write this in shorter form:

```
SUM := 0;
for I := 1 to N do
    SUM := A[I] + SUM;
```

The earliest compiled language to come into wide use was FORTRAN, which was developed in the 1950s. Variations of this language continue to be popular today, and the compilers have become refined and efficient. Here is the FORTRAN code to add the column of numbers:

```
      SUM = 0
      do 100  I = 1,N,1
      SUM = A[I] + SUM
100   continue
```

Notice various differences with Pascal, including punctuation and formating. The second line of code is a looping statement, which says "do all the statements from here to the statement label 100 for the values of *I* from 1 to *N* incrementing 1 each time." FORTRAN was developed before structured programming evolved, and programmers relied on statement labels and "go to" statements for program control. More recent versions of FORTRAN have included features for structured programming.

A later development was "programming language one," or PL/1. This language is famous for its large number of automatic features and its syntactic variety. For example, in most languages, if *I* and *R* are declared to be integer and real, respectively, then one cannot do the assignments $I := R$ and $R := I$ because of type incompatibilities. However, PL/1 allows such intermixing of types and automatically does conversions. PL/1 is a structured language with many resemblances to Pascal, as is evident from its code:

```
SUM = 0;
I = 1;
do while (I <= N);
    SUM = A(I) + SUM;
    I = I + 1;
    end;
```

A problem with PL/1, however, is that its many features result in an immensely complicated compiler and, possibly, slow execution times.

A very popular language in current use is C. Because it has features that give the programmer more exact control over the details of the computation, is often used by professional programmers in systems programming work. Here is the column sum program:

```
SUM = 0;
I = 1;
while (I <= N)
    {SUM = A[I] + SUM;
    I++;}
```

The while statement loops through all the statements between the brackets { }. The *I*++ statement causes *I* to increment by one.

A later upgrade of C, called C++, includes the object-oriented programming constructions that were described at the end of chapter 4. In C++, we will assume there is an adder object called *get_sum* with a method called *add_numbers*. Then the code in C++ to add up array *A* would be simply

```
SUM = get_sum.add_numbers(A,N);
```

Of course, none of this would work unless the programmer has created the object and its method properly. The object will be a member of a class with the name *Adder*:

```
class Adder
       {
       public:
           Adder();
           int add_numbers(int[],int);
       };
```

The method must be defined as follows:

```
Adder::add_numbers(int numbers[], int num_numbers)
       {
       int sum = 0;
       for (int i = 1; i <= num_numbers; i++)
           {sum += numbers[i];}
       return sum;
       }
```

Then we must create the object *get_sum* to be from the class *Adder* and this is done in the program with the declaration

```
Adder get_sum;
```

Another popular language in recent years is BASIC, which is widely used on personal computers. However, this language is in disfavor with many computer scientists because of its reliance on the "go to" statement for control and the weakness of its subroutine feature. A recent and dramatic upgrade of the language was completed in the mid-1980s, and this change eliminated many of the original problems. The new language is called True Basic. Here is its column sum code:

```
let SUM = 0
let I = 1
do while I <= N
    let SUM = A(I) + SUM
    let I = I + 1
loop
```

More recently, Visual Basic has come into popular use. It is well known for its easy access to graphical features and some object-oriented capabilities.

After this short look at five different languages, you may believe they all are the same except for punctuation and formatting. In fact, these and most other popular languages (ALGOL, COBOL, ADA, etc.) are in the same family, and their similarities enable programmers to move from one to the other with relative ease. A competent programmer with one language can usually begin writing simple programs in another after a single day of study. Competence in the new language will usually come within a few weeks. Of course, for the initiated, the differences in these languages become noticeable. In a particular environment, one of these languages may be far more desirable than the others because of some feature—perhaps its fast execution, its ease of interface with other languages, or its allowed data structure forms.

However, there are some important languages that do not fall into the same family as Pascal. APL is one such language; it features a large number of single symbol operators that manipulate arrays. The column sum program is written in APL as

```
SUM <- +/A
```

which means, "add up the numbers in array $A$, putting the result into *SUM*." Larger programs can be created by assembling a sequence of operators. Here is a program to compute prime numbers:

```
PRIMES N (2=+/[1]0=(ₜN)o.|ₜN)/ₜN
```

The powerful operators of the language enable a programmer to obtain a lot of computation with just a few symbols. The programs, however, are typically somewhat difficult to read.

Another well-known language outside the Pascal family is LISP, a language designed for symbolic rather than numerical computation. Its constructs make it easy to build and manipulate complicated structures, such as trees. It uses recursion heavily for control in the manner explained near the end of chapter 4. It is sometimes useful for assembling a prototype program quickly in a situation where execution time may not be critical. The column sum program can be written in LISP as follows:

```
f(A) = (cond ((atom A) 0)
    (T (plus (car A) (f (cdr A)))))
```

Here is a paraphrase of this program, which adds up the list $A$:

```
f(A) = on the condition that A has length 0, return 0
    otherwise, add the first entry of A to
        f(A with first entry removed) and return the answer
```

The explanation for recursive computations of this type appears near the end of chapter 4.

Another important language is Prolog, which uses a declarative style rather than an imperative form for programs. Note that all of the languages discussed elsewhere in this book and almost all languages in regular use are imperative in nature. Most programs are of the form

```
Do this.
Do that.
Do something else.
    etc.
```

Thus, the programmer uses the program to tell the machine what to do. Prolog programs, however, are of the form

```
This is a fact.
That is a fact.
Something else is a fact.
    etc.
```

Using Prolog, the programmer does not tell the machine how to do a calculation. The program merely states facts, and the machine automatically finds the facts needed to answer a question.

Here is an example of how Prolog is used. We will state four facts about height relationships:

```
fact(jill, tallerthan, sally).
fact(sally, tallerthan, renee).
fact(renee, tallerthan, nancy).
fact(nancy, tallerthan, mary).
```

Now we can ask "Who is taller than Mary?" Here is how the question is asked:

```
fact(X, tallerthan, mary).
```

The system will respond with $X = $ nancy. Or we can ask, "Who is taller than whom?"

```
fact(X, tallerthan, Y).
```

The machine will respond:

```
X = jill,  Y = sally
X = sally, Y = renee
X = renee, Y = nancy
X = nancy, Y = mary
```

Actually this feature acts exactly like the database program of chapter 4. It even has the same shortcoming, which is that it does not infer information not explicitly given in the facts.

Prolog also allows much more powerful assertions. We can state generalized facts of the following type:

```
fact(X, tallerthan, Z) :- fact(X, tallerthan, Y), fact(Y, tallerthan, Z).
```

This should be read as "$X$ is taller than $Z$ if $X$ is taller than $Y$ and $Y$ is taller than $Z$." Using the previous four facts and this one, let us again ask the question, "Who is taller than Mary?"

```
fact(X, tallerthan, mary).
```

This time the system will use all the original information plus the generalized fact to infer new facts:

```
X = nancy
X = renee
X = sally
X = jill
```

Thus, the Prolog system assembles the answer using the total of the facts given. Even though the programmer has not explicitly indicated how to do the computation, it has done a kind of inference that our database program could not do, which makes it an extremely useful language.

A programming language of this type is quite different from Pascal and other languages, even when used in ordinary computations. Here is a Prolog program to add a list of numbers:

```
f(0,[ ]).
f(S,[X|Y]) :- f(Z,Y), S is X + Z.
```

The first fact says, "$f$ associates 0 with the list with no entries." The second fact says, "$f$ associates $S$ with a list beginning with $X$ and ending with a list $Y$ of other entries if $f$ associates $Z$ with $Y$ and $S$ is $X+Z$." In other words, the sum $S$ is found by adding up everything $Y$ but the first entry $X$ in the list $[X|Y]$ to obtain $Z$. Then $X$ is added to $Z$ to obtain the result $S$. (This is another recursive program that can be understood only if recursion (chapter 4) is understood.) To add numbers, we simply type

```
f(X,[7,3,9,2]).
```

and the system will respond $X=21$.

Many languages are available to computer scientists, and an experienced programmer must choose which to use in a given application. Some languages resemble Pascal in form but have special characteristics that make them better or worse than Pascal, depending on the situation. Other languages are dramatically different, and they have different strengths and weaknesses.

### Exercises

1. Make up a table with a column for each of the eight languages discussed here. Fill in the table as well as you can, giving the following information for each language: form of assignment statements, punctuation for statement termination, form of looping construction, the addition operator, length of the sample code in number of characters, strengths, and weaknesses.

2. Study the section on recursion in chapter 4 and then show how the LISP program for addition works. *(atom A)* is true if *A* is a list of length zero. The function *(car A)* returns the first entry of list *A*, and the function *(cdr A)* returns *A* with its first entry removed.

3. Using your knowledge of recursion, analyze the Prolog program for addition. The notation $L = [X|Y]$ means that *L* is a list of objects where *X* is the first entry on the list and *Y* is the list containing the rest of the entries of *L*.

## Summary (B)

This chapter has explained a methodology for translating one language to another. It described translation rules that build a linkage between two languages. Each rule has two parts—a syntactic part and a semantic part. The syntactic parts of a rule are used to discover the form of a sentence in the source language; we find a way to generate the source language sentence from an initial symbol such as $\langle s \rangle_1$, and the rules needed to do the generation identify the parts of the source statement. For example, the discovery that the multiplication rule R5 is needed at a particular point to generate a Pascal statement is an indication that a multiplication is to be done, and the rule discovers what is to be multiplied.

Once it is known which syntactic rules generate the source statement, the structure of that statement is known, and its translation can be determined. This is done by the semantic portions of the rules that were used in the syntactic analysis. A straightforward substitution and combination of these semantics definitions yields the result, the translation into the object language. These ideas were demonstrated in the first several sections by the rules R1 to R5, which were used to translate some Pascal assignment statements to assembly language. In a later section, rules R6 to R9 were introduced and we learned how to translate complete code segments, including some loops, into assembly language.

A translation program from a source language such as Pascal to a lower-level language such as P88 assembly language is called a *compiler*. The compiler is composed of the translation rules, the code to use the rules to do the syntactic and semantic analyses, and many other routines to optimize the code, send messages to the user, and so forth.

Another way to use a computer language on a computer, besides compiling it, is to use an *interpreter* for it. Interpreters are programs that execute a source-language program without any initial translation. From the user's point of view, they may seem to function in the same way as compilers, although their execution time will be slower. Many times interpreters are able to produce debugging information that will aid the programmer who is developing new code. Their principles of operation are beyond the scope of this book.

This chapter completes the section of the book that describes the mechanisms of a computer hardware and software system necessary to run a program in a language like Pascal. We have traveled from the program at the highest level, through the architecture of the machine, to the switching circuits and the electron flows at the very lowest level. We will summarize by once again tracing all processing for the single Pascal statement

```
Z := (X + Y)
```

Using the rules R1 through R5 of this chapter, this statement is translated or compiled into equivalent assembly language:

```
COPY AX,X
ADD AX,Y
COPY CN1,AX
COPY AX,CN1
COPY Z,AX
```

These instructions are then translated in a process called *assembly* into a set of binary codes, which we have written as

```
* COPY AX,X   *
* ADD AX,Y    *
* COPY CN1,AX *
* COPY AX,CN1 *
* COPY Z,AX   *
```

but which really look something like this:

```
00101101
01001010
00100111
00101111
00100001
```

These are loaded into the memory of the machine, and when they are used the instruction pointer gives their location. Chapter 8 catalogs the events associated with their execution.

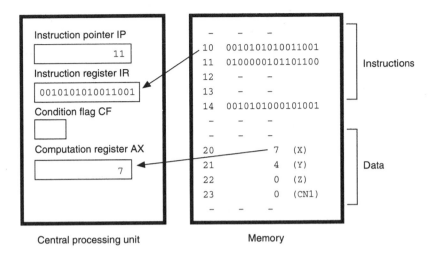

Central processing unit                 Memory

At a more detailed level, you can examine the ways the commands are decoded and carried out. Each instruction is decoded as explained at the end of chapter 7, and circuits of the type examined there are used to do the calculation. For example, the second instruction in the example is an *add* instruction, and a complete circuit for adding is given. Here is a simplified version of that circuit:

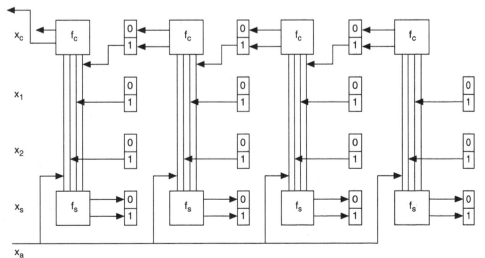

The machine must contain such circuits for all machine instructions, add, copy, multiply, and so forth. These circuits are made up of many tiny switching circuits constructed from semiconductors, as described at the end of chapter 7. Hundreds of thousands of such circuits are packed on a silicon chip, using microscopic doping and etching processes. In these chapters 7, 8, and 9, we have covered all the mechanisms for a computation, from the Pascal statement at the highest level to the movement of the electrons in the semiconductors at the subatomic level.

# 10    Virtual Environments for Computing

## Use Your Imagination (A)

This book has presented a variety of computing processes including editing, graphics generation, and data storage and retrieval. Now it is time to create an environment within which we can comfortably do those things. We can create almost any kind of environment; almost anything we can imagine, we can program.

Suppose, for example, we think of computing as a hallway with a series of rooms that we might enter. Then we can have the computer draw on the screen a hallway and a series of doors that open to places where we can do certain kinds of computing. We might have a room for editing, a room for compiling programs, and a room where mail is handled. We can think of computing as just going down the hall and choosing a room.

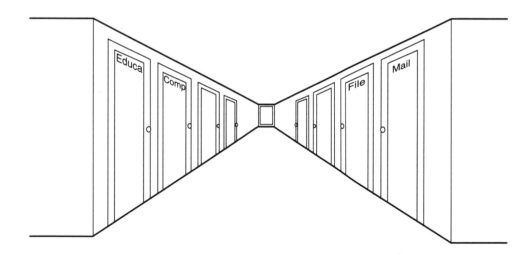

If we enter the room for editing, we will find objects and things to do related to editing. It might look something like this:

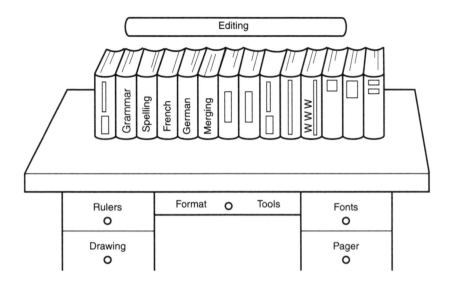

If we decide to compile a program, that room would have whatever objects we might need for compiling. (What would you suggest for that room?)

If we think of computing another way, we can build some other model. For example, we could think of the systems inside the machine as tools. We could think of computing as the process of grabbing tools and applying them to a job. We grab an editor to create a program. Then we grab a compiler to translate the program and an execution system to run the program. Maybe we use a debugging tool to find errors and then a mail facility to send the final program to our course instructor.

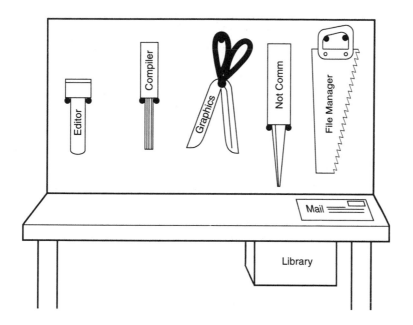

On the other hand, maybe we are uncomfortable with the machine and want it to be our friend. We can build a model that smiles at us in a friendly way and greets us with a warm hello. It responds to our smiles and spoken requests.

Or maybe we think of computing as a menu of choices and we want an easy way to make our selections. This model is the basis of many current computing systems.

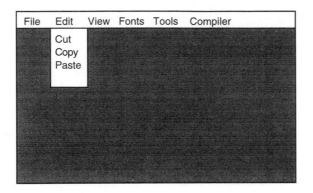

Whatever computing environment we choose, we can program the machine to look that way. We learned in earlier chapters how to get the machine to draw a picture. We can use those methods to draw any picture on the screen and create the environment for computing that we want. If the machine has audio capabilities, we can also program it to provide us with an audio environment, and if it controls any other aspect of our surroundings, we can program it to use these as well. If we have a wearable three-dimensional head display, we can program that to make us feel like we are actually inside the world we coded into the computer.

The environment we program using visual, audio, and possibly other media is called a *virtual environment*. One of the great ideas of computer science is that we can use computers to create such environments to make ourselves more comfortable, to improve our efficiency, or to give ourselves the chance to experience something that we could not easily experience otherwise.

This chapter is a study of *operating systems*, the programs that deliver virtual environments. If you have been writing the programs discussed in earlier chapters, you are already familiar with an operating system like Windows something, DOS, a Macintosh operating system, or UNIX. So you have already done many of the things we will discuss here, such as create a program with an editor, compile it, run it, use mail, and store files.

The purpose of this chapter is not to teach you about some specific operating system, but to teach you that an operating system is just another program and, of course, you already know a great deal about such programs. In fact, you know so much that you could write many parts of an operating system without much help. For example, you have written several command-control loops that receive commands from a user and execute them, and this is one of the main functions of an operating system. In order to help you understand the principles of operating systems, the author, with the help of some students, has created one in Pascal which is available from the Internet, as described in the introductory chapter. That operating system will be the object of our study here, and you should obtain a copy of it and try it for yourself. As with all operating systems, it does not come up to the standards we might like in this chapter or that you might like for your own purposes. Where this occurs, you are invited to upgrade its performance in any way you wish.

**Exercise**

1. Design an interface for computing that you would like to have for your own machine and that does not resemble interfaces you have seen before.

## A Virtual Environment for Computing (B)

Let us now create an environment for computing in the world of great ideas in computer science. We will make any choices that seem to be fun and convenient at the moment. If you would like to do it differently, you can study some programming and do it your own way.

The first thing a computer system usually does is to identify the user and to check that his or her entry is legal. So let us draw a picture on the screen and ask the user to type his or her user identifier and password:

Login: _____
Password: _____

For current purposes, assume that the user logs in with an identifier, say "awb," and password, say "a," and proceeds to enter the world of computation.

Let us adopt the decision that when a person computes, he or she is going to either request a function, manipulate a file, or call for a system action. Our virtual environment for computing can present a series of bubbles with these three names and let the user choose which one.

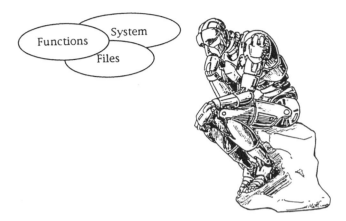

When the user makes a selection, just to keep things simple, let us say that an ordinary menu appears with a series of choices:

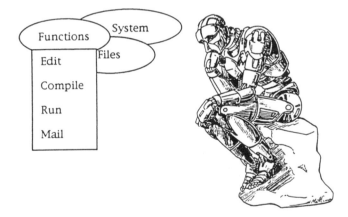

Since the user will surely need an editor, a reasonable decision is to bring in the editor from chapter 2. We will just add a few instructions to make that editor completely general before we insert it into the system. First, an *append* instruction is needed that will enable the user to append lines to the end of the existing document.

Here is how it will look when "awb" types in a program:

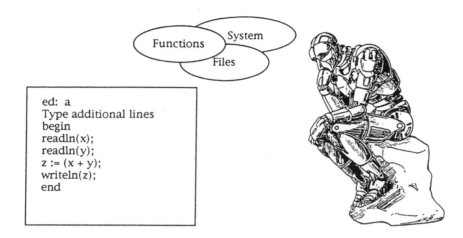

```
ed: a
Type additional lines
begin
readln(x);
readln(y);
z := (x + y);
writeln(z);
end
```

This program is written in the form of the Pascal programs described in the translation chapter, chapter 9. Our compiler in the current system will compile only a very limited class of programs. The lone period in the sixth line of the program is a message to the editor that the user has finished typing. The system responds with

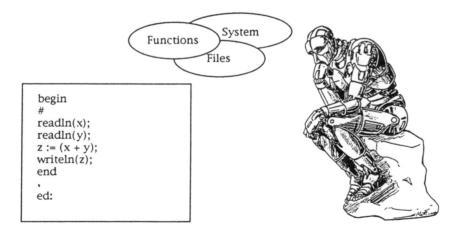

```
begin
#
readln(x);
readln(y);
z := (x + y);
writeln(z);
end
.
ed:
```

This shows that the program has been entered properly. The # represents the cursor; it designates the position where changes can be made. The user can employ the commands *i*, *d*, *c* from chapter 2, as described in that chapter. The editor needs some other commands for controlling the cursor:

```
f    forward
b    backward
p    previous
n    next
```

These will enable the user to get around the text to modify it.

The last new command for the editor will be *s* to save the text that has been created on a disk. (Disks will be described in the next section.) Here is what it will look like to the user:

```
ed:s
Give the filename.
pascaltest
```

Now we should check whether the program has really been stored by leaving the editor and checking the directory. We select *Dir* from the system command submenu.

```
ed:q
```

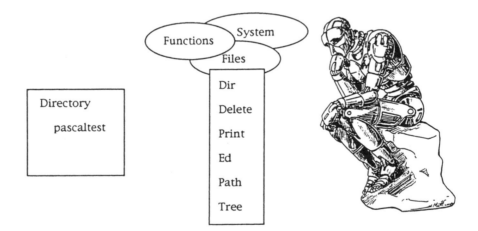

The directory command asks the system to list all programs associated with the directory for the name "awb." The response indicates that one program, *pascaltest*, is now in that directory. Ordinarily this would be stored on a disk, but our system has an array called *disk* and that is where the file is actually stored.

We now might wish to retrieve this program and make changes to it. We do this in the usual way, by calling the editor and using a *g* to "get" it back.

```
ed: g
Give the filename.
pascaltest
begin
#
readln(x);
readln(y):
z := (x+y);
writeln(z);
end
```

Before we add a compiler, mail facility, and various other capabilities to our virtual environment, we will discuss the computer hardware, the *operating system*, and their roles in providing this virtual environment.

**Exercise**

1. Revise your editor from chapter 2 so that it will have all the capabilities shown in this section.

## Hardware Pragmatics (A)

We wish to build a software system called an *operating system* that can deliver all the above behaviors and more to the user. The task of the operating system is to provide a bridge between the hardware and the higher level behaviors. This section will review basic hardware facts, some of which you may have gathered from earlier chapters or from other experiences, and later sections will describe the operating system itself.

The two main parts of the computer are the central processing unit (CPU) and the memory. The CPU has the job of executing instructions that do such things as bring in data from the memory, manipulate them, and store them back into the memory. There are usually a hundred or more instructions for a CPU, and they are typically designed to process a fixed amount of data in each operation. That is, there will be some number $N$, and each CPU instruction will copy or manipulate $N$ bits of data. For many early processors, $N$ was 8 or 16, but more recently, most have $N$ of 32 or 64. Many large mainframe machines process 32 or 64 bits per operation, but a variety of other sizes have also been built.

Memory is usually constructed with very large numbers of tiny electric circuits, each of which can hold a 0 or a 1. A single binary digit of information (a 0 or a 1) is called a bit, and the usual module of memory is the byte, which ordinarily contains eight bits. This is a convenient size because most coding schemes allocate one byte per character.

Thus, a one million byte memory can hold a million characters. Typical machines will have a few hundred thousand (K) of bytes up to many millions of bytes (megabytes). For example, a machine with 128,000 bytes of memory is said to have a 128K memory, and a machine with 128 million bytes is said to have 128 megabytes of memory.

When a program or a set of data is not being used, it is typically stored on a *disk*. These disks are coated with a ferrous material and hold information using magnetism as does an ordinary tape recorder. A *disk drive* spins the disk and either reads information from or stores information on the disk surfaces. A *floppy disk* is a disk made of thin plastic material that can be carried around with its stored information and inserted into the machine's floppy disk drive if the information, programs or data, is needed. A variation on the magnetic disk is the *CD-ROM* (compact disk- read only memory) that can hold huge amounts of data and is often used to hold large data bases or programs. A *hard disk* is a high precision disk permanently mounted in a closed case. A floppy disk can store possibly a few hundred K bytes up to many megabytes of data. Typical CD-ROM disks hold 660 megabytes. Hard disks can store from a few dozen megabytes to many thousands of megabytes. (A thousand megabytes is called a *gigabyte*.)

The information on a disk is organized into *files*. A file contains either a program, a set of data, or both, and is moved around the computer as a unit in the same way that an envelope of pages might be handed around an office. A file can be stored on a disk, it can be brought into the computer memory, it can be modified in the machine, it can be stored back on the disk, it can be printed, or it can be transmitted on a network. A file will always have a name so it can be referred to in commands.

An *input-output* device is a special purpose hardware system to deliver and receive information for the computer. An example of such a device is a printer, which has machinery to manipulate paper and place figures or text on a page. (Most printers actually have their own internal computers and will have a memory to store the information that is to be printed and a central processor to control the printer functions: receive the characters and graphics from an external source, manipulate the hardware to print them out, and send messages to the external source giving the status of the job.) Other examples of input-output devices are scanners that lift information from a page and code it in electronic form for computer manipulation, sound input-output devices, robotic arms, and wearable head displays.

**Exercise**

1. Find the nominal hardware specifications for your machine. How many bits are processed by a machine instruction? How many machine instructions are there and what is their speed? What is the size of the memory and disk system? Is there a *cache* memory on your machine? What is a cache memory? How many bytes fit on a floppy disk on your system?

## The Operating System (B)

The *operating system* is the computer program that provides the virtual environment that we examined in the previous sections and that executes the actions that the user requests. It not only gives the user convenient visual and other media images with comfortable means for interaction, it also carries out immensely complicated and detailed actions inside the machine that will complete the task. This section will describe many major functions of the operating system.

In order to appreciate the operating system, it is useful to consider what a computer would look like without it. You would have a memory with no entries in it, empty computer registers, empty disk files, a display with no information, and input-output devices that do not work. All these devices would be dead because they are all driven by programs. Furthermore, you would have no way to enter programs because even the process of reading a program requires software, the input-output drivers that operate the input-output devices. Here is our symbolic representation of the computer hardware in its naked and useless state.

| Disk | CPU | Memory | I-O Devices |
|------|-----|--------|-------------|

The operating system is a large program with subroutines to operate and manage the devices of the hardware system. Each device has an array of commands that control its operation and special formatting rules for transmitting information to and from its local memory. Thus, a printer might require a special activation code to prepare to print and it might return a status code to indicate its readiness to proceed. It might receive a sequence of, say, 1024 printable characters to begin its job and then send a message when it has printed them and is ready for more. The operating system enables the user to print documents without knowing any of these details. It simply receives the request to print and then executes the actions needed to complete the job. The other devices have their own characteristics that can be learned from their associated manuals, and they must be programmed individually to function properly.

Symbolically, we will represent the operating system, which contains these programs and a lot of others to be described below, as a layer of software that separates the users from the hardware. When we want to use any of these devices, we will issue commands to the operating system and it will deliver the proper instruction sequences to the device.

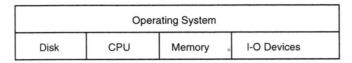

The operating system is read into the computer main memory from a disk or other external source by a special hardwired program in the machine called the *boot strap* code. Loading the operating system brings the computer to life. (It is called *booting the system*.)

The operating system provides four major kinds of services to the user, which we will examine next.

### 1. Providing Access to Computing Functions

The most important task of the operating system is to provide the user with access to computing functions. Some of the functions of the operating system can be better understood if we consider the example of the editor. To the user, it is simply an object on the screen to be selected. To the operating system, the editor is a piece of code on a storage device with an address, a size, and maybe several special characteristics such as communications requirements with other programs or internal parameters to be set. (You wrote an editor in chapter 2, so you know what an editor really is.) When the user calls for the activation of the editor, the operating system must find that code and locate a place in the memory to put it. Then it must move that code into memory and set up communication between it and the user so that an edit can take place.

The operating system has access to many special programs, like the editor, that enable it to do its jobs. These may include the compilers for various languages, a mail system, and many other subsystems. Let us revise our diagram to take this into account:

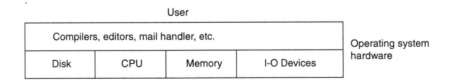

### 2. Providing a File System

A second major function of the operating system is to provide a *file system* to organize and manage files. When any program creates a file, it will be able to call on the file system to store it. If any program later needs that file, it will be able to request the file system to retrieve it. The file system can also be asked to move, rename, or delete files, or to provide a listing of them. An example file system will be described in a later section.

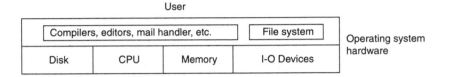

## 3.   Providing a Secure Computing Environment

A third major function of the operating system is to provide security. There are three important kinds of security. (1) *Computing resources protection.* The system can store user identifiers and passwords and prevent unauthorized persons from obtaining service from the machine. (2) *Internal file and function protection.* The system can prohibit a user from accessing data or from using unauthorized functions. The system can also prevent the user from either purposely or accidentally interfering with other running programs. (You would not want the print routines on your computer to stop functioning because you made an error in your Pascal code.) The storage areas where code and data exist that are not meant to be under the user's control also need to be protected. (3) *Protection from hardware failure.* Another kind of security relates to the safety of your programs and data in case of a failure of the machine. Here it is necessary to store the contents of the files in the machine on a permanent medium, such as a tape or floppy disk. Usually such backups are performed manually by the operators of the computer using file-handling facilities provided by the operating system.

We will repeat our diagram from above but to represent the idea of security, we will greatly strengthen the lines dividing the major parts. That is, no subsystem or person is allowed to damage any other entity in the process of a computation. All subparts should have secure boundaries.

User

| Compilers, editors, mail handler, etc. | | | File system |
|---|---|---|---|
| Disk | CPU | Memory | I-O Devices |

Operating system hardware

## 4.  Providing for Time Sharing

The final major function of the operating system that will be discussed here is the management of *time sharing*. We as users may not need or want at one time all the computing capabilities that our machine fetch-execute cycle can offer. While our program is not running, the machine will still be grabbing instructions from memory and executing them. Perhaps we should organize things so that another user can be running a program while we look at a printout or decide what to do next.

We will define a *process* to be our program or any program on the machine in some state of execution. Our process may be running and computing answers for us; it may have stopped to wait for us to type in the next item of data; or it may have been temporarily halted by the operating system while some other job is being done. Whatever its state, our program will have many needs and the operating system will have the job of providing them. First of all, our program will need a place to reside in memory and the operating system will find such a place that is not currently being used and place our program there. Next, if the program needs additional memory for execution, the operating system will find that. If the program needs to access files on the disk system, either for reading or writing, the operating system will make the necessary accesses. If the program needs to send items to the printer or receive data from some outside device, it will transmit requests to the operating system, which will carry out the proper protocols to get the job done.

A process will continue to execute until an *interrupt* occurs. An interrupt is a halting of the current computation to allow for other processing and it can come from various sources. The operating system can initiate an interrupt to allow some other user to have computation time. An external device, that has information-processing needs, such as a printer, can initiate an interrupt. For example, the printer may have completed output of the lines it was given and may be calling for the next segment of data. The computer hardware may also initiate an interrupt because an error condition like a register overflow has occurred. A variety of interrupt types can occur in most machines and an algorithm selects which ones to honor and in what order.

When the system interrupts a process, it must store all information related to its state of computation so that the process can be continued later without error. It must store the state of the program data, a note of which program instruction is to be executed next, and the contents of certain machine registers. Later the system will be able to raise this process to high priority, restore register contents, and continue the computation at the correct next instruction.

The idea of time sharing is that the operating system will have the ability to keep track of many processes simultaneously. It will sequentially service each process, giving it fetch-execute cycles and other support that it may need. If the machine is very fast, as most modern machines are, the operating system may be able to keep many processes running without the individual users ever realizing that they do not have complete control of the machine. In fact, the picture should be as follows: The machine will have many processes in some state of execution at one time. Each of these will have its own segment of memory and its own current status and needs. One process may be in midcalculation and waiting to get a chance to use some more cycles; another may have come to a stopping point until it gets its next data item from its user; another may have just sent a block of characters to the printer and will send more when the printer is ready; another may have finished its computation and will be removed from memory when the operating system gets back to it. In the meantime, the operating system will have a priority schedule that will tell it what to do. It will give one program a *time slice* of several milliseconds, then another, and another. At each point, it will check the status of that particular program and supply it with its momentary needs before going on to the next.

Let us assume a subroutine exists called *chooseprocess* that uses some method to decide which of many processes to execute next. *Chooseprocess* will have one argument, *chosenprocess*, where it will place the number of the process that it has chosen. Also, assume that there is a routine *executeprocess* that activates a process and carries out its instructions for a short period of time. *Executeprocess* will have one argument, the process that it is to execute. Then the operating system's task will be to carry out the following loop endlessly:

```
chooseprocess (chosenprocess);
while chosenprocess > 0 do
    begin
    executeprocess (chosenprocess);
    chooseprocess (chosenprocess);
    end;
```

It may be that a number of processes are initiated by a single user sitting at one terminal. Perhaps the user will want to start a search in a database for an obscure fact, initiate a long printing job, compile a large program, and answer mail, all at the same time on a single machine. The user might create a window or two on the screen to monitor each process as it proceeds.

But many processes are created by the operating system itself. These processes are often initiated to service the needs of existing processes. For example, a process may call for a print of certain data and the operating system may create a process to pass the user's data from his or her program to the printer with whatever special formatting and commands are needed. Simultaneously, that same user program might need some other service, such as the access to a given disk file. This could cause a need for a second extra process that would be created by the operating system for this program. That is, the single program could involve the running of its own process and several others simultaneously. In addition to user-spawned extra processes, the operating system could create special processes related to its own tasks. For example, it might back up the file system onto a permanent storage medium periodically for security reasons or initiate communication with outside systems to receive and send mail or news.

In summary, the operating system can be thought of as the keeper of the resources of the computing environment and the benevolent provider for the processes. It tirelessly selects process after process and executes each one for a short time before moving on to the next. As it does its work, new processes come into existence and old ones occasionally disappear. But the operating system's only job is to keep grabbing processes and executing them.

Our final representation of the operating system shows the addition of several users to remind us that the operating system can keep track of many users and processes simultaneously:

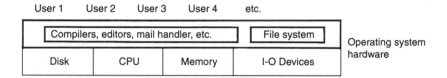

Exercises

1. Log in to the machine on which you have been doing your programming and run through a typical programming session: Create a program, store it, compile and run it, print it out. But as you do these things, write down every command you give to the operating system and describe with the command the functions the operating system is delivering to you and the devices it is using. Describe all the processes that are running besides the ones that you have coded with your own program.

2. List all the operating commands that you know and what their functions are.

3. Describe the file system on your computer. What are the commands that you need to store, print, delete, and otherwise access those files?

## Time Sharing in Action (B)

Returning to our virtual environment for computing, let us create a second process and time share with the program-editing process described above. Specifically, we can access the system call on the screen and select the *foreground* option. This command will bring to the foreground, the screen we are looking at, any process we wish to examine. When it brings in a new process, the old one will disappear into the background, but we will be able to bring it back with the *foreground* command.

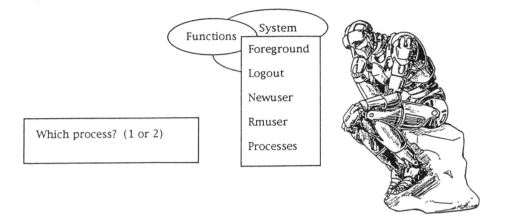

We will call the activities of "awb" listed above "process 1." "Process 2" will be those of some other user. Let us go to process 2 and log in a second user, say "bwb,"

with password "b." This user decides to create and send a message to "awb".

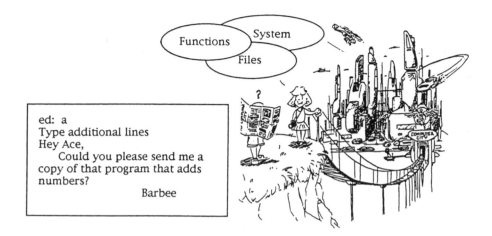

This file can be saved in the usual way:

```
ed: s
Give the filename.
T1
ed: q
```

The mail facility is called by the menu item *mail* under the *Functions* heading. It enables the user to either send mail or read incoming mail. We need not examine those details here, but we will assume they have been done.

After sending the message, "bwb" can use a command called *processes* to examine the states of all running processes.

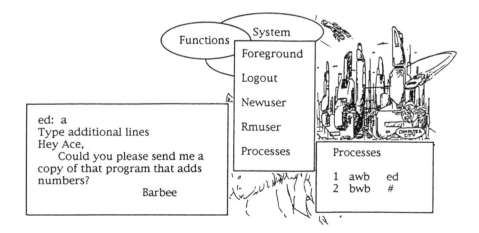

There are two active processes, and this command gives the logged user for each one and the name of the process. Specifically, user "awb" is currently running the editor and user "bwb" is not using any program.

Let us now switch back to process 1 using the *foreground* item under the heading *System* and attend to the Pascal program that was created. We will compile the program *pascaltest* (that we typed earlier) and examine the results of the compilation.

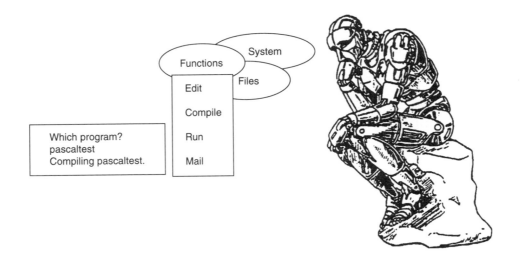

We will assume with this system that compilation requires a long time. The compiler will do its work as a background process and in the meanwhile, the prompt tells "awb" that he can do other work.

"Awb" checks all running processes again:

```
Processes
1          awb    #
2          bwb    #
3    sys   compiling
```

He sees his background compile job is listed. If "awb" checks his mail, he sees that something has come in from "bwb."

After reading his mail, "awb" receives the message

```
Compilation complete.
```

and he looks again at his directory.

Directory

```
pascaltest     1     6
#bwb           7     5
$c-out        12    11
```

The new files are the message that came from "bwb" and the object code from the compiler stored in the file $c-out. "Awb" examines this object code with the editor.

```
ed: g
Which file?
$c-out

IN    AX
#
COPY X,AX
IN    AX
COPY Y,AX
COPY AX,X
ADD   AX,Y
COPY CN1,AX
COPY AX,CN1
COPY Z,AX
COPY AX,Z
OUT   AX
```

If he decides that the object code correctly expresses the meaning of the original program *pascaltest*, he can exit the editor and run the code. He uses it to add up the numbers 74 and 155.

```
Input:     74
Input:     155
Output:    229
```

A last point of interest is what happens to the process listing when a logout occurs. When user "awb" logs out using the *Logout* option under *Functions*, the system removes the "awb" process and, if we check the *Processes* option, we see that only "bwb" remains on the system.

Processes

```
1    bwb    #
```

When the "awb" process was terminated, other lower level processes moved up to take its place. The foreground process 1 is now "bwb" instead of "awb."

**Exercise**

1. To demonstrate the time-sharing feature, you might open a window on your system and get a process running. Then open several more and get processes running on them. Another technique is to log in several different users, as described in this section.

# Files (B)

Processes, of course, have the task of manipulating information and this information is usually organized as files. A file may be stored on the disk system, brought into the memory, modified in a computation, sent abroad on a network, or read or printed by an input-output device. A file may contain data, a program, or both.

Files are usually accessed through a directory, as illustrated above. The user can display the directory and choose a file.

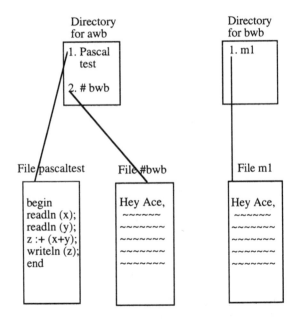

File systems commonly allow for the creation of directories within directories, which leads to the creation of a tree:

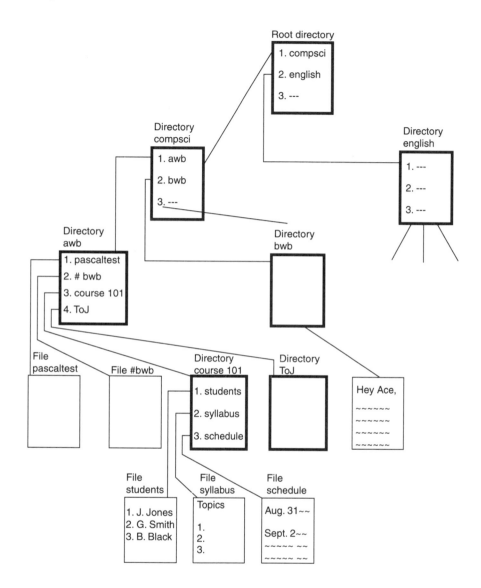

Here the whole file system emanates from a single root directory. Each directory, shown with a bold rectangle, lists a set of directories or files that can be found immediately below it in the hierarchy. Descending branches terminate when files are reached. These are shown with nonbold rectangles. One common naming system simply traces the branches down the tree. Thus, the full name of our sample Pascal program would be */compsci/awb/*

*pascaltest*. Processes managed by the operating system have the job of creating, manipulating, reorganizing, or deleting the various files and directories in this file system.

The usual manner of working with files is to issue an *open* command to the operating system saying that a particular file is to be accessed. Then a sequence of read or write operations directed at that file can either copy information from or add information to that file. Finally, when the accesses are complete, a *close* command can be issued to the operating system telling it to break off that communication.

The file system usually includes a security mechanism that allows or disallows access to the various directories and files. For example, a directory and all its subdirectories and files might be closed to all users except its owner. Or certain directories and their associated files might be read by anyone but security locks could prevent their modification. Thus, an academic department might allow anyone to read the schedule of courses for the coming semester but would make it impossible for readers to change that schedule. However, *superuser* status enables computer administrative personnel to access all files in the system in order to do maintenance and repair on the system.

Once the tree of directories and files has been created, it can be used in a variety of ways. For example, when a floppy disk is loaded into a drive, the system can grow a new subtree on the tree that holds the directories and files from the disk. As another example, sometimes input-output devices are made to look like files so they can be accessed using the same system calls that are used for manipulating files. Thus, reading from an input device might be represented internally as if that device were simply a file to be read like any other file.

**Exercise**

1. Assuming the name of the Pascal program in the above file system is */compsci/awb/ pascaltest*, give the names of all the other files in that tree.

---

## Exploring the File System (B)

The tree-shaped file system shown above can be traversed and examined with a new set of commands:

```
cd    change directory
path  list the path to the current directory
tree  list the tree of directories below the current one
```

We can begin our exploration with *cd* to the root directory: *cd /* Then we can touch *tree* on the menu and get a listing of the tree of directories below the root. It will show directories and not files in order to keep the printout simple.

```
tree
compsci
    awb
            course101
            ToJ
    bwb
english
    black
    jones
```

If we select *path*, we get a listing of the directories traversed from the root to the current directory. In the root node, requesting path obtains just /.

Next we can move to one of the directories below the root, say *compsci*. The command is *cd compsci*. Here *path* will yield /*compsci* and *tree* will yield

```
awb
    course101
    ToJ
bwb
```

This gives the rest of the directory tree that remains below this node. Moving on, *cd course101* will go to a lower directory. Here the path will be /*compsci*/*awb*/*course101* and *tree* will give nothing. *Dir* will give all the files in the *course101* directory:

```
students
syllabus
schedule
```

Let us examine the contents of the directory *ToJ:cd* /*compsci*/*awb*/*ToJ* Woooops! We get a message "Access denied." An author must have personal information that he or she wishes to protect from the world. It has been protected from us, but there are other users who can look at all directories and files and would be able to enter the *ToJ* directory. They have the login "Supervisor" and are presumably in charge of maintaining the system software. So no file is ever completely safe from absolutely everyone.

This completes the exploration of the tree of files. The next section will examine the command interpreter for the operating system.

**Exercises**

1. If a person on the above system selects the commands *cd* /*compsci*/*awb*, then *tree* followed by *path*, what will be printed out?

2. Study the file system available on your machine. Find as many files as you can and check some of their contents. How does the security mechanism work on your operating system?

## The Command Interpreter (B)

The user sees very little of the operating system and the primary interactions are through the *command interpreter*. The command interpreter, sometimes called the *shell*, receives the user requests and makes calls to the operating system to get them handled. The requests may be typed or they may be menu selections, as we have demonstrated in this chapter.

Our coverage of the command interpreter will be confined to presenting a simplified version of the one on our system. It is the procedure given below which has these parameters:

user            *This identifies the user in the current process.*
chosenprocess   *This identifies the process number under which the command interpreter is being invoked.*

The code follows. The bracketed numbers indicate explanatory notes that follow the code.

```
procedure commandinterpreter (var user:stringDB;var
                              chosenprocess:integer);
    var
        command,syscom,s:stringDB;
        i,j:integer;
    begin
    menuinput(command);                {1}
    if command = 'help' then
        begin
        swriteln('Commands');          {2}
        swriteln('compile     compiles m-Pascal');
        swriteln('delete      deletes a file');
        swriteln('dir         displays directory');
        swriteln('ed          calls the editor');
        swriteln('hurry       executes background');
        swriteln('logout      logs out');
        swriteln('mail        activates mail');
        swriteln('me          identifies user');
```

```
          swriteln('newuser      creates new user');
          swriteln('rm user      removes user');
          swriteln('run          runs assembly code');
          swriteln('print        prints a file');
          swriteln('processes    displays processes');
          swriteln('foreground   selects process');
          end;
     if command = 'compile' then        {3}
          begin
          swriteln('Which file?');
          sreadln(s);                    {4}
          syscom := 'compile';
          systemcall(syscom,s,chosenprocess);
          end;
     if command = 'delete' then         {3}
          begin
          swriteln('Which file:');
          sreadln(s);
          syscom := 'delete';
          systemcall(syscom,s,chosenprocess);
          end;
     if command = 'dir' then            {5}
          begin
          swriteln('Directory');
          getusernum(chosenprocess,j);
          i := 1;
          while i <= numfilename[j] do  {6}
              begin
              swrite(filename[j,i]);
              swrite(' ');
              swriteint(fileaddress[j,i]);
              swrite(' ');
              swriteint(filelength[j,i]);
              swriteln(' ');
              i := i + 1;
              end;
          end;
     if command = 'logout' then         {3}
          begin
          syscom := 'logout';
          systemcall(syscom,user,chosenprocess);
          end;
```

```
      if command = 'mail' then              {3}
         begin
         syscom := 'mail';
         systemcall(syscom,user,chosenprocess);
         end;
      if command = 'processes' then       {5}
         begin
         i := 1;
         while i <= numprocesses do       {6}
            begin
            writeln(puser[i],' ',prunningcommand[i],' ',
               pdata[i],' ',ppending[i]);
            i := i + 1;
            end;
         end;
      if command = 'foreground' then      {5}
         begin
         writeln('Which process? (1 to ',(numprocesses + 1), ')');
         readln(foreground);
         displayscreen(foreground);
         end;
      if command = 'ed' then              {5}
         begin
         nummemory[chosenprocess] := 0;
         edit(chosenprocess,nummemory[chosenprocess]);
         end;
      if command = - - - - - -

       {Etc.}
      end;                                {7}
```

## Notes

1. We assume a subroutine is available by the name *menuinput* that receives a user-selected command from the menu bubbles on the screen.

2. The *swrite* and *swriteln* routines are similar to *write* and *writeln* in ordinary Pascal. The difference is that the characters to be printed are sent to the appropriate process, which may or may not be showing on the screen. Thus, when an *swrite* or *swriteln* is executed, if the current process is in the foreground, the characters will show on the screen; if the

current process is in the background, the characters will be sent to a hidden screen, which might be viewed later.

3. Many commands to the command interpreter result in immediate calls to the operating system. The procedure *systemcall* simulates the operating system. It is given as arguments a command (*syscom*), a variable containing a string, and a variable telling which process is being executed.

4. The *sreadln* routine is similar to *readln* except that it supports the same hidden screen capability as described in 2. This instruction receives the user command.

5. The command interpreter can handle some commands immediately without calls to the system.

6. This program violates a rule advocated in the other chapters of this book. Some variables are used that are neither listed as subroutine parameters or as subroutine declared variables. They are called *global variables* and they are declared in the main program. In a program as complex as this, a resort to some global variables helps to keep the number of listed parameters under control. This is not a practice recommended for new programmers, however.

7. The command interpreter releases control to the operating system after doing a single command. This is as if it were interrupted after completing each command so that other processes may be serviced. In a more realistic operating system, control could pass from the current process to another at any time rather than at such convenient points.

Many command interpreters allow more complex commands than the ones shown here. For example, a notation introduced in the UNIX operating system enables the user to direct data to or from a program. Thus, if *run p1* is the command to execute program *p1* and print the results on the display, then *run p1 > file2* is the command to execute *p1* and send the results to *file2*. Or *run p1 < file1* is the command to execute *p1* using *file1* as input. Or *run p1 > file2 < file1* requests that *p1* be executed with *file1* as input and *file2* as output.

**Exercise**

1. Create a new operating system command called *nextprocess*. This command will jump to the next process in numerical order, whatever it is. Thus, if the current process is process 2 and *nextprocess* is invoked, then the current process will become process 3. If the current process is greater than *numprocesses* + *1*, then *nextprocess* will select process 1.

## Contention for Memory and Paging (C)

The advent of time sharing (sometimes called *multiprogramming*) puts new demands on the computer memory. If only a single program is to run on a machine and there is enough memory to run that program, we used to feel that we could run that program and the story was simple. However, when there are many programs in contention to run on one machine, suddenly the memory space to hold them seems scarce and we must look carefully at how we are using that space.

As an example, consider a program *A* which, for our purposes, will be divided into six parts, *A1*, *A2*, ..., *A6*. We will call these six parts *pages*, and think about that program's use of the memory as it runs. (These pages will be convenient partitions for the purposes of machine internal functioning and will have no correspondence to the ordinary pages of our computer printout.) First, let us say, page *A1* runs for a while, then page *A2*, and so forth. Possibly at some point, page *A1* will run again or *A2* will run again, and these repetitions could recur many times. The point is that when *A1* is running, the memory that holds *A2* and beyond is holding unused and unneeded code and when another section is running, the memory holding *A1* is being wasted.

A good solution to this problem is to create a partitioning scheme that separates every program into pages and keeps only a few pages of each running program in memory at a time. The operating system then can run one program (process) for a short time, then another, then another, and so forth, giving each its appropriate time slice. The currently active pages of each program can all be resident in the memory simultaneously and the inactive pages can be kept on the disk ready to be brought in as needed. The picture then looks something like the following, where three running programs *A*, *B*, and *C* are resident on the disk and the active pages from each are loaded into the memory. The operating system can run the active pages of the three programs, first one, then the other, and bring in new pages for each program as needed.

Disk

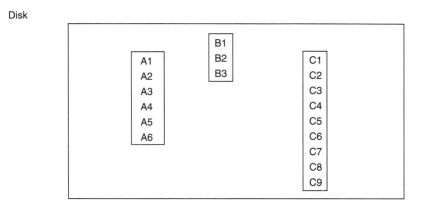

Memory

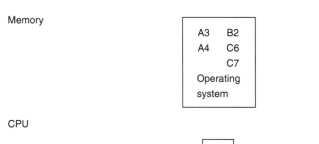

CPU

The act of moving programs or pages in and out of memory is called *swapping*. Sometimes a machine gets caught in a very wasteful mode where it spends too much of its time swapping. This is called *thrashing* and it occurs when the new pages brought in result in calls for other new pages, which result in calls for more pages, and so forth.

An important by-product of the paging and swapping scheme is that individual programs no longer need to be small enough to fit into memory. We can have a 30 megabyte program that runs on a machine with a 10 megabyte memory. We say the machine has a large *virtual memory*, because its memory seems large even though it may actually be small.

**Exercises**

1. Consider the following program. Suppose that it is to be divided into five roughly equal pages and that the computer memory is so small that only one page will fit at a time. Show how to divide it and describe how much swapping will be done in the process of its execution. Assume that the routines *sub1*, *sub2*, and *sub3* are defined elsewhere.

Repeat the exercise dividing it into four roughly equal pages. Repeat it again dividing it into three, and then two, roughly equal pages.

```
program pages;
var
     i,N: integer;
begin
N := 1000000;
i := 1;
while i <= N do
    begin
    sub1;
    i := i + 1;
    end;
i := 1;
while i <= N do
    begin
    sub2;
    i := i + 1;
    end;
i := 1;
while i <= N do
    begin
    sub3;
    i := i + 1;
    end;
end.
```

2. In the figure above, assume that programs *A*, *B*, and *C* are to be run simultaneously. Assume that *A* is linear, executing *A1* through *A6* in a sequence and then halting; however, we do not know how long *A* will take. Assume that *B* executes similarly. Assume that *C* executes *C1* through *C3* once, then a loop consisting of *C4* through *C6* with a million repetitions, then the linear sequence *C7* to *C9* once. How should the pages be loaded into the memory in order to minimize swapping, assuming that the memory will hold no more than six pages at one time.

---

## Summary (B)

The facade that the machine presents to the user is completely programmable. Therefore the designer of a system can decide what image he or she wants the user to have and can write the code to make it happen. The designer thus creates a virtual environment for the user. The purpose of the virtual environment is to enable the user to function more efficiently and comfortably.

The operating system is the program that presents the user with the facade; it translates the user's commands into low-level instruction sequences that can be carried out by the hardware. The primary concepts related to operating systems are the idea of the process and the idea of the file system. Processes are the programs in active execution at any given time; the operating system's central loop simply keeps grabbing processes and executing them according to some priority schedule. The file system maintains the files stored on the machine and makes them available to the operating system.

The study of hardware and software involves an examination of a series of levels of abstraction. The actual computations occur in the electric circuits where voltages and currents tell the story of what is happening. But when we discuss computation at the register level, we seldom mention the electricity; we usually talk about a representation of the register contents in a binary form:

```
0100001101011111
```

At a higher level of abstraction, we might discuss a computation at the assembly-language level, in which case the same register contents might appear as

```
ADD  AX,X
```

The next level of abstraction is the programming level, which is Pascal in this book. In Pascal, we might write

```
Z := (X + Y);
```

At the level of the operating system, the entities being manipulated are programs and files. Here we might type something like

```
run pascaltest
```

In order to understand computer science, it is necessary to deal with all these levels of abstraction.

Another view of the abstraction hierarchy is as a set of *virtual machines*. A virtual entity in computer science is an entity that seems to exist because of the view presented by the machine but which does not exist in reality. For example, when we program in Pascal, the machine looks like a Pascal machine. It seems to understand Pascal statements and responds as if that were its native language. When we are using another language, say assembly language, Prolog, or C++, the machine appears to become, respectively, an assembly language, Prolog, or C++ machine. These are examples of virtual machines created by the authors of the language-processing facilities for the convenience and efficiency of users.

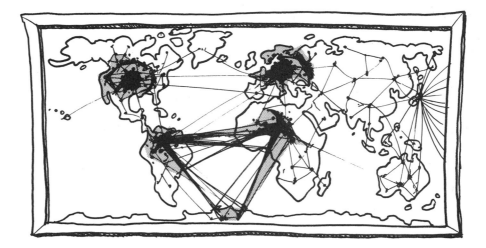

# 11    Computer Communications

Dietolf Ramm

---

## Exploration (A)

On the way back from a concert in New York City by your favorite rock group, you are almost cut off by an 18-wheeler with a huge trailer. You fume for a while, planning all kinds of revenge. You are sorry that you always seem to be fresh out of photon torpedoes just when that kind of thing happens. There is another way. Why not send a letter to the President of the United States noting your dislike of any laws allowing vehicles bigger than yours on the nation's highways? It is no longer necessary to get out paper, envelope, and stamps to do this. All you need to do is log into your networked computer and send electronic mail (*e-mail*) with your thoughts on this matter. You simply type the following:

```
mail president@whitehouse.gov
Subject: Big, bad trucks
Dear Mr. President
I'm afraid of the big bad trucks. Please help!
Sincerely,
Red
.
```

You are in luck and the President would like to discuss your concerns with you in person. He replies that due to the upcoming governor's conference in Seattle, the meeting will have to be there and he asks you to suggest a nice place for lunch. Before making a reservation at one of those outdoor establishments near the Space Needle, you want to

---

Note: If you wish to try out the things in this chapter, you need access to a UNIX workstation that is connected to the Internet.

find out what the weather will be. The latest weather forecast can be displayed by typing

```
weather sea
```

where *sea* is the code for the Seattle area. A typical response is shown below.

```
Weather retrieval script, version 2.2
Connecting to downwind.sprl.umich.edu...connected

|
Weather Conditions at 4 PM PDT on 15 JAN for Seattle, WA.
Temp(F) Humidity(%) Wind(mph) Pressure(in) Weather
======================================================================
466
FQUS1 KSEA 152342
LFPSEA
WAZ001-160530-

SEATTLE TACOMA EVERETT AND VICINITY FORECAST
NATIONAL WEATHER SERVICE SEATTLE WA
400 PM PST SUN JAN 15

.TONIGHT...OCCASIONAL SHOWERS DECREASING LATE, OTHERWISE MOSTLY CLOUDY.
LOWS IN THE UPPER 30S. SOUTH WIND 5 TO 15 MPH, DECREASING OVERNIGHT.
.MONDAY...SCATTERED SHOWERS AND PATCHY MORNING FOG. PARTLY SUNNY
PERIODS. HIGHS MID 40S. LIGHT SOUTH WIND.
.MONDAY NIGHT...PARTLY CLOUDY BECOMING MOSTLY CLOUDY LATE. SLIGHT CHANCE
OF RAIN LATE. LOWS 30S.
.TUESDAY...RAIN DEVELOPING. HIGHS MID 40S.

.<                   TEMPERATURE    /  PRECIPITATION
SEATTLE              38  45  35  44 / 60  40  20  60
The National Weather Service information is provided by the University
of Michigan Weather Underground project and the National Science
Foundation-funded Unidata project, from a data feed broadcast by
Alden/Zephyr Electronics, Inc.
```

These are just a few examples of the opportunities afforded by the Internet. Our goals in this chapter are to get a better understanding of how this marvelous network operates and to learn how to use it.

## Layers and Local Area Networks (LANs) (B)

One recurring theme in computing is *layers*. We looked at issues raised by two layers of programming when we studied Pascal and assembly-language programming, and now we will deal with the problems raised by layers in communications software. The bottom layer is the actual hardware used for communications. The systems at this low level are often described as *Local Area Networks* or *LANs*. Two common low-level methods for computer communications are *Ethernet* and *Token Ring*. Ethernet was developed by the Xerox Corporation and has become a standard. It is called a *bus* architecture because many computers share the same communication line or *bus*, as illustrated below.

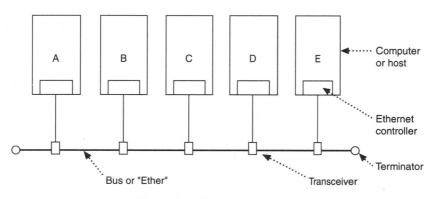

An Ethernet-based local area network (LAN)

In this figure, the letters A through E designate computers (also called *hosts*). Each computer contains an Ethernet controller with a connection to the bus.

The network works like many people trying to communicate in a large room. Judy might wait until the room is quiet and then say, "John, how did you like the book?" Everyone can hear the question, although it is intended for John and, in polite company, only John will listen. Then he might wait for a quiet moment and reply, "Judy, the book was great!" As long as everyone is polite and orderly, any two people in the room can communicate, although no more than two can communicate at any one time. Even though everyone can hear all messages, all listeners are expected to ignore messages not intended for them.

The Ethernet works like this except that the signals on the bus are electrical and the bus takes the form of a piece of coaxial cable. (You may have seen coaxial cable in your cable TV hookup or in the cable connecting your VCR to your TV.) The message length is limited to keep any two computers from monopolizing the bus, and each Ethernet controller is guaranteed a unique address by the manufacturers, who have an agreement among themselves. The address is like a serial number and takes the form of a 12-digit hexadecimal (base 16 arithmetic) number written in the following form:

```
5A   34   B2   31   90   1C
```

With a unique address, messages can always have an unambiguous destination. It would not be like the example given earlier, where John would have problems if there were more than one Judy in the room.

Another problem dealt with at this low level is *collisions*. Even in polite company, two people may start talking at exactly the same time. For Ethernet, this is called a collision. Ethernet controllers can detect a collision and know that this means that the data are likely to be garbled. In this case, each controller wishing to use the bus waits for a random amount of time before attempting to communicate again. This so-called random back-off makes it unlikely that one collision is immediately followed by another one.

A concept used with Ethernet and other computer communications is that of breaking a message into smaller chunks. Since messages have a maximum length, larger messages must be broken down into smaller segments, called *packets*. As illustrated below, each packet includes important control information, including the destination address (where it is going) and the source address (where it came from).

| dest addr | source addr | message | check info |
|-----------|-------------|---------|------------|

The format of an Ethernet packet

Think of it as taking a manuscript and mailing it on several standard postcards. Each has independent address information on the front. At the destination, all postcards can be ordered and the manuscript reassembled. To aid this, each packet also includes sequencing information. This idea is illustrated here:

| dest addr | source addr | Four score and | check info |
|-----------|-------------|----------------|------------|

| dest addr | source addr | seven years ago, | check info |
|-----------|-------------|------------------|------------|

| dest addr | source addr | our forefathers | check info |
|-----------|-------------|-----------------|------------|

| dest addr | source addr | brought forth | check info |
|-----------|-------------|---------------|------------|

. . .

Note that there is a potential security problem in the Ethernet communications method, since every controller on the bus can see every message, regardless of its destination. Standard software causes controllers to ignore all messages not intended for that computer, but users may be able to obtain rogue software that does not follow that convention. Although this is in effect wiretapping and is illegal, such software is not too hard to obtain since it does have legitimate trouble-shooting applications. Therefore, we leave this hardware level with a warning. Unless you are sure of the other machines and users on your local Ethernet, what you are typing may be monitored. Of course, you should keep this in a healthy perspective. Your phone may be tapped, with a court order or illegally; police may intercept your mail if they have a warrant; and, of course, a thief can easily take something out of your mailbox.

### Exercises

1. Suppose there are five people on an Ethernet. Each has a message to send to each other person and each message requires one second to send. If they all send their messages as fast as possible, how long will it take to get them all transferred over the network?

2. Suppose you were to send the first section of this chapter to a friend on postcards that can hold only 200 characters. How many postcards would you need? How would you format them to be sure that they reach your friend and that they can be reassembled in the correct order?

## Wide Area Networks (B)

Once we have mastered the idea of a network, we can consider the possibility of connecting several networks together. As an example, we can connect two Ethernet-based networks, Network 1 with hosts A, B, C, and D and Network 2 with hosts W, X, Y, and Z, as shown below. They are connected using Network 3. (Network 3 could have many more connections but we will consider only the two shown.) To accomplish this, we have set up machine A with two Ethernet controllers and connections to Networks 1 and 3. Machine W also has two controllers, one for Network 2 and one for Network 3.

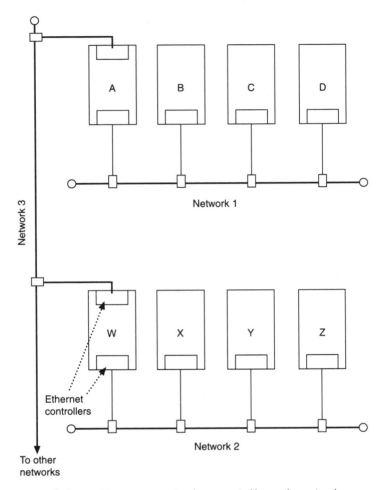

An internet: two or more networks connected by another network

A machine connected to more than one network is sometimes called a *gateway* machine. (We can also buy a special-purpose piece of hardware called a *router* to accomplish this.) You can now see how these gateway machines can be used to enable universal communication. Machine C, for example, can now communicate with machine X by using gateways A and W. A message from C intended for X would first go from C to A using Network 1. Then A would forward it, using Network 3, to W. W would then forward the message, via Network 2, to X. If the message is long enough, it would consist of a number of packets, each taking the same route.

A collection of networks connected together is called an *internet*. In recent years, a very large collection of interconnected networks has evolved, and it is called the *Internet*. It is the basis for what has come to be called the *information superhighway*.

Ethernets are designed to be fairly fast, but they have certain size restrictions. Under ideal conditions, an Ethernet can be almost a mile long, but hardware and software constraints often reduce that to several hundred feet. This means that an internet consisting of only Ethernet-based networks would have to be fairly small physically, or it would take a very large number of "hops" from gateway to gateway to cover very large distances. However, it is possible to replace the Ethernet in Network 3 with other communications hardware. Such hardware, often leased from a common carrier, can provide connections over very large distances. The principles are similar to those used with Ethernet. Information is sent in the form of one or more packets, and each packet includes appropriate addressing and other control information.

### Exercises

1. Suppose you are dealing with Ethernets that can each handle only four computers. Tell how many such nets you would need to connect 100 such machines and tell how you would connect them. Assume that one machine can connect to no more than two networks simultaneously.

2. Define a *network transfer* to be the passage of a message from one network to another through a gateway machine. Suppose that you wish to connect 100 machines with the networks of problem 1 such that the largest number of network transfers required to get a message from any one machine to any other machine is as small as possible. More specifically, find $k$ such that no two machines are more than $k$ transfers apart and such that no smaller value for $k$ would have this property. How would you do it?

## The Internet Protocol Layer (B)

We have discussed one physical communications medium, Ethernet, in some detail. We have mentioned Token Ring (essentially a competing product) as another possibility, and there are others. For example, *Asynchronous Transfer Mode (ATM)* is a transmission medium that can handle very large amounts of material over long distances. But typical users, who may not know all these details, will still be able to use the network because of a layer of software called the *Internet Protocol* or *IP*. This layer provides a standard way of handling packets of information regardless of whether the underlying transport mechanism is Ethernet, Token Ring, or some other system.

Each computer (or host) is given an IP address, regardless of how it is connected. IP packets look a lot like Ethernet packets with a source and destination address. If you know the IP address of the host you want to contact, the software will do the rest. It will automatically choose the appropriate networks (Token Ring, Ethernet, or whatever). The IP layer makes all networks seem the same.

If an IP packet is sent over an Ethernet, the complete IP packet is treated as data by the Ethernet packet. In other words, we have a packet within a packet. The (somewhat stretched) analogy is that if we send our manuscript on postcards to a person in France but that person is on a business trip in Belgium, a secretary might put the postcards into envelopes with French stamps and forward them to Belgium.

## More on Addressing (C)

You have probably seen the words "address" or "addressing" often enough in the last few pages to guess that there is something important here. We use addresses all the time in everyday life and often there are alternate ways to address the same location. For example, "The White House" and "1600 Pennsylvania Avenue" would both work with the U.S. Postal Service in Washington, D.C. Terms like "presidential residence" would probably also work. If you were already nearby and giving directions, you could use "third house on the right," "house on the corner," or "the white house with the columns—you can't miss it." If you are a courier delivering something, it will all eventually translate down to walking a certain number of steps, turning right or left, taking more steps, and so forth. The upshot of this is that we deal with any number of addressing schemes, and in the end we have to translate these into action.

When dealing with computer networks, we also need to be aware that there are several different ways of addressing things. In the end, when Ethernet is involved, all addressing has to be translated to the 12-digit hexadecimal number unique to the Ethernet controller you are trying to reach. Fortunately, we don't have to memorize such addresses, since there are other addressing methods that are better suited for human use, and with the help of computer software, we can use higher level, more descriptive, addresses.

Let us use a high-level address and follow the process that gets us to the right place. Assume we are sending a message to Tom at the University of California at Berkeley. If his login ID on his computer is

```
TOM
```

and the machine he is using is named

```
SIGMA
```

then we might type

```
mail  tom@sigma.berkeley.edu
```

This uses a high-level addressing scheme called a *domain* address. The domain address is a hierarchical addressing scheme going (left to right) from local to general (just like a typical mail address). For the United States, the last portion is one of these:

com    (commercial)
net    (network)
edu    (educational institution)
org    (organization)
mil    (military)
gov    (government)

or a state code. International extensions to this scheme end in a country code. Other levels are appropriately descriptive; their number is dependent on the size and complexity of the organization covered. The leftmost entry of the domain address is often the name of the host machine, *sigma* in the example, on which the user reads his or her e-mail.

This statement will cause a query to be sent to the machine SIGMA at Berkeley. There it will probably encounter a piece of software called the *name server*, which will produce a lower-level address called the IP address (discussed above). This IP address is a number of the form 128.123.34.56 (4 decimal numbers, each ranging from 0 through 255, separated by periods). For all practical purposes, throughout the Internet this IP address uniquely identifies the computer and the network. (Actually, more accurately, it identifies the connection point of a computer to a network. A gateway machine has more than one IP address. Most computers have only one connection point, and thus only one IP address.)

Again, the beauty of the IP address is that it is independent of the kind of hardware it is used for. The actual lower-level hardware may be Ethernet, or Token Ring, or some other communication method. Since everything has an IP address, once we have the address we can start sending packets to our destination using the actual physical medium. Again, let us assume Ethernet. In this case, an IP packet is carried as data in an Ethernet packet that uses the 12-hexadecimal digits for addressing. Since the translation to other addresses is done automatically, we don't have to worry about it. In our message to Berkeley, the software will figure out the addresses of the various Ethernet controllers that may be involved. If other types of communications hardware are also involved, then the addressing specific to that method will automatically be utilized.

**Exercise**

1. Determine the e-mail addresses of several friends in your town and in distant towns. Send them messages.

## Other Applications (A)

Our main illustrations of the Internet so far have been e-mail and, briefly, getting a weather map. Here are two more useful applications.

### News

The interchange of information of general interest by computer started when two graduate students at Duke University got together with a graduate student from the University of North Carolina at Chapel Hill and started posting general information for others to read. The connections between the computers were made via modems over dial-up phone lines, and the students began to develop software for posting and sending news. Soon several Duke computers were involved, and the system went national when AT&T Bell Labs in New Jersey became the first non-North Carolina site. This system, dubbed *Usenet*, grew rapidly and now has participants all over the world. You can read news by typing "rn" and following the instructions. Other programs to organize your news reading are also available.

### Using Remote Computers

If you have accounts on a remote computer that is on the Internet, you can log into it using the *telnet* command. For example, you can type

```
telnet info.berkeley.edu
```

and provide your user id and password to log into the machine named *info*. If you just want to download files from such a computer, you use the *file transfer protocol* or *ftp* by typing

```
ftp info.berkeley.edu
```

and providing your id and password and then using the appropriate download commands (e.g., *get filename*). Many Internet sites provide public information by allowing any person to log in using the user id *anonymous* and his or her own e-mail address as the password. This is called *anonymous ftp*.

### Exercises

1. Try out the news facility on your local machine.

2. Use the telnet feature to access data at another computer installation.

## Exploring the Internet (A)

Over the years, many computer programmers learned to use basic tools like *telnet* and *ftp* to gather information from other computers. It became common for computer sites to keep special archives of programs and other information available for downloading. Some archives are sponsored by computer clubs or the government, and others by institutions and individuals. Scientists often keep copies of their latest publications on the computer so that other scientists can get copies of them.

As the kind of person using the Internet became less expert, tools were developed to make it easier to get information from other sites. Now many information services are available over the Internet. These have names (often acronyms) like WAIS, Gopher, and World Wide Web. These are meant to be user-friendly and allow the Internet to be navigated by someone with a minimum of computer skills. New mechanisms have also been set up to make information available to people who do not have accounts on the machine.

One popular system is the World Wide Web, which provides a method for organizing information in computer files in a standard way, including references to other sources of information. Information on the World Wide Web can be accessed by a number of programs, called *browsers*, specifically designed to make this process as painless as possible. Frequently used programs are *Mosaic*, *Netscape*, and *Lynx*. The first two require a high-quality display system with good graphics, but Lynx makes it practical to access web information on systems with minimal or even no graphics.

These programs use a feature called *hypertext* that allows you to follow the references from one information source to another. In hypertext, certain words are highlighted (by underlines or different colors). By moving your cursor to such a word with your mouse and clicking, you go to another "page" associated with that word; that page will probably have other highlighted words, and so on. You will usually find other words in boxes that you can click on to back up, quit, or do something else. You can invoke Mosaic, Netscape, or Lynx by typing *mosaic*, *netscape*, or *lynx*.

### Exercise

1. Find out what network-access software is available on your local facility and use it to explore the Internet.

## Problems in Paradise (C)

The time has come to discuss a more sober side of communications. Ease in communications brings with it the increased chance that security or confidentiality may be compromised. For our purposes, security involves the integrity of the message. Having the message altered or destroyed is a breach of security. Confidentiality relates to whether an unauthorized person can gain access to the information. No harm to the information is implied. Of course, in most cases we desire both security and confidentiality.

To be fair, other means of communication have the same problems. The national mail service is relatively secure only because the government is willing to put a lot of police power behind insuring the security of your mail. There is, in fact, very little that keeps your neighbor from getting the mail out of your mailbox or from listening to your telephone conversations. Cellular phone use and satellite long distance circuits have made the phone even less secure than it may once have been.

The problems related to the privacy of computer communications are twofold. First, there are, unfortunately, a large number of computer users who consider breaching computer security a game or a challenge. The laws are there, but enforcement is sometimes difficult and not many people have been caught and punished. Second, there is the nature of bus-oriented systems like Ethernet, where the communications channel is shared. Proper software does not allow users to eavesdrop, but many users can easily get or write rogue software that lets them "listen in" on everything being sent on the local Ethernet segment. Since the hardware to listen is "required" for proper operation, there is almost no way, short of physically observing the perpetrator, of detecting that eavesdropping is taking place.

The two most common ways of ensuring privacy turned out to raise problems of their own. In the first way, encryption, the sender of a message encrypts the message using a *secret key*. The receiver of the message must then supply that *key* to decode the message on the target machine. The problem is that the keys must somehow be shared between sender and receiver. Since the computer communications channel is assumed to be compromised, they must be exchanged by some other method, such as telephone or mail (assuming that they are secure).

In the second common way of ensuring privacy, password security, the computer network allows users to log into a remote computer if they have the proper password. However, if someone (let us call this person the *cracker*) is eavesdropping, he or she can "watch" what password is typed. At some other time, the cracker can log into that remote machine, pretending to be the user (this is called a "replay" attack), and do whatever the user could have done—use computer time, read files, delete files, and so forth. The cracker can also send mail, pretending to be the user. The implications are clearly serious, and complicated schemes using encryption have been devised to avoid having passwords go over the network in a readable form.

The password problem is a special case of a more general problem—that of authentication. For example, the university registrar gets a message from an instructor stating that John Smith's grade for the course was incorrect and should be changed from a C to an A. How does the registrar know that the message came from the instructor? Is it a forgery? A stock broker receives a message to buy or sell stocks. Is it genuine? Having special passwords or conventions may not be sufficient, since someone could have been eavesdropping the last time passwords were exchanged or conventions discussed.

## A Solution: The Secure Arbiter

One widely used solution to the password problem was developed at MIT in the Athena Project and is called Kerberos (after the mythical two-headed dog guarding the entrance to Hades). Using a physically secure arbiter of passwords (the Kerberos server), your computer can send essentially encrypted versions of your password to the remote machine. More accurately, the Kerberos server sends a "shared secret" encrypted by your password to the machine you are attempting to log in on. If the password you type in can decrypt this "shared secret," your password is assumed to be correct. Your password is thus never sent across the network while logging in.

To completely defeat the "replay attack," this encryption involves the time of day, so that just replaying a previously encrypted message recorded from eavesdropping will not work, since the correct encrypted message will change with time. It does require that all the computers in the network be synchronized and agree on the time of day (within certain tolerances).

## Another Solution: Public Key Encryption

One of several more general solutions to the confidentiality problem is *public key encryption*, which arose from the discovery of encryption-decryption techniques that use one key to encrypt and a different key to decrypt. It is like having one key to lock your house and a different one to unlock it. In this scheme, the locking key is published. If this ever catches on, you can imagine the equivalent of a telephone directory in which you can look up someone's public key. (In practice, since keys must be rather long to provide security, it will probably have to be a computerized equivalent of a telephone book.) If you want to send a secret message to, say, Joe Jones, you would use Joe's published key to encrypt the message. However, since only Joe has the other key, used for decryption, only Joe can read this message. If someone wants to send a secret message to you, they would use your published key to encrypt the message. You would then use your secret decryption key to read the message.

Free software to support this scheme has recently been published by MIT and is called PGP, which stands for Pretty Good Privacy. There was a dispute over copyright and patent infringement, but the latest version is legal (as long it is used within the United States and not exported) and is free for noncommercial use.

**Exercise**

1. Design a procedure for encrypting your own messages. Write down a procedure that will decode messages that have been scrambled by your encryption procedure. Encrypt a message and ask a friend who does not know your scheme to try to discover what the message is.

## Summary (B)

A revolution in society is now taking place because of the spread of computer networks. People are learning to contact each other with extreme ease and at great distances, and are gaining access to tremendous stores of data, which they are using for both traditional and creative new purposes. The ultimate effects of the new networks are impossible to predict.

A computer network is a set of computers and a communication system that allows them to interact. A machine sends a message by properly packaging and addressing the data and releasing it to the net. Often the message is so large that it must be broken into a set of packets that must make their way individually to the destination and then be reassembled.

Computer networking opens up a myriad of problems related to security and confidentialty because the messages in transit are readable by many other machines on the network. Standard software should prevent unauthorized access to messages in transit, but programs do exist that enable unethical and illegal perusal of messages. A common method for attempting to guarantee security and confidentiality is to encrypt messages before sending them. But there is not likely to be any foolproof method for guaranteeing security under all circumstances.

OUR UNITED NATIONS DELEGATION IS TO VISIT THE 300 LARGEST CITIES OF AFRICA OVER A 3-YEAR PERIOD.

WE NEED TO KNOW THE SHORTEST PATH THAT BEGINS IN CAIRO, GOES TO ALL THE CITIES, AND RETURNS TO CAIRO IN THE END.

WELL... IF YOU WANT THE VERY SHORTEST PATH, YOU'LL NEED TO TRANSPORT ME TO ANOTHER SOLAR SYSTEM.

WHY?!

BECAUSE THE SUN HERE WILL BURN OUT BEFORE I CAN FINISH!

# 12     Program Execution Time

## On the Limitations of Computer Science (A)

In the first five chapters of this book, we studied programming. After one has a reasonable degree of experience in programming, it is quite common to become extremely confident in one's ability to program absolutely anything. Programmers will often announce, "If you tell me what you want done, I can code it for you." At the end of Chapter 4, we discussed the Church-Markov-Turing thesis, which hypothesizes that any procedure that can be precisely explained can be coded in any standard programming language.

It therefore may be surprising to learn that there are many calculations that cannot be done. This chapter and the ones that follow will examine a number of problems whose solutions would be extremely useful but that computer scientists have not been able to solve. We will examine the current limitations of the field and the topic areas of current research.

There are three major reasons why many useful calculations cannot be done:

1. The execution time of the program may be too long. Instead of simply running the program and reading the answer after a few seconds, the program may require a year or even a century or more to find the answer. This may happen even with the fastest and most modern computer.
2. The problem may be what computer scientists call *noncomputable*. There are problems that no computer program can solve using current technologies or any technologies that can be foreseen. Many of these problems are of great practical interest and they seem to block certain kinds of progress.
3. We may not know how to write the program to solve the problem. There are many problems that could conceivably be solved with present-day machines and languages, but the methods are not known for solving them. Many of these are subproblems in the field of artificial intelligence, questions related to how to make machines "understand"

language, visual data, and other concepts, how to make machines learn, and other tasks.

These three limitations of computer science are the concern of this and later chapters. In this chapter, we will study the execution time of programs and limitation 1. In chapter 13, we will examine parallel machine architectures that make it possible to speed up some computations. Chapter 14 will present the fundamental facts of noncomputability and will give examples of important problems that are unsolvable by any known method. Chapter 15 will give an overview of the field of artificial intelligence, a study of problems that may be solvable but seem beyond our current abilities.

## Program Execution Time (A)

Ideally, a computation happens quickly. We type the input to the machine, wait for no more than a few seconds, and then see the answer printed. Most of the programs examined in this book run this fast, and in a learning environment the execution time of programs is not usually a problem. But in the real world of industry, government, and research laboratories, program execution time is a matter of great concern. The quantity of data that needs to be processed can become astronomical, and even the fastest machines can require hours, days, or even years to complete tasks.

It is no longer satisfactory simply to write a program and run it until the job is done. It has become important to predict how much time a specific calculation will require before it is attempted. Before a government service attempts to sort the Social Security Numbers of taxpayers, it needs to know how many hours, months, or years of computer time may be needed to complete the job. Before a power company attempts to compute the most efficient routing of power lines around a region, it must estimate how many hours, months, or years of machine time will be expended. The cost of the calculation may be prohibitive, forcing managers to look for alternative ways to manage their data and make their decisions.

This chapter will examine the execution times of some programs and estimate how long they would require to handle large blocks of data. The concept of a *tractable* computation will be introduced; this is a calculation which can usually be completed on even large blocks of data within "reasonable" amounts of time. Then some *intractable* calculations will be introduced that can require astounding amounts of computation for almost any problem. We will discover that computations divide themselves roughly into two classes: those that can be done with reasonable expenditures of time and those that cannot be realistically completed except for small examples. Since problems in both classes are quite common in practical situations, these limitations are of substantial importance.

## Tractable Computations (B)

For the moment, a *tractable computation* should be understood intuitively as a calculation that can be done within a reasonable amount of time, even if large amounts of data are to be processed. A more precise definition of this term will be given later in this section.

We will begin the study by examining a particular computation, the task of collecting the names of all people with a specified height and weight. We assume three arrays are given, *name*, *height*, and *weight*, which hold in position *i*, respectively, the name, height, and weight for a particular person. For example, suppose the arrays contain information for six people; they might look as follows:

| Name | | Height | | Weight | |
|---|---|---|---|---|---|
| 1 | John Jones | 1 | 67 | 1 | 120 |
| 2 | Sue Black | 2 | 67 | 2 | 131 |
| 3 | Bill Smith | 3 | 73 | 3 | 166 |
| 4 | Frank Doe | 4 | 68 | 4 | 140 |
| 5 | Jean White | 5 | 67 | 5 | 131 |
| 6 | Nancy Blike | 6 | 71 | 6 | 162 |

In other words, John Jones has a height of 67 inches and a weight of 120 pounds, and the other five persons have the heights and weights shown. The program will store these arrays and receive two pieces of information, a target height and a target weight. The program will then print the names of all people who have this target height and weight. A sample execution of the program would begin by first reading in all the entries in the arrays shown above. Then it would proceed as follows:

```
Computer:  Give the target height.
User:      67
Computer:  Give the target weight.
User:      131
Computer:  The list of all persons with the specified height and weight
           is:
               Sue Black
               Jean White
```
End of search.

Let us examine a program written to do this task:

```
program PersonSearch;
type
```

```
      stringarray100 = array[1..100] of string;
      realarray100 = array[1..100] of real;
var
      name:stringarray100;
      height, weight:realarray100;
      n,i:integer;
      targetheight, targetweight: real;
begin
{ Put code here to enter data into the arrays. }
{ Assume that entries 1 to n have been        }
{ filled with data in the three arrays.       }
writeln('Give target height.');
readln(targetheight);
writeln('Give target weight.');
readln(targetweight);
writeln('The list of persons with specified target height
      and weight is:');
i := 1;
while i <= n do
      begin
      if (targetheight = height[i]) and
         (targetweight = weight[i]) then
           writeln(name[i]);
      i := i + 1;
      end;
writeln('End of search.');
readln;
end.
```

As you can see, this program is capable of holding the information for up to one hundred people. Throughout this chapter, the symbol *n* will be used to measure the size of the task being undertaken; in this example, *n* will represent the number of people whose records must be examined. For the above example, *n* is 6 and for the given program, *n* may not exceed 100 unless the type declarations are changed.

The loop in the program examines sequentially *weight[1]* and *height[1]*, then *weight[2]* and *height[2]*, and so forth, printing out the associated name whenever the examined values both equal the target values.

The execution time for the program has two parts, the part required to fill the arrays and type in the target values and the part required to perform the looping computation. We will consider only the second portion; it is that part of the execution where the search through the data takes place. Thus, we are measuring the time required to examine the records of *n* people to find all cases that meet the two requirements. We are measuring the amount of time elapsed between the printing of the two messages: "The list of persons with specified height and weight is:" and "End of search."

A version of this program was entered into a computer and measurements were made of its search times. It was assumed that the number of persons might equal the number of students in a small university, up to 10,000 people. The results showed that this is a very inexpensive calculation, even for this large number of people.

| Number of people, $n$ | Execution time in seconds, $t$ |
|---|---|
| 2500 | 1.275 |
| 5000 | 2.550 |
| 7500 | 3.825 |
| 10000 | 5.100 |

Ten thousand people can be checked in about five seconds on this particular machine.

These values can be graphed showing that they form a straight line, and algebraic methods can be used to find an equation for the line. In fact, the execution time in seconds for the program will be represented by $t$, and in this case, one can show that $t = 5.1*10^{-4}*n$.

The reader should check to see that if values of $n$ from the table are entered into this equation, then the associated times $t$ in the table will be computed. Checking the second entry in the table, where $n = 5000$, $t = 5.1*10^{-4}*5000 = 2.55$.

Here is the graph:

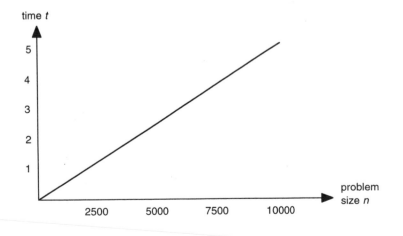

It is often difficult to find formulas to compute execution times, as was done here, but if they can be found they are very useful. For example, one might ask how long it would take to run this program on the total population of a large country. Let us assume $n = 300$ million, and the execution time can be computed to be 153,000 seconds or 42.5 hours. This program can search the whole population of that country in just a couple of days. It is a good example of an easily tractable computation. (In this example, we have ignored the problem of how to fit the records of so many people onto a single computer. We only address the issue of execution time here, the severest constraint in most situations.)

Let us examine another computation, the process of sorting numbers into ascending order. That is, suppose an array A has values as shown:

|   | A  |
|---|----|
| 1 | 47 |
| 2 | 12 |
| 3 | 46 |
| 4 | 10 |
| 5 | 41 |
| 6 | 33 |
| 7 | 44 |
| 8 | 86 |

How long does it take a computer to put these numbers into order?

|   | A  |
|---|----|
| 1 | 10 |
| 2 | 12 |
| 3 | 33 |
| 4 | 41 |
| 5 | 44 |
| 6 | 46 |
| 7 | 47 |
| 8 | 86 |

At the end of chapter 4 we studied a program called "quicksort" that can do this task, and we can examine its running time here. Again, considering populations of the size of a small university, this program was run for values of $n$ up to 10000. The following table gives the values obtained:

| Number of people, $n$ | Execution time in seconds, $t$ |
|---|---|
| 2500 | 59.261 |
| 5000 | 129.021 |
| 7500 | 202.745 |
| 10000 | 279.042 |

Assuming that sorting names is roughly as time-consuming as sorting numbers, we could use this type of program to alphabetize the names of ten thousand students in slightly over four minutes. This is another example of a tractable computation.

These values can also be graphed, as shown below, but the result is not quite a straight line. However, we can still use algebraic techniques (not discussed in the book) to obtain an approximate formula for execution time in seconds: $t = 2.1*10^{-3}*n*\log_2 n$.

The function $\log_2 n$ commonly occurs in algebra and computer science. Some of its values are given here:

| $n$ | $\log_2 n$ |
|---|---|
| 1 | 0 |
| 2 | 1 |
| 4 | 2 |
| 8 | 3 |
| 16 | 4 |
| 32 | 5 |
| 2500 | 11.2877 |
| 5000 | 12.2877 |
| 7500 | 12.8727 |
| 10000 | 13.2877 |

We can check that the formula agrees with the values in the table. Thus, at $n = 5000$, $t = 2.1*10^{-3}*5000*12.2877 = 129.021$.

On the following graph, which shows the run time for both sorting and searching, we can see that although sorting is far more expensive than searching, it is still classified as tractable.

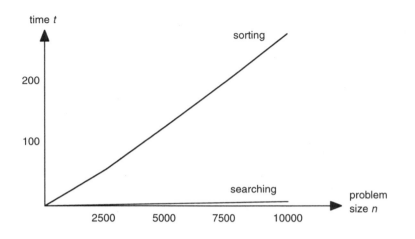

Now we calculate the cost of running this program on a huge population. Using the fact that if $n = 300$ million then $\log_2 n = 28.1604$, the formula gives the sorting time as 205.34 days. This is a long time, but remember that the job is huge. If a government service wants to do this calculation, they will presumably use large computers rather than our desktop model, and such machines might run a hundred or more times faster than our formula would suggest. So the calculation probably could be reduced to a couple of days. Thus, we can see that sorting is a tractable computation.

We are now able to give a more precise definition of tractability, the definition used by most computer scientists. A computation will be called *tractable* if its timing formula is a polynomial on $n$ (and possibly $\log_2 n$). Such polynomials are sums of terms of the form $a^*n^b$ or $a^*n^{b*}(\log_2 n)^c$ where $a$, $b$, and $c$ are fixed numbers. For example, the following formulas give timings for tractable computations:

$t = 3^*n^2$
$t = 4^*n^3 + 16^*n^2 + 7^*n + 8$
$t = 4^*n^{2*}\log_2 n + 3^*n$
$t = 17^*(\log_2 n)^2 + n$

You can check that the execution times for the above search and sort programs have the required form and thus qualify officially as tractable computations.

In contrast to tractable computations, there are intractable ones with timing formulas that do not conform to the definition in the previous paragraph. An example is the timing formula that includes an $n$ in the exponent as in $t = 6^n$. In this case, $t$ increases in a profoundly different manner than in tractable situations and at a much faster rate as $n$ is increased. The next section will give an example of an intractable computation.

**Exercises**

1. Run the following program for various values of $n$. Graph its execution time versus $n$. The formula for execution time should have this form where C and D are numbers that you must determine: $t = C + Dn$.

    What values do the constants C and D have for this program on your computer? How long would it take your program to count to 300 million?

```
program E1;
var
     i,n:integer;
begin
readln(n);
i := 1;
while i <= n do
    begin
    writeln(i);
    i := i + 1;
    end;
writeln('Done.');
readln;
end.
```

2. Repeat exercise 1 for the following program. The execution-time equation should have this form: $t = C + Dn^2$

```
program E2;
var
     i, j, k, n:integer;
begin
readln(n);
i := 1;
j := 1;
while j <= n do
    begin
    k := 1;
    while k <= n do
        begin
        writeln(i);
        i := i + 1;
        k := k + 1;
        end;
```

```
    j := j + 1;
    end;
writeln('Done.');
readln;
end.
```

3. The program of problem 2 was constructed by nesting a loop inside another loop. Revise that loop to have three nested loops instead of two and find a formula for its execution time.

4. The program to find all individuals of given height and weight will run faster if the data in the arrays are organized in a special way. Can you find that special way and show how to revise the program to run faster? Can you find a formula for its execution time and estimate the time required to process all the people in the United States?

---

## Intractable Computations (B)

A computation is called intractable if its execution time increases with increasing *n* faster than any polynomial of the form described in previous section. An example of an intractable computation is the generation of all the orderings of a set of *n* objects. (These orderings are called *permutations*.) As an example, suppose we have the three letters A, B, and C and we wish to find all their orderings. The first ordering is just A, B, C. Another one is A, C, B. Here is a list of all the orderings of these three letters. There are six of them.

A, B, C
A, C, B
B, A, C
B, C, A
C, A, B
C, B, A

A program is given in the exercises below that will compute these orderings or permutations. Following the method of the previous section, let us run the program for several values of *n* and find a function that will estimate the run time. (Actually, the code shown will need some modifications related to the size of the set being reordered. We will not describe those changes here.) We will run the program on the usual values and graph the observed timings.

| Number of objects, *n* | Execution time in seconds, *t* |
|---|---|
| 2500 | ? |
| 5000 | ? |
| 7500 | ? |
| 10000 | ? |

Strangely, the measurement is not successful and the program apparently runs forever when started on these values. What is wrong? Perhaps the program will not work if *n* is large.

In fact, there is a solution and the program will solve it even for a large *n*, but the execution time is long. Let us run the program on some small values of *n* and see how fast the run time grows.

| Number of objects, *n* | Execution time in seconds, *t* |
|---|---|
| 1 | less than 1 second |
| 2 | less than 1 second |
| 3 | less than 1 second |
| 4 | less than 1 second |
| 5 | less than 1 second |
| 6 | 3.19 seconds |
| 7 | 22.57 seconds |
| 8 | 3.05 minutes |
| 9 | 27.87 minutes |

Adding these data to the graph of the previous section, we can see that a new phenomenon is occurring. The time to complete the task at $n = 9$ is greater than it was for sorting at $n = 10,000$. Furthermore, it is climbing on a line that is nearly straight up:

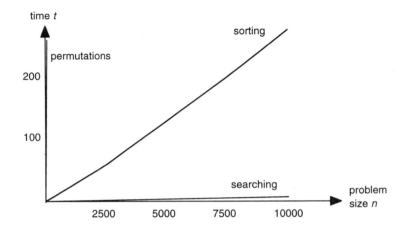

We can find a formula to estimate the timing in seconds for this program: $t = 4.6 \cdot 10^{-3} \cdot n!$

This comes from the fact that the number of orderings of $n$ objects is $n!$ (which is called $n$ *factorial*). Thus, in the case of the three characters A, B, and C, the number of orderings is $3! = 1 \cdot 2 \cdot 3 = 6$, as was observed above. We can use a well known computation in mathematics called Sterling's formula to get a more easily understood version of the time estimate: $t = 4.6 \cdot 10^{-3} \cdot (2\pi n)^{1/2} (n/e)^n$, where $\pi$ and e can be approximated by 3.14159 and 2.71828. Then we can evaluate $t$ for increasing values of $n$ and see what computer scientists mean when they call something "intractable."

| $n$ | $t$ (approximate) |
|---|---|
| 10 | 4.64 hours |
| 11 | 2.13 days |
| 12 | 25.50 days |
| 13 | 331.53 days |
| 14 | 12.71 years |
| 15 | 191 years |
| 16 | 3,052 years |
| 17 | 51,882 years |
| 18 | 933,883 years |
| 19 | 17,743,767 years |
| 20 | 354,875,356 years |
| 21 | 7,452,382,483 years |
| 22 | 163,952,414,630 years |

The time required to do 14 objects is several years, to do 15 objects is a couple of centuries, and to do 18 is a period longer than all of recorded history. Physicists say that the sun will burn out in a few billion years, so the machine would not be able to do 22 objects unless it were moved to a different solar system. The history of the universe since the "big bang," as theorized by cosmologists, is a mere 15 billion or so years, not enough to time to do 22 objects.

In contrast with the examples of the previous section where the calculations were completed for $n$ of 10,000 or even 300,000,000, in the current example $n$ may not exceed even a few dozen. There is no comparison between the run times of tractable problems and the computation discussed here.

We might hope that future technology will circumvent the problem of intractability. Large numbers of faster machines all working together may someday make it possible to handle even the problem discussed here for large $n$. Unfortunately, there is little hope that technology will help with such problems. Suppose a rather substantial improvement in machines enabled them to run a thousand times faster. Suppose, furthermore, that a way were found to break the problem into small parts so that a thousand such machines could all work in parallel on the solution. Even with this one millionfold increase in effort, it would only be possible to solve problems with half a dozen more objects than is currently possible.

Finally, a question arises concerning the importance of this result. How many managers of contemporary industry really want to compute all the orderings of a set of objects? As we will discover in the following section, this computation is at the heart of some very important kinds of problems and its efficient solution would be very valuable. There are also many computations very different in kind from this one but with similar execution times. So a study of these problems presents a set of issues that are common over a large class of computations. The next section will describe several of them.

**Exercise**

1. Type the following program and test it on your machine. A legal input is a string of characters without separators. For example, if you want it to do the orderings of the characters A, B, and C as shown above, just type the string ABC. Run the program on some short strings of lengths 2 to about 6 and draw a graph of execution time versus $n$ for your machine. Can you find a formula for its execution time? (You will have difficulty reading this code unless you have read the section on recursion in chapter 4. But you can do this experiment without understanding it in detail.)

```
{A program to list all of the orderings (permutations) of a set of  }
{   characters.                                                      }
{Input: A string of characters.                                     }
{Output: A set of strings giving every possible reordering of the   }
```

```
{   characters in the original string. For example, if the input is }
{   ABC, then the output will be ABC, ACB, BAC, BCA, CAB, CBA.       }
{Method of operation: The program maintains two strings, original   }
{   and target. Original begins by holding the original string and  }
{   as the target string is constructed, characters are moved from  }
{   original to target. The program makes every possible choice     }
{   for what character should be in the first position, then every  }
{   possible choice from the characters left for the second         }
{   position, etc.                                                  }

program P1;
var
    permstring,blank:string;

procedure permutation(var target,original:string);
    {This routine finds all rearrangements of the characters in    }
    {   original, and concatenates them to the right end of the     }
    {   string in target.                                          }
    var
        i:integer;
        target1,original1:string;
    begin
    if length(original)=0 then        {If original has no characters,}
        writeln(target);             {then print target.           }
    else
        begin                               {Otherwise, for each i, move }
        i := 1;                             {i-th character of original  }
        while i <= length(original) do {to right end of target and  }
                begin                       {do a recursive call.       }
                target1 := target + original[i];
                original1 := copy(original,1,i-1) +
                    copy(original,i+1,length(original)-i);
                permutation(target1,original1);
                i := i + 1;
                end;
        end;
    end;

begin                                       {Begin the main program.}
writeln('Input a string of characters.');
```

```
readln(permstring);                          {Read the original string.}
blank := '';                                 {We build on an empty string.}
writeln('The set of permutations:');
permutation(blank,permstring);                       {Find all orderings.}
writeln('Done.');
readln;
end.
```

## Some Practical Problems with Very Expensive Solutions (B)

We will now examine three problems that appear to be as expensive to solve computationally as finding all the orderings of *n* objects. The problems address the issues of finding minimum cost paths on a flat plane, the most efficient coverage of an area with odd shaped parts, and the discovery of the minimum number of colors for doing a certain kind of graph coloring.

### Finding the Minimum Cost Path

Suppose a traveling salesperson wishes to visit a series of cities, beginning at his or her home city, driving to visit each of the other cities exactly once, and then returning home. Suppose further that there are a total of six cities, as shown below. The question is: Which route should he or she follow in order to achieve the shortest possible trip?

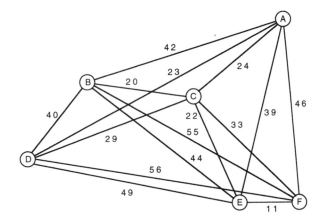

A route might start at city A and then proceed sequentially to cities B, C, D, E, F, and back to A. The distance traveled is easy to compute:

| | |
|---|---|
| From A to B | 42 |
| From B to C | 20 |
| From C to D | 29 |
| From D to E | 49 |
| From E to F | 11 |
| From F to A | 46 |
| Total | 197 |

But is this the shortest possible distance? Perhaps some other route would be better and the goal is to find it.

One way to find the shortest route is to find all routes, compute their lengths, and then select the optimum one. Here are a few of the routes that might be tried and their respective lengths:

| Route | Length |
|---|---|
| AECDBFA | 231 |
| ACBDEFA | 190 |
| ABFEDCA | 210 |
| AEFDCBA | 197 |
| AFDECBA | 235 |

The minimum one found here has a length of 190 but there may be even shorter paths.

This calculation has a strange resemblance to the one we were doing in the last section. We start at a city, then we try an ordering of the cities that are left, then we return to our home city. So we must do a calculation for every possible ordering of the cities that are not the home city. There are $n - 1$ of them so there must be $(n - 1)!$ such paths. Actually, if we count going around a loop in one direction as the same as going around it in the other direction, we should divide by 2. So the number of paths is

```
s = (n-1)!/2 = ((n-1)*(n-2)* . . . *1)/2 .
```

For $n = 6$ cities, we must check

```
s = (5*4*3*2*1)/2 = 60
```

different paths to solve the problem, which is clearly an extremely expensive calculation.

This is called the *Traveling Salesperson Problem* and it has been studied by many researchers over the past three decades. Some substantially better algorithms have been discovered, but even the best yield only intractable calculations, as they were defined in the previous section. (The details of such methodologies are beyond the scope of this book.) If we were to write a program to implement any such procedure, the time chart would look very similar to the one for computing all the orderings. Some problems have been solved for cases where *n* is a few hundred cities or more, but the amount of computer time was large. Problems where *n* ranges in the thousands are completely out of the question unless they are special cases of some kind.

The Traveling Salesperson Problem is of great importance for two reasons:

1. Many practical problems involve finding such shortest-path solutions. This is the problem we face when setting up a truck route or an electric power distribution system.
2. The Traveling Salesperson Problem is a member of a class called the *NP-complete* problems. The NP-complete problems are an important class in that they include many problems of practical significance. It has been shown that if a polynomial-time algorithm can be found for solving any member of the class, then any other problem in the NP-complete class will also be solvable in polynomial time. Thus, if someone were able to find a way to solve the Traveling Salesperson Problem in tractable time, all the other problems in the class would also become tractable.

It is widely conjectured that no algorithm can solve the Traveling Salesperson Problem in tractable (or polynomial) time. Scientists have tried for many years either to prove that it cannot be solved in tractable (polynomial) time or to find a tractable (polynomial) algorithm to solve it. So far they have been unable to achieve either result and this stands as one of the great unsolved problems in the field. In computer science jargon, the question is "Does P equal NP?" That is, does the class of problems solvable in polynomial time equal the class of problems in NP such as the Traveling Salesperson Problem.

### Finding the Best Coverage of an Area

Suppose we have the following positive integers: 3, 21, 25, 31, 45, 57, 77, 87. We wish to find a subset of these integers that comes as close as possible to adding up to 110 but that does not exceed 110. For example, we could try the subset {3, 31, 57}. This adds up to 91. Or we could try another one, {45, 57}; it adds up to 102. What about {25, 87}? It adds up to 112, but this exceeds the allowed maximum of 110. Let us be systematic and write down several possibilities:

| Subset | Sum | Sum is 110 or below |
|--------|-----|---------------------|
| {3, 31, 57} | 91 | |
| {45, 57} | 102 | |
| {25, 87} | 112 | no |
| {31, 77} | 108 | |
| {3, 21, 25, 31} | 80 | |
| {21, 87} | 108 | |
| etc. | | |

The best solution that we have found is a sum of 108, and we found two ways to get it. You should try some other sums and see if you can do better.

This problem is an example of the *Subset Sum Problem*, which is a special case of the much studied *Knapsack Problem*, and it is important for many reasons. First, it is a solution to the following practical question. Assume the set of integers represents the lengths of some boards you need to build a certain structure. You have purchased a board that is 110 units long and you wish to cut boards for your structure with as little waste as possible. Which set of boards should you choose so that as little will be left of the 110-unit board as possible?

A second reason the Subset Sum Problem is important is that a two-dimensional version of it is also common. If you have a set of oddly shaped objects, which ones should you choose and how should you arrange them in order to cover a given rectangular area maximally?

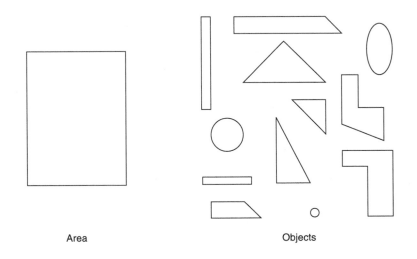

Area                    Objects

Here is a solution to that problem and you can see that it is very difficult to find:

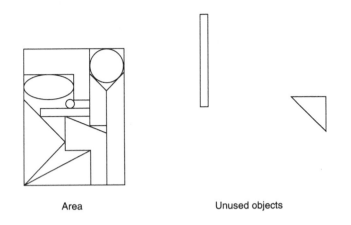

Area                                Unused objects

Since the linear board problem is a special case of this two-dimensional problem, this problem must be at least as expensive to solve.

It turns out that the Subset Sum Problem is in the NP-complete class and thus has all the properties of those problems. We should not be too surprised at this since we have been solving it by looking at all subsets of $n$ objects and there are $2^n$ of them. Thus, it is not known whether there is a tractable solution for this problem; it is generally believed that there is not. We can expect to find only very expensive (intractable) solutions to it, and consequently, we can expect to find only very expensive (intractable) solutions to the two-dimensional problem. (Many parlor games and puzzles that test our intelligence are problems whose only known solutions are very expensive.)

### Finding the Best Coloring of a Graph

Consider the task of assigning a color to each of the circular nodes in the graph below.

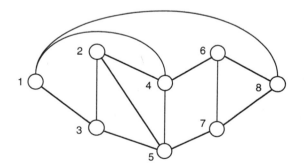

The *Graph Coloring Problem* is to find the coloring of all the nodes such that no two connected nodes have the same color and such that the minimum number of colors has been used.

Let us begin working on a solution by simply using a different color on every node. Call the colors C1, C2, C3, ..., C8. Then we can color the first node with C1, the second node with C2, and so forth, for the rest of the nodes. We can write this down as follows:

```
1. C1, 2. C2, 3. C3, 4. C4, 5. C5, 6. C6, 7. C7, 8. C8
```

This is a coloring such that no two connected nodes have the same color, but it uses too many colors. We can find a better solution.

Let us try using fewer colors. Perhaps we should color node 8 the same as node 1:

```
1. C1, 2. C2, 3. C3, 4. C4, 5. C5, 6. C6, 7. C7, 8. C1
```

This has fewer colors but it is not acceptable because nodes 1 and 8 are connected.

Let us try another coloring with node 7 colored the same as node 1.

```
1. C1, 2. C2, 3. C3, 4. C4, 5. C5, 6. C6, 7. C1, 8. C8
```

This uses only seven colors and it is otherwise acceptable. But we should try to reduce it again. Can we get it down to six colors? What is the minimum number of colors?

The Graph Coloring Problem is another example of an NP-complete problem. Again, we can expect any algorithm that solves it will be intractable unless some new and unexpected discovery is made.

**Exercises**

1. Can you find a better solution to the six-city Traveling Salesperson Problem than the one given above?

2. If you wish to solve the Traveling Salesperson Problem for ten cities, how many different orderings of the cities do you have to examine in order to get the best one? How many do you have to examine in the case of twenty cities?

3. Can you find a better solution to the example of a Sum Subset Problem than the one given above?

4. Find the solution to the Sum Subset Problem for the following set of integers: 11, 23, 34, 57, 90, 110, 331, 366, 423, 462, 622, 801, 1277. The target number is 1435 and your job is to find the subset with the largest sum that is not greater than 1435. How many subsets exist for this set of $n = 13$ integers? Do you need to examine them all?

5. Find the optimum solution to the Graph Coloring Problem shown above.

6. Suppose the graph for the Traveling Salesperson Problem is examined as a Graph Coloring Problem. What is the minimum number of colors needed to color it?

7. Give an example of a practical problem that is equivalent to solving the Graph Coloring Problem.

## Diagnosing Tractable and Intractable Problems (B)

Let us look again at the tractable and intractable problems given above and try to determine some common features of each. Perhaps there are some rules that will help diagnose new problems we encounter as either tractable or intractable. We will speak here only in an intuitive way and try to catch the flavor of the two kinds of problems. We will not be giving "iron-clad" rules for making decisions, but rather suggesting workable guidelines.

Tractable problems can often be characterized as those in which the data items are processed one at a time and not looked at again. As an example, in a sorting problem you might find the smallest number in the array and put it into the first location. It need not be examined again. Then you find the second smallest item and put it into the second location. It need not be referenced again. And so forth. Many tractable computations have this flavor.

Another feature of tractable problems is that you often know examples where they have been solved for large $n$. Is it possible to schedule 10,000 students for their classes while meeting certain acceptability criteria? Yes, we know of many times when this has been done. So this problem appears to be tractable.

NP-complete problems often have the characteristic that you cannot process a given item and simply be done with it. For example, in the Traveling Salesperson Problem, you might decide to start at city A and then go to D. Then you might go to C and then on to E. No matter what decisions you make, you can never be sure that the first decision to go from A to D was correct. You might have to go back and try to start by going from A to C. Later you might decide to try going from A to E first or something else.

The same thing happens with the Subset Sum Problem. If you decide that the 25 is not going to be used in your current guess of the solution, you can never set it aside permanently because later you might decide to use it.

NP-complete problems often have a kind of cut-and-try flavor about them. Examine the NP-complete problems given above again. In each case, we studied the data as a unit and tested it for acceptability. Then we examined some other way of doing the whole problem and tested it. There were always many ways to try to find a solution, and this resulted in the large computation times.

These NP-complete problems are all intractable using known algorithms, and we can expect them to stay that way unless some amazing discovery is made. So the characteristics we have been observing for NP-completeness are, in effect, signs of intractability.

You should study these examples and others and try to develop an intuition for what constitutes tractability and intractability. For most common situations, you should be able to guess correctly. But in some cases, it takes a Ph. D. and years of experience to discover the answer.

**Exercise**

1. In each case, study the problem and then use the guidelines given above to classify the problem as well as you can as either tractable or intractable.
    (a) The 10-th from largest integer in a set of $n$ integers is to be found. (Assume that $n$ is greater than 10.)
    (b) A set of $n$ positive integers is to be divided into two parts, and the sum of the integers in one part is to equal the sum of the integers in the other.
    (c) A set $Q$ of $n$ positive integers is to be examined to determine whether any subset of $Q$ adds up to equal one of the other integers in $Q$.
    (d) A set of $n$ integers is to be examined to determine whether any two of them are the same.
    (e) A set of $n$ integers is to be added up where $n$ is greater than one billion.
    (f) A set of $n$ rectangles of various sizes is to be assembled to cover, without overlap, a large given rectangle.
    (g) An ordinary jigsaw puzzle with $n$ pieces is to be assembled.
    (h) A path is to be found through a set of cities that touches every city exactly once and has minimum length. Notice that there is no home city in this problem or any need to complete the loop.

## Approximate Solutions to Intractable Problems (C)

We decided that the Traveling Salesperson Problem is very expensive to solve if the number of cities is greater than a few dozen. However, there are plenty of salespeople who seem to solve the problem on a regular basis and without much trouble. How can this be? The answer is that the realistic salesperson does not worry about finding the smallest possible path. Any path that is not too wasteful will do.

We can accomplish the same thing with computers. In this section, we will not require the best solution but only a reasonable one. As an illustration, let us return to the Traveling Salesperson Problem and try again. We can propose that the following algorithm will obtain a good enough path through the cities.

1. Select the home city.
2. From the current city, choose the shortest path leading out to a city that has not yet been visited. Follow that path to the next city. If there are still unvisited cities, repeat step 2 again.
3. Connect the final city back to the home city.

Following this algorithm, we might start at city A and note that the nearest unvisited city is D. From D, the nearest unvisited city is C; from C the nearest unvisited city is B, and so forth. This calculation is very fast, and it may lead to an acceptable solution. But it certainly is not likely to find the best answer. Many other fast algorithms have been developed, and they are often better than the one we proposed here. However, their complexity prevents our examining them in this chapter.

Here is a way to get an approximation for the Subset Sum Problem. Write down all subsets of size 3 or less. Add to each as many remaining items in the list as is possible (using any selection process) without exceeding the given limit. Choose the one with the largest sum. It has been shown that if this procedure is followed, the resulting sum will be at least 3/4 of the size of the optimum answer.

**Exercises**

1. Returning to the Traveling Salesperson Problem, find the length of the path discovered by the approximate algorithm of this section when you start at home city A. How does it compare with the best other solution that you have found?

2. Repeat problem 1 starting at home city B.

3. Here is another Traveling Salesperson Problem: The cities are A, B, C, and D, and the distances are 1 between A and B, 2 between A and C, 10,000 between A and D, 1 between B and C, 2 between B and D, and 1 between C and D. Starting at city A, use the approximation algorithm to solve this problem. Can you make any general statements about this approximation after doing this problem?

4. Using the approximate algorithm given in this section, repeat the example of a Subset Sum Problem given in the section "Some Practical Problems."

5. Repeat the example of a Subset Sum Problem given as problem 4 in the exercises in the section "Some Practical Problems." Use the approximate algorithm given above.

6. Find an approximate algorithm for the Graph Coloring Problem.

## Summary (B)

This chapter began by noting that there are three reasons why it may not be possible to do a desired calculation. The first of these reasons, studied here, is that the amount of machine time required to do the calculation may be unrealistically large. Later chapters will examine the other reasons.

The study of execution times leads to the concepts of "tractable" and "intractable" computations. The former class leads to reasonable execution times in most cases even if large amounts of data are processed. The latter class usually results in astronomically huge computation times if problems of nontrivial size are attempted. Both kinds of calculations are important in practice.

Our study leads to the idea of NP-complete problems that are intractable by all known algorithms. Whether there will ever be tractable means for calculating them remains an unsolved problem. Most observers guess that they are intrinsically intractable.

But even if it turns out that the NP-complete problems can be solved in tractable time, there are other problems that are provably intractable. An example of one of these is the problem of computing all the permutations of $n$ objects. Since there are $n!$ such permutations, this will always be an intractable computation.

Some seemingly intractable computations are amenable to approximate solutions that can be computed in acceptable time and are accurate enough for many purposes. Many of these problems and their approximate solutions are the object of recent research in computer science.

An interesting survey of work on the Traveling Salesperson Problem appears in an article cited below, "Exact Solution of Large Asymmetric Traveling Salesman Problems" by Donald L. Miller and Joseph F. Pekny. This article describes a number of approximation methods that have achieved solutions to $n$ city problems with $n$ in the ranges of thousands or hundreds of thousands. It describes in detail an algorithm that finds exact solutions for some special-case problems of similar sizes.

It is possible that a calculation cannot be completed because it requires astronomical amounts of memory. In practice, however, this is an uncommon situation and will not be discussed further in this book.

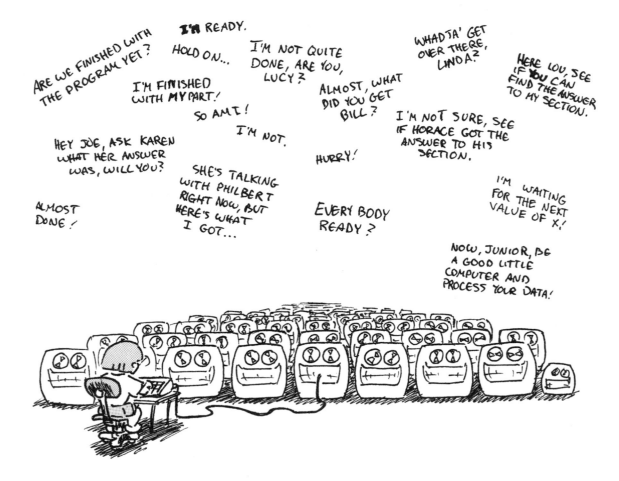

# 13 Parallel Computation

## Using Many Processors Together (A)

Execution time can be a serious problem, as we learned in chapter 12. An excessively long computation can cause inconvenience and missed deadlines; it may even become useless if it is not completed on time. This is the case, for example, in computing the trajectory for a space vehicle course correction or in calculating inventory requirements for the next day's assembly operations. If the figures are not computed on schedule, the usefulness of the calculation is lost.

Computations must be completed on time, but the speed of even the fastest machine is limited. A minimum amount of circuitry is needed to do a calculation, and electricity can travel through wires no faster than the speed of light. We can make the calculation go faster by shrinking the circuit to smaller and smaller dimensions, but this is a process that cannot go on forever.

Another way to speed up a calculation is to divide it into parts and let several processors work on it together. This is called *parallel computation*, and in this chapter we will study computers that are especially designed to do parallel computations. They have many processors, possibly of the kind described in chapter 8, each doing its own part. They communicate as needed for the purposes of the task, and in most cases, they complete their work many times faster than a single-processor machine.

The next section will describe a parallel machine and show how it can be used to solve two problems from the previous chapter: the retrieval of individuals with specified height and weight and the Traveling Salesperson Problem. Later sections will describe a sorting methodology for parallel machines, problems that arise when the parallelism is of limited degree, communication schemes for parallel machines, and a new type of parallel computer, the connectionist machine.

## Parallel Computation (B)

Parallel computation requires a parallel computer, and the first model to be studied here will be composed of 100 machines placed in row. These machines, which are nearly identical to the processor studied in previous chapters, will process a version of Pascal that has been slightly modified to account for the parallelism. All will read from a single input source, as shown below, and simultaneously write to a very fast output device. They are numbered from 0 to 99.

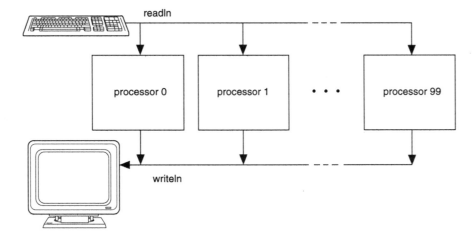

Let us first program this parallel machine to solve the problem of finding all individuals with a given height and weight. We will begin by assuming the number of individuals *n* is 100 or fewer so that one processor can be allocated to each individual. (We will later address the more general problem when *n* may be large.)

Each processor has its own copy of *targetheight* and *targetweight*, and each processor holds the height, weight, and name of a particular person. Here is the program to do the computation. A copy of the following code is loaded into every one of the 100 processors:

```
program ParallelPersonSearch;
var
    targetweight, targetheight, weight, height: real;
    name: string;
begin
{Put code here to enter data into weight, height, and name}
{for a single individual.}
```

```
processor 0 writeln('Give the target height.');
all readln(targetheight);
processor 0 writeln('Give the target weight.');
all readln(targetweight);
if (targetheight = height) and (targetweight = weight) then
   this processor writeln(name);
end.
```

The *readln* and *writeln* statements are prefixed to indicate which of the 100 processors do the operation.

The functioning of the 100 processors as they do this computation is clear. First, each processor loads the weight, height, and name of one individual in a sequence of operations that does not interest us here. If there are fewer than 100 individuals, some of the processors will receive null values for height, weight, and name. Then processor 0 prints the message, "Give the target height." Next all processors receive a value from the input, the target height. Then processor 0 prints "Give the target weight" and all processors receive a second value, the target weight. Finally, each processor compares the target values with the values it stores for one person; if they match, it prints that person's name. The output device will print all the names received from all the processors.

The *readln* and *writeln* statements have prefix operators that designate which of the 100 processors will do the action. If this code is running, for example, on processor 13 and it encounters *processor 0 writeln*, it should ignore the statement and go on. If it encounters *all readln* or *this processor writeln*, it should do the operation.

The timing of this parallel computation is dramatically faster than in the sequential computation in the previous chapter. Instead of finding the individuals in time

$$t_{sequential} = 5.1 * 10^{-4} * n$$

as before, the computation runs as fast as if there were only one individual in the database:

$$t_{parallel} = 5.1 * 10^{-4} * 1$$

The dramatic speedup that we were looking for has been obtained:

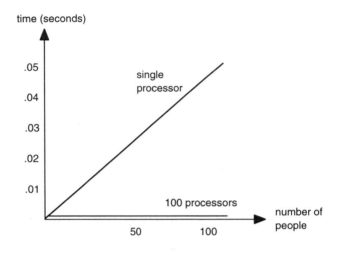

Of course, it is important to remember that these results pertain to a computation where there is a separate processor for each individual. The more general case when there may not be enough processors for all individuals will be examined later.

The Traveling Salesperson Problem provides an interesting second illustration of parallel computation. The methodology will be to have each processor compute a different ordering for the cities and add up the length of the associated path. Then the paths computed by the different processors are compared and the best one is reported.

We will not examine the details of this program here, but will use the fact that the execution time for calculating one path can be estimated to be about

$$t_{parallel} = 5 * 10^{-3} * n$$

which is enormously faster than the sequential version. If we have enough processors so that every possible path will be computed on one of them, $t_{parallel}$ will give a rough estimate of the total time required for a parallel machine to solve this problem. We will assume that a reasonable time estimate for computing the exact solution to the Traveling Salesperson Problem on a single processor machine can be made by using the formula for computing permutations:

$$t_{sequential} = 4.6 * 10^{-3} * n!$$

Again, the power of parallel computing is dramatic, as is shown on the graph for values of $n = 1, 2, \ldots, 6$:

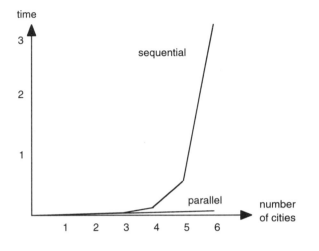

We are tempted to check how long the calculation would be for 22 cities using this parallel computation if we had enough processors. In the previous chapter, we discovered that our sequential machine would not finish the calculation before the sun burns out. Here we find

$$t_{parallel} = 5 * 10^{-3} * 22 = 0.11 \text{ second}$$

Hurrah! The infamous Traveling Salesperson Problem has been crushed by a parallel machine. But let us check further. The parallel machine will need $(n - 1)!/2$ processors, one for each step in the solution. This can be computed to be around $10^{19}$ processors. Thus, if we laid our machine out across the face of the earth, including the oceans, we would have to squeeze at least two dozen processors into every square inch to build a large enough machine.

Here is the program that computes the length of one path of the Traveling Salesperson Problem. After it computes a sum, it passes it to another set of processors which compare its results with those of the many other processors that have done other paths and choses the best. It assumes that the number of the current processor is in a location called *proc-num* and it employs a subroutine *findperm* that uses the processor number to decide which permutation it is to explore. Thus, every processor will explore a different permutation. The program stores the distances from city to city in an array called *distance*.

```
program TSP;
type
    intarray100 = array[1..100] of integer;
    realarraysquare = array[1..100,1..100] of real;
```

```
var
    permarray:intarray100;
    distance:realarraysquare;
    n,homecity,currentcity:integer;
    sum:real;
begin
{Input n and the array of all n cities and their distances.}
findperm(procnum,permarray);
sum := 0;
i := 1;
homecity := permarray[1];
currentcity := homecity;
while i <= n-1 do
    begin
    sum := sum + distance[currentcity,permarray[i+1]];
    currentcity := permarray[i+1];
    i := i + 1;
    end;
sum := sum + distance[currentcity,homecity];
{Send sum to a comparator processor which will work with other   }
{processors to decide the minimum sum and its associated permutation.  }
end.
```

This section has shown how two computations from the previous chapter can be spread out across a parallel architecture to obtain dramatic improvements in execution time. All of these observations, of course, have assumed that *n* is small and the number of processors is unlimited in comparision. Unfortunately not all computations are as easy to speed up as these two examples, as we will see in the next section. The section after that will examine execution times when *n* is large compared to the number of processors.

**Exercises**

1. Show how to program the parallel machine to find which two people in a room have the same birthday or if there are two such people. Assume that there are no more than 100 people in the room.

2. Show how to program the parallel machine to compute all the prime numbers between 1 and 100.

3. Show how to program the parallel machine to do the database program in chapter 4.

4. Show how the parallel program for the Traveling Salesperson Problem solves the problem in the case of four cities. How many processors are needed? What is the task of each processor?

5. Describe how to program the parallel machine to finish the Traveling Salesperson Problem after the sums of all the paths are computed by the many processors. Code must be written to examine these sums and find the smallest one.

## Communicating Processes (B)

The problems of the previous section divided across a set of processors in a simple way. Now, however, we will study a more difficult problem, the sorting of integers when they are distributed across our 100-processor machine. In this case, we will need both communication between the processes and the ability to pass the integers up and down the line.

Let us assume there are $n$ integers located in processors 0 through $n - 1$ where $n$ is 100 or less. Each processor will have a location *num*, which contains one of the numbers in the list. It will also contain $n$, an index $i$, and its own processor number:

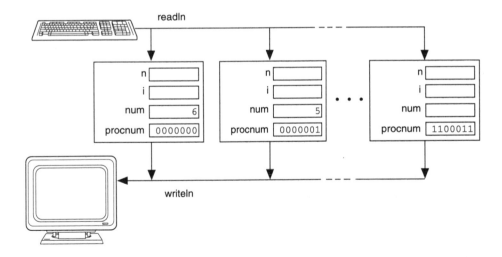

The sorting algorithm will require that each processor, except the first, examine the number in the processor to its left. If the other number is larger than its own, it will exchange them. This operation will be repeated with $n$ repetitions, at which time the numbers should become sorted with the lowest in processor 0 and the largest in processor $n-1$. Here is the program:

```
program ParallelSort;
var
    i,num,n,procnum: integer;
begin
{Put code here to read num and n.}
if (procnum > 0) and (procnum <= n-1) then
    begin
    i := 1;
    while i <= n do
        begin
        if num(left neighbor) > num(this processor) then
            exchange num(left neighbor) and
                    num(this porcessor);
        i := i + 1;
        end;
    end;
end.
```

Let us examine this program in action. Suppose $n$ is 3, and the first three processors contain 6, 5, and 4:

| num | 6 | 5 | 4 |
|---|---|---|---|
| procnum | 00 | 01 | 10 |

Program *ParallelSort* will run simultaneously on these three processors. On the first, it will do nothing, since *procnum* = 00. The second and third processors will each see that their left neighbors have larger numbers, and they will exchange their own numbers with their left neighbors. Thus, processor 01 will put 5 into processor 00 and 6 into itself. Processor 10 will put 4 into processor 01 and 5 into itself. Error! Processor 01 has just had both a 6 and a 4 loaded into its *num* location. Both processors 00 and 10 also have 5s. Something is wrong here. We thought we were going to end up with the numbers sorted like this:

| num | 4 | 5 | 6 |
|---|---|---|---|
| procnum | 00 | 01 | 10 |

Instead, we ended up with this:

| num | 5 | ? | 5 |
|---|---|---|---|
| procnum | 00 | 01 | 10 |

Apparently the computations of one processor confuse those of its neighbor. Each processor looks at its own number and its left neighbor's and decides whether to do an exchange. But by the time it chooses to do the exchange, its own number and its neighbor's may both have changed. It cannot check any value and be sure it will stay that way because other processes may change it. This seemingly straightforward program is fraught with problems.

The solution is to have a set of flags called *semaphores* that guard locations from being changed by any but a selected single processor. That processor will maintain control over the specified locations until its job is done, and then it will change the flags to indicate that it has released the associated locations to other processors. This system of guards can become complicated, but it will restore sanity to the parallel computation.

Let us put a flag with each *num* location; the flag will be a location containing a value of 0 or 1. Then we will follow the rule that a processor will be able to access and change its own *num* only if its flag is 1. If its flag is 0, it will not be allowed to affect its own *num* because that location will be controlled by its neighbor on the right. Of course, a processor will never be able to exchange its *num* value with its left neighbor unless it controls both. Its flag must be 1, and its left neighbor must have a flag that is 0. We indicate in this table the conditions under which processor $i$ can do an exchange. We say its activity is "on" if these conditions are met. Otherwise it is "waiting," or "off" if it is processor 0:

| num | — | — |
|---|---|---|
| flag | 0 | 1 |
| procnum | $i-1$ | $i$ |
| *activity* | *waiting* | *on* |

After a processor completes a cycle, it should change its own flag and its left neighbor's to release them to other processors. There will be two exceptions to this rule, however: The flag of processor 0 should always be 0 since it never needs to do exchanges with its left neighbor, and the flag of the last processor that holds data should always be set at 1 since it has no right neighbor to take control.

We can examine this strategy by repeating the above sort. We will initialize the first flag at 0, the last flag at 1, all flags of other even-numbered processors at 0, causing them to wait, and all flags of other odd-numbered processors at 1, turning them on:

| num | 6 | 5 | 4 |
|---|---|---|---|
| flag | 0 | 1 | 1 |
| procnum | 00 | 01 | 10 |
| *activity* | *off* | *on* | *waiting* |

Remember that a processor never comes on unless its own flag is 1 and its left neighbor is 0. Thus, only one of the three processors has the flag configuration to go on; it is processor

01, and it will see that its left neighbor has *num* larger than its own *num* and exchange them. Also, it will change its own flag. (It would change the flag of its left neighbor if that processor were not the leftmost one.)

| | | | |
|---|---|---|---|
| num | 5 | 6 | 4 |
| flag | 0 | 0 | 1 |
| procnum | 00 | 01 | 10 |
| *activity* | *off* | *waiting* | *on* |

This puts processor 01 in the "waiting" state but releases processor 10 to compare its *num* with its left neighbor. Processor 10 then finds the left neighbor's value larger and executes an exchange. Finally, it would change its own flag and its left neighbor's flag, but since it is the right-most processor, it changes only its neighbor's flag:

| | | | |
|---|---|---|---|
| num | 5 | 4 | 6 |
| flag | 0 | 1 | 1 |
| procnum | 00 | 01 | 10 |
| *activity* | *off* | *on* | *waiting* |

Now process 01 is "on" again, and it can do another compare, an exchange, and a flag change. This completes the sort:

| | | | |
|---|---|---|---|
| num | 4 | 5 | 6 |
| flag | 0 | 0 | 1 |
| procnum | 00 | 01 | 10 |
| *activity* | *off* | *waiting* | *on* |

Once this flagging strategy is designed, one can revise the parallel sorting program to work properly.

```
program ParallelSortWithFlags;
var
     i,n,num,flag,procnum: integer;
begin
{Put code here to read num and n.}
{We assume that procnum holds the processor number.}
if procnum is even then
    flag := 0
else
    flag := 1;
if (procnum = n-1) then
    flag := 1;
```

```
if (procnum > 0) and (procnum <= n-1) then
    begin
    i := 1;
    while i <= n do
        begin
        wait until flag(this processor)=1 and
            flag(left neighbor)=0;
        if num(left neighbor) > num (this processor) then
            exchange num(left neighbor) and
                num(this processor);
        if procnum > 1 then change flag in processor on left;
        if procnum < n-1 then change flag in this processor;
        i := i + 1;
        end;
    end;
end.
```

A common phenomenon in parallel computation occurs when one processor is waiting for another to complete its job while the other is waiting for the first to complete its job. Each processor waits and waits and neither ever takes another step. This is called *dead-lock*, and it is a major concern for designers of parallel computations. In our sorting program, a processor waits until its flag and its left neighbor's flag have the correct configuration before it does anything. You should study the sorting algorithm and determine whether it is ever possible for it to reach a deadlock.

Finally, we should examine the execution time of this algorithm. The program executes its loop $n$ times so the timing formula has the form

$$t_{parallel} = C^* n$$

where $C$ is some constant value. We noted in chapter 12 that it is possible to sort numbers in time

$$t_{sequential} = C'^* n^* \log_2 n$$

where $C'$ is a constant. Since $\log_2 n$ is not a very large number, we see that $t_{parallel}$ is not a lot faster than $t_{sequential}$. If we are using $n$ processors, we would like to see a speedup by a factor of $n$, so this sorting algorithm is disappointing. It is like hiring a hundred people to help pick apples in your orchard and finding that they get the job done only seven times faster than a single person would have. There are better parallel sorting methods that obtain greater speedups, but they are more complex than the one shown here and are beyond the scope of this book.

In this section, we have found that not all computations are easily divided for parallel execution, and that whenever the programming involves interprocess communication, the code can become very complex. Therefore, improvements in execution time may not be as large as we would hope.

**Exercises**

1. Suppose that the list of numbers 7,2,9,6,4,1,5,4 is spread out across processors 000 to 111 in the parallel machine and that they are to be sorted. Show how the program *ParallelSortWithFlags* would complete this sort. Show all the processors with their values for *num*, *flag*, and *procnum* at the moment when the computation is initialized. Then show them again after each significant step.

2. Suppose that a programmer codes the sorting program given above but makes one error: The flags are all initialized at zero. How will the program function in this situation? What new concept introduced in this section will apply here?

3. A sequence of $n$ characters, where $n$ is 100 or less, is spread across the parallel machine, with one character in each processor. Show how to program the processors so that a user can type in a short string of characters and find all the places where it appears in the original character sequence. The machine is to type out the numbers of the processors that hold the initial characters of the discovered substrings.
   As an example, suppose the initial string is "abcbc" so that it is stored as follows:

   | character | a | b | c | b | c |
   |-----------|-----|-----|-----|-----|-----|
   | procnum | 000 | 001 | 010 | 011 | 100 |

   If the user types "bc," the system will find two occurrences of this substring and print the location of their initial characters: 001, 011.

## Parallel Computation on a Saturated Machine (B)

The previous studies assumed that $n$ was small enough to allow the computation to be divided among the available processors in a convenient manner. For the data retrieval problem, it was assumed that there was a processor for every individual, and for the Traveling Salesperson Problem, it was assumed there was a processor for every ordering of the cities. In cases like this, where there are enough processors to divide the problem optimally, we say the computation does not *saturate* the machine.

Realistically, however, we must expect that $n$ will often be large, that we will not have as many processors as we could use effectively, and that it will probably be necessary to revise the organization of the code. When the processors are saturated, the programming becomes more complicated, and some of the improvement in execution time is lost. This section will investigate these two effects of parallel computation on a saturated machine.

Returning to the retrieval problem, let us now assume that there may be thousands of individuals whose records are spread across the 100 processors. If we put 1 percent of the total population on each of the processors, each processor will search its own 1 percent, and the results of the 100 separate computations will be a search of the complete population.

Here is the program revised to handle up to 1000 individuals on each processor:

```
program SaturatedParallelPersonSearch;
type
    stringarray1000 = array [1..1000] of string;
    realarray1000 = array [1..1000] of integer;
var
    name: stringarray1000;
    height, weight: realarray1000;
    m,i: integer;
    targetheight, targetweight: real;
begin
{Put code here to find the number m of individuals to be stored in    }
{this processor and then read in the data for those individuals.      }
processor 0 writeln('Give the target height.');
all readln(targetheight);
processor 0 writeln('Give the target weight.');
all readln(targetweight);
i := 1;
while i <= m do
    begin
    if (targetheight = height[i]) and
        (targetweight = weight[i]) then
            this processor writeln(name[i]);
    i := i+1;
    end;
end.
```

The execution time for this program can be discovered by carefully considering a series of cases. Suppose there are 100 or fewer individuals. This was the case considered earlier, and the execution time was the same as handling one individual on a sequential machine:

$$t_{1-100} = 5.1 * 10^{-4} * 1$$

If there are between 101 and 200 individuals, they can be distributed among the processors, with two on some and one on the others. The execution time is the same as the sequential machine with two individuals:

$$t_{101-200} = 5.1 * 10^{-4} * 2$$

The trend is now clear:

$$t_{201-300} = 5.1 * 10^{-4} * 3, \text{ and so on.}$$

The result gives us a lesson about computing on a saturated machine. The incredible speedup that was apparent when there were enough processors is gone, but the machine is still much faster than a sequential computation. At best, a machine with 100 processors will be 100 times faster than one with a single processor:

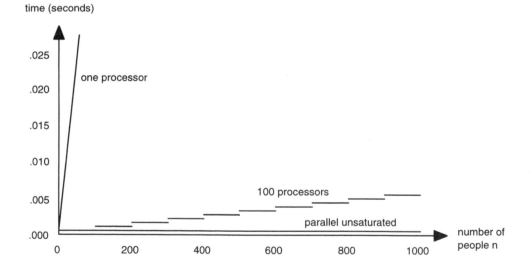

A similar situation occurs with the Traveling Salesperson Problem. If $n!$ is larger than 100, then we can no longer afford the luxury of putting one ordering of the cities on each processor. Instead, each processor must compute 1 percent of all the orderings, and this could be a large number. The execution time graph rises slowly if $n!$ is 100 or less, but it rises exponentially for larger $n$, as in the sequential case. It is at best 100 times faster than a single processor. Unfortunately, this is not sufficient to convert an intractable computation into a tractable one.

The sorting algorithm can also be programmed for large lists, but it, too, has additional complexities. Furthermore, the timing advantage, which was difficult to achieve in the unsaturated case, cannot be maintained.

In summary, parallel computations offer the possibility of huge speedups in computation time, especially in the cases of problems that partition easily into many parts and where high degrees of parallelism are available. However, the introduction of parallelism often results in great increases in program complexity and for many problems does not yield dramatic increases in speed.

**Exercises**

1. Build a chart summarizing the results of this chapter. It should have two columns—one for tractable and one for intractable computations. It should have two rows—one for computations on unsaturated machines and one for computations on saturated machines. In each case, describe the degree of speedup that parallel computation can achieve.

2. Carefully analyze the speedup that can be achieved for the Traveling Salesperson Problem on the 100-processor machine in the case where $n$ is greater than 6. Draw a graph of execution time versus $n$, and compare it with the cases of unsaturated parallel execution and sequential (one-processor) execution.

## Variations on Architecture (B)

A variety of different interconnection schemes is possible for parallel machines. Processors may be organized in straight lines, like our model in the previous sections, but they can also be organized in a ring, a grid, a hypercube, a completely connected set, or in any of a multitude of other ways:

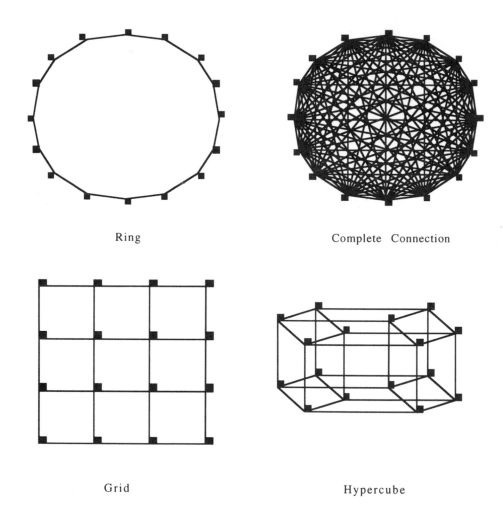

Ring                                    Complete  Connection

Grid                                    Hypercube

Although the simpler schemes like the ring and grid are easier to build, the more complicated ones offer greater potential performance.

   One simple measure of performance is the number of transfers required for information
to reach the most distant points in a network. For example, with 16 processors in a ring
connection, as shown above, the most widely separated nodes are on the opposite sides of
the ring, and the transfer of information from one to the other requires 8 movements
along communication lines. In general, a ring of *n* processors will require $n/2$ transfers to
move information between the most distant processors. The following table gives distances between the farthest processors for the four configurations shown:

| Configuration | Number of Processors | | |
|---|---|---|---|
| | 16 | 10,000 | n |
| Ring | 8 | 5000 | n/2 |
| Grid | 6 | 198 | $2n^{(1/2)} - 2$ |
| Hypercube | 4 | 14 | $\log_2 n$ |
| Complete connection | 1 | 1 | 1 |

The parallel machine described in previous sections in which each processor has its own program to manipulate its own data is known as a *Multiple-Instruction Multiple-Data* (*MIMD*) machine. Each processor can have a completely different piece of code, giving total flexibility to the programmer who organizes the calculation. Another common design is the *Single-Instruction Multiple-Data* (*SIMD*) machine, where one program controls all the processors in the array. It broadcasts its commands to the complete network, which marches in lockstep. This architecture is common in designs where there are many processors, tens of thousands of them, and therefore little possibility of generating individualized code for each one.

This brings up another issue in parallel architectures, the degree of *granularity* in the parallelism. A machine it said to have *coarse* granularity if it has large processors at each node and relatively little communication, as in our model. It will have only a few processors, say a few hundred at most, and each will have full instruction sets and a large memory—100,000 bytes or more. Granularity can also be *fine*, using as many as hundreds of thousands of tiny processors with very tight communication with each other. The next section will give an example of a parallel computer with very fine granularity.

### Exercises

1. Suppose a three-dimensional cubical grid is proposed as a machine architecture:

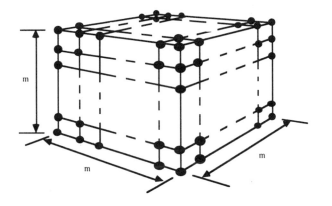

A cube might have *m* nodes along any edge and $m^3$ nodes in all. Fill in the table given above for shortest distance between most distant nodes.

2. Could you run the three problems discussed in this chapter on SIMD machines? Discuss each one, and show how it would succeed or fail.

3. Propose a parallel architecture not described in this chapter, and investigate its properties.

---

## Connectionist Architectures (C)

There has been excitement in recent years over a new kind of computer, the *connectionist* machine. These machines might have millions of tiny nodes, each capable of only very primitive calculation, and a massive connection scheme, with large arrays of nodes communicating wholesale with each other. These architectures are inspired by studies of the physiology of the human brain, and some researchers believe they carry out computations in a similar way. We will study one simple design for a connectionist machine here, and refer you to a fast-growing literature for additional readings.

Our connectionist architecture is typical of many of those currently under investigation and will be organized as an *N* by *N* square grid of nodes where *N* may be in the hundreds. Each node will receive an input from every other of the $N^2$ nodes, so the network is completely connected. Complete connectivity is not needed for many algorithms, but it will provide us with some interesting examples.

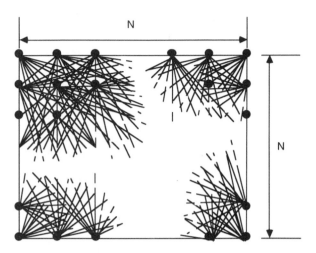

Each node will receive either a 1 or −1 from every other node. It will multiply each of its inputs (1 or −1) by a real value called a *weight* and then add up the results. The node will output 1 if this sum is greater than some constant *c*, and it will output −1 otherwise. This node will then send its output (1 or −1) to all the other nodes, which will simultaneously be recomputing their own outputs and broadcasting them to their neighbors. If the nodes could talk as they compute, there would be a tremendous din from their simultaneous chattering.

As an illustration of a single-node computation, consider the following four-node grid and the calculation of the output of its upper leftmost node. In this figure, the output of each node is shown on the node. All communication links are omitted except those needed for this example.

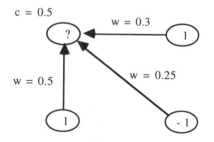

The upper left node will receive the three inputs, multiply them by appropriate weights *w*, and add them.

$$0.3^*(1) + 0.25(-1) + 0.5(1)$$

The sum is 0.55. Since this is larger than $c = 0.5$ for this node, it will output a 1:

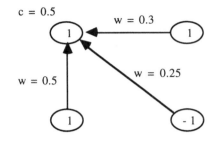

After the upper left output becomes 1, it is transmitted as input to all the other nodes, and they can compute their new outputs.

Consider next a larger version of this machine, a 3 by 3 system. Suppose the upper left node is connected as shown:

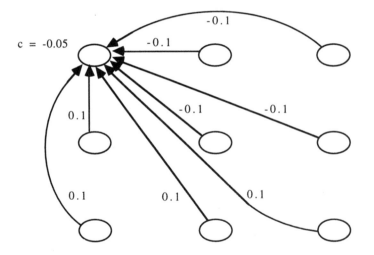

This complex information related to the node can be more economically represented in an array:

|      | −0.05 |      |
|------|-------|------|
| 0    | −0.1  | −0.1 |
| 0.1  | −0.1  | −0.1 |
| 0.1  | 0.1   | 0.1  |

This array shows the values of all the arcs from other nodes back to the upper left node. It contains a zero in the upper left corner because it has no transition to itself. The number above the array represents the constant $c$.

Remember that there are nine nodes, each with transitions coming into it. Thus, the whole connectionist machine can be represented by nine such arrays. Here they are for this sample machine:

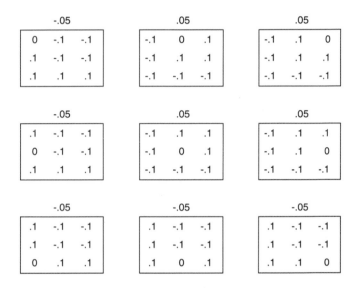

|      | -.05 |      |   |      | .05 |      |   |      | .05 |      |
|------|------|------|---|------|-----|------|---|------|-----|------|
| 0    | -.1  | -.1  |   | -.1  | 0   | .1   |   | -.1  | .1  | 0    |
| .1   | -.1  | -.1  |   | -.1  | .1  | .1   |   | -.1  | .1  | .1   |
| .1   | .1   | .1   |   | -.1  | -.1 | -.1  |   | -.1  | -.1 | -.1  |

|      | -.05 |      |   |      | .05 |      |   |      | .05 |      |
|------|------|------|---|------|-----|------|---|------|-----|------|
| .1   | -.1  | -.1  |   | -.1  | .1  | .1   |   | -.1  | .1  | .1   |
| 0    | -.1  | -.1  |   | -.1  | 0   | .1   |   | -.1  | .1  | 0    |
| .1   | .1   | .1   |   | -.1  | -.1 | -.1  |   | -.1  | -.1 | -.1  |

|      | -.05 |      |   |      | -.05 |      |   |      | -.05 |      |
|------|------|------|---|------|------|------|---|------|------|------|
| .1   | -.1  | -.1  |   | .1   | -.1  | -.1  |   | .1   | -.1  | -.1  |
| .1   | -.1  | -.1  |   | .1   | -.1  | -.1  |   | .1   | -.1  | -.1  |
| 0    | .1   | .1   |   | .1   | 0    | .1   |   | .1   | .1   | 0    |

This specifies all the weights and constants for the machine. If you wish to know the weight from node $i,j$ to node $k,l$, first go to the $k,l$ array and then select the $i,j$ entry in it.

Once the machine is specified, we can compute with it. Let us set the outputs of all the nodes and see what happens. (In the following diagrams, the details of the connections are omitted.)

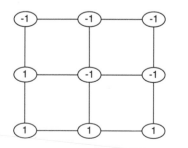

All the nodes will receive inputs from all the other nodes, and they will compute new outputs. Examining the upper left corner, we can compute the next output by adding the weights times the inputs on all lines:

$$(-.1)(-1) + (-.1)(-1) + (.1)(1) + (-.1)(-1) + (-.1)(-1) + (.1)(.1) + (.1)(1) + (.1)(1)$$

$$= 0.8$$

Since 0.8 is larger than $-.05$, we see that this node will have a new value of 1:

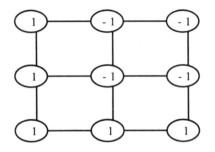

We can also compute new values for the other entries. In this case, they remain unchanged because they have reached stable values. If we consider the original configuration to be the input, then this final stable configuration is the output. Thus, the input

|    |    |    |
|----|----|----|
| $-1$ | $-1$ | $-1$ |
| 1  | $-1$ | $-1$ |
| 1  | 1  | 1  |

resulted in this output

|    |    |    |
|----|----|----|
| 1  | $-1$ | $-1$ |
| 1  | $-1$ | $-1$ |
| 1  | 1  | 1  |

Let us think of these nodes as neurons on a visual plane and assume 1 represents black and $-1$ represents white. Then an input of

has yielded an output of

This will be written as

Now we can experiment with this machine by repeatedly setting the inputs to be some image that interests us and then allowing all the nodes to recompute their values repeatedly until a stable configuration is found:

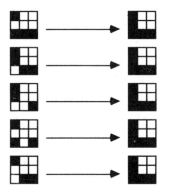

It appears that every pattern that vaguely resembles an L shape will yield an L shape. Also, many patterns that contain mere fragments of the L pattern also yield the L shape:

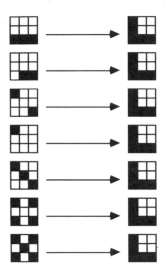

But some configurations lead to something else:

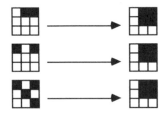

The L shape is much preferred, and all configurations that look vaguely like an L result in an L being formed. In fact, this machine is a recognizer of the L shape, and it attempts to make an L out of anything it encounters.

As you study the particular weights given above, you can discern the L shape coded among them. However, as we shall see later, the weights can be revised so that this machine can also recognize many other patterns. When this occurs, the weights begin to look like random numbers, yet the L and other patterns will still be coded into them.

This ability to bring forth a total image after observing only fragmentary evidence, called *associative memory*, is believed by many to be a key aspect of intelligent behavior. Our own memories are triggered by fragments: the name of an absent friend might evoke the face, which will, in turn, evoke some particular evening, and so on. The model of connectionist machines was derived as an analog to the brain, and its behavior seems reminiscent of our own.

Another characteristic of connectionist machines that resembles a biological system is that no particular weight or node is critical to the recognition. Because of the way the information about the L is spread across the machine, the weights can be varied somewhat randomly without greatly affecting behavior. If there are a few small changes, the pattern recognition will degrade relatively little. If large changes are made, more loss of function will occur, but the basic behavior will probably still not be disabled.

To summarize, we began with a nine-node connectionist computer with its weights specified in a set of arrays. We examined its input-output characteristics and discovered that it strongly prefers one particular output configuration. Whenever fragmentary information appears that may suggest that pattern, the machine will generate it as its output. This output may require many iterations of the basic node computation, but the final stable behavior will be that pattern. Connectionist architecture was modeled on the human brain, and these machines resemble biological systems in their ability to bring forth a total image after observing only fragmentary evidence and in the relative stability of this behavior.

A final attractive characteristic of the connectionist approach is that the computer need not be programmed. It can be trained to recognize patterns, which is the subject of the next section.

### Exercises

1. Suppose a 3 by 3 image with all four corners black and all other squares white is presented to the connectionist machine described above. Calculate the new values of all node outputs to determine the output image.

2. Change some of the weights in the 3 by 3 connectionist machine and determine whether its ability to recognize an L has degraded.

## Learning the Connectionist Weights (C)

Suppose we want the 3 by 3 connectionist machine to recognize some pattern, say L, but we don't know the appropriate values for the weights. The usual strategy is to assume that all the weights are zero and to consider each one individually and try varying it slightly. If the system performs better when a weight is slightly larger or smaller, that change is made. Then additional small changes are repeatedly made and tested for all the weights until they creep to new values that yield satisfactory results.

To see how this is done, return to the example of the upper left node, but this time assume all weights are zero:

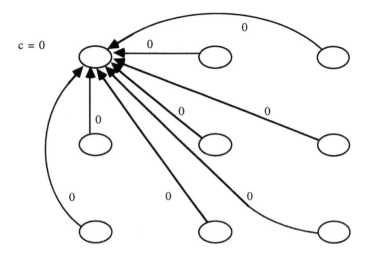

The goal of our procedure is to find values for the weights so that they prefer to output the L shape.

The target pattern has this form

| 1 | −1 | −1 |
| 1 | −1 | −1 |
| 1 | 1 | 1 |

and we want to find values that tend to compute a 1 in the upper left corner when given the other values shown. Assume the first weight to be examined is the one leading from the middle node in the top row to its left neighbor. We will increase it by 0.1 and then decrease it by 0.1, each time checking whether the change of weight helps or hinders the desired result (that the output in the upper left corner is a 1). Summing the eight values from the other nodes, we obtain the following:

If the weight is 0.1 then

$$(.1)(-1) + (0)(-1) + (0)(+1) + (0)(-1) + (0)(-1) + (0)(1) + (0)(1) + (0)(1) = -.1$$

Since $-.1$ is less than $c = 0$, the output is computed to be $-1$. This is not the desired output for the upper left corner.

If the weight is $-0.1$ then

$$(-.1)(-1) + (0)(-1) + (0)(1) + (0)(-1) + (0)(-1) + (0)(1) + (0)(1) = 0.1$$

Since 0.1 is greater than $c = 0$, the output is computed to be 1, which is the desired result. Of the two values tried, only the second was successful, so it is selected:

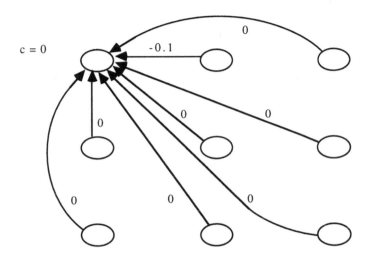

Reexamining this computation, we can see that $w = -0.1$ will be preferred over $w = 0.1$ because the goal is to maximize the summation. Since the weight $w$ is being multiplied by the pattern value at that cell, $-1$, $w = -0.1$ will do the job better than $w = 0.1$ because $-0.1$ results in a positive contribution to the sum. This generalizes as follows: When computing weights on arcs leading to a cell with a 1, all weights coming from cells with 1 should be incremented, and all weights coming from cells with $-1$ should be decremented.

A similar rule can be derived when the arcs lead to a cell with a value of $-1$. In this case, all weights coming from cells with $-1$ should be incremented, and all weights coming from cells with 1 should be decremented.

Let us see how these rules apply to finding more weights. Consider the weight on the arc from the upper right node. Its pattern value is $-1$, so its weight should be decremented. Its new value will be $-0.1$. Consider the weight on the arc from the node just below the upper left corner. This node has pattern value 1 so its arc weight should be increased. Its new value will be 0.1:

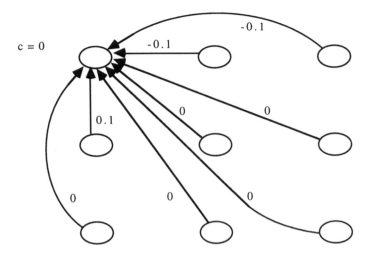

If we carry out this procedure for the rest of the weights, and a similar one is used to compute the constants *c* where variations of +0.05 and −0.05 are used, the result is the set of weights and constants shown in the previous section for the L recognizer. More complicated and less intuitive methods are sometimes used in computing these weights, but the method given here is easier to understand and gives satisfactory results for the purposes of our study. Typically, in realistic situations where many patterns are to be recognized, this weight computation must be repeated many times before satisfactory values are found. The weights and constants will slowly migrate to acceptable values as the computation is repeated. This process of slowly evolving a satisfactory set of weights and constants is called *learning*. (Other types of learning will be examined in chapter 15.)

Presenting the connectionist machine with many different patterns to learn is called *training* the machine. Now that our machine has "learned" the L pattern, let us train it on a T. If we begin with the values of the weights and constants as shown for the L pattern and modify them again in the same way using the T pattern,

$$
\begin{array}{rrr}
1 & 1 & 1 \\
-1 & 1 & -1 \\
-1 & 1 & -1 \\
\end{array}
$$

then a new set is derived:

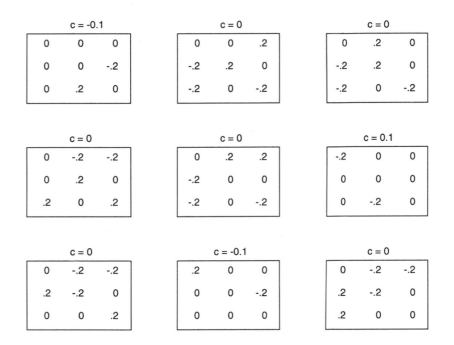

|  c = -0.1  |
|---|---|---|
| 0 | 0 | 0 |
| 0 | 0 | -.2 |
| 0 | .2 | 0 |

|  c = 0  |
|---|---|---|
| 0 | 0 | .2 |
| -.2 | .2 | 0 |
| -.2 | 0 | -.2 |

|  c = 0  |
|---|---|---|
| 0 | .2 | 0 |
| -.2 | .2 | 0 |
| -.2 | 0 | -.2 |

|  c = 0  |
|---|---|---|
| 0 | -.2 | -.2 |
| 0 | .2 | 0 |
| .2 | 0 | .2 |

|  c = 0  |
|---|---|---|
| 0 | .2 | .2 |
| -.2 | 0 | 0 |
| -.2 | 0 | -.2 |

|  c = 0.1  |
|---|---|---|
| -.2 | 0 | 0 |
| 0 | 0 | 0 |
| 0 | -.2 | 0 |

|  c = 0  |
|---|---|---|
| 0 | -.2 | -.2 |
| .2 | -.2 | 0 |
| 0 | 0 | .2 |

|  c = -0.1  |
|---|---|---|
| .2 | 0 | 0 |
| 0 | 0 | -.2 |
| 0 | 0 | 0 |

|  c = 0  |
|---|---|---|
| 0 | -.2 | -.2 |
| .2 | -.2 | 0 |
| .2 | 0 | 0 |

Presumably after training on both an L and a T, these values code both images. Let us now run the machine on a series of test inputs:

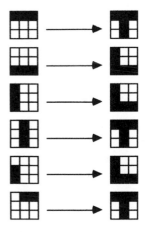 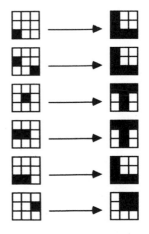

We can see that the machine recognizes as an L any image with even the vaguest resemblance to an L, and does the same for a T. Only one of the test inputs yields a non-L, non-T response.

You might examine the weights and constants and ask where the L and the T are stored. The answer is that they are stored everywhere, in the sense that each weight contributes in a small way to all decisions. From another point of view, they are nowhere, because small perturbations on individual weights will have little effect on total performance.

The examples here are extremely simple and serve only to demonstrate principles. A more realistically sized machine would have a grid with tens of thousands of nodes, as well as auxiliary arrays with more tens of thousands to do background computation. Training could involve thousands of examples, and the learning process could involve thousands of iterations to get the weights to converge to yield acceptable behaviors.

Larger systems are often studied in terms of *energy*. Given a set of weights and constants, a cell in the pattern is said to have energy

$E = c - s$ if the cell contains a 1 and

$E = -(c - s)$ if it contains $-1$.

The energy of a pattern is the sum of the energy of all the cells.

The concept of energy is quite useful for the understanding of large systems. Suppose a system has not been trained so that all weights and constants are at initial values. Then all patterns will have the same energy:

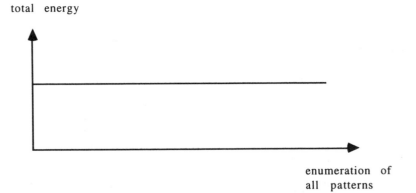

The effect of training is to lower the energy for training patterns and their variations. Thus, if a system is trained on two patterns, there will be two regions of lowered energy:

total  energy

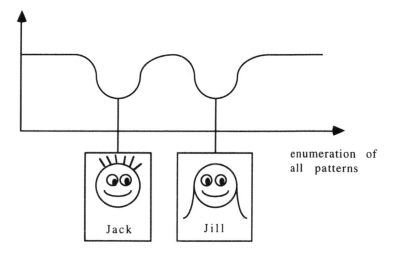

Once training is complete, we can present a fragment of an image to the system as input. This pattern will appear somewhere on the energy curve:

total  energy

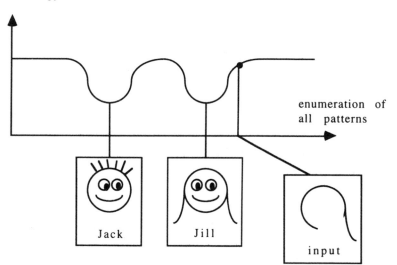

Then we can study the connectionist machine computation algorithm of the previous section to determine what it will do. Careful examination reveals that it tends to change cell outputs in the direction of reducing total pattern energy. Thus, in this example, the system will find its output by changing the values of individual cells in the direction of the nearby energy valley. In this case, it would converge on and output the image and name of Jill.

We can do a similar energy analysis of the L-T recognizer. The L and T will appear in energy valleys, and when the system is started with an input, it will compute iteratively until the pattern is reached in the nearest valley. A fragment of an L will migrate on the energy curve downward toward the bottom of the L valley. A fragment of a T will migrate toward the bottom of the T valley. Other fragments will migrate in unpredictable directions.

Connectionist systems are also capable of generalizing from examples. From images of many faces they can, for instance, form a general image of face: a mouth, two eyes, a nose, and so forth. Then when presented with a partial image, they can construct a whole. For a discussion of this and other connectionist phenomena, you can consult the specialized literature.

### Exercises

1. Use the set of weights and constants derived from the training set of L and T to determine the output if the input pattern is black in the upper left cell and white otherwise.

2. Vary the weights and constants and repeat the computation of problem 1. How big must the changes be to cause the system to make a different decision?

3. Compute the total energy of the input pattern in problem 1. Compute the energy of the output pattern in problem 1. Notice that the second value should be less than the first.

4. Compute the total energy for patterns identical to and varying from the basic L pattern using the weights and constants computed for the L and T training set. Draw a graph showing total energy for patterns of varying nearness to the basic L shape.

5. Study the values of the constants $c$ for the L recognizer and for the L-T recognizer. Can you discover the algorithm used to learn these values?

6. Train the 3 by 3 connectionist system on two patterns of your choosing and then test their performance.

7. The connectionist computation presented here tends to seek a minimum energy. However, we do not give a proof that this behavior will always occur. J. Hopfield has shown that machine processing is guaranteed to seek minimum total energy if the ma-

chine is built such that the weight from node $i,j$ to node $k,l$ always equals the weight back from node $k,l$ to $i,j$. Revise the algorithms presented here to adhere to this restriction.

---

## Summary (B)

Parallel computation appears to be the only way to increase machine speed once limits of technology have been reached for traditional machines. Some problems divide naturally into parts that can be spread across a parallel architecture, and dramatic speedup is often possible, especially if the number of processors is large compared to the size of the problem. But other problems may be hard to speed up under any conditions. With a limited degree $N$ of parallelism, as occurs on realistic machines, the speedup can be no greater than a factor of $N$, and even this is often hard to achieve.

Parallel architectures can vary on many dimensions, including the degree and format of connectivity, the organization of the processors, and the granularity of the parallelism.

A recent trend in computing has been the development of connectionist machines whose architecture was inspired by studies of the human brain. Large numbers of extremely simple computing devices are assembled in highly interconnected arrays. These machines are trained through the presentation of sample data, and their prominent characteristics include the ability to do associative retrieval, to complete fragmentary information, and to maintain robust behavior despite perturbations of their mechanisms. The success of these new machines shows the importance of research in brain biology for computer science.

# 14  Noncomputability

## Speed is Not Enough (A)

Chapter 12 taught us the unpleasant lesson that some important calculations are not possible because their execution times are too long. We may hope for faster machines and for new discoveries that will result in greater improvements in performance. Perhaps someday a computer will be built that will do as much work in one second as the combined effort of all the world's current machines could do in a billion years. But the sad lesson we will learn in this chapter is that computing speed will not be enough to solve many important problems. There exists a class of problems called *noncomputable* that have been shown to be unsolvable by any computer within the current paradigm of modern computing. This mystical and elusive class of problems will be the concern of this chapter.

In the next section, we will study an argument that shows that there are functions that cannot be computed by any Pascal program (or by any other known language). This proof will be simple and convincing. It will solidify the main idea of this chapter, but it will have one shortcoming: it will not show us an example of a noncomputable function. The following sections will give a series of ideas that will lead to further understanding of the concept of noncomputability and will include examples of noncomputable problems. The final section will give a proof that one of the examples is, in fact, noncomputable.

## On the Existence of Noncomputable Functions (B)

We will call a function *computable* if a Pascal program exists that can compute it. In this chapter, we will consider functions that read a positive integer and output a positive integer. Four examples of computable functions are $f_1, f_2, f_3$, and $f_4$, as shown in the table below.

| f₁ | | f₂ | | f₃ | | f₄ | |
|---|---|---|---|---|---|---|---|
| **Input** | **Output** | **Input** | **Output** | **Input** | **Output** | **Input** | **Output** |
| 1 | 2 | 1 | 7 | 1 | 6 | 1 | 100 |
| 2 | 4 | 2 | 8 | 2 | 6 | 2 | 100 |
| 3 | 6 | 3 | 9 | 3 | 6 | 3 | 100 |
| 4 | 8 | 4 | 10 | 4 | 6 | 4 | 4 |
| 5 | 10 | 5 | 11 | 5 | 6 | 5 | 5 |
| 6 | 12 | 6 | 12 | 6 | 6 | 6 | 6 |

The first function doubles its input and can be computed by this program:

```
program q1;
var
    x:integer;
begin
readln(x);
writeln(2*x);
readln;
end.
```

The second function adds six to its input:

```
program q2;
var
    x:integer;
begin
readln(x);
writeln(x+6);
readln;
end.
```

Similarly, the third and fourth functions are easy to program:

```
program q3;
var
    x:integer;
begin
readln(x);
writeln(6);
readln;
end.
```

```
program q4;
var
    x:integer;
begin
readln(x);
if x < 4 then
    writeln(100)
else
    writeln(x);
readln;
end.
```

Sometimes functions are defined to be computable if they can be programmed in some language other than Pascal, but since any general-purpose programming language can be translated into any other, the definitions are equivalent. The class of computable functions includes all the functions studied thus far in this book and almost every function encountered in high school or early college mathematics.

A *noncomputable* function is any function that cannot be computed by any Pascal program. Initially you might suspect that there is no such thing—that every function can be computed. The fact that noncomputable functions exist is a profound and fascinating discovery.

The argument that noncomputable functions exist is straightforward. It states that there are many more functions than there are programs, so it is not possible to have a program for every function. There must be functions that do not have any corresponding programs, and they are the noncomputable functions.

This argument is easy to understand if we propose for the moment the rather extreme assumption that there exist in the world only three programs—$P_1$, $P_2$, and $P_3$—and the four functions listed above. We may not know which program computes which function, but it is clear that no matter how the programs are paired with the functions, there will always be at least one function left unmatched. This leftover function is the noncomputable one. For example, if $P_1$ computes $f_4$, $P_2$ computes $f_1$, and $P_3$ computes $f_2$, then $f_3$ would be a noncomputable function.

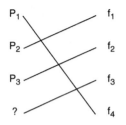

However, in practice there are more than three Pascal programs. There are infinitely many of them, so our argument needs to be refined. Let us list only the programs that read an integer and print an integer. The first in the list will be a shortest such program. Following the conventions of this book, the shortest possible program that reads an integer and prints an integer is as follows. It has a program name of length one, a variable name of length one, and the minimum statements to read and print integer values. (We continue the convention of requiring a *readln* statement just prior to the end.)

```
program p;
var
      x:integer;
begin
readln(x);
writeln(0);
readln;
end.
```

Other programs are equally short, as measured by the number of characters:

```
program p;
var
      x:integer;
begin
readln(x);
writeln(1);
readln;
end.

program p;
var
      x:integer;
begin
readln(x);
```

```
writeln(2);
readln;
end.


    -

    -


program p;
var
    x:integer;
begin
readln(x);
writeln(9);
readln;
end.

program p;
var
    x:integer;
begin
readln(x);
writeln(x);
readln;
end.
```

This is all the programs of this length (except for the renaming of identifiers), but if an additional character is allowed, more programs can be listed:

```
program p;
var
    x:integer;
begin
readln(x);
writeln(10);
readln;
end.
```

```
Etc.
```

We can sequentially list every program of one size, then every one of the next size, then the next, and so forth, in an endless chain of programs. Every Pascal program that reads an integer and prints an integer will appear somewhere in the list and thus prove that this set of programs is a countable set, as defined in chapter 3. These programs can be placed in a row!

Let us place these programs in a row and draw a link from each program to the function it computes:

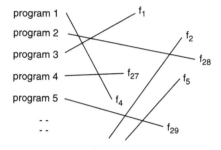

If every function were computable and thus had a link to some program, we could move the functions along their links and put them, too, in a row.

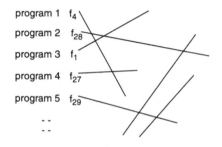

However, we learned in chapter 3 that it is not possible to put all the functions in a row. Since the set of all functions is not countable, we cannot link every function with a program. Some functions do not have programs, so functions must exist that are not computable.

Summarizing once again, not all functions can be computed because there are not enough programs to cover them all. Some functions do not have associated programs that can compute them.

But what is an example of a function that cannot be computed? The next sections will provide background and some very important examples of such functions.

**Exercises**

1. The set of functions that receive a finite set of binary inputs and compute a single binary output was studied in chapter 7. These are the kind of functions that we can build switching circuits for. Are these functions all computable, as defined in this chapter? Give a careful and complete justification for your answer.

2. Consider the set of functions that receive a positive integer and output a binary integer—a 0 or a 1. Are these functions all computable? Give a careful and complete justification for your answer.

## Programs That Read Programs (B)

Our goal is to find computations that cannot be done by any Pascal program. It would be interesting to specify a calculation that inputs integers and is noncomputable, but the most commonly encountered and easily understood examples of noncomputability involve programs that read other programs and print something:

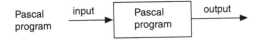

For the purposes of this section, assume that the programs input by other programs are simply sequences of statements separated by spaces, all typed on a single line. Thus the program called *A* that is usually typed as

```
program A;
var
    x:integer;
begin
readln(x);
writeln(2*x);
readln;
end.
```

will be written on a single line as

```
program A; var x:integer; begin readln(x); writeln(2*x); readln; end.
```

If we type this one-line program into our usual compiler, it will compile and execute the program normally. We will also assume that these programs have no subroutine calls.

Let us write a program that can read programs like *A* and do something with them. Let us call the program *B* and specify that *B* will read a program and tell us whether the program it has read has an "if" in it. Thus, if *B* reads *A*, it types "Has no if." However, if *B* reads one of the decision-tree programs of chapter 1, it prints "Has an if in it." (We will assume all programs can be typed on a single line. If we attempt to account for multiple-line programs, our programs that read programs will be distractingly complex. Here is *B*:

```
program B;
var
    p:string;
begin
writeln('Type in a program.');
readln(p);
if pos('if',p) > 0 then
    writeln('Has an if in it.')
else
    writeln('Has no if.');
readln;
end.
```

Since the concept of a program reading other programs is strange, it may be helpful to type *B* into a machine and become comfortable using it. For example, try running *B* on *A* and other sample programs. What happens if *B* is run on *B*?

We will examine other programs that read programs, but first we will introduce *the halting problem*. As we noticed in chapter 2, some programs have the peculiar behavior that they run forever; they never halt. *C* is such a program:

```
program C;
var
    x:integer;
begin
readln(x);
while x = x do
    x := x;
writeln(x);
readln;
end.
```

This code will continue looping as long as $x$ equals itself. But $x$ always equals itself, so this program never halts, regardless of what input is read.

Some programs may halt in some cases and fail to halt in others. The following code, $D$, will halt and print the input if it is less than or equal to 10. Otherwise, it will never halt:

```
program D;
var
    x:integer;
begin
readln(x);
while x > 10 do
    x := x;
writeln(x);
readln;
end.
```

Most programs in this book halt on all inputs. Failure to halt is usually considered an undesirable property. *The halting problem* for computer programs thus addresses the question of whether a program halts on specific inputs or on all inputs.

We might like to write a program that reads other programs and checks whether they halt. Let us call the program $E$ and design it to determine, if possible, whether a program will halt on all inputs. If $E$ reads a program and finds that it will halt on every input, $E$ will type the message "Halts on all inputs." Otherwise $E$ will output "Not known whether it halts":

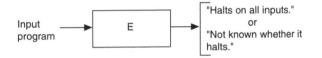

How can we write the program $E$? This could be a complicated undertaking, but only a simple version will be attempted here. We will note, as a start, that if a program has no *while* loops (and, by assumption, no subroutine calls), then it can be composed only of input-output statements, assignment statements, and *if* statements. But such a program would surely always halt because such statements always execute and pass control to the next statement. The program *end* will be reached directly. The only way that nonhalting behavior can occur is if a loop captures control and never terminates, as occurs in $C$. A simple strategy for writing $E$ is to have it check whether *while* appears anywhere in the input program. If $E$ finds there is no *while* statement in its input program, it can be sure the program will halt on all inputs. If $E$ does find *while* statements, it will not be able to guarantee any halting property. $E$ can be written as follows:

```
program E;
var
    p:string;
begin
writeln('Type in a program.');
readln(p);
if pos('while',p) > 0 then
    writeln('Not known whether it halts.')
else
    writeln('Halts on all inputs.');
readln;
end.
```

Again, *E* is best understood if it is typed into a machine. It can then be run on various input programs, such as *A* through *E* of this section, and will return the appropriate answers.

Unfortunately, *E* is more simplistic than we might desire. It does not give us any useful information beyond whether the string "while" appears in a given program, and we would actually like a definitive answer. Does the program halt on every input or does it not? We wish to create a new program *F* and require that it be able to read any program and halt after a finite time with the correct answer: Either the given input program halts on all inputs or it does not.

The next section will describe the construction of *F*.

**Exercises**

1. Write a program that reads another program and tells whether the program is known never to print anything. If your program cannot determine for sure whether the input program prints anything, it should give a message stating this.

2. Write a program that reads another program and gives its length.

3. Write a program that reads a program and then determines whether every variable declared actually appears in the main part of the program. If a variable is found that never appears after the declaration, your program prints its name.

## Solving The Halting Problem (B)

The next task is to see how to write program *F*. *F* will have lines of code that can check the halting characteristics of any input program. *F* will check many features related to halting behavior and if it finds a proof that a given program will or will not always halt, it will print the appropriate message and stop.

The organization of *F* will be as shown below; the input program will be read, and then a series of cases will be examined. When a case is found that indicates the halting or nonhalting behavior of a given program, the appropriate message is printed, and all later cases are skipped:

```
program F;
var
    p,solutionfound,case1holds, . . . . :string;
begin
writeln('Type in a program.');
readln(p);
solutionfound := 'false';
if solutionfound='false' then
    begin
    case 1 code
    if case1holds = 'true' then
        begin
        writeln( put result 1 here );
        solutionfound := 'true';
        end;
    end;
if solutionfound='false' then
    begin
    case 2 code
    if case2holds = 'true' then
        begin
        writeln( put result 2 here );
        solutionfound := 'true';
        end;
    end;

        –
        –
        –
```

```
if solutionfound='false' then
    begin
    case n code
    if casenholds = 'true' then
        begin
        writeln( put result n here );
        solutionfound := 'true';
        end;
    end;
end.
```

Thus, *F* can be completed as soon as all the cases are known. We will now consider them in sequence.

### Case 1

The easiest phenomenon to cover is that addressed by *E*, the case where "while" does not appear anywhere in the input program. Here we know the message to be printed is "Halts on all inputs," so the case 1 portion of the *F* program is as follows:

```
if solutionfound='false' then
    begin
    if pos('while',p) > 0 then
        case1holds := 'false'
    else
        case1holds := 'true';
    if case1holds = 'true' then
        begin
        writeln('Halts on all inputs.');
        solutionfound := 'true';
        end;
    end;
```

### Case 2

A second easy phenomenon occurs in any program with a *while* loop that has "true" as a test. If the loop is ever entered, it will run forever, and this is a situation where *F* should print "Does not halt on all inputs." Program *G* provides an example of this case:

```
program G;
var
    x:integer;
begin
readln(x);
```

```
while true do
    x := x;
writeln(x);
readln;
end.
```

The case 2 portion of *F* should be:

```
if solutionfound = 'false' then
    begin
    Code that checks for a while loop
    that is entered and has true as a test .
    if case2holds = 'true' then
        begin
        writeln('Does not halt on all inputs.');
        solutionfound := 'true';
        end;
    end;
```

## Case 3

A slightly more complicated case is represented by *C*, where a test is made in the loop but the test always produces a true result. If the loop is entered, the repetitions will not terminate. This is another situation in which *F* can return a "no halt" message. The case 3 portion of *F* can be written as follows:

```
if solutionfound = 'false' then
    begin
    Code that checks for a while loop that is
    entered and has a test that is provably
    always true.
    if case3holds = 'true' then
        begin
        writeln('Does not halt on all inputs.');
        solutionfound := 'true';
        end;
    end;
```

## Case 4

*D* provides an example of another interesting class of programs. This is similar to case 3 except that it may not be clear whether the loop-exit test will pass on the first encounter.

In the case of *D*, the exit will occur if the input is not greater than 10. In other examples, more complicated situations may occur, and it will be necessary to check whether any input could exist such that the loop exit will fail. Here is an example of the wide variety of constructions that might appear:

```
program H;
var
    x,y:integer;
begin
readln(x);
if x = 1772 then
    y := 1
else
    y := 0;
while y = 1 do
    x := 1;
writeln(x);
readln;
end.
```

Handling such examples is a complex undertaking that will not be considered at length here.

## Case 5

Another increment in complexity occurs if the loop test includes more than one variable. Here is a program that halts on all inputs, but it is not so easy to discover this:

```
program I;
var
    x,y:integer;
begin
readln(x);
y := 2*x;
while y > x do
    begin
    x := x + 2;
    y := y + 1;
    end;
writeln(x);
readln;
end.
```

This is more complex than case 4 and will not be considered further here.

Other cases that need to be considered are where three or more variables appear in the test or where very complex tests occur, as in this case:

```
while ((x*z+3) > z - (Y/(Z1*Z2 + 4))) and (X*(YY/Z1) <> YY+Z1+Z2) do
```

Loops may also be nested to two or three or more levels, and there may also be deeply convoluted amalgamations of multiple *if* and *while* constructions. There may also be *while* loops with complicated indexing rules that could be mixed an arbitrary number of times with earlier constructions.

So the job of writing a program *F* that will determine whether other programs halt is very difficult. Perhaps it could be a person's life's work! In fact, mathematicians have shown that no matter how many cases are considered and regardless of how completely each case is handled, the job will never be done. There will always be more cases, and there will always be more code to write on the new cases. *No finite program can be written that will check other programs and halt in a finite time giving a solution to the halting problem.* Thus, the goal of finding a noncomputable problem has been achieved. The proof that no program can exist that meets the specifications of *F* will be given later in this chapter.

In summary, we say that the halting problem is not computable. This does not mean that we cannot discover the halting characteristic of a particular program, since we have already determined the halting behavior for many programs. What it does mean is that there is no single finite program *F* that will answer the halting question for all programs.

As an illustration, if *F* could exist, what would it do if it were given the following program *J*:

```
program J;
var
    x:integer;
begin
readln(x);
while x > 1 do
    begin
    if (x div 2) * 2 = x then
        x := x div 2
    else
        x := 3 * x + 1;
    writeln(x);
    end;
readln;
end.
```

If this program reads 17, it will print 52, 26, 13, 40, 20, 10, 5, 16, 8, 4, 2, 1 and halt. We can give it thousands of other positive integers and probably discover it halts on them also. But will *J* halt on *every* positive integer? It is not likely that anyone knows, and there is no sure way to find out.

It is possible that someone will discover a way to solve the halting problem for *J*, but then we will not have to look far to find another program whose halting problem is not understood. There is no single program (or method) for solving all halting problems.

**Exercises**

1. Find a class of programs that halt on all inputs and that we have not discussed. Show how you have solved the halting problem for this class.

2. Find a class of programs that fail to halt on some input and that we have not discussed. Show how you can be sure that each program will fail to halt.

3. Run program *J* on a number of inputs and observe its behavior. Do you believe that it halts on all inputs? Can you solve the halting problem for program *J*?

4. Find a program whose halting behavior is extremely difficult to determine.

---

## Examples of Noncomputable Problems (B)

Suppose the instructor of a computer programming course wishes to have his or her students' programs checked automatically. A reasonable strategy would be for the instructor to write a master program that solves the assigned problem and then to check whether each student's submission is equivalent to the master. In order for two programs to be equivalent, they must print the same result for every input. The checking program would read the two solutions: the instructor's master and the student's submission. Then it would print the appropriate answer, either "The two programs are equivalent," or "They are not equivalent."

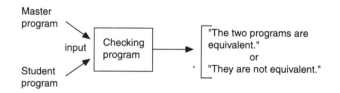

The analysis of this problem proceeds very much like the analysis of the halting problem in the previous section. It is often possible to determine that two programs are equivalent, as with

```
program A;
var
    x:integer;
begin
readln(x);
writeln(2*x);
readln;
end.
```

and

```
program A;
var
    x:integer;
begin
readln(x);
writeln(x+x);
readln;
end.
```

It is also easy to show that two programs are not equivalent, as with program *A* and the following program:

```
program AA;
var
    x:integer;
begin
readln(x);
writeln(3*x);
readln;
end.
```

However, there are many cases in which the discovery of equivalence is an exceedingly subtle, if not impossible, matter. Consider these two programs, *K* and *L*, and the difficulty in determining their equivalence, assuming that the only inputs are positive integers:

```
program K;
var
    x: integer;
```

```
begin
readln(x);
while x > 1 do
    begin
    if (x div 2) * 2 = x then
        x := x div 2
    else
        x := 3 * x + 1;
    end;
writeln(1);
readln;
end.
```

and

```
program L;
var
    x:integer;
begin
readln(x);
writeln(1);
readln;
end.
```

The first program, *K*, may halt on all inputs and print 1. It seems to do this but we have no way of being sure that it always does. If it does, it is equivalent to *L*; otherwise it is not.

If we attempt to write a checking program, we will run into a series of cases like those in the previous section and we will not be able to complete the task. The *equivalence problem* is another example of a noncomputable calculation.

There are large numbers of problems related to programs that are noncomputable, like the halting problem and the equivalence problem. Suppose we want a program to check whether programs print something on every possible input. For some programs this is easy, but for others, like *K*, it is very difficult. This is a noncomputable problem. Suppose you want a program to determine whether a specific line of code is always executed in other programs for all possible inputs. This is also a noncomputable problem. For example, does *K* execute the instruction *writeln(1)* for every (positive integer) input? Suppose you want a program to determine whether other programs double their input. This again is noncomputable.

In fact, almost every problem related to the behavior of programs is noncomputable in the sense described here. Almost every question related to halting, equivalence, printing, correctness, or any other behavioral property is unanswerable for the class of all programs. Anyone who proposes to write a program to check for property X in the behavior of other programs is probably attempting the impossible:

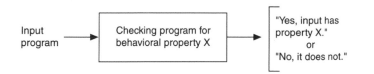

Many computations that do not relate to programming languages are similarly noncomputable. For example, the Post Correspondence Problem described in chapter 2 is such a computation. There is no program that will read every Post Correspondence Problem and halt after a finite time, either giving the solution to the problem or giving the message that there is no solution. Another class of noncomputable computations relates to the answerability of questions about database queries.

Are there any questions about programs that are computable? Yes, we can write programs to check almost any syntactic feature of programs. We can write programs that will measure the length of programs, the number of statements, the number of character A's, the number of arithmetic expressions, and many other things. We can write a program that will read a sequence of characters and tell whether it is a Pascal program or not. (The Pascal compiler does this.) We can write a program that will compute almost any property of the sequence of characters that make up the program. But we usually cannot write a program that will discover any general property of the program's execution when it is functioning as a program.

### Exercises

1. We will categorize functions in three different ways: noncomputable, computable-tractable, and computable-intractable. Study each proposed computation listed below and classify it, as well as you can, in one of the three ways.
   (a) A program that reads a list of *n* numbers and finds whether any one of those numbers is the sum of any two or more of the others.
   (b) A program that reads a program of length *n* and tells the number of characters that will be printed if that program is run on the input of 17.
   (c) A program that reads a program of length *n* and prints "tractable" if the program computes a tractable computation; otherwise, it prints "intractable."
   (d) A program that reads *n* numbers and prints the largest one.
   (e) A program that reads a program of length *n* and translates it into machine language.
   (f) A program that reads a Pascal program of length *n*. If there is a way to rearrange the characters of this program so that they become a legal P88 assembly-language program, the program prints "yes." Otherwise, it prints "no."
   (g) A program that reads a program of length *n* and tells how many legal Pascal statements are in the program.

2. The Church-Markov-Turing thesis described in chapter 4 states that any computation that we can describe can be computed. In this chapter, we have described some computations that we claim cannot be computed. What is the problem here?

## Proving Noncomputability (C)

The above sections argued that programs to solve problems like the halting problem are impossible to write, but they gave no proof of this impossibility. This section will present a classical proof that the halting problem is not computable. The other examples from the last section can be derived from this basic result.

The method of proof will be by contradiction. We will assume that the halting problem is solvable and that a program has been found that solves it. We will study the ramifications of this assumption and come across ridiculous conclusions. We will decide that since the assumption that a program exists to solve the halting problem leads to something obviously false, it must be that such a program does not exist.

The proof begins with the assumption that we have a Pascal subroutine called *halt* that reads two things—a program $p$ and its input $x$. We will assume that *halt* will run for a finite amount of time, and then it will return its answer in *result*. Either it will return *result* = "Halts," indicating that program $p$ halts on input $x$, or it will return *result* = "Does not halt," indicating that $p$ will run forever if given input $x$:

```
procedure halt(var p,x,result:string);
    var . . .
    begin
    Body of the halt routine.
    if . . . then
        result := 'Halts.'
    else
        result := 'Does not halt.';
    end;
```

(This program is more specific than $F$ (discussed earlier) in that it inputs both a program and that program's input. This program returns "Halts" if $p$ halts on input $x$, whereas $F$ reads only $p$ and prints "Halts on all inputs" if $p$ halts on all inputs. The subroutine *halt* checks only one input for program $p$ while $F$ checks all inputs. This difference will be discussed at the end of this section.) We do not know the details of the subroutine *halt*. We assume that someone has filled them in and wonder what the consequences are.

Next we will write two subroutines that will help with this proof. One is called *selfhalt*, and the other is *contrary*. The former will input a program $p$ and then call the subroutine *halt* to find whether $p$ halts with itself as an argument:

```
procedure selfhalt(var p,result:string);
    var
        answer:string;
    begin
    halt (p, p, answer);
    if answer = 'Halt.' then
        result := 'Halts on self.'
    else
        result := 'Does not halt on self.';
    end;
```

The second program, *contrary*, is designed to justify its name. It reads a program *p* and runs *selfhalt* to determine whether *p* halts on itself. If *p* does halt on itself, then *contrary* will never halt. If *p* does not halt on itself, then *contrary* will halt immediately:

```
procedure contrary(var p:string);
    var
        answer:string;
    begin
    selfhalt(p, answer);
    if answer = 'Halts on self.' then
        while true do
            answer := 'x';
    end;
```

This is all extremely simple. (It is also very strange.) But a real collision with reality occurs when *contrary* is allowed to run with itself as input. Let us analyze very carefully what happens.

Assume that *p* is the subroutine *contrary* listed above. Also assume that this routine *contrary* is executed with input *p*. Thus, we are running *contrary* on itself. Let us see what happens. The first statement of *contrary* is *selfhalt (p,answer)*. Consider two cases:

1. Suppose *selfhalt* stops and returns the result *answer* = "Halts on self." Then the second statement of *contrary* will check this and go into an infinite loop. That is, if it is found using *selfhalt* that *contrary* halts on itself, then *contrary* will run forever on itself. The infinite loop *while true do answer* := 'x'; ensures this. This is a contradiction. The routine *contrary* cannot both halt on itself and not halt on itself.
2. Suppose *selfhalt* stops and returns the result *answer* = "Does not halt on self." Then the second statement of *contrary* will be a test that fails, and *contrary* will halt immediately. Thus, we conclude that if *contrary* does not halt on itself (as determined by routine *selfhalt*), then it will halt on itself, an equally ridiculous conclusion.

This concludes the proof by contradiction. We began by assuming that the program *halt* could exist as defined. Then the subroutine *contrary* was defined (with its subroutine *selfhalt*, which depends on *halt*). Then it was shown that if *contrary* halts on itself, then it does not halt on itself, and if it does not halt on itself, then it halts on itself. Something is wrong with this argument. But every step is simple and logically sound. The only step lacking justification is the assumption that *halt* can exist. We conclude that it cannot exist.

This proof of the noncomputability of the *halt* function may seem like mathematical magic because it is so involuted in its structure. It is, however, the classical mathematical proof translated into the notation and vocabulary of this book.

Once we have proved that *halt* cannot exist, we can prove many other noncomputability results. As an illustration, consider the program *F* discussed earlier. This program, if it could exist, would read a program and tell whether it halts on all inputs. Since *halt* cannot exist, how can *F* exist?

The proof is by contradiction: If *F* did exist, then we could build *halt*, and this result has been shown to be impossible. Assume the program whose halting problem is to be solved has this form:

```
procedure p(var z:string);
    begin
    Pascal code that uses variable z.
    end;
```

Then *halt* can be constructed as follows:

```
procedure halt(var p, x, result:string)
    Code which removes variable z from the
        argument of p and replaces it with a new
        variable that appears nowhere in subroutine
        p. Call the new variable newz.
    Code which inserts a new statement at the
        beginning of p: z := (contents of x)
    F(p, answer);
    if answer = "Halts on all inputs." then
        result := 'Halts.'
    else
        result := 'Does not halt.';
    end;
```

Here is how *halt* works. Assume it is called with *p* containing the subroutine *p* shown above and with *x* containing the input for *p*. First *halt* modifies *p* so that it has this form:

```
procedure p (var newz:string);
    begin
    Pascal code which uses variable z.
    end;
```

Notice that this new version of *p* acts the same regardless of what its argument is. Variable *newz* is never used in the code. Notice also that this version has a bug in it because *z*, which previously received its input from the argument, now has no value. The next piece of code in *halt* fixes this error; it puts a statement into *p* that properly loads *z*. Now *p* has this form:

```
procedure p(var newz:string);
    begin
    z := The contents of x is placed here.
    Pascal code which uses variable z.
    end;
```

The new subroutine *p* functions the same regardless of its input *newz* because *newz* is never used, and it does exactly what the old *p* would have done using the input in *x*. Thus, if the old *p* would have halted on *x*, the new *p* will halt on all inputs. If the old *p* would have run forever on *x*, the new *p* will run forever on all inputs.

Next *halt* calls *F* running on this modified program. According to the specifications of *F*, it will stop after a finite time and return the result "Halts on all inputs," if the revised *p* will halt on all inputs, and "Does not halt on all inputs," otherwise. But if the revised *p* halts on all inputs, the original *p* would halt on *x*, so *halt* should return "Halts." If the revised *p* fails to halt on all inputs, the original *p* would not halt on *x*, so *halt* should return "Does not halt." Summarizing, we have seen that if *F* could exist, then *halt* could be constructed, and this is impossible. This concludes the proof that the problem that *F* is specified to solve is noncomputable.

### Exercises

1. Do a hand-simulation of program *contrary* when it is run with program *B* as an input. Repeat with program *E* as an input.

2. Use the methodology of this section to prove that the following problem is non-computable: A program that reads a program and, after a finite time, the output tells whether the input program will ever print anything.

---

## Summary (B)

We began this chapter by asserting that there are numerical functions that cannot be computed by any Pascal program. Then we gave a proof of this assertion. The proof showed that there are noncomputable functions but it failed to provide even one example. Numerical examples are difficult to explain, so we moved our study to a new domain—programs that read programs.

Here it was found that if one program is to read another program and determine almost any property of its execution behaviors, there is a good chance that noncomputability will be encountered; the proposed program will not be constructable using Pascal (or any other language that has been invented or proposed). Thus, programs cannot be written to determine the halting, equivalence, printing, correctness, or almost any other behavioral property of programs. This is an extremely important result for computer scientists because one of their main jobs is to write programs that manipulate other programs, and many of the goals they set for themselves may not be achievable.

However, problems related to the syntax of programs very often are computable and examples of this appear throughout this book. We can, for example, write programs that look for character sequences in other programs or that measure their syntactic properties. Programs can also read other programs and translate them into another language, as shown in chapter 9.

This chapter and chapter 12 have shown two types of computations that cannot be done using current or proposed technologies. The next chapter will study another class of very difficult problems.

# 15    Artificial Intelligence

## The Dream (A)

The final frontier to be examined here concerns our limitations as programmers. As we move into the next century, it is reasonable to ask how large, how complex, how broad in capabilities, and ultimately, how intelligent programs can become. If we consider any program in this book, we wonder how many improvements could be made to strengthen its capabilities and increase its usefulness. Could the program be improved to handle a larger class of problems? Could it be revised to make more subtle inferences? Could it be designed to create alternative plans and to evaluate them and select the best one? Could the program recognize its own shortcomings and modify itself to give better performance?

Consider the database program that was used to help the inspector solve a mystery. We have already noticed its lack of ability to infer new facts from the given information, and a method for addressing this problem was suggested near the end of the translation chapter. But how extensive could this inference mechanism actually be? For example, the system could be given the fact that every person must be somewhere at every instant of time, and then it could attempt to infer the whereabouts of every individual at critical times. It could formulate a plan for solving the crime by seeking a proof for each individual's story in relation to the key events. The program would no longer be a passive provider of information but an active developer of theories. Perhaps the program could handle a variety of English syntax instead of simple noun-verb-noun formats. We might, in addition, design mechanisms to remember successful strategies and then use them to improve the system's subsequent performances. Finally, we would want the system to be general enough in its design to manage various information-processing problems, not simply solve a crime.

Such is the dream of *artificial intelligence*: that machines may be programmed to become more and more powerful until their abilities equal or exceed those of humans. The artificial intelligence researcher looks on the human mind as an example of a very powerful computer, and his or her goal is to write programs so that electronic machines can achieve the abilities of biological systems. Attempts have been made to develop machine systems that converse in natural language, solve puzzles, play games, understand visual images, walk on legs and manipulate the environment with hands, compose music, create new mathematics, and perform many other tasks. The argument is that electronic computers should be able to do whatever the human mind can do.

The difference between human and machine capabilities seems to depend on the complexity of the task. If efficient programs are written, computers can do the job much better than we can: they can add numbers, billions of them per second, and they can remember facts better, billions of them, without making an error. But if the problem is very complex, either programs will be too slow to run efficiently or the codes will be so complicated that no one knows how to write them. So the question is not whether computers or humans have better information-processing abilities, but rather which problems are handled better by machines and which by humans.

To put this into perspective, we can draw a rough graph, giving task complexity on the horizontal axis and estimating human and computer capabilities on the vertical axis:

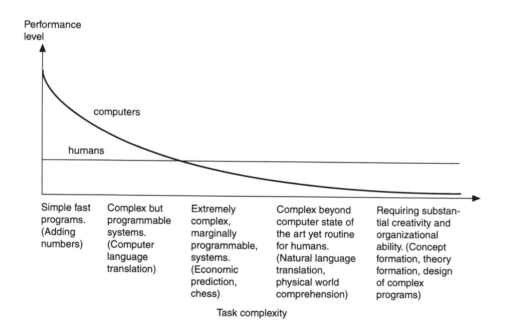

Machines clearly dominate in all situations where moderate-sized programs can be devised that run at acceptable speeds. No sensible person would propose that standard industrial information-processing, such as computer language translation or payroll computations, should be done by humans. However, machines are clearly inferior for tasks mentioned on the right half of the graph, such as in natural language translation, concept formation and any kind of scientific theory formation.

Human performance is much more evenly balanced across the spectrum of activities. Humans are moderately competent at simple tasks, such as adding numbers, at all the intermediate levels of complexity, and even at concept formation and the most complex tasks.

This graph, of course, cannot be taken too seriously, since none of the terms is well-defined, but it gives us a perspective from which to view research in artificial intelligence. The usual definition of intelligence is represented by the horizontal axis, where higher degrees of intelligence correspond to points farther to the right. When humans and machines are being discussed, the definition of "intelligent behavior" typically begins somewhere around the crossover point for the machine and human performance curves. The goal of artificial intelligence researchers is to raise the level of the machine curve in the regions on the right.

As researchers attack more difficult problems, they develop new intellectual paradigms. This chapter introduces the most important ones—the concepts of *knowledge* and *reasoning*. *Knowledge structures* are composed of the same primitives we have discussed in earlier chapters, but now we will think of them as a whole rather than as one memory unit at a time. The way we conceptualized reasoning will also change. Instead of dealing with simple computations, like addition or copy operations, we will discuss steps in a reasoning process, like inferring a new fact, that may involve many such individual operations. An examination of these concepts, which will enable us to approach more difficult problems, will provide the starting point for our study of artificial intelligence.

We will begin by examining knowledge—its representation, the meaning of the word *understand*, the uses of knowledge, and methods for acquiring knowledge. Then we will discuss reasoning as a concept, including the methodologies of heuristic programming with applications to game playing and expert-system design. Finally, the summary sections will discuss the state of the art in artificial intelligence.

---

## Representing Knowledge (B)

We will define *knowledge* as the set of facts and relationships, called *data items*, that pertain to an object or event. For example, our knowledge of a particular chair includes data items like its position, its material, its color, its size and shape, its owner, its cost, its age, its history, and its current use. A particular data item is a part of our knowledge of the chair if there is a processing task related to the chair that references that item. Thus, we might want to use the chair, move it, describe it, or change it, and the data items that are required to do these things comprise our knowledge of the chair.

If a computer is to perform operations on an object, it must have not only the required knowledge, but also the ability to access it efficiently. There are many ways of organizing knowledge, and the method we will describe in this chapter uses *semantic networks*. A semantic network is a set of labeled nodes with labeled arcs connecting them. The nodes can be used to represent objects, names, properties, and other entities, and the arcs can show the relationships between these entities. Here is a semantic network that partially describes a chair that has been given the formal label *a1*:

A Semantic Network

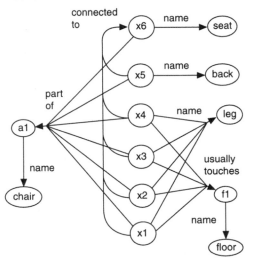

This network describes an object called *a1*, represented by the node at the middle left of the diagram. Following the arrow down, we see that the name of this object is "chair." There are six other objects in the diagram, labelled *x1*, *x2*, ..., *x6*, and they have pointers labelled "part of" aimed at *a1* because they are part of the object labelled *a1*. We can tell what these six objects are by their labels—some are legs, and there is a back and a seat— and we can see the relationships of these objects to each other and to other objects. Some are connected, and the legs "usually touch" the floor.

Because this diagram gives us a way to represent a more complex type of object than a number or string, it enables us to manipulate inside a computer the kinds of objects that we would expect an intelligent agent to manage. But how can we store this semantic network in the machine? A method for doing it is to notice that every arc can be specified by listing its initial node, its arc label, and its final node:

```
x1    partof    a1
x2    partof    a1
       -
       -
       -
a1    name      chair
       -
       -
    etc.
```

This list contains all the information in the network and is suitable for storage. In fact, we are experts at handling facts in three-tuple form because we studied this format extensively in chapter 4. (For the remainder of this chapter, we will continue to draw networks as shown above, and you can fill in implementation details, if needed, by referencing chapter 4.)

Knowledge can be represented in the machine by using methods other than semantic networks. One common technique is to write down a set of logical statements containing the significant relationships; another is to specify the objects and relationships with an ordinary programming language such as Pascal, LISP, or Prolog; a third way is to store information in actual pictorial images. In this chapter, however, the only representation scheme will be semantic networks because they are the easiest to visualize and use in the tasks that we will study.

The next several sections will discuss the concept of knowledge understanding, a method for learning new knowledge, structures for large knowledge modules, and an example of the usefulness of knowledge in understanding natural language.

## Exercises

1. Remove one of the arcs between two nodes on the chair network shown above. Describe the object that it represents after the change.

2. Draw a semantic network to represent a typical house. It should include the walls, the roof, the windows, the doors, a chimney, and so forth. The network should show connectivity, support relationships, and some functional knowledge, such as where to enter.

---

## Understanding (B)

Suppose the knowledge structure of the chair is stored in the machine and an image from the outside world is stored in a memory region near it:

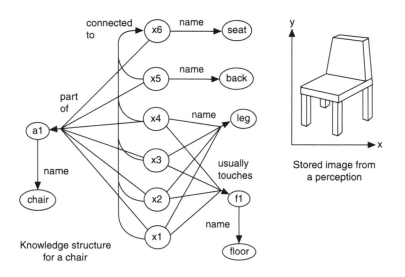

Knowledge structure
for a chair

Stored image from
a perception

We would like to be able to use the knowledge to make sense of the image. If a computer can successfully associate the items in the knowledge structure with the regions and lines in the picture, it will be able to name the object, name its parts, and check whether the appropriate relationships hold. We will say that the machine *understands* this image if it can find the correct linkage between these two structures, the knowledge and the image.

Let us follow the process of searching for an understanding of the image. Where, for example, is the seat of the chair? We will link the node *x6* associated with the seat with a randomly selected region in the image:

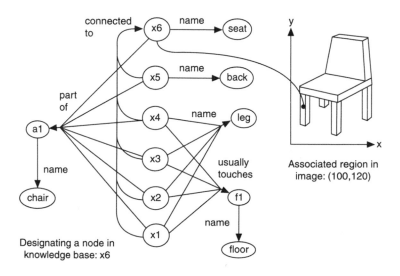

Designating a node in
knowledge base: x6

Associated region in
image: (100,120)

Assume that the selected region is specified by the coordinates of its central point $(x,y) = (100,120)$. Then we will store this linkage in a table:

| Nodes in knowledge base | Associated region in image |
|---|---|
| x6 | (100,120) |

Good! We have begun to understand the image as a chair by identifying the seat.

Examining the knowledge structure, we see that five objects are connected to the seat. In order to confirm the linkage that has been made, let us scan the periphery of the selected region in the image and find those five objects. Unfortunately, a search of the surrounding areas yields only one obviously connected part. Perhaps the linkage is incorrect.

Let us break the linkage and try connecting it to other regions. Other attempts may lead to the same result, but eventually the following linkage will be tried:

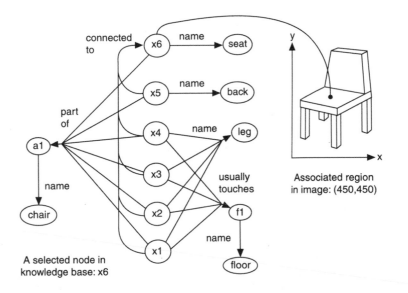

Again, understanding requires continuous confirmation of as many associated relationships as possible. Perhaps the region designated (100,120) can be associated with some other node. Since it touches the floor, we will propose that it is *x3*. Examining *x3* further, the knowledge base asserts that *x3* is connected to *x6*. Can this be confirmed in the image? Yes. All linkages thus far appear to be consistent with expectations given by the knowledge base. Carrying this process on, three more objects can be identified as legs, and one can be identified as the back. In fact, a satisfactory linkage has been found between the nodes of the knowledge structure and the regions of the image. The predicted relationships given in the semantic net are confirmed, and the system can assume that the knowledge structure has been correctly related to the image:

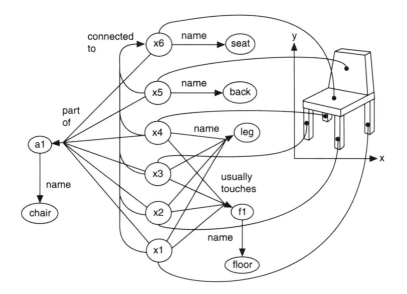

When the system has correctly made these linkages, we say that it *understands* the image, and all its knowledge related to the chair can be used. The system can now find the name of the object of which the identified regions are parts. It follows the *partof* links to *al* and traces the name link to "chair." The system can now output

```
"This is a chair."
```

Furthermore, it can follow the *name* links for all the parts and name them. If a use link existed, it could follow it to discover the function of this object. It could also follow ownership, cost, history, location and other links, if present, to obtain as much additional information about the chair as its knowledge base holds.

In summary, the understanding of an image with respect to a body of knowledge involves finding a set of self-consistent links between the parts of the knowledge structure and the parts of the perceived image. After such a linkage is made, the machine can follow arcs in its knowledge base to obtain as many useful facts as it needs to perform a task.

Of course, linkages may be made incorrectly. Then misunderstandings will occur, and incorrect inferences might be made. For example, in the following case, the machine may incorrectly conclude that an oaken object has been discovered that will be useful for sitting:

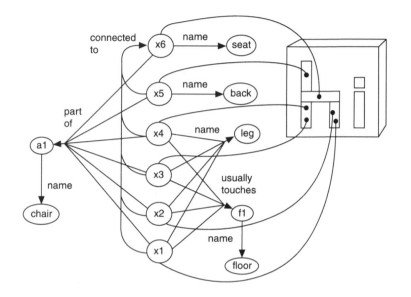

A being may also fail to understand a perception although its knowledge is adequate. The discovery of the proper linkages may also involve a calculation outside its repertoire. Either a teacher or additional computational exploration will be necessary to achieve understanding:

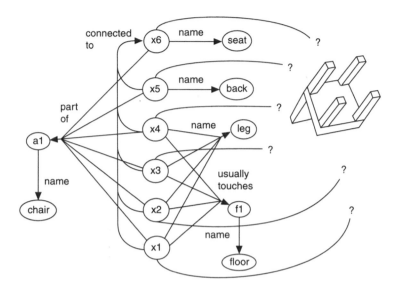

Whether computers can truly understand anything is an interesting philosophical question. However, if we accept the above definition of understanding, then we need to know only whether there are domains where significant knowledge can be stored and whether machines are capable of properly relating such knowledge to perceived images. (We will define *perception* as a sequence of characters typed on the keyboard or read from an incoming line.) On the first issue, it is clear that a computer can store relevant information on large sets of objects and their interrelationships—for instance, the objects in a room or the people in an organization. On the second issue, we have just seen an example of a machine successfully applying a knowledge structure to a perception of a chair.

As another example of computer understanding, consider the task accomplished by a processor for a computer language such as Pascal. The processor sets up linkages between the language constructs and the string of symbols that comprise the program. On the knowledge side, the machine has representations for such entities as keywords, identifiers, expressions, statements, registers, and machine language. On the perception side, the system receives a string of characters that needs to be understood. The process of understanding involves finding the objects and relationships in the perceived string that were predicted by the knowledge of the language. This linking of internal structures to the string represents the understanding of that string as a program.

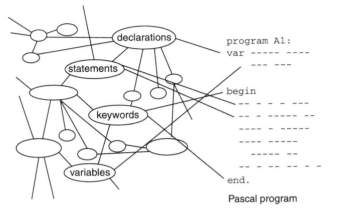

```
program A1:
var ----- ----
        --- ---

begin
-- - - - ---
-- - ----- --
---- - -----
---- -----
----- --
-- - -- -- - -
end.
```
Pascal program

Language knowledge

While the processor will completely understand the input string as a program, it may not understand additional meanings the user has intended. Thus there may be variables that have particular meanings to the user, such as dollars earned. These cannot be known to the processor. However, if the machine had this additional knowledge, it could conceivably understand these facts as well.

At this point, we might begin to believe that machines can understand absolutely everything. After all, is it not reasonable to assume that all knowledge is representable in some kind of computer language? And is it not also reasonable to assume that if there is a linkage between that knowledge and perceptions, a computer could eventually find it? The discovery of the linkage might require much time, but the computer should be able to find it.

However, careful reflection will lead us to the opposite conclusion: There are kinds of knowledge that can probably never be satisfactorily represented in machines. The most important example is the knowledge of our own humanity—the knowledge that comes from being born human, growing up, and surviving in the world. We have all had parents, friends, and loved ones, and we have shared experiences with them over the years. We have struggled hard, suffered anguish, celebrated our successes, and wept over our failures. All of these experiences build cumulatively in our psychobiological selves into an immense complex of memories and feelings. These are the kinds of knowledge that cannot be satisfactorily stored in a machine.

When a friend says, "My baby just spoke her first word" or "My cousin died yesterday," we link these experiences to our own memories to understand them. We have plenty of representations for the emotions and ramifications of the statements, and our understanding involves our linking to them.

If we built a simulation of human experience and emotion into a machine, could we claim that it, too, understoods these uniquely human utterances? We could have nodes for pain, hope, fear, love, and stored remembrances of associated events. They could be connected in complex ways, and the system might seem to understand and respond, "Wonderful!" or "I am sorry" at appropriate times. But the simulation will probably lack authenticity, and at best, it will never be more than a simulation. It is not likely that humans will ever agree that machines can understand the human experience.

In summary, this section defines understanding as a matching of knowledge with perception, and shows that machines are capable of this behavior in many domains. However, it argues that machines will probably never be able to understand some things, such as human emotion, in any satisfactory way.

### Exercises

1. Draw a picture of a typical house and its associated semantic net. Explain the process a machine would go through when using the network to "understand" the image of the house.

2. Suppose the chair network of this section were used to try to understand your house image of exercise 1. What processing would take place, and what mechanism would prevent the machine from recognizing your house as a chair?

3. Suppose a computer program is designed to receive digitized versions of paintings by the masters. Then it is supposed to "understand" these paintings and comment on them. What will the machine possibly be able to do and what will it probably fail to do?

4. A computer program has been designed to write music. Comment on the nature of music as a human endeavor and the role that music written by machines may play.

5. Discuss the replaceability of humans by machines. Does the use of automated bank tellers foreshadow a day when most interactions between businesses and the public will be done by machine? Could teachers, counselors, or judges be replaced by machines? In what situations is a machine preferred and when is a human preferred?

## Learning (B)

Now that we understand the fundamental issues of knowledge, our task is to discover how to build adequate stores of it. One way to build a knowledge base in a machine is to prepare it in an appropriate form to be read directly as data. Another way is to have the system *learn* the knowledge; that is, it uses its own mechanisms to acquire and properly format its knowledge. This latter method is highly desirable if it can be achieved because the task of assembling knowledge is difficult.

We will study two kinds of learning in this chapter: *rote learning* and *concept learning*. *Rote learning* refers to the most primitive kind of knowledge acquisition; information from the outside world is coded into internal formats and stored in a relatively raw form. The amount of memory space used is roughly proportional to the amount of information acquired. *Concept learning* is a much more profound type of knowledge acquisition because it attempts to build a small construction to represent a large amount of data. It attempts to find a summary that properly describes a multiplicity of data items. A learned concept may use relatively little memory in comparison to the amount of data it represents.

Chapter 13 examined connectionist networks that, theoretically, can achieve both kinds of learning, but we will use more conventional models of computing in this chapter. We will begin with an examination of rote learning and show improvements in a basic mechanism that will lead to concept learning.

Suppose that a being has no concept of a "chair." The being has never seen one and has never encounted the term *chair*. Suppose further that it is presented with this image:

We must assume, however, that the being can distinguish some primitive elements in the scene, if not the chair. Let us say that it distinguishes a group of oaken boards, but does not recognize the configuration. Then its internal representation would indicate little more than the existence of the recognized objects:

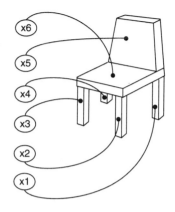

Assume that someone says, "This is a chair." This utterance tells the intelligent being the assembly of wooden boards has enough importance to have a name. It then notes the elements more carefully, assigns them a representation as a group, and attaches the name "chair":

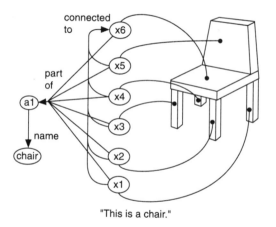

"This is a chair."

For further comprehension, we will assume the teacher also names the components of the chair and demonstrates its use for sitting. Then the system would increase its knowledge structure to account for these additional data:

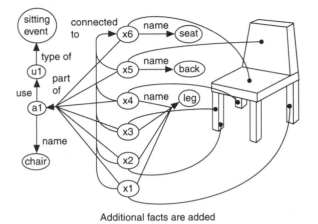

Additional facts are added

Thereafter, when the system sees this object, it will recognize it as a "chair."

This is an example of what we will call *rote learning*. A single data item has been observed, and a memory representation has been created for it. The system could similarly be given other objects to learn and name, such as a table, a lamp, a stool, a puppy dog, and so forth. Each new object has its own configuration and its own structure. If a thousand such objects were learned like this, a thousand such representations would be created.

Suppose a computer is given the following image and asked to identify it:

It would probably fail because it had no way to build a correspondence between the image and any internal representation. The image would not match a description of a table, a lamp, a puppy dog, or any other object in the system's memory. It could not be a chair because a chair must have six major components, and this has only five. The system could not understand this image with respect to its knowledge base.

Let us now indicate to the system that this new image is also a "chair." Let us similarly name its parts and demonstrate it as a useful auxiliary for sitting. The system now has two representations for "chair":

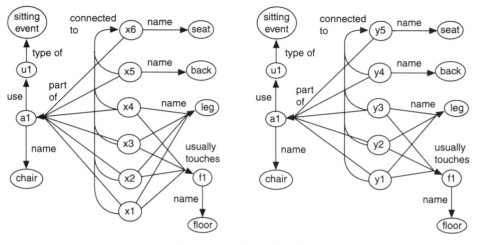

Two representations of "chair"

At this point, the system has two choices: It could continue its rote-memory strategy for learning and store both these representations, or it could attempt to combine them by generalizing. Let us pursue this second strategy and note that these two diagrams are identical except for the number of legs. So they can be merged if the difference between numbers of legs can be accounted for:

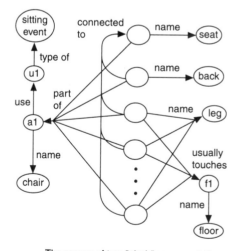

The merge of two "chair" representations

The new representation asserts that something is a chair if it has a seat, a back, is useful for sitting, and has any number of legs.

A merger of this kind is called *concept formation*, and it has a number of advantages. First, it saves memory space because it enables the system to store information for more than one data item. In fact, an unlimited number of data items can have a single representation, as is the case with our own concept of chair. Second, the merged representation allows the system to deal with new situations. Thus, the system can recognize objects as chairs, whether they have one leg or no legs or a thousand legs, as long as they meet the other prerequisites for chairs. The general concept has much greater usefulness than individual instances of rote memory.

Concept formation of this type also has some dangers. An attribute may be observed in a few examples and falsely generalized. For example, a system might find that the winners of several U. S. presidential elections were taller than their major adversaries. On this basis, it might conclude that the tallest candidate will always win, a typical but not necessarily reliable observation.

This section has described the acquisition of knowledge through rote memory and through concept-formation processes that enable a system to generalize from specific instances. The result of learning can be an extremely large knowledge structure, which we will discuss in the next section.

### Exercise

1. Draw semantic networks for two kinds of vehicles, say a car and a truck. Show how to merge the two networks to obtain a more general description of a vehicle.

---

## Frames (B)

The large knowledge structures that evolve with extensive learning, are called *frames*, and they are hypothesized to be of central importance in intelligent thought. They are necessarily complicated and include a variety of notations, indicating, for example, which relationships are obligatory, which are typical, which are possible although unusual, and which strange collections of relationships may occur. In our own memories, frames may be built up over the years through a process of hundreds or thousands of concept-learning merges. These merges result in huge numbers of auxiliary and extraneous connections that may include variations on the original template, as well as seemingly unlimited numbers of related facts—history, associations, usages, special relationships, and long lists of other facts.

As an illustration, consider how much most people can say about their knowledge of chairs. They can talk in considerable detail about the variety of chairs they have seen. They can describe chairs that are in their home, chairs they remember from schools or museums or theaters, chairs that were comfortable, chairs that were broken, and other chairs. They can tell innumerable stories about chairs in their lives, chairs in literature or movies, and chairs in history. They can probably describe in detail the construction of chairs, their materials, their finish, where they are built and sold, how much they cost, and much more.

Therefore, a semantic network that represents something close to our own knowledge of the concept "chair" will be a very large structure. It will include tens of thousands of nodes and arcs. Whenever we need information related to chairs, this frame will be called upon for understanding and for guiding action.

Researchers hypothesize that intelligent beings must have hundreds or even thousands of such modules and that thinking involves activating them as they are needed. This leads to the view of the intelligent being as a kind of frame-shuffling machine. Perceptions from the world impinge on numerous frames, and a few of those frames become successful in understanding those perceptions. Those activated frames prompt the being to appropriate action, which leads to new perceptions, possible confirmation of current frame activity, and perhaps the activation of additional frames. The being is seen as perpetually grabbing frames that enable understanding, responding as dictated by those frames, receiving new perceptions, activating additional frames, responding further, and so forth.

Consider the actions of a woman walking down a hall. Researchers might describe the sequence of actions as follows: A walking frame is activated to coordinate the eyes and muscular activities to achieve the walking behavior. A hall frame enables her to understand the visual images. Suppose she turns into an office. The turning and the visual door frames are activated to enable this movement. Suppose she meets her brother. Then a frame for him is activated along with the frame for friendly conversation. He mentions the weather and the weather frame is activated so she can understand the appropriate words: rain, snow, cold, slippery, and so on. She sees a newspaper on a nearby desk with the headline "Commission Appointed to Study Deficit." The politics and deficit frames come into action to permit relevant conversation: presidential proclamations, the appearance of positive actions, or the requirements for large annual interest payments. The friendly conversation frame interrupts to indicate that the interaction should end. The woman leaves the office, moving through the door frame, and returning again to the walking and hall frames.

The frames system is called a *memory-rich* theory because it emphasizes the importance of memory and access to complex structures. According to this theory, in perceiving the world and responding to it, we depend more on remembrance than on inference or other reasoning mechanisms. It asserts that the actions and thoughts of a person walking down a hall, meeting another person, conversing, and leaving are primarily governed by fast, efficient memory-access methods. The claim is that the person did not calculate much to get the legs to move, to understand the visual images, or to converse.

One of the main arguments for memory-rich theories is that the elements of the human mind-computer are too slow to do such a large amount of sequential computation. The neurons of the brain respond in a time on the order of milliseconds, and the actions of a human are too fast to allow for much more than memory access. For example, a tennis player observing a ball at a distance of 30 feet approaching at 30 miles per hour will have a fraction of a second to respond, which is time for only a few hundred sequential neural cycles. The computation for an appropriate response includes the need to perceive the ball, calculate its trajectory, and activate a myriad of muscular responses throughout the whole body. It would seem that this is too much computation to complete in so few cycles, even with tremendous parallelism. The memory-rich theory proposes that the player amalgamates the experiences of thousands of incoming balls into a massive frame for hitting balls. When the next ball approaches, this huge structure comes into action to monitor the perceptions, to predict the trajectory, and to drive the body to hit the ball back. The player depends more heavily on remembrance than on calculation to return the ball properly.

This section and previous sections have concentrated on concepts of knowledge representation and learning. The next sections will show applications of some of these ideas to processing natural language, general problem solving, and game playing.

**Exercises**

1. Specify as well as you can all the details of the outside of some particular building. Then go and observe the building and check the accuracy of your memory. How many of the details did you remember correctly? How many details were supplied by your general frame for all buildings? Did you "remember" some details that were not actually there but were filled in by your general frame for buildings?

2. Explain the meaning of the sentence "Make a wish." Then describe in some detail a frame for the events of a typical American birthday party. Suppose events have occurred that bring to the speaker's and hearer's mind the birthday party frame, and then the sentence "Make a wish" is uttered. What new meaning does this sentence have in the context of the party frame? What knowledge will the hearer associate with this sentence that would not have been possible without the party frame? Who spoke the sentence? Who was it directed to? Why was it spoken? What other events are associated with this action? What other sentences might be uttered in this environment, and how would the frame aid in understanding them? Is it possible to understand these sentences without the frame?

## An Application: Natural Language Processing (B)

In order to show an application of these ideas, we will examine methods for processing English-language sentences in the presence of a knowledge base. Suppose that the machine is in a place called *room1* and that it has a full representation of the objects in the room and in its world. These objects include chairs *a1*, *a2*, and *a3*.

active  frame

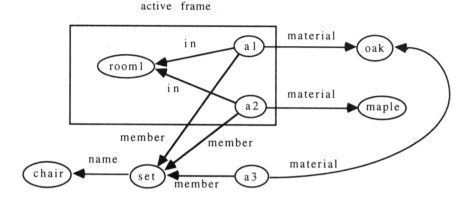

We assume the only active frame contains the set of objects in *room1*, but we list one object outside the frame to remind ourselves that there are other objects. A node is included, called *set*, which stands for the set of all chairs. Objects *a1, a2,* and *a3* are members of that set.

Using this model, we will study methods for handling three kinds of sentences: declarative sentences, questions, and imperative sentences. The function of a declarative sentence is to transmit information to the hearer, in this example, the machine. A declarative sentence will enable the machine to add new nodes and/or transitions to its knowledge base. The purpose of a question is to solicit information from the knowledge base. A question specifies what information is to be retrieved, and the machine's task is to find it and generate a proper answer. An imperative sentence causes the machine to find the objects in the knowledge base that are referenced in the sentence and then to carry out the specified actions on those objects. This may involve making some associated changes in the knowledge.

Considering declarative sentences first, assume someone says, "Nancy owns the oak chair," in the context of our knowledge base. The following is a small grammar in the style of chapter 9 that is capable of generating this sentence:

**Syntax**                    **Semantics**

S => NP VP.                   $M(S) = glue(M(NP),M(VP))$

NP => PROPN                   $M(NP) = M(PROPN)$

VP => V NP                    $M(VP) = glue(M(V),M(NP))$

NP => ART NP1                 $M(NP) = M(NP1)$

NP1 => ADJ NP1               $M(NP1) = glue(M(ADJ),M(NP1))$

NP1 => N                      $M(NP1) = M(N)$

PROPN => Nancy               $M(PROPN) =$

V => owns                     $M(V) =$

ADJ => oak                    $M(ADJ) =$

N => chair                    $M(N) =$

ART => the

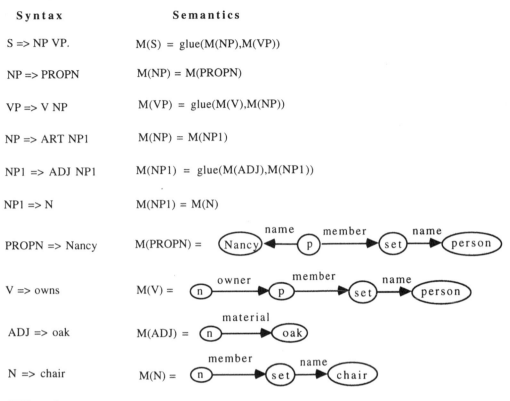

(The *glue* function in the semantics rules will be used to join separate graphs together.)
The declarative sentence will be processed as follows:

Declarative Sentence Processor:
1. The grammar rules with their semantic components are used to create a semantic network representing the sentence meaning. This network will be called *M(S)* where *S* stands for the sentence.
2. The active frame for the sentence processing is selected. This is called the *focus*. It specifies the portion of the knowledge base that will be used in the processing.
3. A match is found between objects specified in *M(S)* and objects in the knowledge base.
4. Additional nodes and linkages specified by the sentence are added to the knowledge base.

The sentence "Nancy owns the oak chair" will result in the addition of several nodes and linkages to the knowledge base. These will specify that a person named Nancy is associated with chair *a1* by the "owns" relationship. We will now examine these steps in detail.

Consider step 1 first. Beginning with *S*, we must find a generation of the target sentence. Associated with each rule application is the semantic function that will be used in creating the meaning representation *M(S)*.

| Generation | Syntactic Rule | Semantic Rule |
|---|---|---|
| S | S => NP VP. | M(S) = glue(M(NP),M(VP)) |
| NP VP. | NP => PROPN | M(NP) = M(PROPN) |
| PROPN VP. | VP => V NP | M(VP) = glue(M(V),M(NP)) |
| PROPN V NP. | NP => ART NP1 | M(NP) = M(NP1) |
| PROPN V ART NP1. | NP1 => ADJ NP1 | M(NP1) = glue(M(ADJ),M(NP1)) |
| PROPN V ART ADJ NP1. | NP1 => N | M(NP1) = M(N) |
| PROPN V ART ADJ N. | PROPN => Nancy | M(PROPN) = Nancy ←name— p —member→ set —name→ person |
| Nancy V ART ADJ N. | V => owns | M(V) = n —owner→ p —member→ set —name→ person |
| Nancy owns ART ADJ N. | ART => the | |
| Nancy owns the ADJ N. | ADJ => oak | M(ADJ) = n —material→ oak |
| Nancy owns the oak N. | N => chair | M(N) = n —member→ set —name→ chair |
| Nancy owns the oak chair. | | |

Following the methodology of chapter 9, we can apply the semantic portions of the above rules:

M(S) = glue(M(NP),M(VP))

 = glue(M(PROPN),M(VP))

 = glue(M(PROPN),glue(M(V),M(NP)))

 = glue(M(PROPN),glue(M(V),M(NP1)))

 = glue(M(PROPN),glue(M(V),glue(M(ADJ),M(NP1))))

 = glue(M(PROPN),glue(M(V),glue(M(ADJ),M(N))))

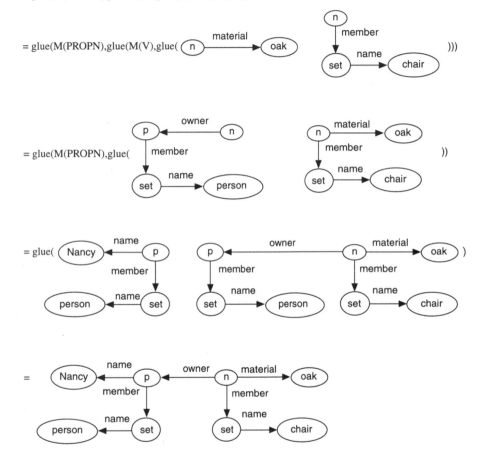

$M(S)$ is a graph that represents the meaning of the original sentence. It states, with nodes and arcs, that Nancy is an entity $p$ that is a member of a set of entities each with the name "person"; that is, Nancy is a person. Furthermore, this person is the owner of object $n$, which is a member of the set of chairs and is made of oak.

 Step 2 of the processing procedure selects the active frame in the knowledge base, the set of objects in *room1*. Then step 3 attempts to match parts of the $M(S)$ graph with parts of the active portion of the knowledge base:

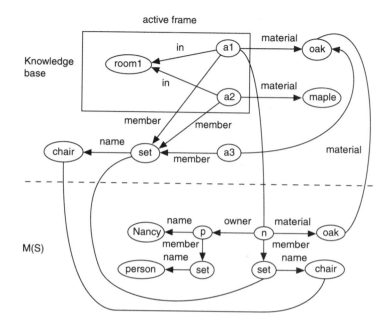

This match seems to imply that *n* in the sentence meaning corresponds to *a1* in the knowledge base. Notice that *n* does not match *a2* because the associated material is wrong. It does not match *a3* because *a3* is not in the active frame.

Once the correspondence has been found between some nodes in *M(S)* and nodes in the knowledge base, the new information in *M(S)* can be accounted for. Step 4 does this by gluing the nodes in *M(S)* that are not found in the knowledge base to the appropriate nodes in the knowledge base:

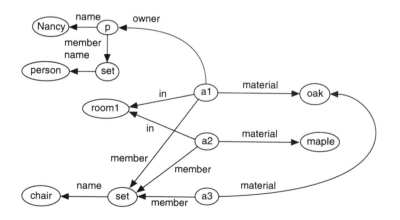

To summarize, the knowledge base at the beginning of this section listed three chairs: *a1*, *a2*, and *a3*. In the context of *room1*, the sentence "Nancy owns the oak chair" was spoken. The meaning graph *M(S)* was generated and matched against the active knowledge-base nodes, those in *room1*. It was determined that *a1* is the object referenced by the noun phrase "the oak chair"; the portion of *M(S)* corresponding to "Nancy owns" was not found in the knowledge base, so it was added. The result of processing the sentence "Nancy owns the oak chair" is the addition of the nodes indicating that Nancy owns *a1*.

In a modern natural language-processing system, a large variety of additional mechanisms are included that cannot be discussed here. Such systems must handle, for example, relative clauses, pronouns, ellipses, and complex syntactic constructions. Furthermore, many contemporary systems use representations other than semantic nets. Thus, while the flavor of the kinds of processing needed to handle natural language utterances is conveyed by the description given here, the details of systems now being built will often be quite different.

Relatively few additions to these mechanisms are needed to enable the system to handle questions. First, we need more rules to handle question syntax:

Q => WH VP                M(Q) = glue(M(WH),M(VP))

WH => who                M(WH) =

Then we need an algorithm for question processing:

Question Processor:
1. Find the meaning graph *M(Q)* for the question.
2. Select the active frame in the knowledge base, the focus.
3. Find a match between parts of *M(Q)* and the active portion of the knowledge base.
4. The question mark in *M(Q)* should match some node in the knowledge base. The system should return as an answer the contents of that matching node.

Using these added rules and the question-handling strategy, you should be able to carry out the processing of "Who owns the oak chair?" You should use the database that exists after the assertion "Nancy owns the oak chair." Most of the steps are similar to those for the previous example. But in the final step, the node with "?" will match the node with "Nancy," indicating that the answer to the question is "Nancy." This processing has some resemblances to the methodology of the database retrieval system in chapter 4.

Finally, we can examine a methodology for processing imperative sentences. Here the system is being asked to find certain objects in the active frame and do something to them. Some additional rules and an imperative-sentence handler are needed:

I => IMPV NP      M(I) = glue(M(IMPV),M(NP))

IMPV = pick up    M(IMPV) =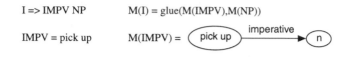

Imperative Sentence Processor:
1. Find $M(I)$.
2. Select the active frame.
3. Match $M(I)$ to the active frame.
4. Apply the action indicated by the imperative verb to the object referenced in the sentence.

   You should be able to complete the details for a sample sentence. Suppose the machine is a robot capable of navigating in the room and picking up objects. Then the command "Pick up the oak chair" will reference *a1*, and proper processing will cause the machine to "pick up *a1*."

   This completes our discussion of mechanisms for processing natural-language input to a computer, but we certainly have not covered all of the interesting topics in natural-language processing. We have not, for example, considered the problem of how the system might generate natural language instead of recognize it. We might like to have the system respond to "Tell me everything you know about the oak chair." The system would then find the object *a1* and create sentences from its associated arcs:

"This chair is in *room1*. It is owned by Nancy ..."

We have also not examined mechanisms for handling indirect requests. Thus, if a person is carrying *a1* out of the room, the sentence "Nancy owns the oak chair" may not mean that the hearer should store this ownership fact in memory. It may really mean, "Put that chair back! It belongs to Nancy."

### Exercises

1. Carry out the details for the processing of "Who owns the oak chair?"

2. Carry out the details for the processing of "Pick up the oak chair."

3. Design grammar rules to enable the processing of the following sentences:

   Nancy owns what?
   What is in this room?
   Don owns the maple chair.
   The oak chair is brown.

4. How would you build a mechanism to respond to the request, "Tell me about the oak chair"?

---

## Reasoning (B)

*Reasoning* is the process of finding or building a linkage from one entity in memory to another. There must be an initial entity, a target entity, and a way of choosing paths from the initial entity toward the target. For example, if the system holds facts about family relationships, it might be asked to determine the relationships between one member and another. If it follows a parent link, a sibling link, and a child link, then it will *reason* that the second individual is a cousin of the first.

Reasoning often discovers existing links, but it can also construct links from the initial entity to the goal. If a system is given some new goal state it can reason a strategy for achieving it by trying to discover a sequence of actions for going from the initial state to the goal. This sequence of actions is the desired linkage between the entities.

The monkey and bananas problem illustrates the complexity of this second type of reasoning. Suppose the following are in a room: a monkey, a chair, and a bunch of bananas hanging from the ceiling. If the goal is for the monkey to get the bananas, it is necessary to find a sequence of actions that begins at the current state and reaches the goal state. In terms of semantic nets, the initial state is represented as follows:

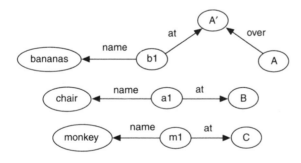

Here $A$, $B$, and $C$ represent positions on the floor below the bananas, the chair, and the monkey, respectively. $A'$ represents a position well above $A$, which is reachable only by standing on the chair. The goal is represented by the following subnet:

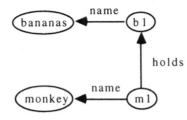

It is desired to achieve a state of the world such that the monkey can hold the bananas (and presumably eat them).

The path from one state to another is a sequence of state-changing operations that will convert the initial state to the target state. Five operations will be available for this problem:

| Operation | Meaning | Preconditions |
|---|---|---|
| go X | monkey goes to X | monkey is not at any $Y'$ (not standing on chair) and monkey is not at X |
| push X | the monkey pushes the chair to X | monkey and chair are at Y and Y is not equal to X |
| climbup | the monkey climbs from current position X to $X'$ | monkey and chair are at same location X |
| grasp | the monkey grasps the bananas | the monkey and bananas are at $X'$ |
| climbdown | monkey climbs from current position $X'$ to X | monkey is at some $X'$ |

The first operation *go X* takes the monkey from its current position to position X. We will consider only three possible values for X: A, B, and C. But this operation cannot be applied if the monkey is already at X or if it is standing on the chair (at some $Y'$). As an illustration, suppose the monkey is at C and we apply operation *go X* to go to A or B. Here are the states achieved in each case:

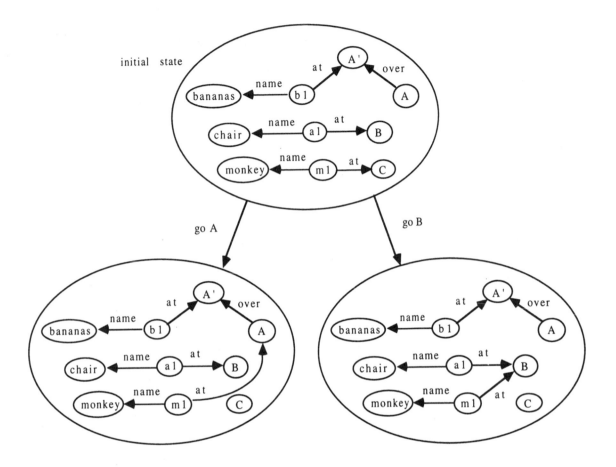

The monkey and bananas problem thus requires that one find the correct sequence of actions from the initial state to any state having the condition that the monkey holds the bananas:

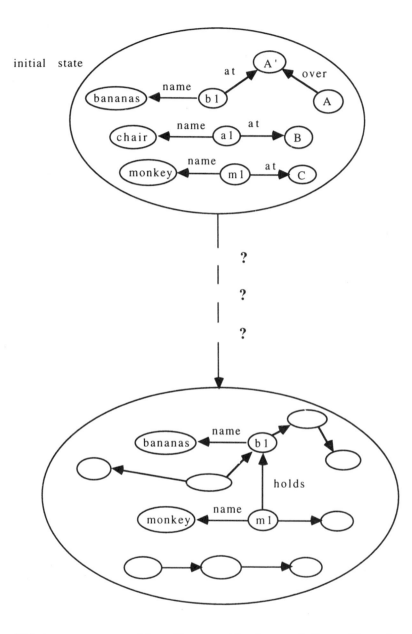

This is not an easy problem. If we consider the set of all possible action sequences, there are many things the monkey could do, and only a few of the possible sequences lead to success:

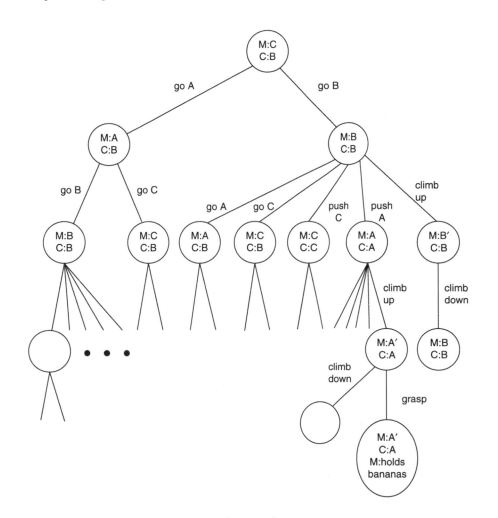

(The semantic net notation is abbreviated here: M: and C: indicate, respectively, the positions of the monkey and the chair.) If the monkey visualizes every possible sequence of actions, it will think for a long time before it finds a successful sequence.

Fortunately, humans have a broad repertoire of remembered tool-using frames, so there is no need for us to do much reasoning in this problem. If the target is not instantly reachable, we can use our memories of successful quests. We might immediately search for tools to help achieve the goal. Or we might remember receiving help from a comrade and call a friend. In the current case, the chair is the only hope for help. Perhaps it could be thrown at the bananas or used as a stick. But if we had no experience using tools and had never seen one used, we would probably have the same difficulty the monkey had reasoning a solution from first principles.

There are very many methods for doing reasoning. We might start at the top of the tree of all possible actions and search down the branches for a goal. We can also reason backwards from the goal toward the initial state. We might believe that the goal cannot be achieved until a certain subgoal is reached, but that subgoal requires some previous achievement, and so forth. Or we might use a kind of distance measure as a guide toward the target: "If I can reach state $S$, I know I will be closer to success. I will do that first and then see what I should do next to reduce further the distance to the goal."

We will examine a search algorithm that tries to find a path by searching downward from an initial node toward the goal. It will work by examining nodes farther and farther down the tree until the goal is found. Nodes that are about to be examined are called *active* nodes; those that have been examined and found not to be goals are called *closed* nodes.

Suppose this tree is about to be searched:

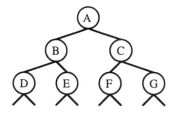

The procedure will begin by marking the top node *active*:

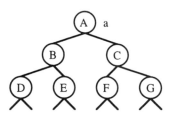

Then this node ($A$) is examined to see if it is a goal. If it is, the search halts. Otherwise its two successors are marked active, and it is marked *closed*:

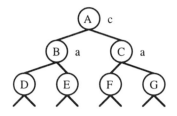

Then one of the active nodes is examined; assume the leftmost one is chosen in this case. If it is not a goal, its successors are marked active, and it is marked closed:

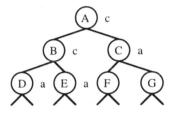

This process continues either until a goal is found or until all nodes of the tree have been examined.

Here is an algorithm for doing this search task. It searches a tree of possible actions until a goal is found. It uses a list, called *ACTIVE*, that stores the set of nodes that need to be examined next. It has a second list, called *CLOSED*, that stores the set of all nodes that have been examined:

```
      begin
(a)   put the initial node on ACTIVE list;
      the CLOSED list begins empty;
      while there are nodes on ACTIVE do
            begin
(b)         remove a node from ACTIVE using criterion C and call it N;
(c)         if N is a goal then
                  begin
                  print "success";
                  print the list of actions on arcs from initial node to N;
                  halt;
                  end.
(d)         find all children nodes of N that are not on ACTIVE or
                  CLOSED and add them to the ACTIVE list;
```

```
(e)      add N to CLOSED;
         end;
      print "failure";
      end.
```

Criterion *C* is the strategy for guiding the search. If no helpful strategy is available, *C* may choose the next node from *ACTIVE* randomly. But if there is a way to gauge the direction that the choice should take, *C* is the mechanism or subroutine that makes the decision.

The monkey and bananas problem can be solved with this search algorithm. We will not discuss immediately how *C* makes selections except to assume that it usually makes good decisions. Here is a trace of the computation:

```
(a) ACTIVE = { (M:C, C:B) }, CLOSED = { }.
(b) Criterion C selects N = (M:C, C:B). ACTIVE becomes empty.
(c) N is not a goal.
(d) Children of N are added to ACTIVE. ACTIVE = { (M:A, C:B),
    (M:B, C:B) }
(e) CLOSED = { (M:C, C:B) }.
(b) Criterion C selects N = (M:A, C:B). ACTIVE is reduced to
    { (M:B, C:B) }
(c) N is not a goal.
(d) The children of N = (M:A, C:B) are (M:B, C:B) and (M:C, C:B). But
    one is on ACTIVE and the other is on CLOSED.
(e) CLOSED = { (M:C, C:B), (M:A, C:B) }
(b) Criterion C selects N = (M:B, C:B ). Active is reduced to { }.
(c) N is not a goal.
(d) The children of N are added to ACTIVE (except for those already on
    CLOSED) ACTIVE = { (M:A, C:A),(M:C, C:C),(M:B', C:B) }
(e) CLOSED = { (M:C, C:B),(M:A, C:B),(M:B, C:B) }
(b) Criterion C selects N = (M:A, C:A) from ACTIVE. ACTIVE =
    { (M:C, C:C), (M:B', C:B) }
(c) N is not a goal.
(d) The children of N not already on ACTIVE or CLOSED are (M:B, C:A),
    (M:C, C:A), (M:A', C:A). These are added to ACTIVE. ACTIVE =
    { (M:C, C:C), (M:B', C:B), (M:B, C:A), (M:C, C:A),(M:A', C:A) }
(e) CLOSED = { (M:C, C:B), (M:A, C:B), (M:B, C:B), (M:A, C:A) }
(b) Criterion C selects N = (M:A', C:A). ACTIVE = { (M:C, C:C), (M:B',
    C:B), (M:B, C:A), (M:C, C:A) }
(c) N is not a goal.
(d) There is only one child of N not already on ACTIVE or CLOSED:
    (M:A', C:A,M holds bananas) ACTIVE = { (M:C, C:C), (M:B', C:B),
    (M:B, C:A), (M:C, C:A), (M:A', C:A, M holds bananas) }
```

```
(e) CLOSED ={(M:C, C:B), (M:A, C:B), (M:B, C:B), (M:A, C:A),
    (M:A', C:A) }
(b) Criterion C selects N = (M:A', C:A, M holds bananas).
(c) N is a goal.
    Print "success".
    Print: go B, push A, climbup, grasp.
    Halt.
```

The selection criterion $C$ greatly affects the operation of this algorithm. You can observe its effects by searching the same tree with different $C$:

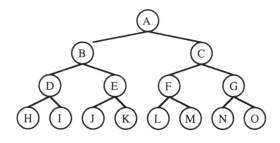

Suppose $C$ always chooses the node on *ACTIVE*, which is shallowest (nearest $A$) and on the left when there are ties. Then the nodes will be selected in the order $A,B,C,D,E,F,G,H,I,J,K,L,M,N,O$. This is called a *breadth-first search* and results in a flat frontier of newly examined nodes that progresses downward on the tree:

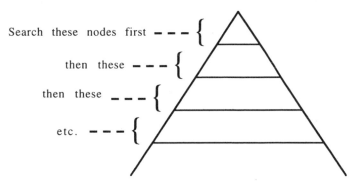

A different strategy is to have $C$ select the deepest node on *ACTIVE*, preferring those on the left if there is a tie. This results in an order that goes to the bottom of the tree very

quickly and then moves across the tree: $A,B,D,H,I,E,J,K,C,F,L,M,G,N,O$. This is called a
*depth-first search*, and it gives a sideways movement for the frontier of new nodes.

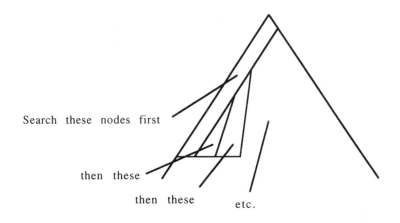

Both strategies are common in applications because they exhaustively cover the whole
tree. If a goal is to be found, they will find it. The only restriction is that for a depth-first
search, the tree must be finite.

But a third strategy is often preferred over both. It assumes the system has some
knowledge about how to find the goal, and node selections are made in the direction of
the earliest possible achievement of the goal. For example, in the monkey and bananas
problem, from the possible positions for the monkey, it might choose those nearest the
bananas. If it were still frustrated in its attempts to reach its goal, it might look for objects
that could be used and bring them also near the bananas. Reexamining the example tree, if
$L$ is a goal node, criterion $C$ might select $A,C,F$, and $L$ in sequence and immediately solve
the problem. If the information were weaker, the algorithm might choose $A,B,C,F,G,M,L$,
solving the problem quickly but with some superfluous excursions. The design of the $C$
function attempts to build in information that will enable the search to go as directly as
possible toward the goal:

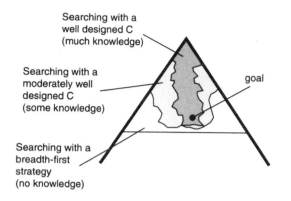

Searching with a
well designed C
(much knowledge)

Searching with a
moderately well
designed C
(some knowledge)

goal

Searching with a
breadth-first
strategy
(no knowledge)

Many times when the *C* function is constructed, the designer is not sure whether the information being programmed will help. If it does help, the system will quickly converge to its solution. If not, the system will wander before finding the goal. In the worst case, the system might never find the goal. When the *C* function is programmed with knowledge that may or may not help find the solution, it is called a *heuristic function*. A heuristic function might suggest that in a navigational situation going toward the goal is usually helpful, or that in a manipulative system trying a tool often helps, or that in a building situation constructing the foundation is typically a good first step. These heuristics often lead effectively toward solutions, but when they fail, a wider search is needed to solve a problem.

**Exercises**

1. Consider a grid of streets, with numbered streets going north and south (First Street, Second Street, etc.) and lettered streets going east and west (A Street, B Street, etc.). Assume one is at the corner of Fifth Street and G Street and wishes to go to the corner of Seventh Street and H Street. Further assume there are four operations E,W,N,S meaning go east one block, go west one block, go north one block, and go south one block, respectively. Show the decision tree with the initial node at the top (the corner of Fifth and G Streets). Show all possible decision sequences of length three. Show the operation of the above search algorithm in the cases where
   (a) *C* chooses a breadth-first search.
   (b) *C* chooses a depth-first search limited to depth three.
   (c) *C* selects the node closest to the direction of the goal.

2. Draw the complete tree of allowable moves to depth two for the Post Correspondence Problem from chapter 2. Show how the search algorithm finds the solution using a breadth-first strategy *C*. Can you invent a better *C* function?

# Game Playing (B)

We next consider reasoning processes that are complicated by an adversary. In a game-playing situation, where the goal is to win, the system searches down the tree of alternative moves, as in the previous section, but it must also account for its opponent's actions. The nature of the search can be seen in the following tree for the game of Nim with 5 squares (The rules for Nim were given in chapter 1.)

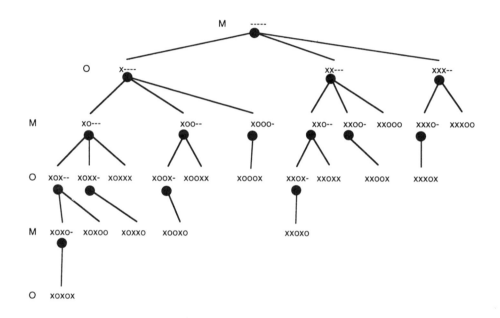

The tree has two kinds of nodes—those labeled M where the machine is to make the move and those labeled O where the opponent is to move. Nodes will be marked W if they are known, by one means or another, to lead to a win for the machine. If the machine is at a node where it sees a win for itself anywhere among the child nodes immediately below it, the machine will move toward that child node:

In fact, we can mark the parent node as a winning node, since the machine is capable of making the move:

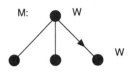

But if the opponent is in the same situation, the move will usually be made away from position W where the machine would win:

For an O node, the position cannot be marked W as a win for the machine unless *all* of the child nodes are marked W:

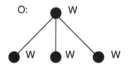

That is, the opponent is not in a position where the machine is guaranteed to win unless all its choices are positions where the machine will win.

These observations lead to a method for analyzing a game. Begin at the bottom of the tree and mark all terminating positions where the machine will win with Ws. Then consider all nodes just above terminating positions. Nodes where the machine is to move that have at least one W-marked child are marked W. Nodes where the opponent is to move are marked W only if all their child nodes are marked W. This process is repeated for layer after layer of nodes up the tree until the top node is reached. If the top node is labeled W, the machine will win the game, and its strategy is to move in the direction of the W at each decision point. If the top node is not labeled W, the machine will not win unless the opponent blunders.

Carrying out this procedure on the 5-Nim game tree, we discover that the machine will win, and its first move should be a single X:

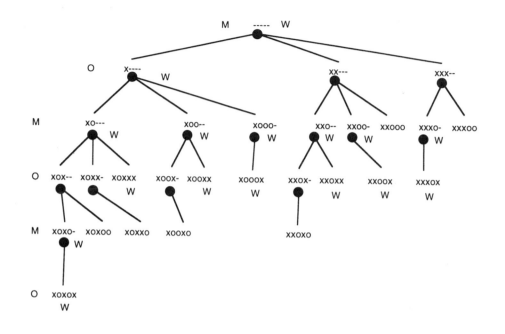

Regardless of what response the opponent gives, the machine will win on the next move.

After some study, we realize that the Nim game of size 5 is not very interesting. The first player always wins, and the moves are so obvious that as soon as we have decided who will play first, we know the winner. Larger Nim games can be solved in the same way if we have a computer fast enough to build the tree and pass the Ws to the top.

Generalizing even further, we can say that any game with the characteristics of Nim can be solved completely by building the tree and passing Ws up from the bottom. But what are those characteristics? First, the game tree must be finite so that it can be completely searched. Second, it should be deterministic (without dice or any other random process) so that all move outcomes are known. Finally, the game must offer both players complete information about the state. (If the opposition holds cards not known to the machine or if other state information is not available, the machine will not know where it is on the tree.) *In summary, any deterministic finite game of complete information can be solved by the procedure given here.* Before play even begins, we can use the above procedure to determine the winner. (Some games allow for the possibility of a draw, but this is easy to account for and is left as an exercise.)

Many common games fit these specifications. For example, chess and checkers are deterministic, finite games of complete information. If we had a machine fast enough to build their complete trees, we could determine the winner before the first move was played and show how to make each move to achieve the guaranteed win. However, these game trees are so large that no one has been able to build them, and so their solutions remain unknown. This is an example of a problem that cannot be solved because the execution time is too great. (These games might seem to be infinite since two players could simply alternate their pieces back and forth forever to achieve unending play. However, there is no need to analyze a game that loops back on its own previous states, since such play results in neither a win nor a loss for the machine.)

The tree-search methodology can be used to play large games like chess and checkers if we can avoid following paths to the end of the game. The usual technique is to have an *evaluation function* that computes a number that estimates the value of a given game state. Then the decision procedure can attempt to reach states of high value. In a game of chess, for example, the procedure could add up the pieces on each side and give greater weight to the stronger pieces like rooks and queens. The value of a position would be the weighted value of the machine's pieces minus the weighted value of the opponent's. The machine would then seek positions with greater piece advantages. Typical chess programs also allot points for positional advantage, such as a castled king or a good pawn structure.

The search tree in this case would look more like the following. The system has constructed move sequences to a constant depth—four in this case—instead of going to the game's end. The game state evaluation is given at each node reached along the bottom.

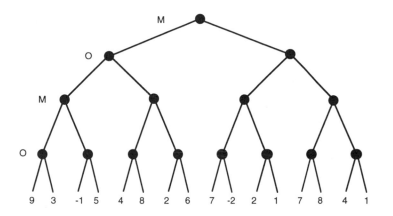

We can compute a value for every other node of the tree. The value of the node at any machine move M is the maximum of the values of its children, on the assumption that it will always try to obtain the best position as scored by the evaluation function. The value of any node at an opponent's move is chosen to be the minimum of its children, on the assumption that the opponent will harm the machine's position as much as possible.

Using these two rules, the values can be passed up from the bottom to obtain a score at the initial node of the tree. This is a process called *minimaxing*:

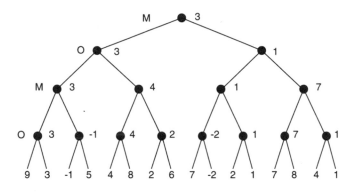

As before, the marker at the tree top shows the best achievable state reachable at the bottom of the tree. The nodes with this value show the machine which move to make at each point to achieve this best value.

The tree search can be shortened by using *tree pruning* strategies that make it possible to omit parts of the calculation. The most powerful technique is *alpha-beta* tree pruning, which uses partial results from the search to prove the uselessness of other portions. An illustration of this is shown in the following tree, where the program has evaluated three board positions below the O nodes:

The first O node will have value 3, and the second 0 node will have value 1 or less. Then the top node, which chooses the maximum of its children, will have value 3. Although one node (marked with ?) has not been evaluated, we know the value of the top node so we can avoid the cost of generating that last node and evaluating its quality. This type of pruning can result in huge savings of time.

Game-playing programs that use limited search with evaluation functions depend on the accuracy of the evaluations. Precise accuracy will lead to excellent play, and moderate accuracy will lead to rambling play. Much recent research in game playing has been centered on the improvement of board evaluations.

**Exercises**

1. At the beginning of this section, a method was described for marking Ws up from the bottom of a game tree to determine whether the first player can force a win. Show how to modify this theory in the case where a game can have three outcomes: win W, loss L, or draw D.

2. Analyze the game of tic-tac-toe and determine whether there is a win, a draw, or a loss for the first player.

3. Assume that the minimax tree shown above has the following values across its nodes at the bottom: $6, -10, 4, 7, 2, 19, -7, 4, 8, -2, -8, 3, 3, 11, 4, -4$. Do a minimax back up to determine the best value that the first player can achieve.

4. Repeat the minimax search shown in this chapter but show that some of the values at the bottom of the tree are not needed to find the value at the tree root. The alpha-beta procedure enables a system to avoid computing some of these values.

---

## Game Playing: Historical Remarks (C)

Game playing has gone through three interesting phases. In the early days of computing, during the 1940s, many programmers believed that computers would win as resoundingly at chess and checkers as they did at adding numbers, since they could search and evaluate thousands of moves while humans looked at only a few dozen. Therefore, when the first programs began to work, their authors were shocked at their incompetence. Even the most bumbling amateurs could beat them, and researchers scrambled to determine why. The answer lay in a combination of two factors, the first arising from the nature of game trees and the second from the nature of the human mind. Chess and checkers have average branching factors around 35 and 7, respectively, so that the number of nodes at depth $i$ is $35^i$ and $7^i$. Even with substantial pruning, programs could examine trees of depth no more than three or four. Humans, on the other hand, seem to have a magical instinct to look at the "right" moves, and human players examined lines of play far deeper than machines did:

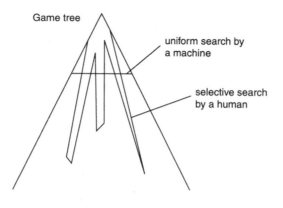

Machines wasted their computation time on huge numbers of positions that humans simply ignored. Human players discovered strong moves with deeper well-guided searches.

This led to the second phase of game-playing research, a period of about two decades when researchers attempted to capitalize on this observation. Uniform search suddenly seemed ridiculous, and a variety of heuristic tree-search methods was developed, including ways to find "hot spots" on the board, play standard tricks on the opponent, and plan long sequences of offensive moves. Although the resulting programs improved over the years and occasionally exhibited spectacular play, they remained poor competitors against competent human players. The programs were able to see many lines of play to a deep level, but they were not finding moves of the quality that humans can find.

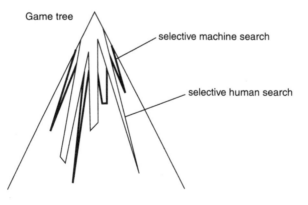

Humans continued to have an instinct for the game that mystified researchers.

Around 1970, the community had another surprise. A group of researchers at North-western University rejected the theory that selective search is the only reasonable approach to game playing. They brought a uniform-search chess program to a national computer championship that defeated all other machines and that continued to defeat all comers for some years afterward. It also played better against humans than any previous program, achieving a good record against amateurs but not master-level players. The researchers had returned to the earlier theory that for the best total game performance, conservative error-free tactical play was more important than occasional spectacular play. The faster machines of the 1970s allowed search depth good enough, about 5 or 6 in chess, to achieve solid play, and within that depth, the machine never made a mistake. If the opponent program ever missed even one key move during the game, the uniform-search program would discover and exploit it.

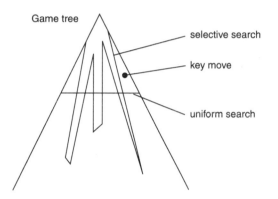

The best chess programs have continued to use this strategy. They examine millions of positions before each move over a relatively uniform tree and use a variety of methods to speed up search and improve evaluation. They are finally able to play at the master level, and they continue to improve each year. However, despite this huge computational effort and four decades of research, they still cannot win the world championship.

In checkers, the story has been similar, but the degree of success has been better. A program called CHINOOK, written by Jonathan Schaeffer and several colleagues at the University of Alberta, played a very close match in 1992 against Marion Tinsley, the reigning world champion in checkers. The program lost in a best-of-40-game match, winning 2 games, losing 4, and drawing 33. In August 1994 the program officially became the world checker champion when Tinsley withdrew for health reasons after drawing six games. The program has also played a second checkers great, Don Lafferty, and has a rather close win-loss record against him. Thus in checkers, it would appear that the machines are closing in on total dominance.

Computer game playing proves an interesting study in computer and human intelligence, giving insights into the nature of each. Computers continue to excel at doing simple activities millions of times, and their best performance is achieved when we are able to organize this activity to obtain useful results. Humans continue to have astonishing, almost mystical abilities to recognize significant patterns and to use them effectively. In game playing, computers and humans have achieved high-performance levels using profoundly different methods.

### Exercise

1. Assume the company you work for is proposing to build an automatic decision-making program for corporate decisions. It will receive information about economic conditions, corporate status, future trends, and so forth. The program is to search the tree of possible decisions for the coming years and decide which sequence of decisions will lead to the best long-term well-being for the firm. Have you learned anything from the history of game playing that will affect your judgment of the current project?

---

## Expert Systems (B)

During the 1970s, artificial intelligence researchers became interested in the reasoning processes of so-called experts. Experts are people who work at specialized jobs over many years and formulate routines for functioning effectively. An expert begins a problem-solving task by looking for key factors and then selects some initial action, perhaps to gather some information, which results in decisions and additional actions until the task is complete. At each stage, the expert seems to use an established formula for action: looking for certain facts, making appropriate conclusions, searching for other information, and so forth. The behaviors seem well formulated, predictable, rule-based, and therefore within the range of computer simulation.

Researchers in expert systems have studied doctors performing routine diagnoses, repairmen diagnosing equipment failures, geologists searching for minerals, and agricultural experts giving advice on crops. These experts have been interviewed at length to discover what they know and how they make decisions. They are led by an interviewer through typical scenarios and asked to explain in detail every thought that helps them reach their conclusions. Then the interviewer, sometimes called a *knowledge engineer*, attempts to construct a model of their knowledge and their reasoning processes.

A common observation of many researchers in this field is that experts often express their knowledge in terms of if-then rules: "If I observe that $X$ and $Y$ are true, I know that condition $Z$ is occurring. If condition $Z$ occurs and $A$ and $B$ are true, I usually prescribe $Q$." In fact, the if-then form of knowledge representation is so common that it has become the basis for many computer programs that attempt to imitate expert behaviors. We will now examine a portion of such a program.

Suppose the Internal Revenue Service of the U.S. Government employs experts to decide when to audit income tax forms and that our task is to build a program to do this job automatically. We will first interview an expert and then attempt to code his or her knowledge in the form of if-then rules. Finally, we will examine a processor of such rules to see how well its actions mimic the expert.

Let us pretend that the following interview takes place:

Interviewer:     When do you prescribe an audit?
Expert:          I often look for something unusual either in the income declarations or in the deductions.
Interviewer:     What kinds of peculiarities are likely to appear in income?
Expert:          The income may be ridiculously low when you consider the person's profession. The other thing I look for is poorly documented income.
Interviewer:     What do you expect in terms of income documentation?
Expert:          The person should either have a W2 form or a systematic method for writing receipts for all funds received.
Interviewer:     Let's go back to deductions. What do you look for there?
Expert:          If I see the person claiming deductions that exceed 20 percent of his or her income, I become suspicious.

A real interview may be complex and go on for many hours, but we will limit ourselves to these few sentences.

We now need to code the knowledge from the interview into a set of if-then rules. The first exchange between the interviewer and the expert yields this rule:

"If the income is unusual or the deductions are unusual, then prescribe an audit."

In abbreviated notation, this rule will be written as

```
IncomeUnusual or DeductionsUnusual ==> Audit
```

The second interaction leads to another rule, which can also be written in concise notation:

```
IncomeNotDoc or IncomeTooLow ==> IncomeUnusual
```

We will assume that *IncomeTooLow* is easy to check. One notes the person's profession and then looks up in a table the minimum expected income for that profession. Let us assume that a function called *CheckData* exists to examine the income tax form and related tables. Then this rule will be written as

```
IncomeNotDoc or CheckData(Income < MinIncome(Profession))
    ==> IncomeUnusual
```

The last part of the interview yields two more rules:

```
CheckData (No W2) and CheckData (No Receipts) ==> IncomeNotDoc
CheckData (Deduction > 0.2 * Income) ==> DeductionsUnusual
```

Next we need an algorithm that will execute these rules like a kind of computer program. The algorithm resembles the search algorithm given above in that it builds a tree beginning at the root node. The function of the computation, however, will not be to find a goal at the bottom of the tree but rather to *achieve* a goal at the root of the tree.

The algorithm uses several ideas that need to be defined. We say a node is *achieved* if a rule leading to it is *satisfied* or if it is a *Checkdata* call that yields "yes." The rules are of two kinds: those that have left-side parts connected by *and* and those with left-side parts connected by *or*. If the left-side parts are connected by *and*, the rule is *satisfied* when all its left-side parts are achieved. If the left parts are connected by *or*, the rule is *satisfied* when at least one of its left parts is achieved. A node is said to be *fully explored* if it is a *CheckData* node and the check has been made or if there are no more rules with this node as a right side that have not been selected and added to the tree. The purpose of the search is to find enough facts to achieve the goal at the root. A list called *ACTIVE* is used as before to store the tree nodes that need to be examined:

```
put the goal node on ACTIVE (For the tax example, this is Audit.)
begin building a tree by creating a root node that contains the goal
while ACTIVE has nodes not fully explored do
    begin
    select an unachieved node on ACTIVE that is not fully explored
    if the node uses CheckData then
        begin
        execute CheckData
        if CheckData returns "yes" then
            mark this node as achieved and mark nodes
            above this node achieved if they are also
            achieved.
        if the root level goal is achieved then
            halt with success.
        end
    else
        begin
        select a rule for achieving this node
        add it to the tree to give a new set of child nodes
        put the tokens on the left side of the rule on ACTIVE
        end
    end
halt with failure
```

Each step of the tree-building process begins by selecting a node on the existing tree (from the *ACTIVE* list). For example, suppose *IncomeNotDoc* is chosen:

Then a rule is selected that is capable of achieving that node:

```
CheckData (No W2) and CheckData(No Receipts) ==> IncomeNotDoc
```

The rule provides the basis for adding more nodes on the tree; each item on the left side of the rule becomes a new node:

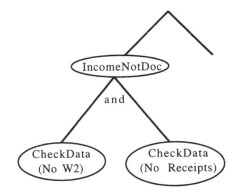

If the algorithm selects a node that is a *CheckData*, it does the data check rather than building more nodes on the tree.

We can now observe the actions of this algorithm on the income tax problem. Suppose the following simplified form has been submitted:

Name:          John Smith
Profession:    Professor
Income:        $60,000 (no W2 or receipts)
Deductions:    $10,000

The algorithm begins by placing *Audit* on the *ACTIVE* list:

```
ACTIVE = {Audit}
```

And it initializes the tree by constructing the root node:

It then enters the loop, selects a node on *ACTIVE*, and selects a rule for achieving this node:

```
IncomeUnusual or DeductionsUnusual => Audit
```

This rule is used as the basis for growing two child nodes on the tree:

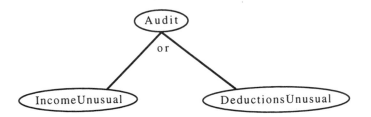

The *ACTIVE* list also receives these terms:

```
ACTIVE = {Audit, IncomeUnusual, DeductionsUnusual}
```

Repeating the loop, suppose the algorithm next chooses *IncomeUnusual* and finds a rule for achieving this node:

```
IncomeNotDoc or CheckData (Income < MinIncome (Profession))
    ==> IncomeUnusual
```

Then more nodes can be grown on the tree, and the appropriate additions can be made to *ACTIVE*:

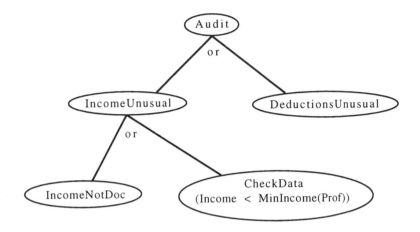

```
ACTIVE = {Audit, IncomeUnusual, DeductionsUnsual, IncomeNotDoc,
      CheckData (Income < MinIncome (Profession))}
```

The third repetition of the loop results in the following change if the *IncomeNotDoc* node is chosen:

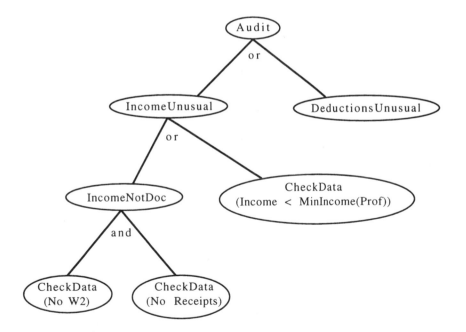

Additional repetitions will eventually result in the *CheckData* nodes at the tree bottom being selected. These will each reference the income tax form, and, for our example, return "yes." So they will be achieved. Their parent nodes will also be achieved, as will each ancestor node to the top. In fact, the algorithm will halt with success; the *Audit* node has been achieved. The program recommends that this income tax form be audited.

The nodes on *ACTIVE* are not removed, because there may be many rules that lead to any given conclusion. If one rule is not successful in achieving a node, perhaps some other one will be.

The tremendous value of such a program is clear. If the programmer correctly encodes the expert's methodology, the system will do the same job much more quickly and accurately, multiplying the effectiveness of the expert manyfold. The automatic system also offers many other advantages. It can be studied for accuracy and improved, possibly beyond the original expert's procedures, and it can be changed easily if the tax law changes. A new employee could also study the system to learn the methodologies.

The system described here is called an *expert system*. Such systems usually have rules like those in our example and a similar execution algorithm. They often have complex node and rule selection heuristics of the kind described in the game-playing section. They may also enable the user to input facts in which he or she has less than perfect confidence, and they may yield answers with less than perfect confidence, as a human expert would do. (For example, a confidence factor with a value somewhere from 0 to 1 might be associated with each fact, where 0 indicates no confidence, 1 indicates complete confidence, and fractions indicate intermediate levels.) Finally, expert systems usually have the ability to print their own reasoning chain, the tree, so that the user can see not only the conclusion, but also what steps led to it.

**Exercises**

1. Show how the tax-audit expert system would handle the following case:
   Name:          John Smith
   Profession:    Professor
   Income:        $60,000   (W2 included)
   Deductions:    $20,000

2. Show how the tax-audit expert system would handle the following case:
   Name:          John Smith
   Profession:    Professor
   Income:        $60,000   (W2 included)
   Deductions:    $5,000

3. Design a set of rules that indicate the prerequisites to your favorite university-level course. The top level goal should be *CourseRecommended*, and the rules should be

designed to achieve this goal if a student meets the criteria that you specify. Demonstrate the use of these rules on typical cases by employing the algorithm for rule execution.

4. Interview an expert in some field, and design a set of rules to emulate the person's behavior when addressing some particular problem.

---

## Perspective (B)

Now that we have learned how to store knowledge in a computer and how a computer can learn, reason, and understand, we should be able to build intelligent machines. If we want to build a machine to understand natural language, it would appear that all we need to do is to store sufficient knowledge and have some linguists compile a set of rules. If we wish to build an image-understanding system, it would appear that all we need is a knowledge base for that domain and appropriate reasoning capabilities. If we want to build machines to invent jokes, compose music, analyze scientific data, interview job applicants, write stories, or create mathematics, we might hope to construct knowledge bases large enough and reasoning systems powerful enough to do these jobs. Humans are capable of all these behaviors, and we have reason to believe that they follow principled methodologies. Computers seem to have ample memory size and speed, so there does not appear to be a lack of computational power.

In fact, computer programs have been written that demonstrate almost every imaginable intelligent behavior. Here is a brief description of some results that appeared as early as 1963 (in *Computers and Thought*, edited by E. Feigenbaum and J. Feldman):

- A checker-playing program uses a tree-search and board-evaluation methodology similar to the one explained in this chapter. The board-evaluation function has the form $f = C_1 X_1 + C_2 X_2 + \cdots + C_{16} X_{16}$ where the $C_i$s are constants to be determined and the $X_i$s are features of the board such as the king advantage, number of pieces in the king row, and number of pieces in the board center squares. The $C_i$s are numbers "learned" during actual play by slowly varying their values until best possible behaviors are achieved. The paper describes a game with "a former Connecticut checkers champion, and one of the nation's foremost players" which the program won by making "several star moves." ("Some Studies in Machine Learning Using the Game of Checkers," A. L. Samuel)
- A program for solving plane geometry problems typical of those taught at the high school level uses a diagram of the geometry problem to guide the search for long proofs heuristically. The use of the diagram reduces the number of child nodes below a typical node from about 1000 to about 5 and thus greatly increases the program efficiency.

This program finds proofs with as many as 20 or more sequential steps that would be difficult for high school students. ("Empirical Explorations of the Geometry Theorem Proving Machine," H. Gelernter, J. R. Hansen, and D. W. Loveland)

- A program answers questions about baseball, such as "Who did the Red Sox lose to on July 5?" or "Did every team play at least once in each park in each month?" The program stores data on baseball games in a tree structure, giving for each month a list of all places, for each place a list of all days, and for each day a list of all games. Answers are obtained by translating the question into a standardized form and then matching it to the tree of data. ("BASEBALL: An Automatic Question Answerer," B. F. Green, Jr., A. K. Wolf, C. Chomsky, and K. Laughery)

- The General Problem Solver, GPS, is a general search program for finding goals using sequences of operators. Utilizing heuristic information to help choose the correct operator at each point, it solves a variety of classical problems. The GPS was studied both as an exercise in artificial intelligence and as a possible model for human intelligence. ("GPS, a Program That Simulates Human Thought," A. Newell and H. A. Simon)

With such impressive results in the early 1960s, researchers expected profound machine intelligence within the next decade or two. An earlier paper by Herbert Simon and Allen Newell had predicted that by 1967, computer programs would win the world chess championship, find and prove some important new mathematical theorem, write music possessing aesthetic value, and be the models for most studies in psychology.

Unfortunately, this optimism proved unfounded. None of the early projects matured to astound the world, and none of the Simon-Newell predictions have come true. Forty years after the original period of great optimism, artificial intelligence remains a science in its infancy with relatively few results applicable to real-world problems. All the systems described are interesting laboratory studies, and many more of them have been undertaken in recent years. But researchers have had great difficulties expanding narrowly defined projects that demonstrate exciting behaviors into large, practical systems capable of what people are willing to call "intelligent."

The problem of building intelligent systems turned out to be much more difficult than early researchers realized. Those who began projects would achieve a fraction of their goals in six months, and then predict that they would achieve all their goals in a few years. They never dreamed that in their whole lifetimes they would not get much farther than their original results. Again and again projects begun with great optimism achieved no more than limited success.

Of course, all of these efforts have been newsworthy and well published over the years. Articles were common in the media in the early days predicting a new age when computers would achieve or surpass human abilities in various fields. Those articles continue to the present day, though we are not much closer to the goal now than we thought we were then.

Why has the field of artificial intelligence failed to produce intelligent machines? We do not know, but we are finally aware that real intelligence involves far more complexity than we ever predicted. It involves vast amounts of knowledge that we do not yet know how to acquire or organize or use. It involves complex reasoning of a kind that we cannot yet comprehend. It probably involves many other mechanisms that we do not even realize are needed. We simply do not understand intelligence.

But some progress has been made. Programs being written as we enter the new century are better than those written in the 1960s. The failures of the early decades have demonstrated what will not work, and able people are applying the most successful methodologies to create better systems for the future. At the risk of oversimplifying a complex picture, a few brief comments are included here about current research in several subfields of artificial intelligence to give a feeling for the current state of the art.

### Automatic Programming

This research area attempts to build systems that will automatically write programs. It assumes the user will give examples of the desired program behavior or will specify with a formal or natural language what the desired program is to do. The system will then write a program to satisfy the user's requirements. Automatic programming systems have been built that reliably create some small LISP programs, three or four lines long, from examples of the target behavior. Systems have also been created that enable a user to specify a program in an interactive session with a formal language, which then will create the target program. A few rather impressive programs have been developed using this approach. However, for general-purpose programming, such systems are usually not as convenient for serious programming as traditional programming languages.

### Expert Systems

Hundreds of these systems have been programmed for industrial and governmental applications. They usually have from a few hundred to a few thousand rules, and if they are properly designed, they can be depended upon to carry out their narrowly defined tasks reliably.

### Game Playing

Chess programs have been developed that can challenge master-level players, and they are improving every year. The best checker program is playing at the level of the best human player and it is still improving. This long-term battle may finally be over. Many other games have been programmed with varying levels of success.

### Image Understanding

Computer systems have been built that are aimed at specific domains, such as aerial photographs or pictures of human faces, and that find and correctly label the significant features a high percentage of the time.

### Mathematical Theory Formation

At least one system built (by Douglas Lenat) can derive new mathematical concepts from more primitive ones. This system was demonstrated in a series of computations where it derived the rudiments of number theory from concepts of set theory. However, it is not clear that the approach is applicable to broader classes of problems.

### Natural Language Understanding

A number of systems have been built that are aimed at specific domains, such as personnel databases or equipment repair tasks, and that deliver proper responses a high percentage of the time. Such systems usually have limited vocabularies, fewer than a thousand words, and limited syntactic capabilities.

### Natural Language Translation

If a system is constructed to understand natural language in a limited domain, it is within the state of the art to convert the system into a translator to some other natural language. Therefore, we can say that natural language translation can be achieved with high accuracy in limited domains where small vocabulary and narrow syntactic variety are adequate. In an application where wide vocabulary and syntactic variety are needed, completely automatic natural language translation is far beyond the state of the art. However, computers are still useful in these translation tasks by parsing input sentences, by displaying word alternatives in the object language that can be selected by a human translator, and by providing convenient editing.

### Learning

The performance of a few systems has been improved by the use of learning mechanisms that optimize parameters, as described in the sections of chapter 13 on connectionist networks. (The Arthur Samuel checker program used this scheme.) Concept-learning mechanisms have been applied to analyzing complex scientific data with the result, in a few cases, that trends or relationships in the data were automatically discovered.

### Speech Recognition

Many systems have been built that enable a user to speak rather than type inputs to the machine. Vocabularies on these systems tend to be limited to a few hundred words, although some systems with vocabulary capabilities up to several tens of thousands of words are becoming operative and moderately reliable. Currently these systems need to be specialized to a particular application in order to give robust behavior. This usually means gathering a large corpus of utterances from the application and building a probabilistic model of the actual word sequences that people use. However, these systems can provide reliable performance in many contemporary environments and can be expected to appear in many products in the next few years.

In summary, researchers have programmed computers to exhibit to a limited extent almost any intelligent behavior—perception, learning, problem solving, language processing, and others. But to achieve any of these behaviors to a large extent or to integrate them to obtain moderately intelligent behavior is very difficult and, in most cases, far beyond the state of the art. The best results have occurred in the environment of narrow domains, where only limited kinds of behaviors were needed and usually where there was tolerance for error.

Some researchers believe that most artificial intelligence subfields face the same central problem of complex representation and reasoning and that if the problem can be solved in one field, it will be solved for all of them. For example, if we could program a machine to process language as well as humans do, then the methodology that made this possible would be applicable to many other problems, such as vision, theorem proving, and automatic programming. Various researchers have called this hypothesis the *Thesis of AI Completeness*, and it is likely to remain controversial for years to come.

In the commercial world, artificial intelligence has had some important successes. In the field of expert systems, large numbers of useful programs have been developed, and they are operating regularly in many enterprises. In natural language processing, some commercial systems have become available, and thousands of people are now able to do some standard tasks, such as access databases with typed natural-language input. Spoken-language systems are beginning to enter the market and their success can be expected to increase. Game-playing programs have become commercially profitable and are widely available. Military strategists are now using many programs for simulation and decision-making that heavily employ artificial intelligence techniques. A lesser noticed but extremely important product of artificial intelligence research is the series of computer languages that were created to do the research. These include LISP, which is widely used as a symbolic programming language, Prolog, which is becoming popular and has even served as a prototype language for the Japanese fifth-generation computer series, and many special languages for programming expert systems.

Finally, we have noticed that there are aspects of human intelligence that will probably remain beyond the programming capacity of researchers for the foreseeable future. First, there is the ability to understand the human condition, which is based upon our life experience. Second, there is the astounding pattern-recognition ability that humans exhibit in game playing, for example. People are able to see in a single position things not visible to a machine in a search of millions of positions. Last, there is the gigantic knowledge base that humans have and the incredible flexibility with which we use it to achieve intelligent behavior.

**Exercises**

1. Assume that you are asked to prepare the specifications for a robot vision and audio output system. The robot is to roam an area too dangerous for humans (because of radiation or other hazards) and report its observations verbally. The vision and audio output system will have three main subsystems: an image processor to find the important features in the scene, a problem-solving system to decide which features are significant enough to describe, and a language planning and output system to enunciate the needed utterances. Prepare specifications for each of the three subsystems that you believe are within the current state-of-the-art.

2. Present arguments for and against the Thesis of AI Completeness.

## Summary (A)

Artificial intelligence is a field of study where researchers attempt to build or program machines with capabilities more complex than have been possible traditionally. These include the abilities to perceive and understand incoming data, learning, processing natural language, and reasoning. The fundamental paradigm for such studies includes the concepts of knowledge and reasoning, which were examined in this chapter.

The knowledge of an object is the set of all information required to deal with it in related processing. Knowledge can be stored in various forms and can be used to understand perception or reasoning processes. Knowledge can be input to a machine by being formatted and read in directly, or it can be acquired by the machine through learning.

Reasoning is the process of finding a sequence of linkages that will lead from one object in memory to another. Often the goal of reasoning is to find a way to change the current state of the world into some desired state. Reasoning is done by selectively searching a tree of possible action sequences until the desired one is found. Many artificial intelligence systems have been built over the years using these ideas, and some of them were described in this chapter.

This section concludes this book, which is a study of what computers are, what they can do, and what they cannot do. The early chapters introduced programming and are primarily a study of what computers can do. After looking at a variety of problems and their solutions, we studied the Church-Markov-Turing Thesis, which asserts that any step-by-step process that we can describe precisely can be programmed on a machine.

The second part of the book examined what computers are so that they may be understood in a deeper way. Specifically, they are simply boxes capable of executing the fetch-execute cycle at a very high speed. Their usefulness comes primarily from the fact that convenient languages can be translated into a form that is amenable to the fetch-execute style of computation. They are made up of millions of tiny switches etched into silicon crystals and organized to store information and compute.

The last part of the book examined advanced topics in computer science. These included the study of execution time and the division of computations into tractable and intractable classes. Parallel computing was introduced as a means for reducing execution time, and some sample problems were studied within this paradigm. We examined one fascinating type of parallel machine, the connectionist network, which spreads information and computation across an array of tiny processors and programs itself through learning. Next we studied noncomputability and attempted to gain enough intuition to recognize a class of functions that, as far as we know, cannot be programmed. Finally, we studied artificial intelligence and the attempts of researchers to build machines that can know, understand, learn, and reason in ways that are reminiscent of human thinking.

# Appendix A

## The Rules for the Subset of Pascal Used in this Book

Here are the rules that generate the Pascal programs in this book. The rules leave out a few details, such as parentheses in arithmetic expressions, nested Boolean expressions, and the formatting that can be included in a *writeln* statement to specify field widths.

Although these rules specify legal syntax for programs, they can also generate some programs that are illegal semantically, such as programs that do not declare variables. You must write code that follows the syntactic constraints given here and also follows the other rules of the language.

A manual on Pascal will include all the syntactic rules of the language, a much larger set than is given here. Usually such rules are given in the form of flowcharts.

### Program

```
<program>    ->    program <identifier>;
                   <type declaration>
                   <variable declaration>
                   <multiple procedures>
                   <compound statement>.
```

### Type Declaration

```
<type declaration>  ->  nothing
<type declaration>  ->  type
                        <identifier> = array[<int>. . <int>] of <type>;
<int>  ->  any integer
```

**Variable Declaration**

```
<variable declaration>  ->  nothing
<variable declaration>  ->  var
                            a sequence of <identifier:type>'s each
                            followed by a semicolon
<identifier:type>  ->  <identifier list> : <type>
<identifier list>  ->  a list of <identifier>'s separated by commas
```

**Type**

```
<type>  ->  string
<type>  ->  integer
<type>  ->  real
<type>  ->  <identifier>
```

**Procedure Declaration**

```
<multiple procedures>  ->  nothing
<multiple procedures>  ->  a sequence of <procedure declaration>'s
<procedure declaration>  ->  procedure <identifier> <parameter list>;
                             <variable declaration>
                             <compound statement>;
<parameter list>  ->  nothing
<parameter list>  ->  (a list of <var declaration>'s separated by
                      semicolons)
<var declaration>  ->  var <identifier:type>
```

**Compound Statement**

```
<compound statement>  ->  begin
                          a sequence of <statement>'s each followed by a
                          semicolon
                          end
```

**Statement**

```
<statement>  ->  <compound statement>
<statement>  ->  writeln(list of <expression>'s separated by commas)
<statement>  ->  readln(<identifier[]>)
<statement>  ->  readln
```

```
<statement>  ->  if <boolean expression> then
                        <statement>
                 else
                        <statement>
<statement>  ->  if <boolean expression> then
                        <statement>
<statement>  ->  <identifier[]>  :=  <expression>
<statement>  ->  while <boolean expression> do
                        <statement>
<statement>  ->  <identifier> <argument list>
```

## Expression

```
<expression>  ->  <string expression>
<expression>  ->  <integer expression>
<expression>  ->  <real expression>
```

## String Expression

```
<string expression>  ->  <identifier[]>
<string expression>  ->  'any string of printable characters'
<string expression>  ->  <string expression> + <string expression>
<string expression>  ->
      copy(<string expression>,<integer expression>,
      <integer expression>)
```

## Integer Expression

```
<integer expression>  ->  any integer
<integer expression>  ->  <identifier[]>
<integer expression>  ->  <integer expression> <intop> <integer
                                expression>
<integer expression>  ->  length(<string expression>)
<integer expression>  ->  pos(<string expression>,<string expression>)
<intop>  ->  one of +, -, *, or div
```

## Real Expression

```
<real expression>  ->  any real number
<real expression>  ->  <identifier[]>
<real expression>  ->  <real expression> <realop> <real expression>
<realop>  ->  one of +, *, -, or /
```

**Boolean Expression**

```
<boolean expression>  ->  <identifier[]> <comp> <expression>
<boolean expression>  ->  true
<comp>  ->  one of >, <, >=, <=, =, or <>
```

**Identifier and Identifier-index**

```
<identifier[]>  ->  <identifier> possibly followed by an <integer
                    expression> in square brackets
<identifier>  ->  a sequence of letters and/or digits that begins with a
                  letter
```

**Argument List**

```
<argument list  ->  nothing
<argument list>  ->  (a list of <identifier[]>'s separated by commas)
```

# Appendix B

## Two Simulation Programs

These programs implement the calculations to illustrate disease contagion and fractal generation, as described in chapter 5.

```
{A demonstration of disease contagion across a linear array.          }

{Inputs: The length of the infection in days, the total time of the   }
{infection plus the following immune period in days, and the number of }
{individuals infected per day by an infectious person.                }

{Outputs: A string of 0s, *s, and 1s for each day indicating the well, }
{ill, and immune individuals.                                         }

{Operation: Array A stores an integer for each member of the          }
{population. If the member is well, the entry is 0. If the member is   }
{infected, the entry is set to 1. For an infected individual, the      }
{entry is increased 1 each day as the infection progresses eventually  }
{returning to 0 when the illness and following immunity are passed.    }

program pop1;
type
    arraytype = array[1..60] of integer;
var
    A:arraytype;
        {This will contain one integer for each individual.}
    i,      {Index for looping.}
    iInc,   {Will contain a pseudo-random number.}
    rate,   {The number of persons infected by ill person per day.}
```

```
infectious,      {The number of days of infectious illness.}
immune:      {Number of days for infection plus immunity.}
integer;
command:string;
```

```
{This procedure assumes individual k is ill and infecting surrounding  }
{persons. It places 1s into the B entries of individuals who are being }
{infected. The number of such individuals is given by rate. The        }
{pseudo-random number iInc is used to decide which individuals will be  }
{infected.                                                             }
procedure infect(var B:arraytype; var k, iInc, rate:integer);
    var
        i,j:integer;
    begin
    i := 1;
    while i <= rate do
        begin
        iInc := ((iInc * 23) mod 31); {Find a new random number.}
        j := k + iInc - 13; {j tells who is being infected.}
        if (j > 0) and (j <= 60) then
            begin
            B[j] := 1; {Indicate the infection.}
            end;
        i := i + 1; {Prepare to infect another.}
        end;
    end;
```

```
{This routine scans the whole array and updates every entry showing    }
{the newly infected individuals and other updates.                     }
procedure update(var A:arraytype; var infectious, immune, iInc,
                                rate:integer);
    var
        k:integer;
        B:arraytype; {We need an extra array B.}
    begin
    k := 1;
    while k <= 60 do {The extra array B is initialized.}
        begin
        B[k] := 0;
        k := k + 1;
        end;
```

```
k := 1;
while k <= 60 do {Mark in B every new infection.}
    begin
    if A[k] > 0 then
        begin
        if (A[k] >= 1) and (A[k] <= infectious) then
            begin
            infect(B,k,iInc,rate);
            end;
        A[k] := A[k] + 1;
        if A[k] > immune then {Also mark some as well.}
            begin
            A[k] := 0;
            end;
        end;
    k := k + 1;
    end;
k := 1;
while k <= 60 do {Find the well individuals.}
    begin
    if A[k] = 0 then
        begin
        A[k] := B[k]; {Mark some as infected.}
        end;
    k := k + 1;
    end;
end;

{Print the string of characters indicating who is well, who is ill,     }
{and who is immune. Also print the associated statistics.               }
procedure outputc(var A:arraytype; var infectious:integer);
    var
        k,Nwell,Nill,Nimmune:integer;
            {Will count the numbers of well, ill, and immune.}
    begin
    Nwell := 0;
    Nill := 0;
    Nimmune := 0;
    k := 1;
    while k <= 60 do                     {Examine each individual.}
        begin
```

```
            if A[k] = 0 then          {If well, print 0.}
                begin
                write('0');
                Nwell := Nwell + 1;
                end;
            if (A[k] > 0) and (A[k] <= infectious) then
                                {If ill, print *.}
                begin
                write('*');
                Nill := Nill + 1;
                end;
            if A[k] > infectious then {If immune, print 1.}
                begin
                write('1');
                Nimmune := Nimmune + 1;
                end;
            k := k + 1;
            end;
        writeln;
        writeln('well ',Nwell,' ill ',Nill,' immune ',Nimmune);
        end;
    begin
    iInc := 2;                 {Initialize pseudo-random number.}
    writeln('Give time of infection.');
    readln(infectious);
    writeln('Give time of infection plus immunity.');
    readln(immune);
    writeln('Give number of individuals infected.');
    writeln(' by each contagious person.');
    readln(rate);
    i := 1;
    while i <= 60 do           {All individuals are well.}
        begin
        A[i] := 0;
        i := i + 1;
        end;
    A[30] := 1;                {Insert one infected person.}
    outputc(A,infectious);         {Display whole population.}
    writeln('Continue?');
    readln(command);
    while command <> 'q' do    {Should we examine another day?}
```

```
      begin
      update(A,infectious,immune,iInc,rate);
      outputc(A,infectious);    {Display new day.}
      writeln('Continue?');
      readln(command);
      end;
readln;
end.
```

```
{A fractal drawing program.                                            }
{Written using Turbo Pascal graphics constructions                     }
{by D. J. Miller.                                                      }

{Inputs: Constants c1 and c2 as described in chapter 5.                }

{Output: The fractal displayed on the terminal screen.                 }

{Operation: Each point on the screen is examined. If its coordinates   }
{result in a converging sequence, it is plotted. Otherwise it is left  }
{uncolored.                                                            }

Program Julia;
uses
    Graph, Crt;
var
    GraphDriver,GraphMode,ErrorCode:integer;
        {Variables used by graphics routine.}
    x, y, x0, y0, x1, y1, z, m, n, c1, c2:real;
    S, T, U, V:string;
    i, j:integer;
    screenXmax, screenYmax, theight, twidth:integer;
        {Real screen parameters.}
    xmax, ymax, xmin, ymin:real;
        {Virtual screen parameters.}

{This function scales and converts an x-coordinate to an integer.     }
function scalex(realx:real) :integer;
    begin
    scalex := round((realx - xmin) / (xmax - xmin) * screenXmax);
    end;

{This function scales and converts a y-coordinate to an integer.      }
function scaley(realy:real):integer;
```

```
    begin
    scaley := screenYmax - round((realy - ymin) / (ymax - ymin) *
            (screenYmax -(3*theight) + 1)));
    end;

{This procedure plots a line. }
procedure plotline(x1,y1,x2,y2:real);
    begin
    moveto(scalex(x1),scaley(y1));
    lineto(scalex(x2),scaley(y2));
    end;

(This procedure writes a string on the graphics screen. }
procedure gwriteln(n:integer;S:string);
    var
        yline:integer;
    begin
    yline := n*theight;
    SetColor(Black);
    while(yline <= (n+1) * theight) do
        begin
        moveto(0,yline);
        lineto(screenXmax,yline);
        yline := yline + 1;
        end;
    SetColor(LightCyan);
    OutTextXY(50,n*theight,S);
    end;

begin
writeln('Input the constants.');
readln(c1);
readln(c2);
            {Standard Turbo graphics initialization.}
GraphDriver := Detect;
InitGraph(GraphDriver,GraphMode,'BGI');
ErrorCode := GraphResult;
if ErrorCode <> grOk then
    begin
    writeln('Graphics error: ', GraphErrorMsg(ErrorCode));
    writeln('Program aborted . . ');
    readln;
```

```
        Halt(1);
        end;
                {Initialize variables.}
screenXmax := GetMaxX;
screenYmax := GetMaxY;
xmax := 200; xmin := 0;
ymax := 200; ymin := 0;
SetTextStyle(DefaultFont, HorizDir, 1);
theight := TextHeight('igyITQq');
twidth := TextWidth('W');
str(c1:10:7,S);
str(c2:10:7,T);
gwriteln(0,'c = ' + S + ' + ' + T + 'i'); {Write c1, c2 values.}
m := 0;
while (m <= 200) do                 {For each x-coordinate.}
    begin
    x0 := -2 + (m/50);
    n := 0;
    while (n <= 100) do             {For each y-coordinate}
        begin                       {on initial half.}
        y0 := 2 - (n/50);
        x := x0;
        y := y0;
        i := 1;
        z := 0;
        while (i <= 20) and (z <= 4) do    {Check convergence.}
            begin
            x1 := (x*x) - (y*y) + c1;
            y1 := (2*x*y) + c2;
            x := x1;
            y := y1;
            z := (x*x) + (y*y);
            i := i + 1;
            end;
        if (z <= 4) then                {If convergence, plot.}
            begin
            PutPixel(scalex(m),scaley(n),15-trunc(z*4));
            PutPixel(scalex(200-m), scaley(200-n),15-trunc(z*4));
                        {Plot other half.}
            end;
```

```
            n := n + 1;
            end;
      m := m + 1;
      end;
gwriteln(2,'END');
readln;
CloseGraph;
end.
```

# Readings

Astrachan, O., *A Computer Science Tapestry: Exploring Programming and Computer Science with C++*, McGraw-Hill, New York, 1997.

Atkinson, K., *Elementary Numerical Analysis*, Second Edition, John Wiley and Sons, New York, 1992.

Brooks, F. P., Jr., *The Mythical Man-Month: Essays on Software Engineering*, Anniversary Edition, Addison-Wesley, Reading, Mass., 1995.

Cheney, W., and Kincaid, D., *Numerical Mathematics and Computing*, Third Edition, Brooks/Cole, Pacific Grove, Calif., 1994.

Comer, D. E., *Internetworking with TCP/IP, Volume I, Principles, Protocols, and Architecture*, Prentice-Hall, Englewood Cliffs, N.J., 1991.

Comer, D. E., and Stevens, D. L., *Internetworking with TCP/IP, Volume II—Implementation and Internals*, Prentice-Hall, Englewood Cliffs, N.J., 1991.

Cooper, D., *Oh! Pascal!*, W. W. Norton & Co., New York, 1997.

Devaney, R. L., *Chaos, Fractals and Dynamics*, Addison-Wesley, Reading, Mass., 1990.

Feibel, W., *Turbo Pascal 7 Handbook*, Osborn McGraw-Hill, New York, 1992.

Feigenbaum, E. A., and Feldman, J. (Editors), *Computers and Thought*, AAAI/The MIT Press, Cambridge, Mass., 1995.

Golub, G. H., and Ortega, J. M., *Scientific Computing and Differential Equations: An Introduction to Numerical Methods*, Academic Press Inc., San Diego, Calif., 1992.

Golub, G. H., and Ortega, J. M., *Scientific Computing: An Introduction with Parallel Computing*, Academic Press Inc., San Diego, Calif., 1993.

Harel, D., *Algorithmics: The Spirit of Computing*, Second Edition, Addison-Wesley, Reading, Mass., 1992.

Haykin, S. S., *Neural Networks: A Comprehensive Foundation*, Macmillan, New York, 1994.

Hopfield, J. J., "Neural Networks and Physical Systems with Emergent Collective Computational Capabilities," *Proceedings of the National Academy of Sciences* (USA) 79, 2554–2558, 1982.

Impagliazzo, J. and Nagin, P., *Computer Science: A Breadth-First Approach with C*, John Wiley and Sons, New York, 1995.

Mano, M. M., *Digital Design*, Second Edition, Prentice-Hall, Englewood Cliffs, N.J., 1991.

Miller, D. L. and Pekny, J. F., "Exact Solution of Large Asymmetric Traveling Salesman Problems," *Science*, vol. 251, February, 1991.

Pattis, R. E., Roberts, J., and Stehlik, M., *Karel the Robot: A Gentle Introduction to the Art of Programming*, Second Edition, John Wiley and Sons, New York, 1994.

Russell, S., and Norvig, P., *Artificial Intelligence: A Modern Approach*, Prentice-Hall, Englewood Cliffs, N.J., 1995.

Sebesta, R. W., *Concepts of Programming Languages*, Third Edition, Addison-Wesley, Reading, Mass., 1996.

Simon, H. A., and Newell, A., "Heuristic Problem Solving: The Next Advance in Operations Research," *Operations Research*, January–February, 1958.

Tannenbaum, A. S., *Modern Operating Systems*, Prentice-Hall, Englewood Cliffs, N.J., 1993.

# Index